Chips From a G

(Volume 4)

Essays Chiefly on the Science of Language

F. Max Müller

Alpha Editions

This edition published in 2024

ISBN : 9789367246092

Design and Setting By
Alpha Editions
www.alphaedis.com
Email - info@alphaedis.com

As per information held with us this book is in Public Domain.
This book is a reproduction of an important historical work. Alpha Editions uses the best technology to reproduce historical work in the same manner it was first published to preserve its original nature. Any marks or number seen are left intentionally to preserve its true form.

Contents

I. INAUGURAL LECTURE, ON THE VALUE OF COMPARATIVE PHILOLOGY AS A BRANCH OF ACADEMIC STUDY. ....- 1 -

II. REDE LECTURE, DELIVERED IN THE SENATE HOUSE BEFORE THE UNIVERSITY OF CAMBRIDGE, ON FRIDAY, MAY 29, 1868.1 ....- 43 -

III. ON THE MIGRATION OF FABLES. A LECTURE DELIVERED AT THE ROYAL INSTITUTION, ON FRIDAY, JUNE 3, 1870. ....- 93 -

IV. ON THE RESULTS OF THE SCIENCE OF LANGUAGE. INAUGURAL LECTURE, DELIVERED IN THE IMPERIAL UNIVERSITY OF STRASSBURG, MAY 23, 1872. ....- 138 -

V. WESTMINSTER LECTURE. ON MISSIONS.1 ....- 164 -

VII. OPENING ADDRESS. ....- 214 -

VIII. LIFE OF COLEBROOKE.1 ....- 239 -

IX. MY REPLY TO MR. DARWIN. ....- 278 -

X. IN SELF-DEFENSE. ....- 302 -

I.
INAUGURAL LECTURE, ON THE VALUE OF COMPARATIVE PHILOLOGY AS A BRANCH OF ACADEMIC STUDY.

DELIVERED BEFORE THE UNIVERSITY OF OXFORD
THE 27TH OF OCTOBER, 1868.

THE foundation of a professorial chair in the University of Oxford marks an important epoch in the history of every new science.1 There are other universities far more ready to confer this academical recognition on new branches of scientific research, and it would be easy to mention several subjects, and no doubt important subjects, which have long had their accredited representatives in the universities of France and Germany, but which at Oxford have not yet received this well-merited recognition.

If we take into account the study of ancient languages only, we see that as soon as Champollion's discoveries had given to the study of hieroglyphics and Egyptian antiquities a truly scientific character, the French government thought it its duty to found a chair for this promising branch of Oriental scholarship. Italy soon followed this generous example: nor was the Prussian government long behind hand in doing honor to the newborn science, as soon as in Professor Lepsius it had found a scholar worthy to occupy a chair of Egyptology at Berlin.

If France had possessed the brilliant genius to whom so much is due in the deciphering of the cuneiform inscriptions, I have little doubt that long ago a chair would have been founded at the *Collège de France* expressly for Sir Henry Rawlinson.

England possesses some of the best, if not the best, of Persian scholars (alas! he who was here in my mind, Lord Strangford, is no longer among us), yet there is no chair for Persian at Oxford or Cambridge, in spite of the charms of its modern literature, and the vast importance of the ancient language of Persia and Bactria, the Zend, a language full of interest, not only to the comparative philologist, but also to the student of Comparative Theology.

There are few of the great universities of Europe without a chair for that language which, from the very beginning of history, as far as it is known to us, seems always to have been spoken by the largest number of human beings,—I mean Chinese. In Paris we find not one, but two chairs for Chinese, one for the ancient, another for the modern language of that wonderful empire; and if we consider the light which a study of that curious form of human speech is intended to throw on the nature and growth of language, if we measure the importance of its enormous literature by the materials which it supplies to the student of ancient religions, and likewise to the historian who wishes to observe the earliest rise of the principal sciences and arts in countries beyond the influence of Aryan and Semitic civilization,—if, lastly, we take into account the important evidence which the Chinese language, reflecting, like a never-fading photograph, the earliest workings of the human mind, is able to supply to the student of psychology, and to the careful analyzer of the elements and laws of thought, we should feel less inclined to ignore or ridicule the claims of such a language to a chair in our ancient university.2

I could go on and mention several other subjects, well worthy of the same distinction. If the study of Celtic languages and Celtic antiquities deserves to be encouraged anywhere, it is surely in England,—not, as has been suggested, in order to keep English literature from falling into the abyss of German platitudes, nor to put Aneurin and Taliesin in the place of Shakespeare and Burns, and to counteract by their "suavity and brilliancy" the Philistine tendencies of the Saxon and the Northman, but in order to supply sound materials and guiding principles to the critical student of the ancient history and the ancient language of Britain, to excite an interest in what still remains of Celtic antiquities, whether in manuscripts or in genuine stone monuments, and thus to preserve such national heir-looms from neglect or utter destruction. If we consider that Oxford possesses a Welsh college, and that England possesses the best of Celtic scholars, it is surely a pity that he should have to publish the results of his studies in the short intervals of official work at Calcutta, and not in the more congenial atmosphere of Rytichin.

For those who know the history of the ancient universities of England, it is not difficult to find out why they should have been less inclined than their continental sisters to make timely provision for the encouragement of these and other important branches of linguistic research. Oxford and Cambridge, as independent corporations, withdrawn alike from the support and from the control of the state, have always looked upon the instruction of the youth of England as their proper work; and nowhere has the tradition of classical learning been handed down more faithfully from one generation to another than in England; nowhere has its generous spirit more thoroughly pervaded the minds of statesmen, poet, artists, and moulded the character of that large and important class of independent and cultivated men, without which this country would cease to be what it has been for the last two centuries, a *res publica*, a commonwealth, in the best sense of the word. Oxford and Cambridge have supplied what England expected or demanded, and as English parents did not send their sons to learn Chinese or to study Cornish, there was naturally no supply where there was no demand. The professorial element in the university, the true representative of higher learning and independent research, withered away; the tutorial assumed the vastest proportions during this and the last centuries.

But looking back to the earlier history of the English universities, I believe it is a mistake to suppose that Oxford, one of the most celebrated universities during the Middle Ages and in the modern history of Europe, could ever have ignored the duty, so fully recognized by other European universities, of not only handing down intact, and laid up, as it were, in a napkin, the traditional stock of human knowledge, but of constantly adding to it, and increasing it fivefold and tenfold. Nay, unless I am much mistaken, there was really no university in which more ample provision had been made by founders and benefactors than at Oxford, for the support and encouragement of a class of students who should follow up new lines of study, devote their energies to work which, from its very nature, could not be lucrative or even self-supporting, and maintain the fame of English learning, English industry, and English genius in that great and time-honoured republic of learning which claims the allegiance of the whole of Europe, nay, of the whole civilized world. That work at Oxford and Cambridge was meant to be done by the Fellows of Colleges. In times, no doubt, when every kind of learning was in the hands of the clergy, these fellowships might seem to have been intended exclusively for the support of theological students. But when other studies, once mere germs and shoots on the tree of knowledge, separated from the old stem and assumed an independent growth, whether under the name of natural science, or history, or scholarship, or jurisprudence, a fair division ought to have been made at once of the funds which, in accordance with the letter, it may be, but certainly not with the spirit of the ancient statutes, have remained for so many years appropriated to the exclusive support of theological learning, if learning it could be called. Fortunately, that mistake has now been remedied, and the funds originally intended, without distinction, for the support of "true religion and useful learning," are now again more equally apportioned among those who, in the age in which we live, have divided and subdivided the vast intellectual inheritance of the Middle Ages, in order to cultivate the more thoroughly every nook and every corner in the boundless field of human knowledge.

Something, however, remains still to be done in order to restore these fellowships more fully and more efficiently to their original purpose, and thus to secure to the university not only a staff of zealous teachers, which it certainly possesses, but likewise a class of independent workers, of men who, by original research, by critical editions of the classics, by an acquisition of a scholarlike knowledge of other languages besides Greek and Latin, by an honest devotion to one or the other among the numerous branches of physical science, by fearless researches into the ancient history of mankind, by a careful collection or revision of the materials for the history of politics, jurisprudence, medicine, literature, and arts, by a life-long occupation with the problems of philosophy, and last, not least, by a real study of theology, or the science of religion, should perform again those duties which in the stillness of the Middle Ages were performed by learned friars within the walls of our colleges. Those duties have remained in abeyance for several generations, and they must now be performed with increased vigor, in order to retain for Oxford that high position which it once held, not simply as a place of education, but as a seat of learning, amid the most celebrated universities of Europe.

"*Noblesse oblige*" is an old saying that is sometimes addressed to those who have inherited an illustrious name, and who are proud of their ancestors. But what are the ancestors of the oldest and proudest of families compared with the ancestors of this university! "*Noblesse oblige*" applies to Oxford at the present moment more than ever, when knowledge for its own sake, and a chivalrous devotion to studies which command no price in the fair of the world, and lead to no places of emolument in church or state, are looked down upon and ridiculed by almost everybody.

There is no career in England at the present moment for scholars and students. No father could honestly advise his son, whatever talent he might display, to devote himself exclusively to classical, historical, or physical studies. The few men who still keep up the fair name of England by independent research and new discoveries in the fields of political and natural history, do not always come from our universities; and unless they possess independent means, they cannot devote more than the leisure hours, left by their official duties in church or state, to the prosecution of their favorite studies. This ought not to be, nor need it be so. If only twenty men in Oxford and Cambridge had the will, everything is ready for a reform, that is, for a restoration of the ancient glory of Oxford. The funds which are now frittered away in so-called prize-fellowships, would enable the universities to-morrow to invite the best talent of England back to its legitimate home. And what should we lose if we had no longer that long retinue of non-resident fellows? It is true, no doubt, that a fellowship has been a help in the early career of many a poor and hard-working man, and how could it be otherwise? But in many cases I know that it has proved a drag rather than a spur for further efforts. Students at English universities belong, as a rule, to the wealthier classes, and England is the wealthiest country in Europe. Yet in no country in the world would a young man, after his education is finished, expect assistance from public sources. Other countries tax themselves to the utmost in order to enable the largest possible number of young men to enjoy the best possible education in schools and universities. But when that is done the community feels that it has fulfilled its duty, and it says to the young generation, Now swim or drown. A manly struggle against poverty, it may be even against actual hunger, will form a stronger and sounder metal than a lotus-eating club-life in London or Paris. Whatever fellowships were intended to be, they were never intended to be mere sinecures, as most of them are at present. It is a national blessing that the two ancient universities of England should have saved such large funds from the shipwreck that swallowed up the corporate funds of the continental universities. But, in order to secure their safety for the future, it is absolutely necessary that these funds should be utilized again for the advancement of learning. Why should not a fellowship be made into a career for life, beginning with little, but rising like the incomes of other professions? Why should the grotesque condition of celibacy be imposed on a fellowship, instead of the really salutary condition of—No work, no pay? Why should not some special literary or scientific work be assigned to each fellow, whether resident in Oxford or sent abroad on scientific missions? Why, instead of having fifty young men scattered about in England, should we not have ten of the best workers in every branch of human knowledge resident at Oxford, whether as teachers, or as guides, or as examples? The very presence of such men would have a stimulating and elevating effect: it would show to the young men higher objects of human ambition than the baton of a field-marshal, the mitre of a bishop, the ermine of a judge, or the money bags of a merchant; it would create for the future a supply of new workers as soon as there was for them, if not an avenue to wealth and power, at least a fair opening for hard work and proper pay. All this might be done to-morrow, without any injury to anybody, and with every chance of producing results of the greatest value to the universities, to the country, and to the world at large. Let the university continue to do the excellent work which it does at present as a teacher, but let it not forget the equally important duty of a university, that of a worker. Our century has inherited the intellectual wealth of former centuries, and with it the duty, not only to preserve it or to dole it out in schools and universities, but to increase it far beyond the limits which it has reached at present. Where there is no advance, there is retrogression: rest is impossible for the human mind.

Much of the work, therefore, which in other universities falls to the lot of the professors, ought, in Oxford, to be performed by a staff of student-fellows, whose labors should be properly organized as they are in the Institute of France or in the Academy of Berlin. With or without teaching, they could perform the work which no university can safely neglect, the work of constantly testing the soundness of our intellectual food, and of steadily expanding the realms of knowledge. We want pioneers, explorers, conquerors, and we could have them in abundance if we cared to have them.

What other universities do by founding new chairs for new sciences, the colleges of Oxford could do to-morrow by applying the funds which are not required for teaching purposes, and which are now spent on sinecure fellowships, for making either temporary or permanent provision for the endowment of original research.

It is true that new chairs have, from time to time, been founded in Oxford also; but if we inquire into the circumstances under which provision was made for the teaching of new subjects, we shall find that it generally took place, not so much for the encouragement of any new branch of scientific research, however interesting to the philosopher and the historian, as in order to satisfy some practical wants that could no longer be ignored, whether in church or state, or in the university itself.

Confining ourselves to the chairs of languages, or, as they used to be called, "the readerships of tongues," we find that as early as 1311, while the Crusades were still fresh in the memory of the people of Europe, an appeal was made by Pope Clement V. at the Council of Vienne, calling upon the principal universities in Christendom to appoint lecturers for the study of Hebrew, Arabic, and Chaldaic. It was considered at the time a great honor for Oxford to be mentioned by name, together with Paris, Bologna, and Salamanca, as one of the four great seats of learning in which the Pope and the Council of Vienne desired that provision should be made for the teaching of these languages. It is quite clear, however, from the wording of the resolution of the Council,[3] that the chief object in the foundation of these readerships was to supply men capable of defending the interests of the church, of taking an active part in the controversies with Jews and Mohammedans, who were then considered dangerous, and of propagating the faith among unbelievers.

Nor does it seem that this papal exhortation produced much effect, for we find that Henry VIII. in 1540 had to make new provision in order to secure efficient teachers of Hebrew and Greek in the University of Oxford. At that time these two languages, but more particularly Greek, had assumed not only a theological, but a political importance, and it was but natural that the king should do all in his power to foster and spread a knowledge of a language which had been one of the most powerful weapons in the hands of the reformers. At Oxford itself this new chair was by no means popular: on the contrary those who studied Greek were for a long time looked upon with great suspicion and dislike.[4]

Henry VIII. did nothing for the support of Arabic; but a century later (1636) we find Archbishop Laud, whose attention had been attracted by Eastern questions, full of anxiety to resuscitate the study of Arabic at Oxford, partly by collecting Arabic MSS. in the East and depositing them in the Bodleian

Library, partly by founding a new chair of Arabic, inaugurated by Pococke, and rendered illustrious by such names as Greaves, Thomas Hyde, John Wallis, and Thomas Hunt.

The foundation of a chair of Anglo-Saxon, too, was due, not so much to a patriotic interest excited by the ancient national literature of the Saxons, still less to the importance of that ancient language for philological studies, but it received its first impulse from the divines of the sixteenth century, who wished to strengthen the position of the English Church in its controversy with the Church of Rome. Under the auspices of Archbishop Parker, Anglo-Saxon MSS. were first collected, and the Anglo-Saxon translations of the Bible, as well as Anglo-Saxon homilies, and treatises on theological and ecclesiastical subjects were studied by Fox, the martyrologist, and others,[5] to be quoted as witnesses to the purity and simplicity of the primitive church founded in this realm, free in its origin from the later faults and fancies of the Church of Rome. Without this practical object, Anglo-Saxon would hardly have excited so much interest in the sixteenth century, and Oxford would probably have remained much longer without its professorial chair of the ancient national language of England, which was founded by Rawlinson, but was not inaugurated before the end of the last century (1795).

Of the two remaining chairs of languages, of Sanskrit and of Latin, the former owes its origin, not to an admiration of the classical literature of India, nor to a recognition of the importance of Sanskrit for the purposes of Comparative Philology, but to an express desire on the part of its founder to provide efficient missionaries for India; while the creation of a chair of Latin, though long delayed, was at last rendered imperative by the urgent wants of the university.

Nor does the chair of Comparative Philology, just founded by the university, form altogether an exception to this general rule. It is curious to remark that while Comparative Philology has for more than half a century excited the deepest interest, not only among continental, but likewise among English scholars, and while chairs of this new science have been founded long ago in almost every university of France, Germany, and Italy, the foundation of a new chair of Comparative Philology at Oxford should coincide very closely with a decided change that has taken place in the treatment of that science, and which has given to its results a more practical importance for the study of Greek and Latin, such as could hardly be claimed for it during the first fifty years of its growth.

We may date the origin of Comparative Philology, as distinct from the Science of Language, from the foundation of the Asiatic Society of Calcutta, in 1784. From that time dates the study of Sanskrit, and it was the study of Sanskrit which formed the foundation of Comparative Philology.

It is perfectly true that Sanskrit had been studied before by Italian, German, and French missionaries; it is likewise perfectly true that several of these missionaries were fully aware of the close relationship between Sanskrit, Greek, and Latin. A man must be blind who, after looking at a Sanskrit grammar, does not see at once the striking coincidences between the declensions and conjugations of the classical language of India and those of Greece and Italy.6

Filippo Sassetti, who spent some time at Goa, between 1581 and 1588, had only acquired a very slight knowledge of Sanskrit before he wrote home to his friends "that it has many words in common with Italian, particularly in the numerals, in the names for God, serpent, and many others." This was in the sixteenth century.

Some of the Jesuit missionaries, however, went far beyond this. A few among them had acquired a real and comprehensive knowledge of the ancient language and literature of India, and we see them anticipate in their letters several of the most brilliant discoveries of Sir W. Jones and Professor Bopp. The père Cœurdoux,7 a French Jesuit, writes in 1767 from Pondichery to the French Academy, asking that learned society for a solution of the question, *"How is it that Sanskrit has so many words in common with Greek and Latin?"* He presents not only long lists of words, but he calls attention to the still more curious fact, that the grammatical forms in Sanskrit show the most startling similarity with Greek and Latin. After him almost everybody who had looked at Sanskrit, and who knew Greek and Latin, made the same remark and asked the same question.

But the fire only smouldered on; it would not burn up, it would not light, it would not warm. At last, owing to the exertions of the founders of the Asiatic Society at Calcutta, the necessary materials for a real study of Sanskrit became accessible to the students of Europe. The voice of Frederick Schlegel roused the attention of the world at large to the startling problem that had been thrown into the arena of the intellectual chivalry of the world, and at last the glove was taken up, and men like Bopp, and Burnouf, and Pott, and Grimm, did not rest till some answer could be returned, and some account rendered of Sanskrit, that strange intruder, and great disturber of the peace of classical scholarship.

The work which then began, was incessant. It was not enough that some words in Greek and Latin should be traced in Sanskrit. A kind of silent conviction began to spread that there must be in Sanskrit a remedy for all evils; people could not rest till every word in Greek and Latin had, in some disguise or other, been discovered in Sanskrit. Nor were Greek, Latin, and Sanskrit enough to satisfy the thirst of the new discoverers. The Teutonic languages were soon annexed, the Celtic languages yielded to some gentle pressure, the Slavonic languages clamored for incorporation, the sacred idiom of ancient Persia, the Zend, demanded its place by the side of Sanskrit, the Armenian followed in its wake; and when even the Ossetic from the valleys of Mount Caucasus, and the Albanian from the ancient hills of Epirus, had proved their birthright, the whole family, the Aryan family of language, seemed complete, and an historical fact, the original unity of all these languages, was established on a basis which even the most skeptical could not touch or shake. Scholars rushed in as diggers rush into a new gold field, picking up whatever is within reach, and trying to carry off more than they could carry, so that they might be foremost in the race, and claim as their own all that they had been the first to look at or to touch. There was a rush, and now and then an ugly rush, and when the armfuls of nuggets that were thrown down before the world in articles, pamphlets, essays, and ponderous volumes, came to be more carefully examined, it was but natural that not everything that glittered should turn out to be gold. Even in the works of more critical scholars, such as Bopp, Burnouf, Pott, and Benfey, at least in those which were published in the first enthusiasm of discovery, many things may now be pointed out, which no assayer would venture to pass. It was the great merit of Bopp that he called the attention away from this tempting field to the more laborious work of grammatical analysis, though even in his Comparative Grammar, in that comprehensive survey of the grammatical outlines of the Aryan languages, the spirit of conquest and centralization still predominates. All languages are, if possible, to submit to the same laws; what is common to all of them is welcome, what is peculiar to each is treated as anomalous, or explained as the result of later corruption.

This period in the history of Comparative Philology has sometimes been characterized as *syncretistic*, and to a certain extent that name and the censure implied in it are justified. But to a very small extent only. It was in the nature of things that a comparative study of languages should at first be directed to what is common to all; nay, without having first become thoroughly acquainted with the general features of the whole family, it would have been impossible to discover and fully to appreciate what is peculiar to each of the members.

Nor was it long before a reaction set in. One scholar from the very first, and almost contemporaneously with Bopp's first essays on Comparative Grammar, devoted himself to the study of one branch of languages only, availing himself, as far as he was able, of the new light which a knowledge of Sanskrit had thrown on the secret history of the whole Aryan family of speech, but concentrating his energies on the Teutonic; I mean, of course, Jacob Grimm, the author of the great historical grammar of the German language; a work which will live and last long after other works of that early period shall have been forgotten, or replaced, at least, by better books.

After a time Grimm's example was followed by others. Zeuss, in his "Grammatica Celtica," established the study of the Celtic languages on the broad foundations of Comparative Grammar. Miklosich and Schleicher achieved similar results by adopting the same method for the study of the Slavonic dialects. Curtius, by devoting himself to an elucidation of Greek, opened the eyes of classical scholars to the immense advantages of this new treatment of grammar and etymology; while Corssen, in his more recent works on Latin, has struck a mine which may well tempt the curiosity of every student of the ancient dialects of Italy. At the present moment the reaction is complete; and there is certainly some danger, lest what was called a *syncretistic* spirit should now be replaced by an *isolating* spirit in the science of language.

It cannot be denied, however, that this isolating, or rather discriminating, tendency has produced already the most valuable results, and I believe that it is chiefly due to the works of Curtius and Corssen, if Greek and Latin scholars have been roused at last from their apathy and been made aware of the absolute necessity of Comparative Philology, as a subject to be taught, not only in every university but in every school. I believe it is due to their works that a conviction has gradually been gaining ground among the best scholars at Oxford, also, that Comparative Philology could no longer be ignored as an important ingredient in the teaching of Greek and Latin; and while a comparative analysis of Sanskrit, Zend, Armenian, Greek, Latin, Gothic, High-German, Lithuanian, Slavonic, and Celtic, such as we find it in Bopp's "Comparative Grammar," would hardly be considered as a subject of practical utility, even in a school of philology, it was recognized at last that, not only for sound principles of etymology, not only for a rational treatment of Greek and Latin grammar, not only for a right understanding of classical mythology, but even for a critical restoration of the very s of Homer and Plautus, a knowledge of Comparative Philology, as applied to Greek and Latin, had become indispensable.

My chief object, therefore, as Professor of Comparative Philology at Oxford, will be to treat the classical languages under that new aspect which they have assumed, as viewed by the microscope of Curtius and Corssen, rather than by the telescope of Bopp, Pott, and Benfey. I shall try not only to give results, but to explain what is far more important, the method by which these results were obtained, so far as this is possible without, for the present at least, presupposing among my hearers a knowledge of Sanskrit. Sanskrit certainly forms the only sound foundation of Comparative Philology, and it will always remain the only safe guide through all its intricacies. A comparative philologist without a knowledge of Sanskrit is like an astronomer without a knowledge of mathematics. He may admire, he may observe, he may discover, but he will never feel satisfied, he will never feel certain, he will never feel quite at home.

I hope, therefore, that, besides those who attend my public lectures, there will be at least a few to form a private class for the study of the elements of Sanskrit. Sanskrit, no doubt, is a very difficult language, and it requires the study of a whole life to master its enormous literature. Its grammar, too, has been elaborated with such incredible minuteness by native grammarians, that I am not surprised if many scholars who begin the study of Sanskrit turn back from it in dismay. But it is quite possible to learn the rules of Sanskrit declension and conjugation, and to gain an insight into the grammatical organization of that language, without burdening one's memory with all the phonetic rules which generally form the first chapter of every Sanskrit grammar, or without devoting years of study to the unraveling of the intricacies of the greatest of Indian, if not of all grammarians,—Pâṇini. There are but few among our very best comparative philologists who are able to understand Pâṇini. Professor Benfey, whose powers of work are truly astounding, stands almost alone in his minute knowledge of that greatest of all grammarians. Neither Bopp, nor Pott, nor Curtius, nor Corssen, ever attempted to master Pâṇini's wonderful system. But a study of Sanskrit, as taught by European grammarians, cannot be recommended too strongly to all students of language. A good sailor may, for a time, steer without a compass, but even he feels safer when he knows that he may consult it, if necessary; and whenever he comes near the rocks,—and there are many in the Aryan sea,—he will hardly escape shipwreck without this magnetic needle.[8,A,B]

It will be asked, no doubt, by Greek and Latin scholars who have never as yet devoted themselves seriously to a study of Comparative Philology, what is to be gained after all the trouble of learning Sanskrit, and after mastering the works of Bopp, and Benfey, and Curtius? Would a man be a better Greek and Latin scholar for knowing Sanskrit? Would he write better Latin and Greek verse? Would he be better able to read and compare Greek and Latin MSS., and to prepare a critical edition of classical authors? To all these questions I reply both *No* and *Yes*.

If there is one branch of classical philology where the advantages derived from Comparative Philology have been most readily admitted, it is etymology. More than fifty years ago, Otfried Müller told classical scholars that that province at least must be surrendered. And yet it is strange to see how long it takes before old erroneous derivations are exploded and finally expelled from our dictionaries; and how, in spite of all warnings, similarity of sound and similarity of meaning are still considered the chief criteria of

Greek and Latin etymologies. I do not address this reproach to classical scholars only; it applies equally to many comparative philologists who, for the sake of some striking similarity of sound and meaning, will now and then break the phonetic laws which they themselves have helped to establish.

If we go back to earlier days, we find that Sanskrit scholars who had discovered that one of the names of the god of love in Bengali was *Dipuc*, i.e. the inflamer, derived from it by inversion the name of the god of love in Latin, *Cupid*. Sir William Jones identified *Janus* with the Sanskrit *Gaṇeśa*, i.e., lord of hosts,9 and even later scholars allowed themselves to be tempted to see the Indian prototype of *Ganymedes* in the *Kaṇva-medhâtithi* or *Kaṇva-mesha* of the Veda.10

After the phonetic laws of each language had been more carefully elaborated, it was but too frequently forgotten that words have a history as well as a growth, and that the history of a word must be explored first, before an attempt is made to unravel its growth. Thus it was extremely tempting to derive *paradise* from the Sanskrit *paradeśa*. The compound *para-deśa* was supposed to mean the highest or a distant country, and all the rest seemed so evident as to require no further elucidation. *Paradeśa*, however, does not mean the highest or a distant country in Sanskrit, but is always used in the sense of a foreign country, an enemy's country. Further, as early as the Song of Solomon (iv. 13), the word occurs in Hebrew as *pardés*, and how it could have got there straight from Sanskrit requires, at all events, some historical explanation. In Hebrew the word might have been borrowed from Persian, but the Sanskrit word *paradeśa*, if it existed at all in Persian, would have been *paradaesa*, the *s* being a guttural, not a dental sibilant. Such a compound, however, does not exist in Persian, and therefore the Sanskrit word *paradeśa* could not have reached Hebrew *viâ* Persia.

It is true, nevertheless, that the ancient Hebrew word *pardés* is borrowed from Persian, viz.: from the Zend *pairidaêza*, which means *circumvallatio*, a piece of ground inclosed by high walls, afterwards a park, a garden.11 The root in Sanskrit is DIH or DHIH (for Sanskrit *h* is Zend *z*), and means originally to knead, to squeeze together, to shape. From it we have the Sanskrit *dehî*, a wall, while in Greek the same root, according to the strictest phonetic rules, yielded τοῖχος, wall. In Latin our root is regularly changed into *fig*, and gives us *figulus*, a potter, *figura*, form or shape, and *fingere*. In Gothic it could only appear as *deig-an*, to knead, to form anything out of soft substances; hence *daig-s*, the English *dough*, German *Deich*.

But the Greek παράδεισος did not come from Hebrew, because here again there is no historical bridge between the two languages. In Greek we trace the word to Xenophon, who brought it back from his repeated journeys in Persia, and who uses it in the sense of pleasure-ground, or deer park.12

Lastly, we find the same word used in the LXX., a[s] garden of Eden, the word having been borrowed ei[ther from] Persia, or taken from the Greek, and indirectly from the [...]

This is the real history of the word. It is an Aryan word, in Sanskrit. It was first formed in Zend, transferred from [that] word into Hebrew and again into Greek. Its modern Persi[...]

All this is matter of history rather than philology. Yet we re[ad in our] best classical dictionaries: "The root of παράδεισος appears [Se]mitic, Arab. *firdaus*, Hebr. *pardês*: borrowed, also, in Sanskrit *paradesa*."13 Nearly every word is wrong.

From the same root DIH springs the Sanskrit word *deha*, body; body, like figure, being conceived as that which is formed or shaped. Bopp identified this *deha* with Gothic *leik*, body, particularly dead body, the modern German *Leiche* and *Leichnam*, the English *lich* in *lich-gate*. In this case the master of Comparative Philology disregarded the phonetic laws which he had himself helped to establish. The transition of *d* into *l* is no doubt common enough as between Sanskrit, Latin, and Greek, but it has never been established as yet on good evidence as taking place between Sanskrit and Gothic. Besides, the Sanskrit *h* ought in Gothic to appear as *g*, as we have it in *deig-s*, dough, and not by a tenuis.

Another Sanskrit word for body is *kalevara*, and this proved again a stumbling-block to Bopp, who compares it with the Latin *cadaver*. Here one might plead that *l* and *d* are frequently interchanged in Sanskrit and Latin words, but, as far as our evidence goes at present, we have no doubt many cases where an original Sanskrit *d* is represented in Latin by *l*, but no really trustworthy instance in which an original Sanskrit *l* appears in Latin as *d*. Besides, the Sanskrit diphthong *e* cannot, as a rule, in Latin be represented by long *â*.

If such things could happen to Bopp, we must not be too severe on similar breaches of the peace committed by classical scholars. What classical scholars seem to find most difficult to learn is that there are various degrees of certainty in etymologies even in those proposed by our best comparative scholars, and that not everything that is mentioned by Bopp, or Pott, or Benfey as possible, as plausible, as probable, and even as more than probable, ought, therefore, to be set down, for instance, in a grammar or dictionary, as simply a matter of fact. With certain qualifications, an etymology may have a scientific value; without those qualifications, it may become not only unscientific but mischievous. Again, nothing seems a more difficult lesson for an etymologist to learn than to say, I do not know. Yet to my mind, nothing shows, for instance, the truly scholarlike mind of Professor Curtius

the very fact for which he has been so often blamed, viz.: his
...g over in silence the words about which he has nothing certain to say.

Let us take an instance. If we open our best Greek dictionaries, we find that the Greek αὐγή, light, splendor, is compared with the German word for eye, *Auge*. No doubt every letter in the two words is the same, and the meaning of the Greek word could easily be supposed to have been specialized or localized in German. Sophocles ("Aj." 70) speaks of ὀμμάτων αὐγαί, the lights of the eyes, and Euripides ("Andr." 1180) uses αὐγαί by itself for eyes, like the Latin *lumina*. The verb αὐγάζω, too, is used in Greek in the sense of seeing or viewing. Why, then, it was asked, should αὐγή not be referred to the same source as the German *Auge*, and why should not both be traced back to the same root that yielded the Latin *oc-ulus*? As long as we trust to our ears, or to what is complacently called common sense, it would seem mere fastidiousness to reject so evident an etymology. But as soon as we know the real chemistry of vowels and consonants, we shrink instinctly from such combinations. If a German word has the same sound as a Greek word, the two words cannot be the same, unless we ignore that independent process of phonetic growth which made Greek Greek, and German German. Whenever we find in Greek a media, a *g*, we expect in Gothic the corresponding tenuis. Thus the root *gan*, which we have in Greek γιγνώσκω, is in Gothic *kann*. The Greek γόνυ, Lat. *genu*, is in Gothic *kniu*. If, therefore, αὐγή existed in Gothic it would be *auko*, and not *augo*. Secondly, the diphthong *au* in *augo* would be different from the Greek diphthong. Grimm supposed that the Gothic *augo* came from the same etymon which yields the Latin *oc-ulus*, the Sanskrit *ak-sh-i*, eye, the Greek ὄσσε for ὄκι-ε, and likewise the Greek stem ὀπ in ὄπ-ωπ-α, ὄμμα, and ὀφ-θ-αλμός. It is true that the short radical vowel *a* in Sanskrit, *o* in Greek, *u* in Latin, sinks down to *u* in Gothic, and it is equally true, as Grimm has shown, that, according to a phonetic law peculiar to Gothic, *u* before *h* and *r* is changed to *aú*. Grimm, therefore, takes the Gothic *aúgô* for *aúhô, and this for *uhô, which, as he shows, would be a proper representative in Gothic of the Sanskrit *ak-an*, or *aksh-an*.

But here Grimm seems wrong. If the *au* of *augô* were this peculiar Gothic *aú*, which represents an original short *a*, changed to *u*, and then raised to a diphthong by the insertion of a short *a*, then that diphthong would be restricted to Gothic; and the other Teutonic dialects would have their own representatives for an original short *a*. But in Anglo-Saxon we find *eáge*, in Old High German *augâ*, both pointing to a labial diphthong, *i.e.* to a radical *u* raised to *au*.14

Professor Ebel,15 in order to avoid this difficulty, proposed a different explanation. He supposed that the *k* of the root *ak* was softened to *kv*, and that *augô* represents an original *agvâ* or *ahvâ*, the *v* of *hvâ* being inserted before the *h* and changed to *u*. As an analogous case he quoted the Sanskrit enclitic particle *ca*, Latin *que*, Gothic **hva*, which **hva* appears always under the form of *uh*. Leo Meyer takes the same view, and quotes, as an analogon, *haubida* as possibly identical with *caput*, originally **kapvat*.

These cases, however, are not quite analogous. The enclitic particle *ca*, in Gothic **hva*, had to lose its final vowel. It thus became unpronounceable, and the short vowel *u* was added simply to facilitate its pronunciation.16 There was no such difficulty in pronouncing **ah* or **uh* in Gothic, still less the derivative form **ahvô*, if such a form had ever existed.

Another explanation was therefore attempted by the late Dr. Lottner.17 He supposed that the root *ak* existed also with a nasal as *ank*, and that *ankô* could be changed to *aukô*, and *aukô* to *augô*. In reply to this we must remark that in the Teutonic dialects the root *ak* never appears as *ank*, and that the transition of *an* into *au*, though possible under certain conditions, is not a phonetic process of frequent occurrence.

Besides, in all these derivations there is a difficulty, though not a serious one, viz.: that an original tenuis, the *k*, is supposed irregularly to have been changed into *g*, instead of what it ought to be, an *h*. Although this is not altogether anomalous,18 yet it has to be taken into account. Professor Curtius, therefore, though he admits a possible connection between Gothic *augô* and the root *ak*, speaks cautiously on the subject. On page 99 he refers to *augô* as more distantly connected with that root, and on p. 457 he simply refers to the attempts of Ebel, Grassmann, and Lottner to explain the diphthong *au*, without himself expressing any decided opinion. Nor does he commit himself to any opinion as to the origin of αὐγή, though, of course, he never thinks of connecting the two words, Gothic *augô* and Greek αὐγή, as coming from the same root.

The etymology of the Greek αὐγή, in the sense of light or splendor, is not known unless we connect it with the Sanskrit *ojas*, which, however, means vigor rather than splendor. The etymology of *oculus*, on the contrary, is clear; it comes from a root *ak*, to be sharp, to point, to fix, and it is closely connected with the Sanskrit word for eye, *akshi*, and with the Greek ὄσσε. The etymology of the German word *Auge* is, as yet, unknown. All we may safely assert is, that, in spite of the most favorable appearances, it cannot, for the present, be traced back to the same source as either the Greek αὐγή or the Latin *oculus*.

If we simply transliterated the Gothic *augô* into Sanskrit, we should expect some word like *ohan*, nom. *ohâ*. The question is, may we take the liberty, which many of the most eminent comparative philologists allow themselves, of deriving Gothic, Greek, and Latin words from roots which occur in

Sanskrit, only, but which have left no trace of their former presence in any other language? If so, then there would be little difficulty in finding an etymology for the Gothic *augô*. There is in Sanskrit a root *ûh*, which means to watch, to spy, to look. It occurs frequently in the Veda, and from it we have likewise a substantive, *oha-s*, look or appearance. If, in Sanskrit itself this root had yielded a name for eye, such as *ohan*, the instrument of looking, I should not hesitate for a moment to identify this Sanskrit word *ohan* with the Gothic *augô*. No objection could be raised on phonetic grounds. Phonetically the two words would be one and the same. But as in Sanskrit such a derivation has not been found, and as in Gothic the root *ûh* never occurs, such an etymology would not be satisfactory. The number of words of unknown origin is very considerable as yet in Sanskrit, in Greek, in Latin, and in every one of the Aryan languages; and it is far better to acknowledge this fact, than to sanction the smallest violation of any of those phonetic laws, which some have called the straight jacket, but which are in reality, the leading strings of all true etymology.

If we now turn to grammar, properly so called, and ask what Comparative Philology has done for it, we must distinguish between two kinds of grammatical knowledge. Grammar may be looked upon as a mere art, and, as taught at present in most schools, it is nothing but an art. We learn to play on a foreign language as we learn to play on a musical instrument, and we may arrive at the highest perfection in performing on any instrument, without having a notion of thorough bass or the laws of harmony. For practical purposes this purely empirical knowledge is all that is required. But though it would be a mistake to attempt in our elementary schools to replace an empirical by a scientific knowledge of grammar, that empirical knowledge of grammar ought in time to be raised to a real, rational, and satisfying knowledge, a knowledge not only of facts, but of reasons; a knowledge that teaches us not only what grammar is, but how it came to be what it is. To know grammar is very well, but to speak all one's life of gerunds and supines and infinitives, without having an idea what these formations really are, is a kind of knowledge not quite worthy of a scholar.

We laugh at people who still believe in ghosts and witches, but a belief in infinitives and supines is not only tolerated, but inculcated in our best schools and universities. Now, what do we really mean if we speak of an infinitive? It is a time-honored name, no doubt, handed down to us from the Middle Ages; it has its distant roots in Rome, Alexandria, and Athens;—but has it any real kernel? Has it any more body or substance than such names as Satyrs and Lamias?

Let us look at the history of the name before we look at the mischief which it, like many other names, has caused by making people believe that whenever there is a name there must be something behind it. The name was invented by Greek philosophers who, in their first attempts at classifying and giving names to the various forms of language, did not know whether to class such forms as γράφειν, γράψειν, γράψαι, γεγραφέναι, γράφεσθαι, γράψεσθαι, γέγραφθαι, γράψασθαι, γραφθῆναι, γραφθήσεσθαι, as nouns or as verbs. They had established for their own satisfaction the broad distinction between nouns (ὀνόματα) and verbs (ῥήματα); they had assigned to each a definition, but, after having done so, they found that forms like γράφειν would not fit their definition either of noun or verb.19 What could they do? Some (the Stoics) represented the forms in ειν, etc., as a subdivision of the verb, and introduced for them the name ῥῆμα ἀπαρέμφατον or γενικώτατον. Others recognized them as a separate part of speech, raising their number from eight to nine or ten. Others, again, classed them under the adverb (ἐπιρρημα), as one of the eight recognized parts of speech. The Stoics, taking their stand on Aristotle's definition of ῥῆμα, could not but regard the infinitive as ῥῆμα, because it implied time, past, present, or future, which was with them recognized as the specific characteristic of the verb (*Zeitwort*). But they went further, and called forms such as γράφειν, etc., ῥῆμα, in the highest or most general sense, distinguishing other verbal forms, such as γράφει, etc., by the names of κατηγόρημα or σύμβαμα. Afterwards, in the progress of grammatical science, the definition of ῥῆμα became more explicit and complete. It was pointed out that a verb, besides its predicative meaning (ἔμφασις), is able to20 express several additional meanings (παρακολουθήματα or παρεμφάσεις), viz.: not only time, as already pointed out by Aristotle, but also person and number. The two latter meanings, however, being absent in γράφειν, this was now called ῥῆμα ἀπαρέμφατον (without by-meanings), or γενικώτατον, and, for practical purposes, this ῥῆμα ἀπαρέμφατον soon became the prototype of conjugation.

So far there was only confusion, arising from a want of precision in classifying the different forms of the verb. But when the Greek terminology was transplanted to Rome, real mischief began. Instead of ῥῆμα γενικώτατον, we now find the erroneous, or, at all events, inaccurate, translation, *modus infinitus*, and *infinitivus* by itself. What was originally meant as an adjective belonging to ῥῆμα, became a substantive, the infinitive, and though the question arose again and again what this infinitive really was, whether a noun, or a verb, or an adverb; whether a mood or not a mood; the real existence of such a thing as an infinitive could no longer be doubted. One can hardly trust one's eyes in reading the extraordinary discussions on the nature of the infinitive in grammatical works of successive centuries up to the nineteenth. Suffice it to say that Gottfried Hermann, the great reformer of classical grammars, treated the infinitive again as an adverb, and, therefore, as a part of speech belonging to the particles. We ourselves were brought up to believe in infinitives; and to doubt the existence of this grammatical entity would have been considered in our younger days a most dangerous heresy.

And yet, how much confused thought, and how much controversy might have been avoided, if this grammatical term of infinitive had never been invented.21,C The fact is that what we call infinitives are nothing more or less than cases of verbal nouns, and not till they are treated as what they are shall we ever gain an insight into the nature and the historical development of these grammatical monsters.

Take the old Homeric infinitive in μεναι, and you find its explanation in the Sanskrit termination *mane*, *i.e. manai*, the native of the suffix *man* (not, as others suppose, the locative of a suffix *mana*), by which a large number of nouns are formed in Sanskrit. From *gnâ*, to know, we have *(g)nâman*, Latin *(g)nomén*, that by which a thing is known, its name; from *gan*, to be born, *gánman*, birth. In Greek this suffix man is chiefly used for forming masculine nouns, such as γνώ-μων, γνώ-μονος, literally a knower; τλή-μων, a sufferer; or as μην in ποι-μήν, a shepherd, literally a feeder. In Latin, on the contrary, *men* occurs frequently at the end of abstract nouns in the neuter gender, such as *teg-men*, the covering, or *tegu-men* or *tegi-men*; *solamen*, consolation; *voca-men*, an appellation; *certa-men*, a contest; and many more, particularly in ancient Latin; while in classical Latin the fuller suffix *mentum* predominates. If then we read in Homer, κύνας ἔτευξε δῶμα φυλασσέμεναι, we may call φυλασσέμεναι an infinitive, if we like, and translate "he made dogs to protect the house;" but the form which we have before us, is simply a dative of an old abstract noun in μεν, and the original meaning was "for the protection of the house," or "for protecting the house;" as if we said in Latin, *tutamini domum*.

The infinitives in μεν may be corruptions of those in μεναι, unless we take μεν as an archaic accusative, which, though without analogy in Greek, would correspond to Latin accusatives like *tegmen*, and express the general object of certain acts or movements. In Sanskrit, at least in the Veda, infinitives in *mane* occur, such as *dā́-mane*, to give, Greek δό-μεναι; *vid-máne*, to know, Greek ϝιδ-μεναι.22

The question next arises, if this is a satisfactory explanation of the infinitives in μεναι, how are we to explain the infinitives in εναι? We find in Homer, not only ἴμεναι, to go, but also ἰέναι; not only ἔμμεναι, to be, but also εἶναι, *i.e.*, ἔσ-εναι. Bopp simply says that the *m* is lost, but he brings no evidence that in Greek an *m* can thus be lost without any provocation. The real explanation, here, as elsewhere, is supplied by the *Beieinander* (the collateral growth), not by the *Nacheinander* (the successive growth) of language. Besides the suffix *man*, the Aryan languages possessed two other suffixes, *van* and *an*, which were added to verbal bases just like *man*. By the side of *dâman*, the act of giving, we find in the Veda *dâ-van*, the act of giving, and a dative *dâ-váne*, with the accent on the suffix, meaning for the giving, *i.e.* to give. Now in Greek this *v* would necessarily disappear, though its former presence might be indicated by the *digamma æolicum*. Thus, instead of Sanskrit *dâváne*, we should have in Greek δοϝέναι, δοέναι, and contracted δοῦναι, the regular form of the infinitive of the aorist, a form in which the diphthong ου would remain inexplicable, except for the former presence of the lost syllable ϝε. In the same manner εἶναι stands for ἐσ-ϝέναι, ἐσ-έναι, ἐέναι, εἶναι. Hence ἰέναι, stands for ἰϝέναι, and even the accent remains on the suffix *van*, just as it did in Sanskrit.

As the infinitives in μεναι were traced back to the suffix *man*, and those in ϝεναι to a suffix *van*, the regular infinitives in εναι after consonants, and ναι after vowels, must be referred to the suffix *an*, dat. *ane*. Here, too, we find analogous forms in the Veda. From *dhûrv*, to hurt, we have *dhûrv-ane*, for the purpose of hurting, in order to hurt; in Rv. IX. 61, 30, we find *vibhv-áne*, Rv. VI. 61, 13, in order to conquer, and by the same suffix the Greeks formed their infinitives of the perfect, λελοιπ-έναι, and the infinitives of the verbs in μι, τιθέ-ναι, διδο-ναι, ἱστα-ναι, etc.

In order to explain, after these antecedents, the origin of the infinitive in ειν, as τύπτειν, we must admit either the shortening of ναι to νι, which is difficult; or the existence of a locative in ι by the side of a dative in αι. That the locative can take the place of the dative we see clearly in the Sanskrit forms of the aorist, *parsháni*, to cross, *nesháni*, to lead, which, as far as their form, not their origin, is concerned, would well match Greek forms like λύσειν in the future. In either case, τύπτε-νι in Greek would have become τύπτειν, just as τύπτε-σι became τύπτεις. In the Doric dialect this throwing back of the final ι is omitted in the second person singular, where the Dorians may say ἀμέλγες for ἀμέλγεις; and in the same Doric dialect the infinitive, too, occurs in εν instead of ειν; *e.g.*, ἀείδεν instead of ἀείδειν. (Buttman, "Greek Gr.," § 103, 10, 11.)

In this manner the growth of grammatical forms can be made as clear as the sequence of any historical events in the history of the world, nay, I should say far clearer, far more intelligible; and I should think that even the first learning of these grammatical forms might be somewhat seasoned and rendered more really instructive by allowing the pupil, from time to time, a glimpse into the past history of the Greek and Latin languages. In English what we call the infinitive is clearly a dative; *to speak* shows by its very preposition what it was intended for. How easy, then, to explain to a beginner that if he translates, "able to speak," by ἱκανὸς εἰπεῖν, the Greek infinitive is really the same as the English, and that εἰπεῖν stands for εἶπενι and this for εἴπεναι, which, to a certain extent, answers the same purpose as the Greek ἔπει, the dative of ἔπος, and therefore originally ἔπεσι.

And remark, these very datives and locatives of nouns formed by the suffix ος in Greek, as in Sanskrit, *es* in Latin, though they yield no infinitives in Greek, yield the most common form of the infinitive in Latin, and may be traced also in Sanskrit. As from *genus* we form a dative *generi*, and a locative *genere*, which stands for *genese*, so from *gigno* an abstract noun would be formed, *gignus*, and from it a dative, *gigneri*, and a locative, *gignere*. I do not say that the intermediate form *gignus* existed in the spoken Latin, I only maintain that such a form would be analogous to *gen-us*, *op-us*, *fœd-us*, and that in Sanskrit the process is exactly the same. We form in Sanskrit a substantive *càkshas*, sight, *càkshus*, eye; and we find the dative of *càkshas*, *i.e.* *càkshase*, used as what we should call an infinitive, in order to see. But we also find another so-called infinitive, *jîvàse*, in order to live, although there is no noun, *jîvas*, life; we find *áyase*, to go, although there is no noun *áyas*, going. This Sanskrit *áyase* explains the Latin *i-re*, as *i-vane explained the Greek ἰέναι. The intention of the old framers of language is throughout the same. They differ only in the means which they use, one might almost say, at random; and the differences between Sanskrit, Greek, and Latin are often due to the simple fact that out of many possible forms that might be used and had been used before the Aryan languages became traditional, settled, and national, one family or clan or nation fancied one, another another. While this one became fixed and classical, all others became useless, remained perhaps here and there in proverbial sayings or in sacred songs, but were given up at last completely, as strange, obsolete, and unintelligible.

And even then, after a grammatical form has become obsolete and unintelligible, it by no means loses its power of further development. Though the Greeks did not themselves, we still imagine that we feel the infinitive as the case of an abstract noun in many constructions. Thus χαλεπὸν εὑρεῖν, difficult to find, was originally, difficult in the finding, or difficult for the act of finding; δεινὸς λέγειν, meant literally, powerful in speaking; ἄρχομαι λέγειν, I begin to speak, *i.e.*, I direct myself to the act of speaking; κέλεαί με μυθήσασθαι, you bid me to speak, *i.e.*, you order me towards the act of speaking; φοβοῦμαι διελέγχειν σε, I am afraid of refuting you, *i.e.*, I fear in the act, or, I shrink when brought towards the act, of refuting you; σὸν ἔργον λέγειν, your business is in or towards speaking, you have to speak; πᾶσιν ἀδεῖν χαλεπόν, there is something difficult in pleasing everybody, or, in our endeavor after pleasing everybody. In all these cases the so-called infinitive can, with an effort, still be felt as a noun in an oblique case. But in course of time expressions such as χαλεπὸν ἀδεῖν, it is difficult to please, ἀγαθὸν λέγειν, it is good to speak, left in the mind of the speaker the impression that ἀδεῖν and λέγειν were subjects in the nominative, the pleasing is difficult, the speaking is good; and by adding the article, these oblique cases of verbal nouns actually became nominatives, τὸ ἀδειν, the act of pleasing, τὸ λέγειν, the act of speaking, capable of being used in every case, *e.g.*, ἐπιθυμια τοῦ πιειν, *desiderium bibendi*. This regeneration, this process of creating new words out of decaying and decayed materials may seem at first sight incredible, yet it is as certain as the change with which we began our discussion of the infinitive. I mean the change of the conception of a ῥῆμα γενικώτατον, a *verbum generalissimum*, into a *generalissimus* or *infinitivus*. Nor is the process without analogy in modern languages. The French *l'avenir*, the future (*Zukunft*), is hardly the Latin *advenire*. That would mean the arriving, the coming, but not what is to come. I believe *l'avenir* was (*quod est*) *ad venire*, what is to come, contracted to *l'avenir*. In Low-German *to come* assumes even the character of an adjective, and we can speak not only of a year to come, but of a to-come year, *de tokum Jahr*.23

This process of grammatical vivisection may be painful in the eyes of classical scholars, yet even they must see how great a difference there is in the quality of knowledge imparted by our Greek and Latin grammars, and by comparative grammar. I do not deny that at first children must learn Greek and Latin mechanically, but it is not right that they should remain satisfied with mere paradigms and technical terms, without knowing the real nature and origin of so-called infinitives, gerunds, and supines. Every child will learn the construction of the accusative with the infinitive, but I well remember my utter amazement when I first was taught to say *Miror te ad me nihil scribere*, "I am surprised that you write nothing to me." How easy would it have been to explain that *scribere* was originally a locative of a verbal noun, and that there was nothing strange or irrational in saying, "I wonder at thee in the act of not writing to me." This first step once taken, everything else followed by slow degrees, but even in phrases like *Spero te mihi ignoscere*, we can still see the first steps which led from "I hope or I desire thee, toward the act of forgiving me," to "I trust thee to forgive me." It is the object of the comparative philologist to gather up the scattered fragments, to arrange them and fit them, and thus to show that language is something rational, human, intelligible, the very embodiment of the mind of man in its growth from the lowest to the highest stage, and with capabilities for further growth far beyond what we can at present conceive or imagine.

As to writing Greek and Latin verse, I do not maintain that a knowledge of Comparative Philology will help us much. It is simply an art that must be acquired by practice, if in these our busy days it is still worth acquiring. A good memory will no doubt enable us to say at a moment's notice whether certain syllables are long or short. But is it not far more interesting to know why certain vowels are long and others short, than to be able to string longs and shorts together in imitation of Greek and Latin hexameters? Now in many cases the reason why certain vowels are long or short, can be supplied by Comparative Philology alone. We may learn from Latin grammar that the *i* in *fīdus*, trusty, and in *fīdo*, I trust, is long, and that it is short in *fĭdes*, trust, and *perfĭdus*, faithless; but as all these words are derived from the same root, why should some have a long, others a short vowel? A comparison of Sanskrit at once supplies an answer. Certain derivatives, not only in Latin but in Sanskrit and Greek too, require what is called *Guṇa* of the radical vowel. In *fīdus* and *fīdo*, the *i* is really a diphthong, and represents a more ancient *ei* or *oi*, the former appearing in Greek πείθω, the latter in Latin *foedus*, a truce.

We learn from our Greek grammars that the second syllable in δείκνῡμι is long, but in the plural, δείκνῠμεν, it is short. This cannot be by accident, and we may observe the same change in δάμνημι and δάμναμεν, and similar words. Nothing, however, but a study of Sanskrit would have enabled us to discover the reason of this change, which is really the accent in its most primitive working, such as we can watch it in the Vedic Sanskrit, where it produces exactly the same change, only with far greater regularity and perspicuity.

Why, again, do we say in Greek, οἶδα, I know, but ἴσ-μεν, we know? Why τέτληκα, but τέτλαμεν? Why μέμονα, but μέμαμεν? There is no recollection in the minds of the Greeks of the motive power that was once at work, and left its traces in these grammatical convulsions; but in Sanskrit we still see, as it were, a lower stratum of grammatical growth, and we can there watch the regular working of laws which required these changes, and which have left their impress not only on Greek, but on Sanskrit, and even on German. The same necessity which made Homer say οἶδα and ἴδμεν, and the Vedic poet *véda* and *vidmás*, still holds good, and makes us say in German, *Ich weiss*, I know, but *wir wissen*, we know.

All this becomes clear and intelligible by the light of Comparative Grammar; anomalies vanish, exceptions prove the rule, and we perceive more plainly every day how in language, as elsewhere, the conflict between the freedom claimed by each individual and the resistance offered by the community at large, establishes in the end a reign of law most wonderful, yet perfectly rational and intelligible.

These are but a few small specimens to show you what Comparative Philology can do for Greek and Latin; and how it has given a new life to the study of languages by discovering, so to say, and laying bare, the traces of that old life, that prehistoric growth, which made language what we find it in the oldest literary monuments, and which still supplies the vigor of the language of our own time. A knowledge of the mere facts of language is interesting enough; nay, if you ask yourself what grammars really are—those very Greek and Latin grammars which we hated so much in our schoolboy days—you will find that they are store-houses, richer than the richest museums of plants or minerals, more carefully classified and labeled than the productions of any of the great kingdoms of nature. Every form of declension and conjugation, every genitive and every so-called infinitive and gerund, is the result of a long succession of efforts, and of intelligent efforts. There is nothing accidental, nothing irregular, nothing without a purpose and meaning in any part of Greek or Latin grammar. No one who has once discovered this hidden life of language, no one who has once found out that what seemed to be merely anomalous and whimsical in language is but, as it were, a petrification of thought, of deep, curious, poetical, philosophical thought, will ever rest again till he has descended as far as he can descend into the ancient shafts of human speech, exploring level after level, and testing every successive foundation which supports the surface of each spoken language.

One of the great charms of this new science is that there is still so much to explore, so much to sift, so much to arrange. I shall not, therefore, be satisfied with merely lecturing on Comparative Philology, but I hope I shall be able to form a small philological society of more advanced students, who will come and work with me, and bring the results of their special studies as materials for the advancement of our science. If there are scholars here who have devoted their attention to the study of Homer, Comparative Philology will place in their hands a light with which to explore the dark crypt on which the temple of the Homeric language was erected. If there are scholars who know their Plautus or Lucretius, Comparative Philology will give them a key to grammatical forms in ancient Latin, which, even if supported by an Ambrosian palimpsest, might still seem hazardous and problematical. As there is no field and no garden that has not its geological antecedents, there is no language and no dialect which does not receive light from a study of Comparative Philology, and reflect light in return on more general problems. As in geology again, so in Comparative Philology, no progress is possible without a division of labor, and without the most general coöperation. The most experienced geologist may learn something from a miner or from a ploughboy; the most experienced comparative philologist may learn something from a schoolboy or from a child.

I have thus explained to you what, if you will but assist me, I should like to do as the first occupant of this new chair of Comparative Philology. In my public lectures I must be satisfied with teaching. In my private lectures, I hope I shall not only teach, but also learn, and receive back as much as I have to give.

NOTES.

NOTE A.
ON THE FINAL DENTAL OF THE PRONOMINAL STEM *tad*.

ONE or two instances may here suffice to show how compassless even the best comparative philologists find themselves if, without a knowledge of Sanskrit, they venture into the deep waters of grammatical research. What can be clearer at first sight than that the demonstrative pronoun *that* has the same base in Sanskrit, Greek, Latin, and German? Bopp places together (§ 349) the following forms of the neuter:—

Sanskrit Zend Greek Latin Gothic

tat   *taḍ.*   τό   *is-tud   thata*

and he draws from them the following conclusions:—

In the Sanskrit *ta-t* we have the same pronominal element repeated twice, and this repeated pronominal element became afterwards the general sign of the neuter after other pronominal stems, such as *ya-t*, *ka-t*.

Such a conclusion seems extremely probable, particularly when we compare the masculine form *sa-s*, the old nom. sing., instead of the ordinary *sa*. But the first question that has to be answered is, whether this is phonetically possible, and how.

If *tat* in Sanskrit is *ta + ta*, then we expect in Gothic *tha + tha*, instead of which we find *tha + ta*. We expect in Latin *istut*, not *istud*, *illut*, not *illud*, *it*, not *id*, for Latin represents final *t* in Sanskrit by *t*, not by *d*. The old Latin ablative in *d* is not a case in point, as we shall see afterwards.

Both Gothic *tha-ta*, therefore, and Latin *istud*, postulate a Sanskrit *tad*, while Zend and Greek at all events do not conflict with an original final media. Everything therefore depends on what was the original form in Sanskrit; and here no Sanskrit scholar would hesitate for one moment between *tat* and *tad*. Whatever the origin of *tat* may have been, it is quite certain that Sanskrit knows only of *tad*, never of *tat*. There are various ways of testing the original surd or sonant nature of final consonants in Sanskrit. One of the safest seems to me to see how those consonants behave before *taddhita* or secondary suffixes, which require no change in the final consonant of the base. Thus before the suffix *îya* (called *cha* by Pâṇini) the final consonant is never changed, yet we find *tad-îya*, like *mad-îya*, *tvad-îya*, *asmad-îya*, *yushmad-îya*, etc. Again, before the possessive suffix *vat* final consonants of nominal bases suffer no change. This is distinctly stated by Pâṇini, I. 4, 19. Hence we have *vidyut-vân*, from *vidyut*, lightning, from the root *dyut*; we have *udaśvit-vân*, from *uda-śvi-t*. In both cases the original final tenuis remains unchanged. Hence, if we find *tad-vân*, *kad-vân*, our test shows us again that the final consonant in *tad* and *kad* is a media, and that the *d* of these words is not a modification of *t*.

Taking our stand therefore on the undoubted facts of Sanskrit grammar, we cannot recognize *t* as the termination of the neuter of pronominal stems, but only *d*;24 nor can we accept Bopp's explanation of *tad* as a compound of *ta* + t, unless the transition of an original *t* into a Sanskrit and Latin *d* can be established by sufficient evidence. Even then that transition would have to be referred to a time before Sanskrit and Gothic became distinct languages, for the Gothic *tha-ta* is the counterpart of the Sanskrit *tad*, and not of *tat*.

Bopp endeavors to defend the transition of an original *t* into Latin *d* by the termination of the old ablatives, such as *gnaivod*, etc. But here again it is certain that the original termination was *d*, and not *t*. It is so in Latin, it may be so in Zend, where, as Justi points out, the *d* of the ablative is probably a media.25 In Sanskrit it is certainly a media in such forms as *mad*, *tvad*, *asmad*, which Bopp considers as old ablatives, and which in *madîya*, etc., show the original media. In other cases it is impossible in Sanskrit to test the nature of the final dental in the ablative, because *d* is always determined by its position in a sentence. But under no circumstances could we appeal to Latin *gnaivod* in order to prove a transition of an original *t* into *d*; while on the contrary all the evidence at present is in favor of a media, as the final letter both of the ablative and of the neuter bases of pronouns, such as *tad* and *yad*.

These may seem *minutiæ*, but the whole of Comparative Grammar is made up of *minutiæ*, which, nevertheless, if carefully joined together and cemented, lead to conclusions of unexpected magnitude.

NOTE B.
DID FEMININE BASES IN *â* TAKE *s* IN THE NOMINATIVE SINGULAR?

I ADD one other instance to show how a more accurate knowledge of Sanskrit would have guarded comparative philologists against rash conclusions. With regard to the nominative singular of feminine bases ending in derivative *â*, the question arose, whether words like *bona* in Latin, ἀγαθά in Greek, *sivâ* in Sanskrit, had originally an *s* as the sign of the nom. sing., which was afterwards lost, or whether they never took that termination. Bopp (§ 136), Schleicher (§ 246), and others seem to believe in the loss of the *s*, chiefly, it would seem, because the *s* is added to feminine bases ending in *î* and *û*. Benfey26 takes the opposite view, viz. that feminines in *â* never took the *s* of the nom. sing. But he adds one exception, the Vedic *gnâ-s*. This remark has caused much mischief. Without verifying Benfey's statements, Schleicher (l.c.) quotes the same exception, though cautiously referring to the Sanskrit dictionary of Boehtlingk and Roth as his authority. Later writers, for instance Merguet,27 leave out all restrictions, simply appealing to this Vedic form *gnâ-s* in support of the theory that feminine bases in *â* too took originally *s* as sign of the nom. sing. and afterwards dropped it. Even so careful a scholar as Büchler28 speaks of the *s* as lost.

There is, first of all, no reason whatever why the *s* should have been added29; secondly, there is none why it should have been lost. But, whatever opinion we may hold in this respect, the appeal to the Vedic *gnâ-s* cannot certainly be sustained, and the word should at all events be obelized till there is better evidence for it than we possess at present.30

The passage which is always quoted from the Rv. IV. 9, 4, as showing *gnâ-s* to be a nom. sing. in *s*, is extremely difficult, and as it stands at present, most likely corrupt:—

Utá gnā́ḥ agníḥ adhvaré utó gṛhá-patiḥ dáme, utá brahmā́ ní sídati.

This could only be translated:—

"Agni sits down at the sacrifice as a woman, as lord in the house, and as priest."

This, however, is impossible, for Agni, the god of fire, is never represented in the Veda as a woman. If we took *gnâḥ* as a genitive, we might translate, "Agni sits down in the sacrifice of the lady of the house," but this again would be utterly incongruous in Vedic poetry.

I believe the verse is corrupt, and I should propose to read:—

Utá agnā́v agníḥ adhvaré.

"Agni sits down at the sacrifice in the fire, as lord in the house, and as a priest."

The ideas that Agni, the god of fire, sits down in the fire, or that Agni is lighted by Agni, or that Agni is both the sacrificial fire and the priest, are familiar to every reader of the Veda. Thus we read, I. 12, 6, agnínâ agníḥ sám idhyate, "Agni is lighted by Agni;" X. 88, 1, we find Agni invoked as ā́-hutam agnáu, etc.

But whether this emendation be right or wrong, it must be quite clear how unsafe it would be to support the theory that feminine bases in *â* ended originally in *s* by this solitary passage from the Veda.

NOTE C.
GRAMMATICAL FORMS IN SANSKRIT CORRESPONDING TO SO-CALLED INFINITIVES IN GREEK AND LATIN.

THERE is no trace of such a term as infinitive in Sanskrit, and yet exactly the same forms, or, at all events, forms strictly analogous to those which we call infinitives in Greek and Latin, exist in Sanskrit. Here, however, they are treated in the simplest way.

Sanskrit grammarians when giving the rules according to which nouns and adjectives are derived from verbal roots by means of primary suffixes (Kṛt), mention among the rest the suffixes *tum* (Pân., III. 3, 10), *se, ase, adhyai, tavai, tave, shyai,* e, *am, tos, as* (IV. 4, 9–17), defining their meaning in general by that of *tum* (III. 3, 10). This *tum* is said to express immediate futurity in a verb, if governed by another word conveying an intention. An example will make this clearer. In order to say he goes to cook, where "he goes" expresses an intention, and "to cook" is the object of that intention which is to follow immediately, we place the suffix *tum* at the end of the verb *pak*, to cook, and say in Sanskrit, vrajati pak-tum. We might also say pâcako vrajati, he goes as one who means to cook, or vrajati pâkâya, he goes to the act of cooking, placing the abstract noun in the dative; and all these constructions are mentioned together by Sanskrit grammarians. The same takes place after verbs which express a wish (III. 3, 158); *e.g.*, icchati paktum, he wishes to cook, and after such words as *kâla*, time, *samaya*, opportunity, *velâ*, right moment (III. 3, 167); *e.g.*, kâlaḥ paktum, it is time to cook, etc. Other verbs which govern forms in *tum* are (III. 4, 65) *śak*, to be able; *dhṛsh*, to dare; *jñâ*, to know; *glai*, to be weary; *ghaṭ*, to endeavor; *ârabh*, to begin; *labh*, to get; *prakram*, to begin; *utsah*, to endure; *arh*, to deserve; and words like *asti*, there is; *e.g.*, asti bhoktum, it is (possible) to eat; not, it is (necessary) to eat. The forms in *tum* are also enjoined (III. 4, 66) after words like *alam*, expressing fitness, *e.g.*, paryâpto bhoktum, alam bhoktum, kuśalo bhoktum, fit or able to eat.

Here we have everything that is given by Sanskrit grammarians in place of what we should call the Chapter on the Infinitive in Greek and Latin. The only thing that has to be added is the provision, understood in Pânini's grammar, that such suffixes as *tum*, etc., are indeclinable.

And why are they indeclinable? For the simple reason that they are themselves case terminations. Whether Pânini was aware of this, we cannot tell with certainty. From some of his remarks it would seem to be so. When treating of the cases, Pânini (I. 4, 32) explains what we should call the dative by *Sampradâna*. *Sampradâna* means giving (δοτική), but Pânini uses it here as a technical term, and assigns to it the definite meaning of "he whom one looks to by any act" (not only the act of giving, as the commentators imply). It is therefore what we should call "the remote object." Ex. Brâhmaṇâya dhanam dadâti, he gives wealth to the Brâhman. This is afterwards extended by several rules explaining that the *Sampradâna* comes in after verbs expressive of pleasure caused to somebody (I. 4, 33); after *ślâgh*, to applaud, *hnu*, to dissemble, to conceal, *sthâ*,31 to reveal, *śap*, to curse (I. 4, 34); after *dhâray*, to owe (I. 4, 35); *spṛh*, to long for (I. 4, 36); after verbs expressive of anger, ill-will, envy, detraction (I. 4, 37); after *râdh* and *îksh*, if they mean to consider concerning a person (I. 4, 39); after *pratiśru* and *âśru*, in the sense of according (I. 4, 40); *anugṛ* and *pratigṛ*, in the sense of acting in accordance with (I. 4, 41); after *parikrî*, to buy, to hire (I. 4, 44). Other cases of *Sampradâna* are mentioned after such words as *namaḥ*, salutation to, *svasti*, hail, *svâhâ*, salutation to the gods, *svadhâ*, salutation to the manes, *alam*, sufficient for, *vashaṭ*, offered to, a sacrificial invocation, etc. (II. 3, 16); and in such expressions as na tvam triṇâya manye, I do not value thee a straw (II. 3, 17); grâmâya gacchati, he goes to the village (II. 2, 12): where, however, the accusative, too, is equally admissible. Some other cases of Sampradâna are mentioned in the Vârttikas; *e.g.*, I. 4, 44, muktaye harim bhajati, for the sake of liberation he worships Hari; vâtâya kapilâ vidyut, a dark red lightning indicates wind. Very interesting, too, is the construction with the prohibitive *mâ*; *e.g.* mâ câpalâya, lit. not for unsteadiness, *i.e.*, do not act unsteadily.32

In all these cases we easily recognize the identity of *Sampradâna* with the dative in Greek and Latin. If therefore we see that Pâṇini in some of his rules states that *Sampradâna* takes the place of *tum*, the so called infinitive, we can hardly doubt that he had perceived the similarity in the functions of what we call dative and infinitive. Thus he says that instead of phalâny âhartum yâti, he goes to take the fruits, we may use the dative and say phalebhyo yâti, he goes for the fruits; instead of yashṭum yâti, he goes to sacrifice, yâgâya yâti, he goes to the act of sacrificing (II. 3, 14–15).

But whether Pâṇini recognized this fact or not, certain it is that we have only to look at the forms which in the Veda take the place of *tum*, in order to convince ourselves that most of them are datives of verbal nouns. As far as Sanskrit grammar is concerned, we may safely cancel the name of infinitive altogether, and speak instead boldly of datives and other cases of verbal nouns. Whether these verbal nouns admit of the dative case only, and whether some of those datival terminations have become obsolete, are questions which do not concern the grammarian, and nothing would be more unphilosophical than to make such points the specific characteristic of a new grammatical category, the infinitive. The very idea that every noun must possess a complete set of cases, is contrary to all the lessons of the history of language; and though the fact that some of these forms belong to an antiquated phase of language has undoubtedly contributed towards their being used more readily for certain syntactical purposes, the fact remains that in their origin and their original intention they were datives and nothing else. Neither could the fact that these datives of verbal nouns may govern the same case which is governed by the verb, be used as a specific mark, because it is well known that, in Sanskrit more particularly, many nouns retain the power of governing the accusative. We shall now examine some of these so-called infinitives in Sanskrit.

DATIVES IN E.

The simplest dative is that in *e*, after verbal bases ending in consonants or *â*, e.g., *dṛśé*, for the sake of seeing, to see; *vid-é*, to know, *paribhveê*,33 to overcome; *śraddhé kám*, to believe.

DATIVES IN AI.

After some verbs ending in *â*, the dative is irregularly (Grammar, §§ 239, 240) formed in *ai*; Rv. VII. 19, 7, *parâdái*, to surrender. III. 60, 4, *pratimái*, to compare, and the important form *vayodhái*, of which more by and by.

ACCUSATIVES IN AM. GENITIVES AND ABLATIVES IN AS. LOCATIVES IN I.

By the side of these datives we have analogous accusatives in *am*, genitives and ablatives in *as*, locatives in *i*.

Accusative: I. 73, 10, śakéma yámam, May we be able to get. I. 94, 3, śakéma tvâ samídhan, May we be able to light thee. This may be the Oscan and Umbrian infinitive in *um*, *om* (*u*, *o*), if we take *yama* as a base in *a*, and *m* as the sign of the accusative. In Sanskrit it is impossible to determine this question, for that bases in *a* also are used for similar purposes is clearly seen in datives like *dábhaya*; *e.g.*, Rv. V. 44, 2, ná dábhaya, not to conquer; VIII. 96, 1, nṛbhyâḥ táraya síndhavaḥ su-pârāḥ, the rivers easy to cross for men. Whether the Vedic imperatives in *âya* (*śâyac*) admit of a similar explanation is doubtful on account of the accent.

Genitive: *vilikhaḥ*, in îśvaro vilikhaḥ, cognizant of drawing; and possibly X. 108, 2, atiskádaḥ bhiyásâ, from fear of crossing.

Ablative: Rv. VIII. 1, 12, purâ âtṛdaḥ, before striking.

Locative: Rv. V. 52, 12, dṛśí tvishé, to shine in glancing(?)

DATIVES IN S-E.

The same termination of the dative is added to verbal bases which have taken the increment of the aorist, the s. Thus from *ji*, to conquer, we have *ji-sh*, and *je-sh*, and from both datival forms with infinitival function. I. 111, 4, té naḥ hinvantu sâtáye dhiyé jishé, May they bring us to wealth, wisdom, victory!

I. 100, 11, apā́m tokásya tánayasya jeshé, May Indra help us for getting water, children, and descendants. Cf. VI. 44, 18.

Or, after bases ending in consonants, *upaprakshé*; V. 47, 6, upa-prakshé vŕshaṇaḥ - - - vadhvā́ḥ yanti áccha, the men go towards their wives to embrace.

These forms correspond to Greek infinitives like λῦσαι and τύψαι, possibly to Latin infinitives like *ferre*, for *fer-se*, *velle* for *vel-se*, and *voluis-se*; for *se*, following immediately on a consonant, can never represent the Sanskrit *ase*. With regard to infinitives like *fac-se*, *dic-se*, I do not venture to decide whether they are primitive forms, or contracted, though *fac-se* could hardly be called a contraction of *fecisse*. The 2d pers. sing. of the imperative of the 1st aorist middle, λῦσαι, is identical with the infinitive in form, and the transition of meaning from the infinitive to the imperative is well known in Greek and other languages. (Παῖδα δ' ἐμοὶ λῦσαί τε φίλην τά τ' ἄποινα δέχεσθαι, Deliver up my dear child and accept the ransom). Several of these aoristic forms are sometimes very perplexing in Sanskrit. If we find, for instance, *stushé*, we cannot always tell whether it is the infinitive (λῦσαι); or the 1st pers. sing. of the aor. Âtmanep. in the subjunctive (for *stushai*), Let me praise (λύσωμαι); or lastly, the 2d pers. sing. Âtmanep. in the indicative (λύῃ). If *stushe* has no accent, we know, of course, that it cannot be the infinitive, as in X. 93, 9; but when it has the accent on the last, it may, in certain constructions, be either infinitive, or 1st pers. sing. aor. Âtm. subj. Here we want far more careful grammatical studies on the language of the Veda, before we can venture to translate with certainty. In places, for instance, where as in I. 122, 7 we have a nominative with *stushé*, it is clear that it must be taken as an infinitive, stushé sâ vâm - - - râtíḥ, your gift, Varuṇa and Mitra, is to be praised; but in other places, such as VIII. 5, 4, the choice is difficult. In VIII. 65, 5, índra griṇîshé u stushé, I should propose to translate, Indra, thou longest for praising, thou desirest to be praised, cf. VIII. 71, 15; while in II. 20, 4, tám u stushe índram tám gr̥ṇîshe, I translate, Let me praise Indra, let me laud him, admitting here, the irregular retention of Vikaraṇa in the aorist, which can be defended by analogous forms such as gŕ-ṇî-sh-áṇi, stŕ̥-ṇî-sh-áṇi, of which more hereafter. However, all these translations, as every real scholar knows, are, and can be tentative only. Nothing but a complete Vedic grammar, such as we may soon expect from Professor Benfey, will give us safe ground to stand on.

DATIVES IN *ÂYAI*.

Feminine bases in *â* form their dative in *âyai*, and thus we find *carâyai* used in the Veda, VII. 77, 1, as what we should call an infinitive, in the sense of to go. No other cases of *carâ* have as yet been met with. A similar form is *jarâyai*, to praise, I. 38, 13.

DATIVES IN *AYE*.

We have next to consider bases in *i*, forming their dative in *áye*. Here, whenever we are acquainted with the word in other cases, we naturally take *aye* as a simple dative of a noun. Thus in I. 31, 8, we should translate *sanáye dhánânâm*, for the acquisition of treasures, because we are accustomed to other cases, such as I. 100, 13, *sanáyas*, acquisitions, V. 27, 3, *saním*, wealth. But if we find, V. 80, 5, *dṛśáye naḥ asthât*, she stood to be seen by us, lit., for our seeing, then we prefer, though wrongly, to look upon such datives as infinitives, simply because we have not met with other cases of dṛśi-s.

DATIVES IN *TAYE*.

What applies to datives of nouns in *i*, applies with still greater force to datives of nouns in *ti*. There is no reason why in IX. 96, 4 we should call *áhataye*, to be without hurt, an infinitive, simply because no other case of *áhati-s* occurs in the Rig-Veda; while *ájîtaye*, not to fail, in the same line, is called a dative of *ájîti-s*, because it occurs again in the accusative *ájîti-m*.

DATIVES IN *TYAI*.

In *ityái*, to go, I. 113, 6; 124, 1, we have a dative of *iti-s*, the act of going, of which the instrumental *ityâ* occurs likewise, I. 167, 5. This *tyâ*, shortened to *tya*, became afterwards the regular termination of the gerund of compound verbs in *tya* (Grammar § 446), while *ya* (§ 445) points to an original *ya* or *yai*.

DATIVES IN *AS-E*.

Next follow datives from bases in *as*, partly with accent on the first syllable, like neuter nouns in *as*, partly with the accent on *as*; partly with Guṇa, partly without. With regard to them it becomes still clearer how impossible it would be to distinguish between datives of abstract nouns, and other grammatical forms, to be called infinitives. Thus Rv. I. 7, 3 we read *dîrghâya cákshase*, Indra made the sun rise for long glancing, *i.e.*, that it might glance far and wide. It is quite true that no other cases of *cákshas*, seeing, occur, on which ground modern grammarians would probably class it as an infinitive; but the qualifying dative *dîrghâya*, clearly shows that the poet felt *cákshase* as the dative of a noun, and did not trouble himself, whether that noun was defective in other cases or not.

These datives of verbal nouns in *as*, correspond exactly to Latin infinitives in *ěre*, like *vivere* (*jîvâse*), and explain likewise infinitives in *âre*, *êre*, and *îre*, forms which cannot be separated. It has been thought that the nearest approach to an infinitive is to be found in such forms as *jîvâse*, *bhiyáse*, to fear (V. 29, 4), because in such cases the ordinary nominal form would be *bháyas-e*. There is, however, the instrumental *bhiyásâ*, X. 108, 2.

DATIVES IN *MANE*.

Next follow datives from nouns in *man*, *van*, and *an*. The suffix *man* is very common in Sanskrit, for forming verbal nouns, such as *kar-man*, doing, deed, from *kar*. *Van* is almost restricted to forming *nomina agentis*, such as *druh-van*, hating; but we find also substantives like *pat-van*, still used in the sense of flying. *An* also is generally used like *van*, but we can see traces of its employment to form *nomina actionis* in Greek ἀγών, Lat. *turbo*, etc.

Datives of nouns in *man*, used with infinitival functions, are very common in the Veda; *e.g.* I. 164, 6, pṛccâmi vidmane, I ask to know; VIII. 93, 8, dâmane kṛtáḥ, made to give. We find also the instrumental case *vidmánâ*, *e.g.*, VI. 14, 5, vidmánâ urushyáti, he protects by his knowledge. These correspond to Homeric infinitives, like ἴδμεναι, δόμεναι, etc., old datives and not locatives, as Schleicher and Curtius supposed; while forms like δόμεν are to be explained either as abbreviated, or as obsolete accusatives.

DATIVES IN *VANE*.

Of datives in *váne* I only know *dāvâne*, a most valuable grammatical relic, by which Professor Benfey was enabled to explain the Greek δοῦναι, i.e., δοϝέναι.34

DATIVES IN *ANE*.

Of datives in *áne* I pointed out (l.c.) *dhûrv-ane* and *vibhv-áne*, VI. 61, 13, taking the latter as synonymous with *vibhvḗ*, and translating, Sarasvatî, the great, made to conquer, like a chariot. Professor Roth, *s.v. vibhván*, takes the dative for an instrumental, and translates "made by an artificer." It is, however, not the chariot that is spoken of, but *Sarasvatî*, and of her it could hardly be said that she was made either by or for an artificer.

LOCATIVES IN *SANI*.

As we saw before that aoristic bases in *s* take the dativaI *e*, so that we had *prák-sh-e* by the side of *pṛc-e*, we shall have to consider here aoristic bases in *s*, taking the suffix *an*, not however with the termination of the dative, but with that of the locative *i*. Thus we read X. 126, 3, náyishṭhâḥ u naḥ nesháni párshishṭhâḥ u naḥ parsháni áti dvíshaḥ, they who are the best leaders to lead us, the best helpers to help us to overcome our enemies, lit. in leading us, in helping us. In VIII. 12, 19, *gṛṇîsháni*, i.e. *gṛ-ṇî-shán-i* stands parallel with *turv-án-e*, thus showing how both cases can answer nearly the same purpose. If these forms existed in Greek, they would, after consonantal bases, be identical with the infinitives of the future.

CASES OF VERBAL NOUNS IN *TU*.

We next come to a large number of datives, ablatives, or genitives, and accusatives of verbal nouns in *tu*. This *tu* occurs in Sanskrit in abstract nouns such as *gâtú*, going, way, etc., in Latin in *adven-tus*, etc. As these forms have been often treated, and as some of them occur frequently in later Sanskrit also, it will suffice to give one example of each:—

Dative in *tave*: *gántave*, to go, I. 46, 7.

Old form in *ai*: *gántavái*, X. 95, 14.

Genitive in *toḥ*: *dâtoḥ*, governed by *îśe*, VII. 4, 6.

Ablative in *toḥ*: *gántoḥ*, I. 89, 9.

Accusative in *tum*: *gántum*. This is the supine in *tum* in Latin.

CASES OF VERBAL NOUNS IN *TVA*.

Next follow cases of verbal nouns in *tvá*, the accent being on the suffix.

Datives in *tvấya*: *hatvấya*, X. 84, 2.

Instrumental in *tvấ*: *hatvấ*, I. 100, 18.

Older form in *tvî́*: *hatvî́*, II. 17, 6; *gatvî́*, IV. 41, 5.

DATIVES IN *DHAI* AND *DHYAI*.

I have left to the end datives in *dhai* and *dhyai*, which properly belong to the datives in *ai*, treated before, but differ from them as being datives of compound nouns. As from *máyaḥ*, delight, we have *mayaskará*, delight-making, *mayobhú*, delight-causing, and constructions like *máyo dádhe*, so from *váyas*, life, vigor, we have *váyaskṛt*, life-giving, and constructions like *váyo dhât*. From *dhâ* we can frame two substantival frame, *dhâ* and *dhi-s*, e.g. *puro-dhâ*, and *puro-dhis*, like *vi-dhi-s*. As an ordinary substantive, *purodhâ* takes the feminine termination *â*, and is declined like *śivá*. But if the verbal base remains at the end of a compound without the feminine suffix, a compound like *vayodhâ* would form its dative *vayodhe* (Grammar, § 239); and as in analogous cases we found old datives in *ai*, instead of *e*, e.g. *parâdai*, nothing can be said against *vayodhai*, as a Vedic dative of *vayodhâ*. The dative of *purodhi* would be *purodhaye*, but here again, as, besides forms like *dṛśaye*, we met with datives, such as *ityai*, *rohishyai*, there is no difficulty in admitting an analogous dative of *purodhi*, viz., *purodhyai*.

The old dative *dhai* has been preserved to us in one form only, which for that reason is all the more valuable and important, offering the key to the mysterious Greek infinitives in θαι, I mean *vayodhái*, which occurs twice in the Rig-Veda, X. 55, 1, and X. 67, 11. The importance of this relic would have been perceived long ago, if there had not been some uncertainty as to whether such a form really existed in the Veda. By some accident or other, Professor Aufrecht had printed in both passages *vayodhaiḥ*, instead of *vayodhai*. But for this, no one, I believe, would have doubted that in this form *vayodhai* we have not only the most valuable prototype of the Greek infinitives in (σ)θαι, but at the same time their full explanation. *Vayodhai* stands for *vayas-dhai*, in which composition the first part *vayas* is a neuter base in *as*, the second a dative of the auxiliary verb *dhâ*, used as a substantive. If, therefore, we find corresponding to *vayodhai* a Greek infinitive βέεσθαι, we must divide it into βέεσ-θαι, as we divide ψεύδεσθαι into ψεύδεσ-θαι, and translate it literally by "to do lying."

It has been common to identify Greek infinitives in σθαι with corresponding Sanskrit forms ending in *dhyai*. No doubt these forms in *dhyai* are much more frequent than forms in *dhai*, but as we can only take them as old datives of substantives in *dhi*, it would be difficult to identify the two. The Sanskrit *dhy* appears, no doubt, in Greek, as σσ, *dh* being represented by the surd θ, and then assibilated by *y*; but we could hardly attempt to explain σθ = θy, because σδ = ζ = δy. Therefore, unless we are prepared to see with Bopp in the σ before θ, in this and similar forms, a remnant of the reflexive pronoun, nothing remains but to accept the explanation offered by the Vedic *vayodhai*, and to separate ψεύδεσθαι into ψεύδεσ-θαι lying to do. That this grammatical compound, if once found successful, should have been repeated in other tenses, giving us not only γράφεσ-θαι, but γράψεσ-θαι, γράψασ-θαι, and even γραφθήσεσ-θαι, is no more than what we may see again and again in the grammatical development of ancient and modern languages. Some scholars have objected on the same ground to Bopp's explanation of *ama-mini*, as the nom. plur. of a participle, because they think it impossible to look upon *amemini*, *amabâmini*, amaremini, *amabimini* as participial formations. But if a mould is once made in language, it is used again and again, and little account is taken of its original intention. If we object to γράψεσ-θαι, why not to κελευσέ-μεναι or τεθνά-μεναι or μιχθή-μεναι? In Sanskrit, too, we should hesitate to form a compound of a modified verbal base, such as *pṛṇa*, with *dhi*, doing; yet as the Sanskrit ear was accustomed to *yajadhyai* from *yaja*, *gamadhyai* from *gama*, it did not protest against *pṛṇadhyai*, *vâvṛdhadhyai*, etc.

HISTORICAL IMPORTANCE OF THESE GRAMMATICAL FORMS.

And while these ancient grammatical forms which supply the foundation of what in Greek, Latin, and other languages we are accustomed to call infinitives are of the highest interest to the grammarian and the logician, their importance is hardly less in the eyes of the historian. Every honest student of antiquity, whether his special field be India, Persia, Assyria, or Egypt, knows how often he is filled with fear and trembling when he meets with thoughts and expressions which, as he is apt to say, cannot be ancient. I have frequently confessed to that feeling with regard to some of the hymns of the Rig-Veda, and I well remember the time when I felt inclined to throw up the whole work as modern and unworthy of the time and labor bestowed upon it. At that time I was always comforted by these so-called infinitives and other relics of ancient language. They could not have been fabricated in India. They are unknown in ordinary Sanskrit, they are unintelligible as far as their origin is concerned in Greek and Latin, and yet in the Vedic language we find these forms, not only identical with Greek and Latin forms, but furnishing the key to their formation in Greece and Italy. The Vedic *vayas-dhâi* compared with Greek βεεσ-θαι, the Vedic *stushe* compared with λυσαι are to my mind evidence in support of the antiquity and genuineness of the Veda that cannot be shaken by any arguments.

THE INFINITIVE IN ENGLISH.

I add a few words on the infinitive in English, though it has been well treated by Dr. March in his "Grammar of the Anglo-Saxon Language," by Dr. Morris, and others. We find in Anglo-Saxon two forms, one generally called the infinitive, *nim-an*, to take, the other the gerund, *to nim-anne*, to take. Dr. March explains the first as identical with Greek νέμ-ειν and νέμ-εν-αι, i.e., as an oblique case, probably the dative, of a verbal noun in *an*. He himself quotes only the dative of nominal bases in *a*, e.g. *namanâya*, because he was probably unacquainted with the nearer forms in *an-e* supplied by the Veda. This infinitive exists in Gothic as *nim-an*, in Old Saxon as *nim-an*, in Old Norse as *nem-a*, in Old High German as *nem-an*. The so-called gerund, to *nimanne*, is rightly traced back by Dr. March to Old Saxon *nim-annia*, but he can hardly be right in identifying these old datival forms with the Sanskrit base *nam-anîya*. In the Second Period of English (1100–1250)35 the termination of the infinitive became *en*, and frequently dropped the final *n*, as *smelle = smellen*; while the termination of the gerund at the same time became *enne*, *(ende)*, *ene*, *en*, or *e*, so that outwardly the two forms appear to be identical, as early as the 12th century.36 Still later, towards the end of the 14th century, the terminations were entirely lost, though Spenser and Shakespeare have occasionally to *killen, passen, delven*, when they wished to impart an archaic character to their language. In modern English the infinitive with *to* is used as a verbal substantive. When we say, "I wish you to do this," "you are able to do this," we can still perceive the datival function of the infinitive. Likewise in such phrases, "it is time," "it is proper," "it is wrong to do that," *to do* may still be felt as an oblique case. But we have only to invert these sentences, and say, "to do this is wrong," and we have a new substantive in the nom. sing., just as in the Greek τὸ λέγειν. Expressions like *for to do*, show that the simple *to* was not always felt to be sufficiently expressive to convey the meaning of an original dative.

WORKS ON THE INFINITIVE.

The infinitive has formed the subject of many learned treatises. I divide them into two classes, those which appeared before and after Wilhelm's excellent essay, written in Latin, "De Infinitivi Vi et Natura," 1868; and in a new and improved edition, "De Infinitivo Linguarum Sanscritæ, Bactricæ, Persicæ, Græcæ, Oscæ, Umbricæ, Latinæ, Goticæ, forma et usu," Isenaci, 1873. In this essay the evidence supplied by the Veda was for the first time fully collected, and the whole question of the nature of the infinitive placed in its true historical light. Before Wilhelm the more important works were Hofer's book, "Vom Infinitiv, besonders im Sanskrit," Berlin, 1840; Bopp's paragraphs in his "Comparative Grammar;" Humboldt's paper, in Schlegel's "Indische Bibliothek" (II. 74), 1824; and his posthumous paper in Kuhn's "Zeitschrift" (II. 245), 1853; some dissertations by L. Meyer, Merguet, and Golenski. Benfey's "Sanskrit Grammar" (1852), too, ought to be mentioned, as having laid the first solid foundations for this and all other branches of grammatical research, as far as Sanskrit is concerned. After Wilhelm the same subject has been treated with great independence by Ludwig, "Der Infinitif im Veda," 1871, and again "Agglutination oder Adaptation," 1873; and also by Jolly, "Geschichte des Infinitivs," 1873.

I had myself discussed some questions connected with the nature of the infinitive in my "Lectures on the Science of Language," vol. ii. p. 15 seq., and I had pointed out in Kuhn's "Zeitschrift," XV. 215 (1866) the great importance of the Vedic *vayodhai* for unraveling the formation of Greek infinitives in σ-θαι.

THE INFINITIVE IN BENGALI.

At a still earlier time, in 1847, in my "Essay on Bengali," I said: "As the infinitives of the Indo-Germanic languages must be regarded as the absolute cases of a verbal noun, it is probable that in Bengali the infinitive in *ite* was also originally a locative, which expressed not only local situation, but also movement towards some object, as an end, whether real or imaginary. Thus the Bengali infinitive corresponds exactly with the English, where the relation of case is expressed by the preposition *to*. Ex. tâhâke mârite âmi âsiyâchi, means, I came to the state of beating him, or, I came to beat him; âmake mârite deo, give me (permission), let me (go) to the action of beating, *i.e.*, allow me to beat. Now as the form of the participle is the same as that of the infinitive, it may be doubted if there is really a distinction between these two forms as to their origin. For instance, the phrase âpan putrake mârite âmi tâhâka dekhilâm, can be translated, I saw him beating his own son; but it can be explained also as, what they nonsensically call in Latin grammar *accusativus cum infinitivo*, that is to say, the infinitive can be taken for a locative of the verbal noun, and the whole phrase be translated, I saw him in the action of beating his own son, (*vidi patrem cædere ipsius filium*). As in every Bengali phrase the participle in *ite* can be understood in this manner, I think it admissible to ascribe this origin to it, and instead of taking it for a nominative of a verbal adjective, to consider it as a locative of a verbal noun."

THE INFINITIVE IN THE DRAVIDIAN LANGUAGES.

I also tried to show that the infinitive in the Dravidian languages is a verbal noun with or without a case suffix. This view has been confirmed by Dr. Caldwell, but, in deference to him, I gladly withdraw the explanation which I proposed in reference to the infinitive in Tamil. I quote from Dr. Caldwell's "Comparative Grammar of the Dravidian Languages," 2d ed. p. 423: "Professor Max Müller, noticing that the majority of Tamil infinitives terminate in *ka*, supposed this *ka* to be identical in origin with *kô*, the dative-accusative case-sign of the Hindi, and concluded that the Dravidian infinitive was the accusative of a verbal noun. It is true that the Sanskrit infinitive and Latin supine in *tum* is correctly regarded as an accusative, and that our English infinitive *to do*, is the dative of a verbal noun; it is also true that the Dravidian infinitive is a verbal noun in origin, and never altogether loses that character; nevertheless, the supposition that the final *ka* of most Tamil infinitives is in any manner connected with *ku*, the sign of the Dravidian dative, or of *kô*, the Hindi dative-accusative, is inadmissible. A comparison of various classes of verbs and of the various dialects shows that the *kâ* in question proceeds from a totally different source."

ON LABIALIZED AND UNLABIALIZED GUTTURALS.

As in my article on *Vayodhai*, published in Kuhn's "Zeitschrift," 1866, p. 215, I had entered a *caveat* against identifying Greek β with Sanskrit ज, I take this opportunity of frankly withdrawing it. Phonetically, no doubt, these two letters represent totally distinct powers, and to say that Sanskrit ज ever became Greek β is as irrational to-day as it was ten years ago. But historically I was entirely wrong, as will be seen from the last edition of Curtius' "Grundzüge." The guttural sonant check was palatalized in the Southeastern Branch, and there became j and z, while in the Northwestern Branch the same g was frequently labialized and became gv, v, and b. Hence, where we have ज in Sanskrit, we may and do find β in Greek.

But after withdrawing my former *caveat*, I make bold to propose another, namely, that the original palatal sonant flatus, which in Sanskrit is graphically represented by j, can never be represented in Greek by β. Whether j in Sanskrit represents an original palatal sonant check or an original palatal sonant flatus can generally be determined by a reference to Zend, which represents the former by j, the latter by z. We may therefore formulate this phonetic law:—

"When Sanskrit j is represented by Zend z̦, it cannot be represented by Greek β."

In this manner it is possible, I believe, to utilize Ascoli's and Fick's brilliant discovery as to a twofold, or even threefold, distinction of the Aryan k, as applied to the Aryan g. They have proved that all Aryan languages show traces of an original distinction between a guttural surd check, k, frequently palatalized in the Southeastern Branch (Sk. c, Zend c) and liable to labialization, in Latin, Greek, Cymric, and Gothic; and another k, never liable to labialization, but changed into a flatus, palatal or otherwise, in Sanskrit, Lithuanian, and Old Slavonic. They showed, in fact,—

Sanskrit. Lith. Slav.	Gadh. Cym.	& Lat.	Greek.	Gothic.
क (च) = k = k, č, = c	= c	= p	= c, qu, = κ, κϝ, κκ, π, ππ, τ, ττ, hv, h.
		= v	=	
श = sz = s	= c	= c	= κ	= h

In the same manner we ought in future to distinguish between a guttural sonant check, g, frequently palatalized in the Southeastern Branch (Sk. j, Zend j), and liable to labialization, like k; and another g, never liable to labialization, but changed into a flatus, palatal or otherwise, in Zend, Lithuanian, and Old Slavonic. As we never have π = श we never have β = ज, if ज in Zend is z̦.

The evidence will be found under Sk. *jan, jabh, jar* (to decay, and to praise), *jush, jñā, jñu, jāmātar, aj, bhrāj, marj, yaj, raj(atam)*.

Gothic *quinô*, Gadh. *ben*, Bœot. βάνα depend on Zend *jeni*; Gadh. *baith-is* on Zend *jaf-ra*. It is wrong to connect σβεσ with *jas*, on account of Zend *z̦as*, and *gyā-ni* with βία, on account of Zend *z̦yā-ni*.

Footnotes to Chapter I:
The Value of Comparative Philology

1. The following statute was approved by the University of Oxford in 1868 (*Statuta Universitatis Oxoniensis*, iv., i., 37. §§ 1–3):—

"1. Professor philologiæ comparativæ a Vice-Cancellario, et professoribus linguarum Hebraicæ, Sanskriticæ, Græcæ, Latinæ, et Anglo-Saxonicæ eligatur. In æqualitate suffragantium rem decidat Vice-Cancellarius.

"Proviso tamen ut si vir cl. M. Müller, M.A., hodie linguarum modernarum Europæ professor Taylorianus, eam professionem intra mensem post hoc statutum sancitum resignaverit, seque professoris philologiæ comparativæ munus suscipere paratum esse scripto Vice-Cancellarium certiorem fecerit, is primus admittatur professor.

"2. Professor quotannis per sex menses in Universitate incolat et commoretur inter decimum diem Octobris et primum diem Julii sequentis.

"3. Professor duas lectionum series in duobus discretis terminis legat, terminis Paschatis et S. Trinitatis pro uno reputatis; scilicet per sex septimanas in utroque termino, et bis ad minimum in unaquaque septimana: atque insuper per sex septimanas unius alicujus termini bis ad minimum in unaquaque septimana per unius horæ spatium vacet instruendis auditoribus in iis quæ melius sine solennitate tradi possunt. Unam porro ad minimum lectionem quotannis publice habeat ab academicis quibuscunque sine mercede audiendam. De die hora et loco quibus hæc lectio solennis habenda sit academiam modo consueto certiorem faciat."

2. An offer to found a professorship of Chinese, to be held by an Englishman whom even Stanislas Julien recognized as the best Chinese scholar of the day, has lately been received very coldly by the Hebdomadal Council of the University.

3. *Liber Sextus Decretalium* (Lugduni, 1572), p. 1027: "Ut igitur peritia linguarum hujusmodi possit habiliter per instructionem efficaciam obtinere, hoc sacro approbante concilio scholas in subscriptarum linguarum generibus ubicunque Romanam curiam residere contigerit, necnon in Parisiensi, et Oxoniensi, Bononiensi, et Salmantino studiis providimus erigendas; statuentes ut in quolibet locorum ipsorum teneantur viri catholici, sufficienter habentes Hebraicæ, Arabicæ, et Chaldææ linguarum notitiam."

4. Greaves, *Oratio Oxonii habita*, 1637, p. 19: "Paucos ultra centum annos numeramus ex quo Græcæ primum literæ oras hasce appulerunt, antea ignotæ prorsus, nonnullis exosæ etiam et invisæ, indoctissimis scilicet fraterculis, quibus religio erat graece scire, et levissimus Atticæ eruditionis gustus hæresin sapiebat."

5. See *Biographia Britannica Literaria*, vol. i. p. 110.

6. M. M.'s *Lectures on the Science of Language*, vol. i. p. 171.

7. Ibid., p. 176.

8. See Notes A and B, pp. 43, 45.

9. See M. M., *Science of Religion*, 1873, p. 293.

10. See Weber, *Indische Studien*, vol. i. p. 38.

11. See Haug, in Ewald's *Biblische Jahrbücher*, vol. vi. p. 162.

12. *Anab.*, i. 2, 7: Ἐνταῦθα Κύρῳ Βασίλεια ἦν καὶ παράδεισος μέγας, ἀγρίων θηρίων πλήρης, ἃ ἐκεῖνος ἐθήρευεν ἀπὸ ἵππου, ὁπότε γυμνάσαι βούλοιτο ἑαυτόν τε καὶ τοὺς ἵππους. Διὰ μέσου δὲ τοῦ παραδείσου ῥεῖ ὁ Μαίανδρος ποταμός κ.τ.λ. *Hell.*, iv. 1, 15: Ἐν περιειργμένοις παραδείσοις κ.τ.λ.

13. See *Indian Antiquary*, 1874, p. 332.

14. Grassmann, Kuhn's *Zeitschrift*, vol. ix. p. 23.

15. Ebel, Kuhn's *Zeitschrift*, vol. viii. p. 242.

16. Schleicher, *Compendium*, § 112.

17. Lottner, Kuhn's *Zeitschrift*, vol. ix. p. 319.

18. Leo Meyer, *Die Gothische Sprache*, § 31.

19. Choeroboscus, B. A., p. 1274, 29: Τὰ ἀπαρέμφατα ἀμφιβάλλεται εἰ ἄρα εἰσὶ ῥήματα ἢ οὐχί. Schoemann, *Rede-theile*, p. 49.

20. Apollonius, *De Constr.*, i. c. 8, p. 32: Δυνάμει αὐτὸ τὸ ῥῆμα οὔτε πρόσωπα ἐπιδέχεται οὔτε ἀριθμούς, ἀλλὰ ἐγγενόμενον ἐν προσώποις τότε καὶ τὰ πρόσωπα διέστειλεν .... καὶ ψυχικὴν διάθεσιν. Schoemann, l.c. p. 19.

21. Note C, p. 47.

22. Benfey, *Orient und Occident*, vol. i. p. 606; vol. ii. pp. 97, 132.

23. *Chips*, vol. iii. p. 134.

24. Dr. Kielhorn in his grammar gives correctly *tad* as base, *tat* as nom. and acc. sing., because in the latter case phonetic rules either require or allow the change of *d* into *t*. Boehtlingk, Roth, and Benfey also give the right forms. Curtius, like Bopp, gives *yat*, Schleicher *tat*, which he supposes to have been changed at an early time into *tad* (§ 203).

25. Weich ist es (*t* oder *d*) wohl im abl. sing., *gafnât* (*gafnâdha*). Justi, *Handbuch der Zendsprache*, p. 362.

26. *Orient und Occident*, vol. i. p. 298.

27. *Entwickelung der Lateinischen Formenlehre*, 1870, p. 20.

28. *Grundriss der Lateinischen Declination*, 1866, p. 9.

29. See Benfey, l.c. p. 298.

30. In the dictionary of Boehtlingk and Roth we read *s.v. gnâ*, "scarce in the singular; nom. sing. seems to be *gnâs*, according to the passage Rv. IV. 9, 4, and Naigh. I. 11, in one , while the other gives the form *gnâ*." Against this, it should be remarked, that it would make no difference whether the MSS. of the Naighaṇṭuka give *gnâ* or *gnâs*. *Gnâ* would be the nom. sing., *gnâs* would be the form in which the word occurs most frequently in the Veda. It is easy to see that the collector of the Naighaṇṭuka allowed himself to quote words according to either principle.

Devarâja, in his commentary on *gnâ*, explains it: "Gamer dhâtor dhâpr̃vasyajyatibhyo naḥ (U. S. III. 6) iti bahulakân napratyayo bhavati ṭilopaś ca; ṭap. Gatyarthâ buddhyarthâḥ jânanti karmeti gnâḥ. Yadvâ gacchati yajñeshu; abhí yajñám gr̥ṇîhi no gnâvaḥ (patnîvaḥ) Rv. I. 15, 3. Chandâṃsi vai gnâ iti brâhmaṇam iti Mâdhavaḥ. Asmấ îd u gnấś cid (Rv. I. 61, 8) ity api; gâyatryâdyâ devapatnya iti sa eva. Tasmâc chandasâm gâyatryâdînâm vâgrûpatvâd gnâvyapadeśaḥ."

In his remarks on Nigh. III. 29, it is quite clear that Devarâja takes *gnâḥ* as a nom. plur., not as a nom. sing. He says: Menâ gnâ iti strîṇâm; ubhâv api śabdau vyâkhyâtau vânnâmasu. Mânayanti hi tâḥ patiśvaśuramâtulâdayaḥ, pûjyâ bhûshayitavyâś ceti smaraṇât. Gacchanty enâḥ patayo patyârthinaḥ. The passage quoted in the Nirukta III. 29, gnâs tvâkr̥ntann apaso 'tanvata vayitryo 'vayan, is taken from the Tâṇḍyabrâhmaṇa I. 8, 9. "O dress! the women cut thee out, the workers stretched thee out, the weavers wove thee."

Thus every support which the Nighaṇṭu or the Nirukta was supposed to give to the form *gnâḥ* as a nom. sing. vanishes. And if it is said *s.v. gnâspati*, that in this compound *gnâḥ* might be taken as a nom. sing., and that the Pada- separates *gnâḥ-patiḥ*, it has been overlooked that the separation in Rv. II. 38, 10, is a mere misprint. See Prâtiśâkhya, 738. The compound *gnâspatiḥ* has been correctly explained as standing for *gnâyâspatiḥ*, and the same old genitive is also found in *jâspatiḥ* and *jâspatyam*. See also Vâjasan. Prâtiśâkhya,

IV. 39. It is important to observe that the metre requires us to pronounce *gnâspati* either as *gnăāspătīh* or as *gănāspătīh*.

There is, as far as I know, no passage where *gnâh* in the Veda can be taken as a nom. sing., and it should be observed that *gnâh* as nom. plur. is almost always disyllabic in the Rig-veda, excepting the tenth Maṇḍala; that the acc. sing. (V. 43, 6) is, however, disyllabic, but the acc. plur. monosyllabic (I. 22, 10). In V. 43, 13, we must either read *gnāh* or *ōshădhīh*.

The beginning of V.43.13c is also given as "ghnā vasāna oṣadhīr". Printed (breve over n, combined breve and macron over i) may be intended to read "gnăâh" or "gănâh" and "oṣadhīh".

31. Sthâ, svâbhiprâyabodhanânukûlasthiti, to reveal by gestures, a meaning not found in our dictionaries. Wilson renders it wrongly by to stay with, which would govern the instrumental. *Śap*, cursing, means to use curses in order to convey some meaning or intention to another person.

32. Wilson's *Sanskrit Grammar*, p. 390.

33. In verbs compounded with prepositions the accent is on the penultimate: *e.g., samídhe, atikráme,* etc.

34. See M. M.'s *Translation of the Rig-Veda*, I. p. 34.

35. Morris, *Historic Outlines of English Accidence*, p. 52.

36. Morris, l.c. p. 177.

II.
REDE LECTURE,
DELIVERED IN THE SENATE HOUSE BEFORE THE UNIVERSITY OF CAMBRIDGE, ON FRIDAY, MAY 29, 1868.[1]

PART I.
ON THE STRATIFICATION OF LANGUAGE.

THERE are few sensations more pleasant than that of wondering. We have all experienced it in childhood, in youth, and in our manhood, and we may hope that even in our old age this affection of the mind will not entirely pass away. If we analyze this feeling of wonder carefully, we shall find that it consists of two elements. What we mean by wondering is not only that we are startled or stunned,—that I should call the merely passive element of wonder. When we say "I wonder," we confess that we are taken aback, but there is a secret satisfaction mixed up with our feeling of surprise, a kind of hope, nay, almost of certainty, that sooner or later the wonder will cease, that our senses or our mind will recover, will grapple with these novel impressions or experiences, grasp them, it may be, throw them, and finally triumph over them. In fact we wonder at the riddles of nature, whether animate or inanimate, with a firm conviction that there is a solution to them all, even though we ourselves may not be able to find it.

Wonder, no doubt, arises from ignorance, but from a peculiar kind of ignorance; from what might be called a fertile ignorance: an ignorance which, if we look back at the history of most of our sciences, will be found to have been the mother of all human knowledge. For thousands of years men have looked at the earth with its stratifications, in some places so clearly mapped out; for thousands of years they must have seen in their quarries and mines, as well as we ourselves, the imbedded petrifications of organic creatures: yet they looked and passed on without thinking more about it—they did not wonder. Not even an Aristotle had eyes to see; and the conception of a science of the earth, of Geology, was reserved for the eighteenth century.

Still more extraordinary is the listlessness with which during all the centuries that have elapsed since the first names were given to all cattle, and to the fowl of the air, and to every beast of the field, men have passed by what was much nearer to them than even the gravel on which they trod, namely, the words of their own language. Here, too, the clearly marked lines of different strata seemed almost to challenge attention, and the pulses of former life were still throbbing in the petrified forms imbedded in grammars and dictionaries. Yet not even a Plato had eyes to see, or ears to hear, and the conception of a science of language, of Glottology, was reserved for the nineteenth century.

I am far from saying that Plato and Aristotle knew nothing of the nature, the origin, and the purpose of language, or that we have nothing to learn from their works. They, and their successors, and their predecessors too, beginning with Herakleitos and Demokritos, were startled and almost fascinated by the mysteries of human speech as much as by the mysteries of human thought; and what we call grammar and the laws of language, nay, all the technical terms which are still current in our schools, such as *noun* and *verb*, *case* and *number*, *infinitive* and *participle*, all this was first discovered and named by the philosophers and grammarians of Greece, to whom, in spite of all our new discoveries, I believe we are still beholden, whether consciously or unconsciously, for more than half of our intellectual life.

But the interest which those ancient Greek philosophers took in language was purely philosophical. It was the form, far more than the matter of speech which seemed to them a subject worthy of philosophical speculation. The idea that there was, even in their days, an immense mass of accumulated speech to be sifted, to be analyzed, and to be accounted for somehow, before any theories on the nature of language could be safely started, hardly ever entered their minds; or when it did, as we see here and there in Plato's "Kratylos," it soon vanished, without leaving any permanent impression. Each people and each generation has its own problems to solve. The problem that occupied Plato in his "Kratylos" was, if I understand him rightly, the possibility of a perfect language, a correct, true, or ideal language, a language founded on his own philosophy, his own system of types or ideas. He was too wise a man to attempt, like Bishop Wilkins, the actual construction of a philosophical language. But, like Leibniz, he just lets us see that a perfect language is conceivable, and that the chief reason of the imperfections of real language must be found in the fact that its original framers were ignorant of the true nature of things, ignorant of dialectic philosophy, and therefore incapable of naming rightly what they had failed to apprehend correctly. Plato's view of actual language, as far as it can be made out from the critical and negative rather than didactic and positive dialogue of "Kratylos," seems to have been very much the same as his view of actual government. Both fall short of the ideal, and both are to be tolerated only in so far as they participate in the perfections of an ideal state and an ideal language.2 Plato's "Kratylos" is full of suggestive wisdom. It is one of those books which, as we read them again from time to time, seem every time like new books: so little do we perceive at first all that is pre-supposed in them,—the accumulated mould of thought, if I may say so, in which alone a philosophy like that of Plato could strike its roots and draw its support.

But while Plato shows a deeper insight into the mysteries of language than almost any philosopher that has come after him, he has no eyes for that marvelous harvest of words garnered up in our dictionaries, and in the dictionaries of all the races of the earth. With him language is almost synonymous with Greek, and though in one passage of the "Kratylos" he suggests that certain Greek words might have been borrowed from the Barbarians, and, more particularly from the Phrygians, yet that remark, as coming from Plato, seems to be purely ironical, and though it contains, as we know, a germ of truth that has proved most fruitful in our modern science of language, it struck no roots in the minds of Greek philosophers. How much our new science of language differs from the linguistic studies of the Greeks; how entirely the interest which Plato took in language is now supplanted by new interests, is strikingly brought home to us when we see how the *Société de Linguistique*, lately founded at Paris, and including the names of the most distinguished scholars of France, declares in one of its first statutes that "it will receive no communication concerning the origin of language or the formation of a universal language," the very subjects which, in the time of Herakleitos and Plato, rendered linguistic studies worthy of the consideration of a philosopher.

It may be that the world was too young in the days of Plato, and that the means of communication were wanting to enable the ancient philosopher to see very far beyond the narrow horizon of Greece. With us it is different. The world has grown older, and has left to us in the annals of its various literatures the monuments of growing and decaying speech. The world has grown larger, and we have before us, not only the relics of ancient civilization in Asia, Africa, and America, but living languages in such number and variety that we draw back almost aghast at the mere list of their names. The world has grown wiser too, and where Plato could only see imperfections, the failures of the founders of human speech, we see, as everywhere else in human life, a natural progress from the imperfect towards the perfect, unceasing attempts at realizing the ideal, and the frequent triumphs of the human mind over the inevitable difficulties of this earthly condition,— difficulties, not of man's own making, but, as I firmly believe, prepared for him, and not without a purpose, as toils and tasks, by a higher Power and by the highest Wisdom.

Let us look then abroad and behold the materials which the student of language has now to face. Beginning with the language of the Western Isles, we have at the present day, at least 100,000 words, arranged as on the shelves of a Museum, in the pages of Johnson and Webster. But these 100,000 words represent only the best grains that have remained in the sieve, while clouds of chaff have been winnowed off, and while many a valuable grain too has been lost by mere carelessness. If we counted the wealth of English dialects, and if we added the treasures of the ancient language from Alfred to Wycliffe, we should easily double the herbarium of the linguistic flora of England. And what are these Western Isles as compared to Europe; and what is Europe, a mere promontory, as compared to the vast continent of Asia; and what again is Asia, as compared to the whole inhabitable world? But there is no corner of that world that is not full of language: the very desert and the isles of the sea teem with dialects, and the more we recede from the centres of civilization, the larger the number of independent languages, springing up in every valley, and overshadowing the smallest island.

Ἴδαν ἐς πολύδενδρον ἀνὴρ ὑλατόμος ἐνθὼν

Παπταίνει, παρεόντος ἅδην, πόθεν ἄρξεται ἔργω.3

We are bewildered by the variety of plants, of birds, and fishes, and insects, scattered with lavish prodigality over land and sea;—but what is the living wealth of that Fauna as compared to the winged words which fill the air with unceasing music! What are the scanty relics of fossil plants and animals, compared to the storehouse of what we call the dead languages! How then can we explain it that for centuries and centuries, while collecting beasts, and birds, and fishes, and insects, while studying their forms, from the largest down to the smallest and almost invisible creatures, man has passed by this forest of speech, without seeing the forest, as we say in German, for the very number of its trees (*Man sah den Wald vor lauter Bäumen nicht*), without once asking how this vast currency could have been coined, what inexhaustible mines could have supplied the metal, what cunning hands could have devised the image and superscription,—without once wondering at the countless treasure inherited by him from the fathers of the human race?

Let us now turn our attention in a different direction. After it had been discovered that there was this great mass of material to be collected, to be classified, to be explained, what has the Science of Language, as yet, really accomplished? It has achieved much, considering that real work only began about fifty years ago; it has achieved little, if we look at what still remains to be done.

The first discovery was that languages admit of classification. Now this was a very great discovery, and it at once changed and raised the whole character of linguistic studies. Languages might have been, for all we know, the result of individual fancy or poetry; words might have been created here and there at random, or been fixed by a convention, more or less arbitrary. In that case a scientific classification would have been as impossible as it is if applied to the changing fashions of the day. Nothing can be classified, nothing can be scientifically ruled and ordered, except what has grown up in natural order and according to rational rule.

Out of the great mass of speech that is now accessible to the student of language, a number of so-called families have been separated, such as the *Aryan*, the *Semitic*, the *Ural-Altaic*, the *Indo-Chinese*, the *Dravidian*, the *Malayo-Polynesian*, the *Kafir* or *Bâ-ntu* in Africa, and the *Polysynthetic* dialects of America. The only classes, however, which have been carefully examined, and which alone have hitherto supplied the materials for what we might call the Philosophy of Language, are the Aryan and the Semitic, the former comprising the languages of India, Persia, Armenia, Greece and Italy, and of the Celtic, Teutonic, and Slavonic races; the latter consisting of the languages of the Babylonians, the Syrians, the Jews, the Ethiopians, the Arabs.

These two classes include, no doubt, the most important languages of the world, if we measure the importance of languages by the amount of influence exercised on the political and literary history of the world by those who speak them. But considered by themselves, and placed in their proper place in the vast realm of human speech, they describe but a very small segment of the entire circle. The completeness of the evidence which they place before us in the long series of their literary treasures, points them out in an eminent degree as the most useful subjects on which to study the anatomy of speech, and nearly all the discoveries that have been made as to the laws of language, the process of composition, derivation, and inflexion, have been gained by Aryan and Semitic scholars.

Far be it from me, therefore, to underrate the value of Aryan and Semitic scholarship for a successful prosecution of the Science of Language. But while doing full justice to the method adopted by Semitic and Aryan scholars in the discovery of the laws that regulate the growth and decay of language, we must not shut our eyes to the fact that our field of observation has been thus far extremely limited, and that we should act in defiance of the simplest rules of sound induction, were we to generalize on such scanty evidence. Let us but clearly see what place these two so-called families, the Aryan and Semitic, occupy in the great kingdom of speech. They are in reality but two centres, two small settlements of speech, and all we know of them is their period of decay, not their period of growth, their descending, not their ascending career, their Being, as we say in German, not their Becoming (*Ihr Gewordensein, nicht ihr Werden*). Even in the earliest literary documents both the Aryan and Semitic speech appear before us as fixed and petrified. They had left forever that stage during which language grows and expands, before it is arrested in its exuberant fertility by means of religious or political concentration, by means of oral tradition, or finally by means of a written literature. In the natural history of speech, writing, or, what in early times takes the place of writing, oral tradition, is something merely accidental. It represents a foreign influence which, in natural history, can only be compared to the influence exercised by domestication on plants and animals. Language would be language still, nay, would be more truly language, if the idea of a literature, whether oral or written, had never entered men's minds; and however important the effects produced by this artificial domestication of language may be, it is clear that our ideas of what language is in a natural state, and therefore what Sanskrit and Hebrew, too, must have been before they were tamed and fixed by literary cultivation, ought not to be formed from an exclusive study of Aryan and Semitic speech. I maintain that all that we call Aryan and Semitic speech, wonderful as its literary representatives may be, consists of neither more or less than so many varieties which all owe their origin to only two historical concentrations of wild unbounded speech; nay, however perfect, however powerful, however glorious in the history of the world,—in the eyes of the student of language, Sanskrit, Greek, and Latin, Hebrew, Arabic, and Syriac, are what a student of natural history would not hesitate to call "*monstra*," unnatural, exceptional formations which can never disclose to us the real character of language left to itself to follow out its own laws without let or hindrance.

For that purpose a study of Chinese and the Turanian dialects, a study even of the jargons of the savages of Africa, Polynesia, and Melanesia is far more instructive than the most minute analysis of Sanskrit and Hebrew. The impression which a study of Greek and Latin and Sanskrit leaves on our minds is, that language is a work of art, most complicated, most wonderful, most perfect. We have given so many names to its outward features, its genders and cases, its tenses and moods, its participles, gerunds, and supines, that at last we are frightened at our own devices. Who can read through all the so-called irregular verbs, or look at the thousands and thousands of words in a Greek Dictionary without feeling that he moves about in a perfect labyrinth? How then, we ask, was this labyrinth erected? How did all this come to be? We ourselves, speaking the language which we speak, move about, as it were, in the innermost chambers, in the darkest recesses of that primeval palace, but we cannot tell by what steps and through what passages we arrived there, and we look in vain for the thread of Ariadne which in leading us out of the enchanted castle of our language, would disclose to us the way by which we ourselves, or our fathers and forefathers before us, entered into it.

The question how language came to be what it is has been asked again and again. Even a school-boy, if he possesses but a grain of the gift of wondering must ask himself why *mensa* means one table, and *mensæ* many tables; why I love should be *amo*, I am loved *amor*, I shall love *amabo*, I have loved *amavi*, I should have loved *amavissem*. Until very lately two answers only could have been given to such questions. Both sound to us almost absurd, yet in their time they were supported by the highest authorities. Either, it was said, language, and particularly the grammatical framework of language was made by *convention*, by agreeing to call one table *mensa*, and many tables *mensæ*; or, and this was Schlegel's view, language was declared to possess an organic life, and its terminations, prefixes, and suffixes were supposed to have sprouted forth from the radicals and stems and branches of language, like so many buds and flowers. To us it seems almost incredible that such theories should have been seriously maintained, and maintained by men of learning and genius. But what better answer could they have given? What better answer has been given even now? We have learnt something, chiefly from a study of the modern dialects, which often repeat the processes of ancient speech, and thus betray the secrets of the family. We have learnt that in some of the dialects of modern Sanskrit, in Bengali for instance,4 the plural is formed, as it is in Chinese, Mongolian, Turkish, Finnish, Burmese, and Siamese, also in the Dravidian and Malayo-Polynesian dialects, by adding a word expressive of plurality, and then appending again the terminations of the singular. We have learnt from French how a future, *je parlerai*, can be formed by an auxiliary verb: "I to speak have" coming to mean, I shall speak. We have learnt from our own language, whether English or German, that suffixes, such as *head* in *godhead*, *ship* in *ladyship*, *dom* in *kingdom* were originally substantives, having the meaning of quality, shape, and state. But I doubt whether even thus we should have arrived at a thorough understanding of the real antecedents of language, unless, what happened in the study of the stratification of the earth, had happened in the study of language. If the formation of the crust of the earth had been throughout regular and uniform, and if none of the lower strata had been tilted up, so that even those who run might read, no shaft from the surface could have been sunk deep enough to bring the geologist from the tertiary strata down to the Silurian rocks. The same in language. Unless some languages had been arrested in their growth during their earlier stages, and had remained on the surface in this primitive state exposed only to the decomposing influence of atmospheric action, and to the ill-treatment of literary cultivation, I doubt whether any scholar would have had the courage to say that at one time Sanskrit was like unto Chinese, and Hebrew no better than Malay. In the successive strata of language thus exposed to our view, we have in fact, as in Geology, the very thread of Ariadne, which, if we will but trust to it, will lead us out of the dark labyrinth of language in which we live, by the same road by which we and those who came before us, first entered into it. The more we retrace our steps, the more we advance from stratum to stratum, from story to story, the more shall we feel almost dazzled by the daylight that breaks in upon us; the more shall we be struck, no longer by the intricacy of Greek or Sanskrit grammar, but by the marvelous simplicity of the original warp of human speech, as preserved, for instance, in Chinese; by the child-like contrivances, that are at the bottom of Paulo-post Futures and Conditional Moods.

Let no one be frightened at the idea of studying a Chinese grammar. Those who can take an interest in the secret springs of the mind, in the elements of pure reason, in the laws of thought, will find a Chinese grammar most instructive, most fascinating. It is the faithful photograph of man in his leading-strings, trying the muscles of his mind, groping his way, and so delighted with his first successful grasps that he repeats them again and again. It is child's play, if you like, but it displays, like all child's play, that wisdom and strength which are perfect in the mouth of babes and sucklings. Every shade of thought that finds expression in the highly finished and nicely balanced system of Greek tenses, moods, and particles can be expressed, and has been expressed, in that infant language by words that have neither prefix nor suffix, no terminations to indicate number, case, tense, mood, or person. Every word in Chinese is monosyllabic, and the same word, without any change of form, may be used as a noun, a verb, an adjective, an adverb, or a particle. Thus *ta*, according to its position in a sentence, may mean great, greatness, to grow, very much, very.5

And here a very important observation has been made by Chinese grammarians, an observation which, after a very slight modification and expansion, contains indeed the secret of the whole growth of language from Chinese to English. If a word in Chinese is used with the *bonâ fide* signification of a noun or a verb, it is called a *full word* (*shi-tsê*); if it is used as a particle or with a merely determinative or formal character, it is called an *empty word* (*hiu-tsê*6). There is as yet no outward difference between full and empty words in Chinese, and this renders it all the more creditable to the grammarians of China that they should have perceived the inward distinction, even in the absence of any outward signs.

Let us learn then from Chinese grammarians this great lesson, that words may become empty, and without restricting the meaning of empty words as they do, let us use that term in the most general sense, as expressive of the fact that words may lose something of their full original meaning.

Let us add to this another observation, which the Chinese could not well have made, but which we shall see confirmed again and again in the history of language, viz.: that empty words, or, as we may also call them, dead words, are most exposed to phonetic decay.

It is clear then that, with these two preliminary observations, we can imagine three conditions of language:—

1. There may be languages in which all words, both empty and full, retain their independent form. Even words which are used when we should use mere suffixes or terminations, retain their outward integrity in Chinese. Thus, in Chinese, *jin* means man, *tu* means crowd, *jin-tu*, man-crowd. In this compound both *jin* and *tu* continue to be felt as independent words, more so

than in our own compound *man-kind*; but nevertheless *tu* has become empty, it only serves to determine the preceding word *jin*, man, and tells us the quantity or number in which *jin* shall be taken. The compound answers in intention to our plural, but in form it is wide apart from *men*, the plural of *man*.

2. Empty words may lose their independence, may suffer phonetic decay, and dwindle down to mere suffixes and terminations. Thus in Burmese the plural is formed by *to*, in Finnish, Mordvinian, and Ostiakian by *t*. As soon as *to* ceases to be used as an independent word in the sense of number, it becomes an empty, or if you like, an obsolete word, that has no meaning except as the exponent of plurality; nay, at last, it may dwindle down to a mere letter, which is then called by grammarians the termination of the plural. In this second stage phonetic decay may well-nigh destroy the whole body of an empty word, but—and this is important—no full words, no radicals are as yet attacked by that disintegrating process.

3. Phonetic decay may advance, and does advance still further. Full words also may lose their independence, and be attacked by the same disease that had destroyed the original features of suffixes and prefixes. In this state it is frequently impossible to distinguish any longer between the radical and formative elements of words.

If we wished to represent these three stages of language algebraically, we might represent the first by RR, using R as the symbol of a root which has suffered no phonetic decay; the second, by $R + \varrho$ or $\varrho + R$, or $\varrho + R + \varrho$ representing by ϱ an empty word that has suffered phonetic change; the third, by $r\varrho$, or ϱr, or $\varrho r \varrho$, when both full and empty words have been changed, and have become welded together into one indistinguishable mass through the intense heat of thought, and by the constant hammering of the tongue.

Those who are acquainted with the works of Humboldt will easily recognize, in these three stages or strata, a classification of language first suggested by that eminent philosopher. According to him languages can be classified as *isolating, agglutinative,*[7] and *inflectional*, and his definition of these three classes agrees in the main with the description just given of the three strata or stages of language.

But what is curious is that this threefold classification, and the consequences to which it leads, should not at once have been fully reasoned out, nay, that a system most palpably erroneous should have been founded upon it. We find it repeated again and again in most works on Comparative Philology, that Chinese belongs to the *isolating* class, the Turanian languages to the *combinatory*, the Aryan and Semitic to the *inflectional*; nay, Professor Pott[8] and his school seem convinced that no evolution can ever take place from *isolating* to *combinatory* and from *combinatory* to *inflectional* speech. We should thus be forced to believe that by some inexplicable grammatical instinct, or by some kind of inherent necessity, languages were from the beginning created as *isolating* or *combinatory*, or *inflectional*, and must remain so to the end.

It is strange that those scholars who hold that no transition is possible from one form of language to another, should not have seen that there is really no language that can be strictly called either isolating, or combinatory, or inflectional, and that the transition from one stage to another is in fact constantly taking place under our very noses. Even Chinese is not free from combinatory forms, and the more highly developed among the combinatory languages show the clearest traces of incipient inflection. The difficulty is not to show the transition of one stratum of speech into another, but rather to draw a sharp line between the different strata. The same difficulty was felt in Geology, and led Sir Charles Lyell to invent such pliant names as *Eocene*, *Meiocene*, and *Pleiocene*, names which indicate a mere dawn, a minority, or a majority of new formations, but do not draw a fast and hard line, cutting off one stratum from the other. Natural growth, and even merely mechanical accumulation and accretion, here as elsewhere, are so minute and almost imperceptible that they defy all strict scientific terminology, and force upon us the lesson that we must be satisfied with an approximate accuracy. For practical purposes Humboldt's classification of languages may be quite sufficient, and we have no difficulty in classing any given language, according to the prevailing character of its formation, as either isolating, or combinatory, or inflectional. But when we analyze each language more carefully we find there is not one exclusively isolating, or exclusively combinatory, or exclusively inflectional. The power of composition, which is retained unimpaired through every stratum, can at any moment place an inflectional on a level with an isolating and a combinatory language. A compound such as the Sanskrit *go-duh*, cow-milking, differs little, if at all, from the Chinese *nieou-jou*, *vaccæ lac*, or in the patois of Canton, *ngau ü*, cow-milk, before it takes the terminations of the nominative, which is, of course, impossible in Chinese.

So again in English *New-town*, in Greek *Nea-polis*, would be simply combinatory compounds. Even *Newton* would still belong to the combinatory stratum; but *Naples* would have to be classed as belonging to the inflectional stage.

Finnish, Hungarian, Turkish, and the Dravidian languages belong in the main to the combinatory stratum; but having received a considerable amount of literary cultivation, they all alike exhibit forms which in every sense of the word are inflectional. If in Finnish, for instance, we find *käsi*, in the singular, hand, and *kädet*, in the plural, hands, we see that phonetic corruption has clearly reached the very core of the noun, and given rise to a plural more decidedly inflectional than the Greek χεῖϱ-ες, or the English *hand-s*. In Tamil, where the suffix of the plural is *gal*, we have indeed a regular combinatory form in *kei-gal*, hands; but if the same plural suffix *gal* is added to *kal*, stone, the euphonic rules of Tamil require not only a change in the suffix, which becomes *kal*, but likewise a modification in the body of the word, *kal* being changed to *kar*. We thus get the plural *karkal* which in every sense of the word is an inflectional form. In this plural suffix *gal*, Dr. Caldwell has recognized the Dravidian *tala* or *dala*, a host, a crowd; and though, as he admits himself in the second edition (p. 143), the evidence in support of this etymology may not be entirely satisfactory, the steps by which the learned author of the Grammar of the Dravidian languages has traced the plural termination *lu* in Telugu back to the same original suffix *kal* admit of little doubt.

Evidence of a similar kind may easily be found in any grammar, whether of an isolating, combinatory, or inflectional language, wherever there is evidence as to the ascending or descending progress of any particular form of speech. Everywhere amalgamation points back to combination, and combination back to juxtaposition, everywhere isolating speech tends towards terminational forms, and terminational forms become inflectional.

I may best be able to explain the view commonly held with regard to the strata of language by a reference to the strata of the earth. Here, too, where different strata have been tilted up, it might seem at first sight as if they were arranged perpendicularly and side by side, none underlying the other, none presupposing the other. But as the geologist, on the strength of more general evidence, has to reverse this perpendicular position, and to re-arrange his strata in their natural order, and as they followed each other horizontally, the student of language too is irresistibly driven to the same conclusion. No language can by any possibility be inflectional without having passed through the combinatory and isolating stratum; no language can by any possibility be combinatory without clinging with its roots to the underlying stratum of isolation. Unless Sanskrit and Greek and Hebrew had passed through the combinatory stratum, nay, unless, at some time or other, they had been no better than Chinese, their present form would be as great a miracle as the existence of chalk (and the strata associated with it) without an underlying stratum of oolite (and the strata associated with it;) or a stratum of oolite unsupported by the trias or system of new red sandstone. Bunsen's dictum, that "the question whether a language can begin with inflections, implies an absurdity," may have seemed too strongly worded: but if he took inflections in the commonly received meaning, in the sense of something that may be added or removed from a base in order to define or to modify its meaning, then surely the simple argument *ex nihilo nihil fit* is sufficient to prove that the inflections must have been something by themselves, before they became inflections relatively to the base, and that the base too must have existed by itself, before it could be defined and modified by the addition of such inflections.

But we need not depend on purely logical arguments, when we have historical evidence to appeal to. As far as we know the history of language, we see it everywhere confined within those three great strata or zones which we have just described. There are inflectional changes, no doubt, which cannot as yet be explained, such as the *m* in the accusative singular of masculine, feminine, and in the nominative and accusative of neuter nouns; or the change of vowels between the Hebrew *Piel* and *Pual*, *Hiphil* and *Hophal*, where we might feel tempted to admit formative agencies different from juxtaposition and combination. But if we consider how in Sanskrit the Vedic instrumental plural, *aśvebhis* (Lat. *equobus*), becomes before our very eyes *aśvais* (Lat. *equis*), and how such changes as *Bruder*, brother, and *Brüder*, brethren, *Ich weiss*, I know, A.S. *wât*, and *Wir wissen*, we know, A.S. *wit-on*, have been explained as the results of purely mechanical, *i.e.*, combinatory proceedings, we need not despair of further progress in the same direction. One thing is certain, that, wherever inflection has yielded to a rational analysis, it has invariably been recognized as the result of a previous combination, and wherever combination has been traced back to an earlier stage, that earlier stage has been simple juxtaposition. The primitive blocks of Chinese and the most perplexing agglomerates of Greek can be explained as the result of one continuous formative process, whatever the material elements may be on which it was exercised; nor is it possible even to imagine in the formation of language more than these three strata through which hitherto all human speech has passed.

All we can do is to subdivide each stratum, and thus, for instance, distinguish in the second stratum the suffixing (R + ϱ) from the prefixing (ϱ + R), and from the affixing (ϱ + R + ϱ) languages.

A fourth class, the infixing or incapsulating languages, are but a variety of the affixing class, for what in Bask or in the polysynthetic dialects of America has the appearance of actual insertion of formative elements into the body of a base can be explained more rationally by the former existence of simpler bases to which modifying suffixes or prefixes have once been added, but not so firmly as to exclude the addition of new suffixes at the end of the base, instead of, as with us, at the end of the compound. If we could say in Greek δείκ-μι-νυ, instead of δείκ-νυ-μι, or in Sanskrit *yu-mi-na-j*, instead of *yu-na-j-mi*, we should have a real beginning of so-called incapsulating formations.9

A few instances will place the normal progress of language from stratum to stratum more clearly before our eyes. We have seen that in Chinese every word is monosyllabic, every word tells, and there are, as yet, no suffixes by which one word is derived from another, no case-terminations by which the relation of one word to another could be indicated. How, then, does Chinese distinguish between the son of the father, and the father of the son? Simply by position. *Fú* is father, *tzé*, son; therefore *fú tzé* is son of the father, *tzé fú*, father of the son. This rule admits of no exception but one. If a Chinese wants to say *a wine-glass*, he puts *wine* first and *glass* last, as in English. If he wants to say *a glass of wine*, he puts *glass* first and *wine* last. Thus *i-pei thsieou*, a cup of wine; *thsieou pei*, a wine-cup. If, however, it seems desirable to mark the word which is in the genitive more distinctly, the word *tchi* may be placed after it, and we may say, *fú tchi tzé*, the son of the father. In the Mandarin dialect this *tchi* has become *ti*, and is added so constantly to the governed word, that, to all intents and purposes, it may be treated as what we call the termination of the genitive. Originally this *tchi* was a relative, or rather a demonstrative, pronoun, and it continues to be used as such in the ancient Chinese.10

It is perfectly true that Chinese possesses no derivative suffixes; that it cannot derive, for instance, *kingly* from a noun, such as *king*, or adjectives like *visible* and *invisible* from a verb *videre*, to see. Yet the same idea which we express by invisible, is expressed without difficulty in Chinese, only in a different way. They say *khan-pu-kien*, "I-behold-and-do-not-see," and this to them conveys the same idea as the English *invisible*, though more exactly *invisible* might be rendered by *kien*, to see, *pou-te*, one cannot, *tí*, which.

We cannot in Chinese derive from *ferrum*, iron, a new substantive *ferrarius*, a man who works in iron, a blacksmith; *ferraria*, an iron mine, and again *ferrariarius*, a man who works in an iron mine. All this is possible in an inflectional language only. But it is not to be supposed that in Chinese there is an independent expression for every single conception, even for those which are clearly secondary and derivative. If an arrow in Chinese is *shi*, then a maker of arrows (in old French *fléchier*, in English *fletcher*) is called an arrow-man, *shi-jin*. *Shui* means water, *fu*, man; hence *shui-fu*, a water man, a water carrier. The same word *shui*, water, if followed by *sheu*, hand, stands for steersman, literally, water-hand. *Kin* means gold, *tsiang*, maker; hence *kin-tsiang*, a goldsmith. *Shou* means writing, *sheu*, hand; hence *shou-sheu*, a writer, a copyist, literally, a writing-hand.

A transition from such compounds to really combinatory speech is extremely easy. Let *sheu*, in the sense of hand, become obsolete, and be replaced in the ordinary language by another word for hand; and let such names as *shu-sheu*, author, *shui-sheu*, boatsman, be retained, and the people who speak this language will soon accustom themselves to look upon *sheu* as a mere derivative, and use it by a kind of false analogy, even where the original meaning of *sheu*, hand, would not have been applicable.11

We can watch the same process even in comparatively modern languages. In Anglo-Saxon, for instance, *hâd* means state, order. It is used as an independent word, and continued to be so used as late as Spenser, who wrote:—

"Cuddie, I wote thou kenst little good,

So vainly t' advaunce thy headlesse hood."

After a time, however, *hâd*, as an independent word, was lost, and its place taken by more classical expressions, such as *habit*, *nature*, or *disposition*. But there remained such compounds as *man-hâd*, the state of man, *God-hâd*, the nature of God; and in these words the last element, being an empty word and no longer understood, was soon looked upon as a mere suffix. Having lost its vitality, it was all the more exposed to phonetic decay, and became both *hood* and *head*.

Or, let us take another instance, The name given to the fox in ancient German poetry was *Regin-hart*. *Regin* in Old High German means thought or cunning, *hart*, the Gothic *hardu*, means strong. This *hart*12 corresponds to the Greek κρατος, which, in its adjectival form of κρατης, forms as many proper names in Greek as *hart* in German. In Sanskrit the same word exists as *kratu*, meaning intellectual rather than bodily strength, a shade of meaning which is still perceivable even in the German *hart*, and in the English *hard* and *hardy*. *Reginhart*, therefore, was originally a compound, meaning "thought-strong," strong in cunning. Other words formed in the same or a very similar manner are: *Peranhart* and *Bernhart*, literally, bear-minded, or bold like a bear; *Eburhart*, boar-minded; *Engil-hart*, angel-minded; *Gothart*, god-minded; *Egin-hart*, fierce-minded; *Hugihart*, wise-minded or strong in thought, the English *Hogarth*. In Low German the second element, *hart*, lost its *h* and became *ard*. This *ard* ceased to convey any definite meaning, and though in some words which are formed by *ard* we may still discover its original power, it soon became a mere derivative, and was added promiscuously to form new words. In the Low German name for the fox, *Reinaert*, neither the first nor the second word tells us any longer anything, and the two words together have become a mere proper name. In other words the first portion retains its meaning, but the second, *ard*, is nothing but a suffix. Thus we find the Low German *dronk-ard*, a drunkard; *dick-ard*, a thick fellow; *rik-ard*, a rich fellow; *gêrard*, a miser. In English *sweet-ard*, originally a very sweet person, has been changed and resuscitated as *sweet-heart*,13 by the same process which changed *shamefast* into *shamefaced*. But, still more curious, this suffix *ard*, which had lost all life and meaning in Low German, was taken over as a convenient derivative by the Romance languages. After having borrowed a number of words such as *renard*, fox, and proper names like *Bernard*, *Richard*, *Gerard*, the framers of the new Romance dialects used the same termination even at the end of Latin words. Thus they formed not only many proper names, like *Abeillard*, *Bayard*, *Brossard*, but appellatives like *leccardo*, a gourmand, *linguardo*, a talker, *criard*, a crier, *codardo*, Prov. *coart*, Fr. *couard*, a coward.14 That a German word *hart*, meaning strong, and originally strength, should become a Roman suffix may seem strange; yet we no longer hesitate to use even Hindustani words as English suffixes. In Hindustani *válá* is used to form many substantives. If *Dilli* is Delhi, then *Dill-válá* is a man of Delhi. *Go* is cow, *go-válá* a cow-herd, contracted into *gválá*. Innumerable words can thus be formed, and as the derivative seemed handy and useful, it was at last added even to English words, for instance in "Competition wallah."

These may seem isolated cases, but the principles on which they rest pervade the whole structure of language. It is surprising to see how much may be achieved by an application of those principles, how large results may be obtained by the smallest and simplest means. By means of the single radical î or *yâ* (originally *ya*), which in the Aryan languages means to go or to send, the almost unconscious framers of Aryan grammar formed not only their neuter, denominative, and causative verbs, but their passives, their optatives, their futures, and a considerable number of substantives and adjectives. Every one of these formations, in Sanskrit as well as in Greek, can be explained, and has been explained, as the result of a combination between any given verbal root and the radical *î* or *yâ*.

There is, for instance, a root *nak*, expressive of perishing or destruction. We have it in *nak*, night; Latin *nox*, Greek νύξ, meaning originally the waning, the disappearing, the death of day. We have the same root in composition, as, for instance, *jîva-nak*, life-destroying; and by means of suffixes Greek has formed from it νεκ-ρός, a dead body, νέκ-υς, dead, and νέκ-υ-ες in the plural, the departed. In Sanskrit this root is turned into a simple verb, *naś-a-ti*, he perishes. But in order to give to it a more distinctly neuter meaning, a new verbal base is formed by composition with *ya*, *naś-ya-ti*, he goes to destruction, he perishes.

By the same or a very similar process denominative verbs are formed in Sanskrit to a very large extent. From *râjan*, king, we form *râjâ-ya-te*, he behaves like a king, literally, he goes the king, he acts the king, *il a l'allure d'un roi*. From *kumârî*, girl, *kûmârâ-ya-te*, he behaves like a girl, etc.15

After raising *naś* to *nâśa*, and adding the same radical *ya*, Sanskrit produces a causative verb, *nâśa-ya-ti*, he sends to destruction, the Latin *nêcare*.

In close analogy to the neuter verb *naśyati*, the regular passive is formed in Sanskrit by composition with *ya*, but by adding, at the same time, a different set of personal terminations. Thus *náś-yá-ti* means he perishes, while *naś-yá-te* means he is destroyed.

The usual terminations of the Optative in Sanskrit are:—

    yâm,   yâs,   yât,   yâma,   yâta,   yus,

or, after bases ending in vowels:—

    iyam,   is,   it,   ima,   ita,   iyus.

In Greek:—

    ιην,   ιης,   ιη,   ιημεν,   ιητε,   ιεν,

or, after bases ending in o:—

    ιμι,   ις,   ι,   ιμεν,   ιτε,   ιεν.

In Latin:—

    iêm   iês   iet   ——   ——   ient,

    îm,   îs,   it,   îmus,   îtis,   int.

If we add these terminations to the root *AS*, to be, we get the Sanskrit *s-yâm* for *as-yâm*:—

    syâm,   syâs,   syât,   syâma,   syâta,   syus.

Greek ἐσ-ίην, contracted to εἴην:—

    εἴην,   εἴης,   εἴη,   εἴημεν,   εἴητε,   εἶεν.

Latin *es-iem*, changed to *siêm*, *sîm*, and *erîm*:—

    siêm,   siês,   siet,[16]   ——   ——   sient.

    sim,   sîs,   sit,[17]   sîmus,   sitis,   sint.

    erîm,   erîs,   erit,   erîmus,   erîtis,   erint.

If we add the other termination to a verbal base ending in certain vowels, we get the Sanskrit *bhara-iyam*, contracted to *bháreyam*:—

    bharêyam, bharês, bharêt, bharêma, bharêta, bharêyus.

in Greek φέρο-ιμι:—

    φέρο-ιμι, φέρο-ις, φέρο-ι, φέρο-ιμεν, φέρο-ιτε, φέρο-ιεν.

in Latin *fere-im*, changed to *ferem*, used in the sense of a future, but replaced[18] in the first person by *feram*, the subjunctive of the present:—

    feram, ferês, feret, ferêmus, ferêtis, ferent.

Perfect Subjunctive:—

    tul-erîm, tul-erîs, tul-erit, tul-erimus, tul-eritis,[19] tul-erint.

Here we have clearly the same auxiliary verb, i or *ya*, again, and we are driven to admit that what we now call an optative or potential mood, was originally a kind of future, formed by *ya*, to go, very much like the French *je vais dire*, I am going to say, I shall say, or like the Zulu

1   2   3   4   1 2 3 4

n g i - y a - k u - t a n d a , I go to love, I shall love.[20]

The future would afterwards assume the character of a civil command, as "thou wilt go" may be used even by us in the sense of "go;" and the imperative would dwindle away into a potential, as we may say: "Go and you will see," in the same sense as, If you go, you will see.

The terminations of the future are:—

Sanskrit:—

    syâmi,   syasi,   syati,   syâmas,   syâtha,   syanti.

Greek:—

    σω,   σεις,   σει,   σομεν,   σετε,   σοντι.

Latin:—

    ero,   erĭs,   erĭt,   erĭmus,   erĭtis,   erunt.

In these terminations we have really two auxiliary verbs, the verb *as*, to be, and *ya*, to go, and by adding them to any given root, as, for instance, *DA*, to give, we have the Sanskrit (*dâ-as-yâ-mi*):—

    dâ-s-yâ-mi, dâ-s-ya-si, dâ-s-ya-ti, dâ-s-yâ-mas, dâ-s-ya-tha, dâ-s-ya-nti,

Greek (δω-εσ-ιω):—

    δώ-σ-ω,[21] δώ-σ-εις, δώ-σ-ει, δώ-σ-ομεν, δώ-σ-ετε, δώ-σ-ουσι.

Latin:—

    pot-ero, pot-erĭs, pot-erit, pot-erimus, pot-erĭtis, pot-erunt.

A verbal form of very frequent occurrence in Sanskrit is the so-called gerundive participle which signifies that a thing is necessary or proper to be done. Thus from *budh*, to know, is formed *bodh-ya-s*, one who is to be known, *cognoscendus*; from *guh*, to hide, *gúh-ya-s*, or *goh-ya-s*, one who is to be hidden, literally, one who goes to a state of hiding or being hidden; from *yaj*, to sacrifice, *yâj-ya-s*, one who is or ought to be worshipped. Here, again, what is going to be becomes gradually what will be, and lastly, what shall be. In Greek we find but few analogous forms, such as ἅγιος, holy, στύγ-ι-ος, to be hated; in Latin *ex-im-i-us*, to be taken out; in Gothic *anda-nêm-ja*, to be taken on, to be accepted, agreeable, German *angenehm*.22

While the gerundive participles in *ya* are formed on the same principle as the verbal bases in *ya* of the passive, a number of substantives in *ya* seem to have been formed in close analogy to the bases of denominative verbs, or the bases of neuter verbs, in all of which the derivative *ya* expresses originally the act of going, behaving, and at last of simple being. Thus from *vid*, to know, we find in Sanskrit *vid-yâ*, knowing, knowledge; from *śi*, to lie down, *śayyâ*; resting. Analogous forms in Latin are *gaud-i-um*, *stud-i-um*, or with feminine terminations, *in-ed-i-a*, *in-vid-i-a*, *per-nic-i-es*, *scab-i-es*; in Greek, μαν-ι-α, ἁμαρτ-ι-α, or ἁμάρτ-ι-ον; in German, numerous abstract nouns in *i* and *e*.23

This shows how much can be achieved, and has been achieved, in language with the simplest materials. Neuter, denominative, causative, passive verbs, optatives and futures, gerundives, adjectives, and substantives, all are formed by one and the same process, by means of one and the same root. It is no inconsiderable portion of grammar which has thus been explained by this one root *ya*, to go, and we learn again and again how simple and yet how wonderful are the ways of language, if we follow them up from stratum to stratum to their original starting-point.

Now what has happened in these cases, has happened over and over again in the history of language. Everything that is now formal, not only derivative suffixes, but everything that constitutes the grammatical framework and articulation of language, was originally material. What we now call the terminations of cases were mostly local adverbs; what we call the personal endings of verbs were personal pronouns. Suffixes and affixes were mostly independent words, nominal, verbal, or pronominal; there is, in fact, nothing in language that is now empty, or dead, or formal, that was not originally full, and alive, and material. It is the object of Comparative Grammar to trace every formal or dead element back to its life-like form; and though this resuscitating process is by no means complete, nay, though in several cases it seems hopeless to try to discover the living type from which proceeded the petrified fragments which we call terminations or suffixes, enough evidence has been brought together to establish on the firmest basis this general maxim, that *Nothing is dead in any language that was not originally alive*; that nothing exists in a tertiary stratum that does not find its antecedents and its explanation in the secondary or primary stratum of human speech.

After having explained, as far as it was possible in so short a time, what I consider to be the right view of the stratification of human speech, I should have wished to be able to show to you how the aspect of some of the most difficult and most interesting problems of our science is changed, if we look at them again with the new light which we have gained regarding the necessary antecedents of all language. Let me only call your attention to one of the most contested points in the Science of Language. The question whether we may assign a common origin to the Aryan and Semitic languages has been discussed over and over again. No one thinks now of deriving Sanskrit from Hebrew, or Hebrew from Sanskrit; the only question is whether at some time or other the two languages could ever have formed part of one and the same body of speech. There are scholars, and very eminent scholars, who deny all similarity between the two, while others have collected materials that would seem to make it difficult to assign such numerous coincidences to mere chance. Nowhere, in fact, has Bacon's observation on this radical distinction between different men's dispositions for philosophy and the sciences been more fully verified than among the students of the Science of Language:—*Maximum et velut radicale discrimen ingeniorum, quoad philosophiam et scientias, illud est, quod alia ingenia sint fortiora et aptiora ad notandas rerum differentias; alia ad notandas rerum similitudines. . . . . . Utrumque autem ingenium facile labitur in excessum, prensando aut gradus rerum, aut umbras.*24 Before, however, we enter upon an examination of the evidence brought forward by different scholars in support of their conflicting theories, it is our first duty to ask a preliminary question, viz.: What kind of evidence have we any right to expect, considering that both Sanskrit and Hebrew belong, in the state in which we know them, to the inflectional stratum of speech?

Now it is quite true that Sanskrit and Hebrew had a separate existence long before they reached the tertiary stratum, before they became thoroughly inflectional; and that consequently they can share nothing in common that is peculiar to the inflectional stratum in each, nothing that is the result of phonetic decay, which sets in after combinatory formations have become unintelligible and traditional. I mean, supposing that the pronoun of the first person had been originally the same in the Semitic and Aryan languages, supposing that in the Hebrew *an-oki* (Assyrian *an-aku*, Phen. *anak*) the last portion, *oki*, was originally identical with the Sanskrit *ah* in *aham*, the Greek ἐγ in ἐγ-ώ, it would still be useless to attempt to derive the termination of the first person singular, whether in *kâtal-ti* or in *ektôl*, from the same type which in Sanskrit appears as *mi* or *am* or *a*, in *tudâ-mi, atud-am, tutod-a*. There cannot be between Hebrew and Sanskrit the same relationship as between Sanskrit and Greek, if indeed the term of relationship is applicable even to Sanskrit and Greek, which are really mere dialectic varieties of one and the same type of speech.

The question then arises, Could the Semitic and Aryan languages have been identical during the second or *combinatory* period? Here, as before, the answer must be, I believe, decidedly negative, for not only are the empty words which are used for derivative purposes different in each, but, what is far more characteristic, the manner in which they are added to the stems is different too. In the Aryan languages formative elements are attached to the ends of words only; in the Semitic languages they are found both at the end and at the beginning. In the Aryan languages grammatical compounds are all according to the formula rǫ; in the Semitic we have formations after the formulas rǫ, ǫr, and ǫrǫ.

There remains, therefore, the first or isolating stage only in which Semitic and Aryan speech might have been identical. But even here we must make a distinction. All Aryan roots are monosyllabic, all Semitic roots have been raised to triliteral form. Therefore it is only previous to the time when the Semitic roots assumed this secondary triliteral form that any community could possibly be admitted between these two streams of language. Supposing we knew as an historical fact that at this early period—a period which transcends the limits of everything we are accustomed to call historical—Semitic and Aryan speech had been identical, what evidence of this union could we expect to find in the actual Semitic and Aryan languages such as we know them in their inflectional period? Let us recollect that the 100,000 words of English, nay, the many hundred thousand words in all the dictionaries of the other Aryan languages, have been reduced to about 500 roots, and that this small number of roots admits of still further reduction. Let us, then, bear in mind that the same holds good with regard to the Semitic languages, particularly if we accept the reduction of all triliteral to biliteral roots. What, then, could we expect in our comparison of Hebrew and Sanskrit but a small number of radical coincidences, a similarity in the form and meaning of about 500 radical syllables, everything else in Hebrew and Sanskrit being an after-growth, which could not begin before the two branches of speech were severed once and forever.

But more, if we look at these roots we shall find that their predicative power is throughout very general, and therefore liable to an infinite amount of specification. A root that means to fall (Sk. *pat*, πἰ-πτ-ω) comes to mean to fly (Sk. *ut-pat*, πέτομαι). The root *dâ*, which means to give, assumes, after the preposition *â*, the sense of taking. The root *yu*, which means to join, means to separate if preceded by the preposition *vi*. The root *ghar*, which expresses brightness, may supply, and does supply in different Aryan languages, derivations expressive of brightness (gleam), warmth (Sk. *gharma*, heat), joy (χαίρειν), love (χάρις), of the colors of green (Sk. *hari*), yellow (*gilvus, flavus*), and red (Sk. *harit, fulvus*), and of the conception of growing (*ger-men*). In the Semitic languages this vagueness of meaning in the radical elements forms one of the principal difficulties of the student, for according as a root is used in its different conjugations, it may convey the most startling variety of conception. It is also to be taken into account that out of the very limited number of roots which at that early time were used in common by the ancestors of the Aryan and Semitic races, a certain portion may have been lost by each, so that the fact that there are roots in Hebrew of which no trace exists in Sanskrit, and *vice versâ*, would again be perfectly natural and intelligible.

It is right and most essential that we should see all this clearly, that we should understand how little evidence we are justified in expecting in support of a common origin of the Semitic and Aryan languages, before we commit ourselves to any opinion on this important subject. I have by no means exhausted all the influences that would naturally, nay necessarily, have contributed towards producing the differences between the radical elements of Aryan and Semitic speech, always supposing that the two sprang originally from the same source. Even if we excluded the ravages of phonetic decay from that early period of speech, we should have to make ample allowances for the influence of dialectic variety. We know in the Aryan languages the constant play between gutturals, dentals, and labials (*quinque*, Sk. *panca*, πέντε, Æol. πέμπε, Goth. *fimf*). We know the dialectic interchange of Aspirate, Media, and Tenuis, which, from the very beginning, has imparted to the principal channels of Aryan speech their individual character (τρεῖς, Goth. *threis*, High German *drei*).25 If this and much more could happen within the dialectic limits of one more or less settled body of speech, what must have been the chances beyond those limits? Considering how fatal to the identity of a word the change of a single consonant would be in monosyllabic languages, we might expect that monosyllabic roots, if their meaning was so general, vague, and changeable, would all the more carefully have preserved their consonantal outline. But this is by no means the case. Monosyllabic languages have their dialects no less than polysyllabic ones; and from the rapid and decisive divergence of such dialects, we may learn how rapid and decisive the divergence of language must have been during the isolating period. Mr. Edkins, who has paid particular attention to the dialects of Chinese, states that in the northern provinces the greatest changes have taken place, eight initial and one final consonant having been exchanged for others, and three finals lost. Along the southern bank of the Yang-tsï-kiang, and a little to the north of it, the old initials are all preserved, as also through Chekiang to Fuh-kien. But among the finals, *m* is exchanged for *n*; *t* and *p* are lost, and also *k*, except in some country districts. Some words have two forms, one used colloquially, and one appropriated to reading. The former is the older pronunciation, and the latter more near to Mandarin. The cities of Su-cheu, Hang-cheu, Ningpo, and When-cheu, with the surrounding country, may be considered as having one dialect, spoken probably by thirty millions of people, *i.e.*, by more than the whole population of Great Britain and Ireland. The city of Hwei-cheu has a dialect of its own, in which the soft initial consonants are exchanged for hard and aspirated ones, a process analogous to what we call *Lautverschiebung* in the Aryan languages. At Fu-cheu-fu, in the eastern part of the province of Kiang-si, the soft initials have likewise been replaced by aspirates. In many parts of the province of Hunan the soft initials still linger on; but in the city of Chang-sha the spoken dialect has the five tones of Mandarin, and the aspirated and other initials distributed in the same manner. In the island of Hai-nan there is a distinct approach to the form which Chinese words assume in the language of Annam. Many of the hard consonants are softened, instead of the reverse taking place as in many other parts of China. Thus *ti*, *di*, both *ti* in Mandarin, are both pronounced *di* in Hai-nan. *B* and *p* are both used for many words whose initials are *w* and *f* in Mandarin. In the dialects of the province of Fuhkien the following changes take place in initial consonants: *k* is used for *h*; *p* for *f*; *m*, *b*, for *w*; *j* for *y*; *t* for *ch*; *ch* for *s*; *ng* for *i*, *y*, *w*, *n* for *j*.26 When we have clearly realized to ourselves what such changes mean in words consisting of one consonant and one vowel, we shall be more competent to act as judges, and to determine what right we have to call for more ample and more definite evidence in support of the common origin of languages which became separated during their monosyllabic or isolating stages, and which are not known to us before they are well advanced in the inflectional stage.

It might be said,—Why, if we make allowance for all this, the evidence really comes to nothing, and is hardly deserving of the attention of the scholar. I do not deny that this is, and always has been my own opinion. All I wish to put clearly before other scholars is, that this is not our fault. We see why there can be no evidence, and we find there is no evidence, or very little support of a common origin of Semitic and Aryan speech. But that is very different from dogmatic assertions, so often and so confidently repeated, that there can be no kind of relationship between Sanskrit and Hebrew, that they must have had different beginnings, that they represent, in fact, two independent species of human speech. All this is pure dogmatism, and no true scholar will be satisfied with it, or turn away contemptuously from the tentative researches of scholars like Ewald, Raumer, and Ascoli. These scholars, particularly Raumer and Ascoli, have given us, as far as I can judge, far more evidence in support of a radical relationship between Hebrew and Sanskrit than, from my point of view, we are entitled to expect. I mean this as a caution in both directions. If, on one side, we ought not to demand more than we have a right to demand, we ought, on the other, not to look for, nor attempt to bring forward, more evidence than the nature of the case admits of. We know that words which have identically the same sound and meaning in Sanskrit, Greek, Latin, and German, cannot be the same words, because they would contravene those phonetic laws that made these languages to differ from each other. *To doom* cannot have any connection with the Latin *damnare*; *to call* cannot be the Greek καλεῖν, the Latin *calare*; nor Greek φαῦλος the German *faul*; the English *care* cannot be identified with Latin *cura*, nor the German *Auge* with the Greek αὐγή. The same applies, only with a hundred-fold greater force, to words in Hebrew and Sanskrit. If any triliteral root in Hebrew were to agree with a triliteral word in Sanskrit, we should feel certain, at once, that they are not the same, or that their similarity is purely accidental. Pronouns, numerals, and a few imitative rather than predicative names for father and mother, etc., may have been preserved from the earliest stage by the Aryan and Semitic speakers; but if scholars go beyond, and compare such words as Hebrew *barak*, to bless, and Latin *precari*; Hebrew *lab*, heart, and the English *liver*; Hebrew *melech*, king, and the Latin *mulcere*, to smoothe, to quiet, to subdue, they are in great danger, I believe, of proving too much.

Attempts have lately been made to point out a number of roots which Chinese shares in common with Sanskrit. Far be it from me to stigmatize even such researches as unscientific, though it requires an effort for one brought up in the very straitest school of Bopp, to approach such inquiries without prejudice. Yet, if conducted with care and sobriety, and particularly with a clear perception of the limits within which such inquiries must be confined, they are perfectly legitimate; far more so than the learned dogmatism with which some of our most eminent scholars have declared a common origin of Sanskrit and Chinese as out of the question. I cannot bring myself to say that the method which Mr. Chalmers adopts in his interesting work on the "Origin of Chinese" is likely to carry conviction to the mind of the *bonà fide* skeptic. I believe, before we compare the words of Chinese with those of any other language, every effort should be made to trace Chinese words back to their most primitive form. Here Mr. Edkins has pointed out the road that ought to be followed, and has clearly shown the great advantage to be derived from an accurate study of Chinese dialects. The same scholar has done still more by pointing out how Chinese should at first be compared with its nearest relatives, the Mongolian of the North-Turanian, and the Tibetan of the South-Turanian class, before any comparisons are attempted with more distant colonies that started during the monosyllabic period of speech. "I am now seeking to compare," he writes, "the Mongolian and Tibetan with the Chinese, and have already obtained some interesting results:—

"1. A large proportion of Mongol words are Chinese. Perhaps a fifth are so. The identity is in the first syllable of the Mongol words, that being the root. The correspondence is most striking in the adjectives, of which perhaps one half of the most common are the same radically as in Chinese; e.g., *sain*, good; *begen*, low; *ic'hi*, right; *sologai*, left; *c'hihe*, straight; *gadan*, outside; *c'hohon*, few; *logon*, green; *hung-gun*, light (not heavy). But the identity is also extensive in other parts of speech, and this identity of common roots seems to extend into the Turkish, Tatar, etc.; e.g., *su*, water; *tenri*, heaven.

"2. To compare Mongol with Chinese it is necessary to go back at least six centuries in the development of the Chinese language. For we find in common roots final letters peculiar to the old Chinese, *e.g.*, final *m*. The initial letters also need to be considered from another standpoint than the Mandarin pronunciation. If a large number of words are common to Chinese, Mongol, and Tatar, we must go back at least twelve centuries to obtain a convenient epoch of comparison.

"3. While the Mongol has no traces of tones, they are very distinctly developed in Tibetan. Csoma de Körös and Schmidt do not mention the existence of tones, but they plainly occur in the pronunciation of native Tibetans resident in Peking.

"4. As in the case of the comparison with Mongol, it is necessary in examining the connection of Tibetan with Chinese to adopt the old form of the Chinese with its more numerous final consonants, and its full system of soft, hard, and aspirated initials. The Tibetan numerals exemplify this with sufficient clearness.

"5. While the Mongol is near the Chinese in the extensive prevalence of words common to the two languages, the Tibetan is near in phonal structure, as being tonic and monosyllabic. This being so, it is less remarkable that there are many words common to Chinese and Tibetan, for it might have been expected; but that there should be perhaps as many in the Mongol with its long untoned polysyllables, is a curious circumstance."27

This is no doubt the right spirit in which researches into the early history of language should be conducted, and I hope that Mr. Edkins, Mr. Chalmers, and others, will not allow themselves to be discouraged by the ordinary objections that are brought against all tentative studies. Even if their researches should only lead to negative results, they would be of the highest importance. The criterion by which we test the relationship of inflectional languages, such as Sanskrit and Greek, Hebrew and Arabic, cannot, from the nature of the case, be applied to languages which are still in the combinatory or isolating stratum, nor would they answer any purpose, if we tried by them to determine whether certain languages, separated during their inflectional growth, had been united during their combinatory stage, or whether languages, separated during their combinatory progress, had started from a common centre in their monosyllabic age. Bopp's attempt to work with his Aryan tools on the Malayo-Polynesian languages, and to discover in them traces of Aryan forms, ought to serve as a warning example.

However, there are dangers also, and even greater dangers, on the opposite shore, and if Mr. Chalmers in his interesting work on "the Origin of Chinese," compares, for instance, the Chinese *tzé*, child, with the Bohemian *tsi*, daughter, I know that the indignation of the Aryan scholars will be roused to a very high pitch, considering how they have proved most minutely that *tsi* or *dci* in Bohemian is the regular modification of *dugte*, and that *dugte* is the Sanskrit *duhitar*, the Greek θυγάτηϱ, daughter, originally a pet-name, meaning a milk-maid, and given by the Aryan shepherds, and by them only, to the daughters of their house. Such accidents28 will happen in so comprehensive a subject as the Science of Language. They have happened to scholars like Bopp, Grimm, and Burnouf, and they will happen again. I do not defend haste or inaccuracy, I only say, we must venture on, and not imagine that all is done, and that nothing remains to conquer in our science. Our watchword, here as elsewhere, should be Festina lente! but, by all means, Festina! Festina! Festina!

PART II.
ON CURTIUS' CHRONOLOGY OF THE INDO-GERMANIC LANGUAGES.

IN a former Lecture on the "Stratification of Language" I ventured to assert that wherever *inflection* has yielded to a rational analysis, it has invariably been recognized as the result of a previous *combination*, and wherever *combination* has been traced back to an earlier stage, that earlier stage has been simply *juxtaposition*.

Professor Pott in his "Etymologische Forschungen" (1871, p. 16), a work which worthily holds its place by the side of Bopp's "Comparative Grammar," questions the correctness of that statement; but in doing so he seems to me to have overlooked the restrictions which I myself had introduced, in order to avoid the danger of committing myself to what might seem too general a statement. I did not say that every form of inflection had been proved to spring from a previous combination, but I spoke of those cases only where we have succeeded in a rational analysis of inflectional forms, and it was in these that I maintained that inflection had always been found to be the result of previous combination. What is the object of the analysis of grammatical inflections, or of Comparative Grammar in general, if not to find out what terminations originally were, before they had assumed a purely formal character? If we take the French adverb *sincèrement*, sincerely, and trace it back to the Latin *sincerâ mente*, we have for a second time the three stages of juxtaposition, combination, and, to a certain extent, inflection, repeated before our eyes. I say, inflection, for *ment*, though originally an independent word, soon becomes a mere adverbial suffix, the speakers so little thinking of its original purport, that we may say of a stone that it falls *lourdement*, heavily, without wishing to imply that it falls *luridâ mente*, with a heavy, lit., with a lurid mind.

If we take the nom. sing. of a noun in Sanskrit, Greek, or Latin, we find that masculine nouns end frequently in *s*. We have for instance, Sk. *veśa-s*, Gr. οἶκο-ς, Lat. *vîcu-s*. These three words are identical in their termination, in their base, and in their root. The root is the Sk. *viś*, to settle down, to enter upon or into a thing. This root, without undergoing any further change, may answer the purpose both of a verbal and a nominal base. In the precative, for instance, we have *viś-yâ-t*, he may enter, which yields to a rational analysis into *viś*, the root *yâ*, to go, and the old pronominal stem of the third person, *t*, he. We reduplicate the root, and we get the perfect *vi-viś-us*, they have entered. Here I can understand that objections might be raised against accepting us as a mere phonetic corruption of *ant* and *anti*; but if, as in Greek, we find as the termination of the third pers. plur. of the perfect ᾶσι, we know that this is a merely phonetic change of the original *anti*,29 and this *anti* has been traced back by Pott himself (whether rightly or wrongly, we need not here inquire) to the pronominal stems *ana*, that, and *ti*, he. These two stems, when joined together, become *anti*,30 meaning *those* and *he*, and are gradually reduced to ᾶσι, and in Sanskrit to *us* for *ant*. What we call reduplication has likewise been traced back by Pott himself to an original repetition of the whole root, so that *vi-viś* stands for an original or intentional *viś-viś*; thus showing again the succession of the three stages, juxtaposition, *viś-viś*, combination *vi-viś*, inflection, the same, *vi-viś*, though liable to further phonetic modification.

Used as a nominal base the same root *viś* appears, without any change, in the nom. plur. *viś-as*, the settlers, the clans, the people. Now here again Professor Pott himself has endeavored to explain the inflection *as* by tracing it back to the pronominal base *as*, in *asau*, *ille*. He therefore takes the plural *viś-as* as a compound, meaning "man and that;" that is to say, he traces the inflection back to a combinatory origin.

By raising the simple base *viś* to *viśa*, we arrive at new verbal forms, such as *viś-â-mi*, I enter, *viś-a-si*, thou enterest, *viś-a-ti*, he enters. In all these inflectional forms, the antecedent combinatory stage is still more or less visible, for *mi*, *si*, *ti*, whatever their exact history may have been, are clearly varieties of the pronominal bases of the first, second, and third persons, *ma*, *tva*, *ta*.

Lastly, by raising *viś* to *veśa*, we arrive at a new nominal base, and by adding to it the stem of a demonstrative pronoun *s*, we form the so-called nom. sing. *veśa-s*, οἶκο-ς, *vicu-s*, from which we started, meaning originally house-here, this house, the house.

In all this Professor Pott would fully agree, but where he would differ, would be when we proceed to generalize, and to lay it down as an axiom, that all inflectional forms *must* have had the same combinatory origin. He may be right in thus guarding against too hasty generalization, to which we are but too prone in all inductive sciences. I am well aware that there are many inflections which have not yielded, as yet, to any rational analysis, but, with that reservation, I thought, and I still think, it right to say that, until some other process of forming those inflections has been pointed out, inflection may be considered as the invariable result of combination.

It is impossible in writing, always to repeat such qualifications and reservations. They must be taken as understood. Take for instance the augment in Greek and Sanskrit. Some scholars have explained it as a negative particle, others as a demonstrative pronoun; others, again, took it as a mere symbol of differentiation. If the last explanation could be established by more general analogies, then, no doubt, we should have here an inflection, that cannot be referred to combination. Again, it would be difficult to say, what independent element was added to the pronoun *sa*, he, in order to make it sâ, she. This, too, may, for all we know, be a case of phonetic symbolism, and, if so, it should be treated on its own merits. The lengthening of the vowel in the subjunctive mood was formerly represented by Professor Curtius as a symbolic expression of hesitation, but he has lately recalled that explanation as untenable. I pointed out that when in Hebrew we meet with such forms as *Piel* and *Pual*, *Hiphil* and *Hophal*, we feel tempted to admit formative agencies, different from mere juxtaposition and combination. But before we admit this purely phonetic symbolism, we should bear in mind that the changes of *bruder*, brother, into *brüder*, brethren, of *Ich weiss*, I know, into *wir wissen*, we know, which seem at first sight purely phonetic, have after all been proved to be the indirect result of juxtaposition and combination, so that we ought to be extremely careful and first exhaust every possible rational explanation, before we have recourse to phonetic symbolism as an element in the production of inflection forms.

The chief object, however, of my lecture on the "Stratification of Language" was not so much to show that inflection everywhere presupposes combination, and combination juxtaposition, but rather to call attention to a fact that had not been noticed before, viz.: that there is hardly any language, which is not at the same time *isolating*, *combinatory*, and *inflectional*.

It had been the custom in classifying languages morphologically to represent some languages, for instance Chinese, as *isolating*; others, such as Turkish or Finnish, as *combinatory*; others, such as Sanskrit or Hebrew, as *inflectional*. Without contesting the value of this classification for certain purposes, I pointed out that even Chinese, the very type of the isolating class, is not free from combinatory forms, and that the more highly developed among the combinatory languages, such as Hungarian, Finnish, Tamil, etc., show the clearest traces of incipient inflection. "The difficulty is not," as I said, "to show the transition of one stratum of speech into another, but rather to draw a sharp line between the different strata. The same, difficulty was felt in Geology, and led Sir Charles Lyell to invent such pliant names as *Eocene*, *Meiocene*, and *Pleiocene*, names which indicate a mere dawn, a minority, or a majority of new formations, but do not draw a fast and hard line, cutting off one stratum from the other. Natural growth and even merely mechanical accumulation and accretion, here as elsewhere, are so minute and almost imperceptible that they defy all strict scientific terminology, and force upon us the lesson that we must be satisfied with an approximate accuracy."

Holding these opinions, and having established them by an amount of evidence which, though it might easily be increased, seemed to me sufficient, I did not think it safe to assign to the three stages in the history of the Aryan languages, the *juxtapositional*, the *combinatory*, and the *inflectional*, a strictly successive character, still less to admit in the growth of the Aryan languages a number of definite stages, which should be sharply separated from each other, and assume an almost chronological character. I fully admit that wherever *inflectional* forms in the Aryan languages have yielded to a rational analysis, we see that they are preceded chronologically by *combinatory* formations; nor should I deny for one moment that *combinatory* forms presuppose an antecedent, and therefore chronologically more ancient stage of mere juxtaposition. What I doubt is whether, as soon as combination sets in, juxtaposition ceases, and whether the first appearance of inflection puts an end to the continued working of combination.

It seems to me, even if we argue only on *à priori* grounds, that there must have been at least a period of transition during which both principles were at work together, and I hardly can understand what certain scholars mean if they represent the principle of inflection as a sudden psychological change which, as soon as it has taken place, makes a return to combination altogether impossible. If, instead of arguing *à priori*, we look the facts of language in the face, we cannot help seeing that, even after that period during which it is supposed that the United Aryan language had attained its full development, I mean at a time when Sanskrit, Greek, and Latin had become completely separated, as so many national dialects, each with its own fully developed inflectional grammar, the power of combination was by no means extinct. The free power of composition, which is so manifest in Sanskrit and Greek, testifies to the continued working of combination in strictly historical times. I see no real distinction between the transition of *Néa pólis*, i.e., new town, into *Neápolis*, and into *Naples*, and the most primitive combination in Chinese, and I maintain that as long as a language retains that unbounded faculty of composition, which we see in Sanskrit, in Greek, and in German, the growth of new inflectional forms from combinatory germs must be admitted as possible. Forms such as the passive aorist in Greek, ἐτέθην, or the weak preterite in Gothic *nas-i-da, nas-i-dédjau*, need not have been formed before the Aryan family broke up into national languages; and forms such as Italian *meco, fratelmo*, or the future *avro*, I shall have, though not exactly of the same workmanship, show at all events that analogous powers are at work even in the latest periods of linguistic growth.

Holding these opinions, which, as far as I know, have never been controverted, I ought perhaps, when I came to publish the preceding Lecture, to have defended my position against the powerful arguments advanced in the meantime by my old friend, Professor G. Curtius, in support of a diametrically opposite opinion in his classical essay, "On the Chronology of the Indo-Germanic Languages," published in 1867, new edition, 1873. While I had endeavored to show that juxtaposition, combination, and inflection, though following each other in succession, do not represent chronological periods, but represent phases, strongly developed, it is true, in certain languages, but extending their influence far beyond the limits commonly assigned to them, Professor Curtius tried to establish the chronological character not only of these three, but of four other phases or periods in the history of Aryan speech. Confining himself to what he considers the undivided Aryan language to have been, before it was broken up into national dialects, such as Sanskrit, Greek, and Latin, he proceeds to subdivide the antecedent period of its growth into *seven* definite stages, each marked by a definite character, and each representing a sum of years in the chronology of the Aryan language. As I had found it difficult to treat Chinese as entirely *juxtapositional*, or Turkish as entirely *combinatory*, or Sanskrit as entirely *inflectional*, it was perhaps not to be wondered at that not even the persuasive pleading of my learned friend could convince me of the truth of the more minute chronological division proposed by him in his learned essay. But it would hardly have been fair if, on the present occasion, I had reprinted my "Rede Lecture" without explaining why I had altered nothing in my theory of linguistic growth, why I retained these three phases and no more, and why I treated even these, not as chronological periods, in the strict sense of the word, but as preponderating tendencies, giving an individual character to certain classes of language, without being totally absent in others. Professor Curtius is one of the few scholars with whom it is pleasant to differ. He has shown again and again that what he cares for is truth, not victory, and when he has defended his position against attacks not always courteous, he has invariably done so, not with hard words, but with hard arguments. I therefore feel no hesitation in stating plainly to him where his theories seem to me either not fully supported, or even contradicted by the facts of language, and I trust that this free exchange of ideas, though in public, will be as pleasant as our conversations in private used to be, now more than thirty years ago.

Let us begin with the *First Period*, which Professor Curtius calls the *Root-Period*. There must have been, as I tried to explain before, a period for the Aryan languages, during which they stood on a level with Chinese, using nothing but roots, or radical words, without having reduced any of them to a purely formal character, without having gone through the process of changing what Chinese grammarians call *full* words into *empty* words. I have always held, that to speak of roots as mere abstractions, as the result of grammatical theory, is self-contradictory. Roots which never had any real or historical existence may have been invented both in modern and ancient collections or *Dhâtupâṭhas*; but that is simply the fault of our etymological analysis, and in no way affects the fact, that the Aryan, like all other languages we know, began with roots. We may doubt the legitimacy of certain chemical elements, but not the reality of chemical elements in general. Language, in the sense in which we use the word, begins with roots, which are not only the ultimate facts for the Science of Language, but real facts in the history of human speech. To deny their historical reality would be tantamount to denying cause and effect.

Logically, no doubt, it is possible to distinguish between a root as a mere postulate, and a root used as an actual word. That distinction has been carefully elaborated by Indian grammarians and philosophers, but it does in no way concern us in purely historical researches. What I mean by a root used in real language is this: when we analyze a cluster of Sanskrit words, such as *yodha-s*, a fighter, *yodhaka-s*, a fighter, *yoddhâ*, a fighter, *yodhana-m*, fighting, *yuddhi-s*, a fight, *yuyutsu-s*, wishing to fight, *â-yudha-m*, a weapon, we easily see that they presuppose an element *yudh*, to fight, and that they are all derived from that element by well-known grammatical suffixes. Now is this *yudh*, which we call the root of all these words, a mere abstraction? Far from it. We find it as *yudh* used in the Veda either as a nominal or as a verbal base, according to suffixes by which it is followed. Thus *yudh* by itself would be a fighter, only that *dh* when final, has to be changed into t. We have *goshu-yúdh-am*, an accusative, the fighter among cows. In the plural we have *yúdh-as*, fighters; in the locative *yudh-i*, in the fight; in the instrumental, *yudh-â*, with the weapon. That is to say, we find that as a nominal base, *yudh*, without any determinative suffixes, may express fighting, the place of fighting, the instrument of fighting, and a fighter. If our grammatical analysis is right, we should have *yudh* as a nominal base in *yúdh-ya-ti*, lit. he goes to fighting, *yudh-*

yá-te, pass.; *(a)-yut-smahi*, aor., either we were to fight, or we were fighters; *yú-yut-sa-ti*, he is to fight-fight; *yudh-ya-s*, to be fought (p. 94), etc. As a verbal base we find *yudh*, for instance, or *yu-yudh-e*, I have fought; in *a-yud-dha*, for *a-yudh-ta*, he fought. In the other Aryan languages this root has left hardly any traces; yet the Greek ὑσμῖν, and ὑσμίνη would be impossible without the root *yudh*.

The only difference between Chinese and these Sanskrit forms which we have just examined, is that while in Chinese such a form as *yudh-i*, in the battle, would have for its last element a word clearly meaning middle, and having an independent accent, Sanskrit has lost the consciousness of the original material meaning of the *i* of the locative, and uses it traditionally as an empty word, as a formal element, as a mere termination.

I also agree with Curtius that during the earliest stage, not of Sanskrit, but of Aryan speech in general, we have to admit two classes of roots, the *predicative* and *demonstrative*, and that what we now call the plural of *yudh*, *yudh-as*, fighters, was, or may have been, originally a compound consisting of the predicative root *yudh*, and the demonstrative root, *as* or *sa*, possibly repeated twice, meaning "fight-he-he," or "fight-there-there," *i.e.*, fighters.

There is another point with regard to the character of this earliest radical stage of the Aryan language, on which formally I should have agreed with Curtius, but where now I begin to feel more doubtful,—I mean the necessarily monosyllabic form of all original roots. There is, no doubt, much to be said for this view. We always like to begin with what is simple. We imagine, as it has been said, that "the simple idea must break forth, like lightning, in a simple body of sound, to be perceived in one single moment." But, on the other hand, the simple, so far as it is the general, is frequently, to us at least, the last result of repeated complex conceptions, and therefore there is at all events no *à priori* argument against treating the simplest roots as the latest, rather than the earliest products of language. Languages in a low state of development are rich in words expressive of the most minute differences, they are poor in general expressions, a fact which ought to be taken into account as an important qualification of a remark made by Curtius that language supplies necessaries first, luxuries afterwards (p. 32). I quote the following excellent remarks from Mr. Sayce's "Principles of comparative Philology" (p. 208): "Among modern savages the individual objects of sense have names enough, while general terms are very rare. The Mohicans have words for cutting various objects, but none to signify cutting simple."31 In taking this view we certainly are better able to explain the actual forms of the Aryan roots, viz., by *elimination*, rather than by *composition*. If we look for instance, as I did myself formerly, on such roots as *yudh*, *yuj*, and *yaut*, as developed from the simpler root *yu*, or on *mardh*, *marg*, *mark*, *marp*, *mard*, *smar*, as developed from *mar*, then we are bound to account for the modificatory elements, such as *dh, g, k, p, d, s, n, t, r*, as remnants of other roots, whether predicative or demonstrative. Thus Curtius compares *tar* or *tra*, with *tras, tram, trak, trap; tri* and *tru* with *trup, trib*, taking the final consonants as modificatory letters. But what are these modificatory letters? Every attempt to account for them has failed. If it could be proved that these modificatory elements, which Curtius calls *Determinatives*, produced always the *same* modification of meaning, they might then be classed with the verbal suffixes which change simple verbs into causative, desiderative, or intensive verbs. But this is not the case. On the other hand, it would be perfectly intelligible that such roots as *mark, marg, mard, mardh*, expressing different kinds of crushing, became fixed side by side, that by a process of elimination, their distinguishing features were gradually removed, and the root *mar* left as the simplest form, expressive of the most general meaning. Without entering here on that process of mutual friction by which I believe that the development of roots can best be explained, we may say at least so much, that whatever process will account for the root *yu*, will likewise account for the root *yuj*, nay, that roots like *mark* or *mard* are more graphic, expressive, and more easily intelligible than the root mar.

However, if this view of the origin of roots has to be adopted, it need not altogether exclude the other view. In the process of simplification, certain final letters may have become typical, may have seemed invested with a certain function or determinative power, and may therefore have been added independently to other roots, by that powerful imitative tendency which asserts itself again and again through the whole working of language. But however that may be, the sharp line of distinction which Curtius draws between the First Period, represented by simple, and the Second Period represented by derivative roots, seems certainly no longer tenable, least of all as dividing *chronologically* two distinct periods in the growth of language.

When we approach the Third Period, it might seem that here, at least, there could be no difference of opinion between Professor Curtius and myself. That Third Period represents simply what I called the first setting in of *combination*, following after the *isolating* stage. Curtius calls it the *primary verbal period*, and ascribes to it the origin of such combinatory forms as *dâ-ma*, give-I, *dâ-tva*, give-thou, *dâ-ta*, give-he; *dâ-ma-tvi*, give-we, *dâ-tva-tvi*, give-you, *dâ-(a)nti*, give-they. These verbal forms he considers as much earlier than any attempts at declension in nouns. No one who has read Curtius' arguments in support of this chronological arrangement would deny their extreme plausibility; but there are grave difficulties which made me hesitate in adopting this hypothetical framework of linguistic chronology. I shall only mention one, which seemed to me insurmountable. We know that during what we called the First Radical Period the sway of phonetic laws was already so firmly established, that, from that period onward to the present day, we can say, with perfect certainty, which phonetic changes are possible, and which are not. It is through these phonetic laws that the most distant past in the history of the Aryan language is connected with the present. It is on them that the whole science of etymology is founded. Only because a certain root has a tenuis, a media, an aspirate, or a sibilant, is it possible to keep it distinct from other roots. If t and s could be interchanged, then the root *tar*, to cross, would not be distinct from the root *sar*, to go. If d and *dh* could vary, then *dar*, to tear, would run together with *dhar*, to hold. These phonetic distinctions were firmly established in the radical period, and continue to be maintained, both in the undivided Aryan speech, and in the divided national dialects, such as Sanskrit, Greek, Latin, and Gothic. How then can we allow an intervening period, during which *ma-tvi*, could become *masi*, *tva-tvi*, *thas*, and the same *tva-tvi* appear also as *sai*? Such changes, always most startling, may have been possible in earlier periods; but when phonetic order had once been established, as it was in what Curtius calls his first and second periods, to admit them as possible, would be, as far as I can judge, to admit a complete anachronism. Of two things one; either we must altogether surrender those chaotic changes which are required for identifying Sanskrit e with Greek μαι, and Greek μαι with *mâ-ma*, etc., or we must throw them back to a period anterior to the final settlement of the Aryan roots.

I now proceed to point out a second difficulty. If Curtius uses these same personal terminations, *masi*, *tvasi*, and *anti*, as proof positive that they must have been compounded out of *ma* + *tva*, and *tva-tva*, before there were any case terminations, I do not think his argument is quite stringent. Curtius says: "If plural suffixes had existed before the coining of these terminations, we should expect them here, as well as in the noun" (p. 33). But the plural of the pronoun *I* could never have been formed by a plural suffix, like the plural of *horse*. *I* admits of no plural, as little as *thou*, and hence the plural of these very pronouns in the Aryan language is not formed by the mere addition of a plural termination, but by a new base. We say *I*, but *we*; *thou* but *you*, and so through all the Aryan languages. According to Curtius himself, *masi*, the termination of the plural, is not formed by repeating *ma*, by saying I and I, but by *ma* and *tva*, I and thou, the most primitive way, he thinks, of expressing *we*. The termination of the second person plural might be expressed by repeating *thou*. "You did it," might have been rendered by "thou and thou did it;" but hardly by treating *thou* like a noun, and adding to it a plural termination. The absence of plural terminations, therefore at the end of the personal suffixes of the verbs, does not prove, as far as I can see, that plurals of nouns were unknown when the first, second, and third persons plural of the Aryan verbs were called into existence.

Again, if Curtius says, that "what language has once learnt, it does not forget again, and that therefore if the plural had once found expression in nouns, the verb would have claimed the same distinction," is true, no doubt, in many cases, but not so generally true as to supply a safe footing for a deductive argument. In so late a formation as the periphrastic future in Sanskrit, we say *dâtâ-smaḥ*, as it were *dator sumus*, not *dâtâraḥ smaḥ*; and in the second person plural of the passive in Latin *amamini*, though the plural is marked, the gender is always disregarded.

Further, even if we admit with Bopp and Curtius that the terminations of the medium are composed of two pronouns, that the *ta* of the third person singular stands for *ta-ti*, to-him-he, that καλύπτεται in fact meant originally hide-himself-he, it does not follow that in such a compound one pronominal element should have taken the termination of the accusative, any more than the other takes the termination of the nominative. The first element in every composition takes necessarily its Pada or thematic form; the second or final element has suffered so much, according to Bopp's own explanation, that nothing would be easier to explain than the disappearance of a final consonant, if it had existed. The absence of case-terminations in such compounds cannot therefore be used as proof of the non-existence of case-terminations at a time when the medial and other personal endings took their origin. On the contrary, these terminations seem to me to indicate, though I do not say to prove, that the conception of a subjective, as distinct from an objective case, had been fully realized by those who framed them. I do not myself venture to speak very positively of such minute processes of analysis as that which discovers in the Sk. first pers. sing. ind. pres. of the middle, tude, I strike, an original *tuda + a + i*, *tuda + ma + i*, *tuda + ma + mi*, tuda + mâ + ma, but admitting that the middle was formed in that way, and that it meant originally *strike-to-me-I*, then surely we have in the first *mâ* an oblique case, and in the compound itself the clearest indication that the distinction between a nominative and an oblique case, whether dative or accusative, was no longer a mystery. Anyhow, and this is the real point at issue, the presence of such compounds as *mâ-ma*, to-me-I, is in no way a proof that at the time of their formation people could not distinguish between *yudh (s)*, nom., a fighter, and *yudh (am)*, acc., a fighter; and we must wait for more irrefragable evidence before admitting, what would under all circumstances be a most startling conclusion, namely, that the Aryan language was spoken for a long time without case-terminations, but with a complete set of personal terminations, both in the singular and the plural. For though it is quite true that the want of cases could only be felt in a sentence, the same seems to me to apply to personal terminations of the verb. The one, in most languages we know, implies the other, and the very question whether conjugation or declension came first is one of those dangerous questions which take something for granted which has never been proved.

During all this time, according to Curtius, our Aryan language would have consisted of nothing but roots, used for nominal and verbal purposes, but without any purely derivative suffixes, whether verbal or nominal, and without declension. The only advance, in fact, made beyond the purely Chinese standard, would have consisted in a few combinations of personal pronouns with verbal stems, which combinations assumed rapidly a typical character, and led to the formation of a skeleton of conjugation, containing a *present*, an *aorist* with an augment, and a *reduplicated perfect*. Why, during the same period, nominal bases should not have assumed at least some case-terminations, does not appear; and it certainly seems strange that people who could say *vak-ti*, speak-he, *vak-anti*, speak-this-he, should not have been able to say *vâk-s*, whether in the sense of speak-there, *i.e.*, speech or speak-there, *i.e.*, speaker.

The next step which, according to Curtius, the Aryan language had to make, in order to emerge from its purely radical phase, was the creation of bases, both verbal and nominal, by the addition of verbal and nominal suffixes to roots, both primary and secondary. Curtius calls this fourth the Period of the *Formation of Themes*. The suffixes are very numerous, and it is by them that the Aryan languages have been able to make their limited number of roots supply the vast materials of their dictionary. From *bhar*, to carry, they formed *bhar-a*, a carrier, but sometimes also a burden. In addition to *bhar-ti*, carry-he, they formed *bhara-ti*, meaning possibly carrying-he. The growth of these early themes may have been very luxuriant, and, as Professor Curtius expresses it, chiefly *paraschematic*. It may have been left to a later age to assign to that large number of possible synonyms more definite meanings. Thus from φέρω, I carry, we have φορά, the act of carrying, used also in the sense of *impetus* (being carried away), and of *provectus*, i.e., what is brought in. Φορός means carrying, but also violent, and lucrative; φέρετρον, an instrument of carrying, means a bier; φαρέτρα, a quiver, for carrying arrows. Φορμός comes to mean a basket; φόρτος, a burden; φορός, tribute.

All this is perfectly intelligible, both with regard to nominal and verbal themes. Curtius admits four kinds of verbal themes as the outcome of his Fourth Period. He had assigned to his Third Period the simple verbal themes ἐσ-τί, and the reduplicated themes such as δίδω-σι. To these were added, in the Fourth Period, the following four secondary themes:—

    (1) πλέκ-ε-(τ)-ι Sanskrit *lipa-ti*

    (2) ἀλείφ-ε-(τ)-ι   ,,   *laipa-ti*

    (3) δείκ-νυ-σι   ,,   *lip-nau-ti*

    (4) δάμ-νη-σι   ,,   *lip-nâ-ti*.

He also explains the formation of the subjunctive in analogy with bases such as *lipa-ti*, as derived from *lip-ti*.

Some scholars would probably feel inclined to add one or two of the more primitive verbal themes, such as

limpa-ti   *rumpo*

limpana-ti λαμβάνε(τ)ι

but all would probably agree with Curtius in placing the formation of these themes, both verbal and nominal, between the radical and the latest inflectional period. A point, however, on which there would probably be considerable difference of opinion is this, whether it is credible, that at a time when so many nominal themes were formed,—for Curtius ascribes to this Fourth Period the formation of such nominal bases as

λόγ-ο, intellect, = *lipa-ti*

λοίπ-ο, left,   = *laipa-ti*

λιγ-νύ, smoke, = *lip-nau-ti*

δάφ-νη, laurel, = *lip-nâ-ti* —

the simplest nominal compounds, which we now call nominative and accusative, singular and plural, were still unknown; that people could say *dhṛsh-nu-más*, we dare, but not *dhṛsh-nú-s*, daring-he; that they had an imperative, *dhṛshnuhí*, dare, but not a vocative, *dhṛshṇo?* Curtius strongly holds to that opinion, but with regard to this period too, he does not seem to me to establish it by a regular and complete argument. Some arguments which he refers to occasionally have been answered before. Another, which he brings in incidentally, when discussing the abbreviation of certain suffixes, can hardly be said to carry conviction. After tracing the suffixes *ant* and *tar* back to what he supposes to have been their more primitive forms, *an-ta* and *ta-ra*, he remarks that the dropping of the final vowel would hardly be conceivable at a time when there existed case-terminations. Still this dropping of the vowel is very common, in late historical times, in Latin, for instance, and other Italian dialects, where it causes frequent confusion and heteroclitism.32 Thus the Augustan *innocua* was shortened in common pronunciation to *innoca*, and this dwindles down in Christian inscriptions to *innox*. In Greek, too, διάκτορος is older than διάκτωρ; φύλακος older than φύλαξ.

Nor can it be admitted that the nominal suffixes have suffered less from phonetic corruption than the terminations of the verb, and that therefore they must belong to a more modern period (pp. 39, 40). In spite of all the changes which the personal terminations are supposed to have undergone, their connection with the personal pronouns has always been apparent, while the tracing back of the nominal suffixes, and, still more, of the case-terminations to their typical elements, forms still one of the greatest difficulties of comparative grammarians.33

Professor Curtius is so much impressed with the later origin of declension that he establishes one more period, the fifth, to which he assigns the growth of all compound verbal forms, compound stems, compound tenses, and compound moods, before he allows the first beginnings of declension, and the formation even of such simple forms as the nominative and accusative. It is difficult, no doubt, to disprove such an opinion by facts or dates, because there are none to be found on either side: but we have a right to expect very strong arguments indeed, before we can admit that at a time when an aorist, like ἔδειχ-σα, Sanskrit *a-dik-sha-t* was possible, that is to say, at a time when the verb *as*, which meant originally to breathe, had by constant use been reduced to the meaning of being; at a time when that verb, as a mere auxiliary, was joined to a verbal base in order to impart to it a general historical power; when the persons of the verb were distinguished by pronominal elements, and when the augment, no longer purely demonstrative, had become the symbol of time past, that at such a time people were still unable to distinguish, except by a kind of Chinese law of position, between "the father struck the child," and "the child struck the father." Before we can admit this, we want much stronger proofs than any adduced by Curtius. He says, for instance, that compound verbal bases formed with *yâ*, to go, and afterwards fixed as causatives, would be inconceivable during a period in which accusatives existed. From *naś*, to perish, we form in Sanskrit *nâśa-yâmi*, I make perish. This, according to Curtius, would have meant originally, I send to perishing. Therefore *nâśa* would have been, in the accusative, *nâśam*, and the causative would have been *nâśamyâmi*, if the accusative had then been known. But we have in Latin34 *pessum dare, venum ire*, and no one would say that compounds like *calefacio, liquefacio, putrefacio*, were impossible after the first Aryan separation, or after that still earlier period to which Curtius assigns the formation of the Aryan case-terminations. Does Professor Curtius hold that compound forms like Gothic *nasi-da* were formed not only before the Aryan separation, but before the introduction of case-terminations? I hold, on the contrary, that such really old compositions never required, nay never admitted, the accusative. We say in Sanskrit, *dyu-gat*, going to the sky, *dyu-ksha*, dwelling in the sky, without any case-terminations at the end of the first part of the compound. We say in Greek, σακέσ-παλος, not σάκοσ-παλος, παιδοφόνος, not παιδαφόνος, ὀρεσ-κῷος, mountain-bred, and also ὀρεσί-τροφος, mountain-fed. We say in Latin, *agri-cola*, not *agrum-cola, fratri-cīda*, not *fratrem-cīda, rēgĭfugium*, not *regis-fugium*. Are we to suppose that all these words were formed before there was an outward mark of distinction between nominative and accusative in the primitive Aryan language? Such compounds, we know, can be formed at pleasure, and they continued to be formed long after the full development of the Aryan declension, and the same would apply to the compound stems of causal verbs. To say, as Curtius does, that composition was possible only before the development of declension, because when cases had once sprung up, the people would no longer have known the bases of nouns, is far too strong an assertion. In Sanskrit35 the really difficult bases are generally sufficiently visible in the so-called Pada, cases, *i.e.*, before certain terminations beginning with consonants, and there is besides a strong feeling of analogy in language, which would generally, though not always (for compounds are frequently framed by false analogy), guide the framers of new compounds rightly in the selection of the proper nominal base. It seems to me that even with us there is still a kind of instinctive feeling against using nouns, articulated with case-terminations, for purposes of composition, although there are exceptions to that rule in ancient, and many more in modern languages. We can hardly realize to ourselves a Latin *pontemfex*, or *pontisfex*, still less *ponsfex* instead of *pontifex*, and when the Romans drove away their kings, they did not speak of a *regisfugium* or a *regumfugium*, but they took, by habit or by instinct, the base *regi*, though none of them, if they had been asked, knew what a base was. Composition, we ought not to forget, is after all only another name for combination, and the very essence of combination consists in joining together words which are not yet articulated grammatically. Whenever we form compounds, such as *railway*, we are still moving in the combinatory stage, and we have the strongest proof that the life of language is not capable of chronological division. There was a period in the growth of the Aryan language when the principle of combination preponderated, when inflection was as yet unknown. But inflection itself was the result of combination, and unless combination had continued long after inflection set in, the very life of language would have become extinct.

I have thus tried to explain why I cannot accept the fundamental fact on which the seven-fold division of the history of the Aryan language is founded, viz., that the combinatory process which led to the Aryan system of conjugation would have been impossible, if at the time nominal bases had already been articulated with terminations of case and number. I see no reason why the earliest case-formations, I mean particularly the nominative and accusative in the singular, plural, and dual, should not date from the same time as the earliest formations of conjugation. The same process that leads to the formation of *vak-ti*, speak-he, would account for the formation of *vak-s*, speak-there, *i.e.*, speaker. Necessity, which after all is the mother of all inventions, would much sooner have required the clear distinction of singular and plural, of nominative and accusative, than of the three persons, of the verbs. It is far more important to be able to distinguish the subject and the object in such sentences as "the son has killed the father," or "the father has killed the son," than to be able to indicate the person and tense of the verb. Of course we may say that in Chinese the two cases are distinguished without any outward signs, and by mere position; but we have no evidence that the law of position was preserved in the Aryan languages, after verbal inflection had once set in. Chinese dispenses with verbal inflection as well as with nominal, and an appeal to it would therefore prove either too much or too little.

At the end of the five periods which we have examined, but still before the Aryan separation, Curtius places the sixth, which he calls the Period of the Formation of Cases, and the seventh, the Period of Adverbs. Why I cannot bring myself to accept the late date here assigned to declension, I have tried to explain before. That adverbs existed before the great branches of Aryan speech became definitely separated has been fully proved by Professor Curtius. I only doubt whether the adverbial period can be separated chronologically from the case period. I should say, on the contrary, that some of the adverbs in Sanskrit and the other Aryan languages exhibit the most primitive and obsolete case-terminations, and that they existed probably long before the system of case-terminations assumed its completeness.

If we look back at the results at which we have arrived in examining the attempt of Professor Curtius to establish seven distinct chronological periods in the history of the Aryan speech, previous to its separation into Sanskrit, Greek, Latin, Slavonic, Teutonic, and Celtic, I think we shall find two principles clearly established:—

1. That it is impossible to distinguish more than *three* successive phases in the growth of the Aryan language. In the first phase or period the only materials were roots, not yet compounded, still less articulated grammatically, a form of language to us almost inconceivable, yet even at present preserved in the literature and conversation of millions of human beings, the Chinese. In that stage of language, "king rule man heap law instrument," would mean, the king rules men legally.

The *second* phase is characterized by the combination of roots, by which process one loses its independence and its accent, and is changed from a full and material into an empty or formal element. That phase comprehends the formation of compound roots, of certain nominal and verbal stems, and of the most necessary forms of declension and conjugation. What distinguishes this phase from the inflectional is the consciousness of the speaker, that one part of his word is the stem or the body, and all the rest its environment, a feeling analogous to that which we have when we speak of *man*-hood, *man*-ly, *man*-ful, *man*-kind, but which fails us when we speak of *man* and *men*, or if we speak of *wo-man*, instead of *wif-man*. The principle of combination preponderated when inflection was as yet unknown. But inflection itself was the result of combination, and unless it had continued long after inflection set in, the very life of language would have become extinct.

The *third* phase is the inflectional, when the base and the modificatory elements of words coalesce, lose their independence in the mind of the speaker, and simply produce the impression of modification taking place in the body of words, but without any intelligible reason. This is the feeling which we have throughout nearly the whole of our own language, and it is only by means of scientific reflection that we distinguish between the root, the base, the suffix, and the termination. To attempt more than this threefold division seems to me impossible.

2. The second principle which I tried to establish was that the growth of language does not lend itself to a chronological division, in the strict sense of the word. Whatever forces are at work in the formation of languages, none of them ceases suddenly to make room for another, but they work on with a certain continuity from beginning to end, only on a larger or smaller scale. Inflection does not put a sudden end to combination, nor combination to juxtaposition. When even in so modern a language as English we can form by mere combination such words as *man-like*, and reduce them to *manly*, the power of combination cannot be said to be extinct, although it may no longer be sufficiently strong to produce new cases or new personal terminations. We may admit, in the development of the Aryan language, previous to its division, three successive strata of formation, a *juxtapositional*, a *combinatory*, and an *inflectional*; but we shall have to confess that these strata are not regularly superimposed, but tilted, broken up, and convulsed. They are very prominent each for a time, but even after that time is over, they may be traced at different points, pervading the very latest formations of tertiary speech. The true motive power in the progress of all language is combination, and that power is not extinct even in our own time.

Footnotes to Chapter II:
Stratification of Language *and* Curtius' Chronology

1. This Lecture has been translated by M. Louis Havet, and forms the first fasciculus of the Bibliothèque de l'École des Hautes Études, publiée sous les auspices du Ministère de l'Instruction Publique. Paris, 1869.

2. See Benfey, *Ueber die Aufgabe des Kratylos*, Göttingen, 1868.

3. Theokritos, xvii. 9.

4. In my essay *On the Relation of Bengali to the Aryan and Aboriginal Languages of India*, published in 1848, I tried to explain these plural suffixes, such as *dig, gaṇa, jâti, varga, dala*. I had translated the last word by *band*, supposing from Wilson's Dictionary, and from the Śabda-kalpa-druma that *dala* could be used in the sense of band or multitude. I doubt, however, whether *dala* is ever used in Sanskrit in that sense, and I feel certain that it was not used in that sense with sufficient frequency to account for its adoption in Bengali. Dr. Friedrich Müller, in his useful abstracts of some of the grammars discovered by the *Novara* in her journey round the earth (1857–59), has likewise referred *dal* to the Sanskrit *dala*, but he renders what I had in English rendered by *band*, by the German word *Band*. This can only be an accident. I meant *band* in the sense of a band of robbers, which in German would be *Bande*. He seems to have misunderstood me, and to have taken *band* for the German *Band*, which means a ribbon. Might *dala* in Bengali be the Dravidian *taḷa* or *daḷa*, a host, a crowd, which Dr. Caldwell (p. 197) mentions as a possible etymon of the pluralizing suffix in the Dravidian languages? Bengali certainly took the idea of forming its plurals by composition with words expressive of plurality from its Dravidian neighbor, and it is not impossible that in some cases it might have transferred the very word *daḷa*, crowd. This *daḷa* and *taḷa* appears in Tamil as *kala* and *gala*, and as Sanskrit *k* may in Sinhalese be represented by *v* (*loka* = *lova*), I thought that the plural termination used in Sinhalese after inanimate nouns might possibly be a corruption of the Tamil *kala*. Mr. Childers, however, in his able "Essay on the formation of the Plural of Neuter Nouns in Sinhalese" (*J. R. A. S.*, 1874, p. 40), thinks that the Sinhalese *vala* is a corruption of the Sanskrit *vana*, forest, an opinion which seems likewise to be held by Mr. D'Alwis (l.c. p. 48). As a case in point, in support of my own opinion, Mr. Childers mentioned to me the Sinhalese *malvaru*, Sanskrit *mâlâ-kâra*, a wreath-maker, a gardener. In Persian both *ân* and *hâ* are remnants of decayed plural terminations, not collective words added to the base.

5. Stanislas Julien, *Exercises Pratiques*, p. 14.

6. Endlicher, *Chinesische Grammatik*, § 122. Wade, *Progressive Course on the Parts of Speech*, p. 102. A different division of words adopted by Chinese grammarians is that into *dead* and *live words, ssè-tsé* and *sing-tsé*, the former comprising nouns, the latter verbs. The same classes are sometimes called *tsing-tsé* and *ho-tsé*, unmoved and moved words. This shows how purposeless it would be to try to

find out whether language began with noun or verb. In the earliest phase of speech the same word was both noun and verb, according to the use that was made of it, and it is so still to a great extent in Chinese. See Endlicher, *Chinesische Grammatik*, § 219.

7. *Agglutinative* seems an unnecessarily uncouth word, and as implying a something which glues two words together, a kind of *Bindevocal*, it is objectionable as a technical term. *Combinatory* is technically more correct, and less strange than agglutinative.

8. Professor Pott, in his article entitled "Max Müller und die Kennzeichen der Sprachverwandtschaft," published in 1855, in the *Journal of the German Oriental Society*, vol. ix. p. 412, says, in confutation of Bunsen's view of a real historical progress of language from the lowest to the highest stage: "So cautious an inquirer as W. von Humboldt declines expressly, in the last chapter of his work on the *Diversity of the Structure of Human Language* (p. 414), any conclusions as to a real historical progress from one stage of language to another, or at least does not commit himself to any definite opinion. This is surely something very different from that gradual progress, and it would be a question whether, by admitting such an historical progress from stage to stage, we should not commit an absurdity hardly less palpable than by trying to raise infusoria into horses or still further into men. [What was an absurdity in 1855 does not seem to be so in 1875.] Mr. Bunsen, it is true, does not hesitate to call the monosyllabic idiom of the Chinese an inorganic formation. But how can we get from an inorganic to an organic language? In nature such a thing would be impossible. No stone becomes a plant, no plant a tree, by however wonderful a metamorphosis, except, in a different sense, by the process of nutrition, *i.e.*, by regeneration. The former question, which Mr. Bunsen answers in the affirmative, is disposed of by him with the short dictum: 'The question whether a language can be supposed to begin with inflections, appears to us simply an absurdity;' but unfortunately he does not condescend, by a clear illustration, to make that absurdity palpable. Why, in inflectional languages, should the grammatical form always have added itself to the matter subsequently and *ab extra*? Why should it not partially from the beginning have been created with it and in it, as having a meaning with something else, but not having antecedently a meaning of its own?"

9. Cf. D. G. Brinton, *The Myths of the New World*, p. 6, note.

10. Julien, *Exercises Pratiques*, p. 120. Endlicher, *Chineseische Grammatik*, § 161. See, also, Nöldeke, *Orient und Occident*, vol. i. p. 759. *Grammar of the Bornu Language* (London, 1853), p. 55: "In the Treaty the genitive is supplied by the relative pronoun *agu*, singularly corroborative of the Rev. R. Garnett's theory of the genitive case."

11. "Time changes the meaning of words as it does their sound. Thus, many old words are retained in compounds, but have lost their original signification. E.g., *'k·eu*, mouth, has been replaced in colloquial usage by *'tsui*, but it is still employed extensively in compound terms and in derived senses. Thus, *k·wai' 'k·eu* a rapid talker, *.men 'k·eu*, door, *,kwan 'k·eu*, custom house. So also *muh*, the original word for eye, has given place to *'yen, tsing*, or *'yen* alone. It is, however, employed with other words in derived senses. E.g., *muh hia·*, at present; *muh luh*, table of contents.

"The primitive word for head, *'sheu*, has been replaced by *.t'eu*, but is retained with various words in combination. E.g., *tseh 'sheu*, robber chief."

Edkins, *Grammar of the Chinese Colloquial Language*, 2d edition, 1864, p. 100.

12. Grimm, *Deutsche Grammatik*, ii. 339.

13. Cf. the German Liebhart, mignon, in Anshelm, 1, 335. Grimm, *Deutsche Grammatik*, iii. 707. I feel more doubtful now as to *sweetard*. Dr. Morris mentions it in his *Historical Outlines of English Grammar*, p. 219; but Koch, when discussing the same derivations in his *English Grammar*, does not give the word. Mr. Skeat writes to me: "The form really used in Middle English is *sweeting*. Three examples are given in Stratmann. One of the best is in my edition of William of Palerne, where, however, it occurs not *once* only (as given by Stratmann), but *four times*, viz.: in lines 916, 1537, 2799, 3088. The lines are:—

> 916 'Nai, sertes, *sweting*, he seide· that schal I neuer.'
>
> 1537 '& seide aswithe· *sweting*, welcome!'
>
> 2799 'Sertes, *sweting*, thæt is soth. seide william thanne.'
>
> 3088 'treuli, *sweting*, that is soth· seide william thane.'

The date of this poem is about A.D. 1360. Shakespeare has both forms, viz.: *sweeting* and *sweet-heart*. Chaucer has *swete herte*, just as we should use *sweet-heart*."

14. Diez, *Grammatik*, ii. 358. Grimm, *Deutsche Grammatik*, i. p. 340, 706.

15. See *Sanskrit Grammar*, § 497. I doubt whether in Greek ἀγγελλω is a denominative verb and stands for ἀγγελ(ο)jω (Curtius, *Chronologie*, p. 58). I should prefer to explain it as ἀνα-γαρ-ίω, to proclaim, as a verb of the fourth class.

16. Lex Repetund. "ceivis romanus ex hac lege fiet, nepotesque — ceiveis romanei justei sunto." Cf. Egger, *Lat, Serm. Vetust. Reliq.*, p. 245. Meunier, in *Mémoires de la Societé de Linguistique de Paris*, vol. i. p. 34.

17. Still used as long by Plautus; of. Neue, *Formenlehre*, ii. p. 340.

18. In old Latin the termination of the first person singular was *em*. Thus Quintilian, i. 7, 23, says: "Quid? non Cato Censorius *dicam* et *faciam*, *dicem* et *faciem* scripsit, eundemque in ceteris, quæ similiter cadunt, modum tenuit? quod et ex veteribus ejus libris manifestum est, et a Messala in libro de s. littera positum." Neue, *Formenlehre*, ii. p. 348. The introduction of *feram*, originally a subjunctive, to express the future in the first person, reminds us of the distinction in English between *I shall* and *thou wilt*, though the analogy fails in the first person plural. In Homer the use of the subjunctive for the future is well known. See Curtius, *Chronologie*, p. 50.

19. Historically the *i* in *tuleritis* should be long in the subjunctive of the perfect, short in the future.

20. Bleek, *On the Concord*, p. lxvi.

21. In δώ-σω, for δωσίω, the *i* or *y* is lost in Greek as usual. In other verbs *s* and *y* are both lost. Hence τενεσίω becomes τενέσω, and τενῶ the so-called Attic future. Bopp, *Vergleich-Grammatik*, first ed., p. 903. In Latin we have traces of a similar future in forms like *fac-so*, *cap-so*, etc. See Neue, *Formenlehre*, ii. p. 421. The Epic dialect sometimes doubles the σ when the vowel is short, αἰδέσσομαι. But this can hardly be considered a relic of the original σι, because the same reduplication takes places sometimes in the Aorist, ἐγέλασσα.

22. See Bopp, *Vergleichende Grammatik*, §§ 897, 898. These verbal adjectives should be carefully distinguished from nominal adjectives, such as Sanskrit *div-yá-s*, divinus, originally *div-i-a-s*, i.e., divi-bhavas, being in heaven; οἰκεῖος, domesticus, originally οἰκει-ο-ς, being in the house. These are adjectives formed, it would

seem, from old locatives, just as in Bask we can form from *etche*, house, *etche-tic*, of the house, and *etche-tic-acoa*, he who is of the house; or from *seme*, son, *semea-ren*, of the son, and *semea-ren-a*, he who is of the son. See W. J. van Eys, *Essai de Grammaire de la Langue Basque*, 1867, p. 16.

23. Bopp, *Vergleichende Grammatik*, §§ 888–898.

24. Bacon, *Novum Organum*, i. 55.

25. Until a rational account of these changes, comprehended under the name of *Lautverschiebung*, is given, we must continue to look upon them, not as the result of phonetic decay, but of dialectic growth. I am glad to find that this is more and more admitted by those who think for themselves, instead of simply repeating the opinions of others. Grimm's Law stands no longer alone, as peculiar to the Teutonic languages, but analogous changes have been pointed out in the South-African, the Chinese, the Polynesian dialects, showing that these changes are everywhere collateral, not successive. I agree with Professor Curtius and other scholars that the impulse to what we call *Lautverschiebung* was given by the third modification in each series of consonants, by the *gh*, *dh*, *bh* in Sanskrit, the χ, θ, φ, in Greek. I differ from him in considering the changes of *Lautverschiebung* as the result of dialectic variety, while he sees their motive power in phonetic corruption. But whether we take the one view or the other, I do not see that Dr. Scherer has removed any of our difficulties. See Curtius, *Grundzüge*, 4th ed., p. 426, note. Dr. Scherer, in his thoughtful work, *Zur Geschichte der Deutschen Sprache*, has very nearly, though not quite, apprehended the meaning of my explanation as to the effects of dialectic change contrasted with those of phonetic decay. If it is allowable to use a more homely illustration, one might say with perfect truth, that each dialect chooses its own phonetic garment, as people choose the coats and trousers which best fit them. The simile, like all similes, is imperfect, yet it is far more exact than if we compare the ravages of phonetic decay, as is frequently done, to the wear and tear of these phonetic suits.

26. Edkins, *Grammar*, p. 84.

27. Having stated this on the authority of Mr. Edkins, one of our best living Chinese scholars, it is but fair that I should give the opinion of another Chinese scholar, the late Stanislas Julien, whose competence to give an opinion on this subject Mr. Edkins would probably be the first to acknowledge. All that we really

want is the truth, not a momentary triumph of our own opinions. M. Julien wrote to me in July, 1868:—

"Je ne suis pas du tout de l'avis d'Edkins qui dit qu'un grand nombre de mots mongols sont chinois; c'est faux, archifaux.

Sain est mandchou et veut dire bon, en chinois *chen*.

begen, low: en chinois *hia*.

itchi, droit; en chinois *yeou*.

sologaï, left, gauche; en chinois *tso*.

c'hihe, straight; en chinois *tchi* (rectus).

gadan, outside; en chinois *waï*.

logon, green; en chinois *tsing*.

c'hohon, few; en chinois *chao*.

hungun, light (not heavy); en chinois *king*.

"Je voudrais bien savoir comment M. Edkins prouve que les mots qu'il cite sont chinois.

"Foucaux a échoué également en voulant prouver, autrefois, que 200 mots thibétains qu'il avait choisis ressemblaïent aux mots chinois correspondants."

M. Stanislas Julien wrote again to me on the 21st of July:—

"J'ai peur que vous ne soyez fâché du jugemont sévère que j'ai porté sur les identifications faites par Edkins du mongol avec le chinois. J'ai d'abord pris dans votre savant article les mots mongols qu'il cite et je vous ai montré qu'ils ne ressemblent pas le moins du monde au chinois.

"Je vais vous en citer d'autres tirés du Dictionnaire de Khienlung chinois mandchou-mongol.

Mongol	Chinois
tegri, ciel	*thien*.
naran, soleil	*ji*.
naram barimoni, éclipse de soleil	*ji-chi*.

saran, lune	*youeï.*
oudoun, étoile	*sing.*
egoulé, nuages,	*yun.*
ayounga, le tonnerre	*louï.*
tchagilgan, éclair	*tien.*
borogan, la pluie	*yu.*
sigouderi, la rosée	*lou.*
kirago, la gelée	*choang.*
lapsa, la neige	*sioue.*
salgin, le vent	*fong.*
ousoun, l'eau	*chouï.*
gal, le feu	*ho.*
siroi, la terre	*thou.*
aisin, l'or	*altan.*

"Je vous donnerai, si vous le désirez, 1000 mots mongols avec leurs synonymes chinois, et je défie M. Edkins de trouver dans les 1000 mots mongols un seul qui ressemble au mot chinois synonyme.

"Comme j'ai fait assez de thibétain, je puis vous fournir aussi une multitude de mots thibétains avec leurs correspondants en chinois, et je défierai également M. Edkins de trouver un seul mot thibétain dans mille qui ressemble au mot chinois qui a le même sens."

My old friend, M. Stanislas Julien, wrote to me once more on this subject, the 6th of August, 1868:—

"Depuis une quinzaine d'anneés, j'ai l'avantage d'entretenir les meilleures relations avec M. Edkins. J'ai lu, anciennement dans un journal que publie M. Léon de Rosny (actuellement professeur titulaire de la langue Japanaise) le travail où M. Edkins a tâché de rapprocher et d'identifier, par les sons, des mots mongols et chinois ayant la même signification. Son système m'a paru mal fondé. Quelques mots chinois peuvent être entrés dans la langue mongole par suite du contact des deux peuples, comme cela est arrivé pour le mandchou, dont beaucoup de mots sont entrés dans la langue mongole en en prenant les terminaisons; mais il ne faudrait pas se servir de ces exemples pour montrer l'identité ou les ressemblances des deux langues.

"Quand les mandchous ont voulu traduire les livres chinois, ils ont rencontré un grand nombre de mots dont les synonymes n'existaient pas dans leur langue. Ils se sont alors emparé des mots chinois en leur donnant des terminaisons mandchoues, mais cette quasi-ressemblance de certains mots mandchous ne prouve point le moins du monde l'identité des deux langues. Par exemple, un préfet se dit en chinois *tchi-fou*, et un sous-préfet *tchi-hien*; les mandchous qui ne possédaient point ces fonctionaires se sont contentés de transcire les sons chinois *dchhifou, dchhikhiyan*.

"Le tafetas se dit en chinois *tcheou-tse*; les mandchous, n'ayant point de mots pour dire tafetas, ont transcrit les sons chinois par *tchousé*. Le bambou se dit *tchou-tze*; ils ont écrit l'arbre (moo) *tchousé*. Un titre de noblesse écrit sur du papier doré s'appelle *tsĕ*; les mandchous écrivent *tche.* Je pourrais vous citer un nombre considérable de mots du même genre, qui ne prouvent pas du tout l'identité du mandchou et du chinois.

"L'ambre s'appelle *hou-pe*; les mandchous écrivent *khôba*. La barbe s'appelle *hou-tse*, ils écrivent *khôsé*.

"Voici de quelle manière les mandchous ont fait certains verbes. Une balance s'appelle en chinois *thien ping*, ils écrivent *p'ing-sé*; puis pour dire peser avec une balance, ils ont fait le verbe *p'ingselembi*; *lembi* est une terminaison commune à beaucoup de verbes.

"Pour dire faire peser, ordonner de peser avec une balance, ils écrivent *p'ingseleboumbi*; *boumbi* est la forme factive ou causative; cette terminaison sert aussi pour le passif; de sorte que ce verbe peut signifier aussi *être pesé avec une balance*.

"Je pourrais citer aussi des mots mandchous auxquels on a donné la terminaison mongole, et *vice versâ*."

These remarks, made by one who, during his lifetime, was recognised by friend and foe as the first Chinese scholar in Europe, ought to have their proper weight. They ought certainly to make us cautious before persuading ourselves that the connection between the northern and southern branches of the Turanian languages has been found in Chinese. On the other hand I am quite aware that all that M. Stanislas Julien says against

Mr. Edkins may be true, and that nevertheless Chinese may have been the central language from which Mongolian in the north and Tibetan in the south branched off. A language, such as Chinese, with a small number of sounds and an immense number of meanings, can easily give birth to dialects which, in their later development, might branch off in totally different directions. Even with languages so closely connected as Sanskrit and Latin, it would be easy to make out a list of a thousand words in Latin which could not be matched in Sanskrit. The question, therefore, is not decided. What is wanted are researches carried on by competent scholars, in an unprejudiced and at the same time thoroughly scientific spirit.

28. If Mr. Chalmers' comparison of the Chinese and Bohemian names for daughter is so unpardonable, what shall we say of Bopp's comparison of the Bengali and Sanskrit names for sister? Sister in Bengali is *bohinî*, the Hindi *bahin* and *bhân*, the Prakrit *bahinî*, the Sanskrit *bhaginî*. Bopp, in the most elaborate way, derives *bohinî* from the Sanskrit *svasr*, sister. Bopp, *Vergleichende Grammatik*, Vorrede zur vierten Abtheilung, p. x.

29. Curtius, *Verbum*, p. 72.

30. Pott, E. F., 1871, p. 21.

31. Dr. Callaway, in his *Remarks on the Zulu Language* (1870), p. 2, says: "The Zulu Language contains upwards of 20,000 words in *bonâ fide* use among the people. Those curious appellations for different colored cattle, or for different maize cobs, to express certain minute peculiarities of color or arrangement of color, which it is difficult for us to grasp, are not synonymous, but instances in which a new noun or name is used instead of adding adjectives to one name to express the various conditions of an object. Neither are these various verbs used to express varieties of the same action, synonyms, such as *ukupata*, to carry in the hand, *ukwetshata*, to carry on the shoulder, *ukubeleta*, to carry on the back."

32. Bruppacher, *Lantlere der Oskischen Sprache*, p. 48. Büchler, *Grundriss der Lateinischen Declination*, p. 1.

33. "Die Entstehung der Casus ist noch das allerdunkelste im weiten Bereich des indogermanischen Formensystems." Curtius, *Chronologie*, p. 71.

34. Corssen, ii. 888.

35. Cf. Clemm, *Die neusten Forschungen auf dem Gebiet der Griechischen Composita*, p. 9.

III.
ON THE MIGRATION OF FABLES.
A LECTURE DELIVERED AT THE ROYAL INSTITUTION, ON FRIDAY, JUNE 3, 1870.

"COUNT not your chickens before they be hatched," is a well-known proverb in English, and most people, if asked what was its origin, would probably appeal to La Fontaine's delightful fable, *La Laitière et le Pot au Lait*.1 We all know Perrette, lightly stepping along from her village to the town, carrying the milk-pail on her head, and in her day-dreams selling her milk for a good sum, then buying a hundred eggs, then selling the chickens, then buying a pig, fattening it, selling it again, and buying a cow with a calf. The calf frolics about, and kicks up his legs—so does Perrette, and, alas! the pail falls down, the milk is spilt, her riches gone, and she only hopes when she comes home that she may escape a flogging from her husband.

Did La Fontaine invent this fable? or did he merely follow the example of Sokrates, who, as we know from the Phædon,2 occupied himself in prison, during the last days of his life, with turning into verse some of the fables, or, as he calls them, the myths of Æsop.

La Fontaine published the first six books of his fables in 1668,3 and it is well known that the subjects of most of these early fables were taken from Æsop, Phædrus, Horace, and other classical fabulists, if we may adopt this word "fabuliste," which La Fontaine was the first to introduce into French.

In 1678 a second edition of these six books was published, enriched by five books of new fables, and in 1694 a new edition appeared, containing one additional book, thus completing the collection of his charming poems.

The fable of Perrette stands in the seventh book, and was published, therefore, for the first time in the edition of 1678. In the preface to that edition La Fontaine says: "It is not necessary that I should say whence I have taken the subjects of these new fables. I shall only say, from a sense of gratitude, that I owe the largest portion of them to Pilpay the Indian sage."

If, then, La Fontaine tells us himself that he borrowed the subjects of most of his new fables from Pilpay, the Indian sage, we have clearly a right to look to India in order to see whether, in the ancient literature of that country, any traces can be discovered of Perrette with the milk-pail.

Sanskrit literature is very rich in fables and stories; no other literature can vie with it in that respect; nay, it is extremely likely that fables, in particular animal fables, had their principal source in India. In the sacred literature of the

Buddhists, fables held a most prominent place. The Buddhist preachers, addressing themselves chiefly to the people, to the untaught, the uncared for, the outcast, spoke to them, as we still speak to children, in fables, in proverbs and parables. Many of these fables and parables must have existed before the rise of the Buddhist religion; others, no doubt, were added on the spur of the moment, just as Sokrates would invent a myth or fable whenever that form of argument seemed to him most likely to impress and convince his hearers. But Buddhism gave a new and permanent sanction to this whole branch of moral mythology, and in the sacred canon, as it was settled in the third century before Christ, many a fable received, and holds to the present day, its recognized place. After the fall of Buddhism in India, and even during its decline, the Brahmans claimed the inheritance of their enemies, and used their popular fables for educational purposes. The best known of these collections of fables in Sanskrit is the Pañcatantra, literally the Pentateuch, or Pentamerone. From it and from other sources another collection was made, well known to all Sanskrit scholars by the name of Hitopadesa, *i.e.*, Salutary Advice. Both these books have been published in England and Germany, and there are translations of them in English, German, French, and other languages.4

The first question which we have to answer refers to the date of these collections, and dates in the history of Sanskrit literature are always difficult points. Fortunately, as we shall see, we can in this case fix the date of the Pañcatantra at least, by means of a translation into ancient Persian, which was made about 550 years after Christ, though even then we can only prove that a collection somewhat like the Pañkatantra must have existed at that time; but we cannot refer the book, in exactly that form in which we now possess it, to that distant period.

If we look for La Fontaine's fable in the Sanskrit stories of the Pañcatantra, we do not find, indeed, the milkmaid counting her chickens before they are hatched, but we meet with the following story:—

"There lived in a certain place a Brâhman, whose name was Svabhâvakṛpaṇa, which means 'a born miser.' He had collected a quantity of rice by begging (this reminds us somewhat of the Buddhist mendicants), and after having dined off it, he filled a pot with what was left over. He hung the pot on a peg on the wall, placed his couch beneath, and looking intently at it all the night, he thought, 'Ah, that pot is indeed brimful of rice. Now, if there should be a famine, I should certainly make a hundred rupees by it. With this I shall buy a couple of goats. They will have young ones every six months, and thus I shall have a whole herd of goats. Then, with the goats, I shall buy cows. As soon as they have calved, I shall sell the calves. Then, with the cows, I shall buy buffaloes; with the buffaloes, mares. When the mares have foaled, I shall have plenty of horses; and when I sell them, plenty of gold. With that gold I shall get a house with four wings. And then a Brâhman will come to my house, and will give me his beautiful daughter, with a large dowry. She will have a son, and I shall call him Somaśarman. When he is old enough to be danced on his father's knee, I shall sit with a book at the back of the stable, and while I am reading the boy will see me, jump from his mother's lap, and run towards me to be danced on my knee. He will come too near the horse's hoof, and, full of anger, I shall call to my wife, "Take the baby; take him!" But she, distracted by some domestic work does not hear me. Then I get up, and give her such a kick with my foot.' While he thought this, he gave a kick with his foot, and broke the pot. All the rice fell over him, and made him quite white. Therefore, I say, 'He who makes foolish plans for the future will be white all over, like the father of Somaśarman.'"[5]

I shall at once proceed to read you the same story, though slightly modified, from the Hitopadeśa.[6] The Hitopadeśa professes to be taken from the Pañcatantra and some other books; and in this case it would seem as if some other authority had been followed. You will see, at all events, how much freedom there was in telling the old story of the man who built castles in the air.

"In the town of Devîkoṭṭa there lived a Brâhman of the name of Devaśarman. At the feast of the great equinox he received a plate full of rice. He took it, went into a potter's shop, which was full of crockery, and, overcome by the heat, he lay down in a corner and began to doze. In order to protect his plate of rice, he kept a stick in his hand, and began to think, 'Now, if I sell this plate of rice, I shall receive ten cowries (kapardaka). I shall then, on the spot, buy pots and plates, and after having increased my capital again and again, I shall buy and sell betel nuts and dresses till I become enormously rich. Then I shall marry four wives, and the youngest and prettiest of the four I shall make a great pet of. Then the other wives will be so angry, and begin to quarrel. But I shall be in a great rage, and take a stick, and give them a good flogging.' . . . . While he said this, he flung his stick away; the plate of rice was smashed to pieces, and many of the pots in the shop were broken. The potter, hearing the noise, ran into the shop, and when he saw his pots broken, he gave the Brâhman a good scolding, and drove him out of his shop. Therefore I say, 'He who rejoices over plans for the future will come to grief, like the Brâhman who broke the pots.'"

In spite of the change of a Brahman into a milkmaid, no one, I suppose, will doubt that we have here in the stories of the Pañcatantra and Hitopadeśa the first germs of La Fontaine's fable.[7,A] But how did that fable travel all the way from India to France? How did it doff its Sanskrit garment and don the light dress of modern French? How was the stupid Brahman born again as the brisk milkmaid, *"cotillon simple et souliers plats?"*

It seems a startling case of longevity that while languages have changed, while works of art have perished, while empires have risen and vanished again, this simple children's story should have lived on, and maintained its place of honor and its undisputed sway in every school-room of the East and every nursery of the West. And yet it is a case of longevity so well attested that even the most skeptical would hardly venture to question it. We have the passport of these stories *viséed* at every place through which they have passed, and, as far as I can judge, *parfaitement en règle*. The story of the migration of these Indian fables from East to West is indeed wonderful; more wonderful and more instructive than many of these fables themselves. Will it be believed that we, in this Christian country and in the nineteenth century, teach our children the first, the most important lessons of worldly wisdom, nay, of a more than worldly wisdom, from books borrowed from Buddhists and Brahmans, from heretics and idolaters, and that wise words, spoken a thousand, nay, two thousand years ago, in a lonely village of India, like precious seed scattered broadcast all over the world, still bear fruit a hundred and a thousand-fold in that soil which is the most precious before God and man, the soul of a child? No lawgiver, no philosopher, has made his influence felt so widely, so deeply, and so permanently as the author of these children's fables. But who was he? We do not know. His name, like the name of many a benefactor of the human race, is forgotten. We only know he was an Indian—a nigger, as some people would call him—and that he lived at least two thousand years ago.

No doubt, when we first hear of the Indian origin of these fables, and of their migration from India to Europe, we wonder whether it can be so; but the fact is, that the story of this Indo-European migration is not, like the migration of the Indo-European languages, myths, and legends, a matter of theory, but of history, and that it was never quite forgotten either in the East or in the West. Each translator, as he handed on his treasure, seems to have been anxious to show how he came by it.

Several writers who have treated of the origin and spreading of Indo-European stories and fables, have mixed up two or three questions which ought to be treated each on its own merits.

The first question is whether the Aryans, when they broke up their pro-ethnic community, carried away with them, not only their common grammar and dictionary, but likewise some myths and legends which we find that Indians, Persians, Greeks, Romans, Celts, Germans, Slaves, when they emerge into the light of history, share in common? That certain deities occur in India, Greece, and Germany, having the same names and the same character, is a fact that can no longer be denied. That certain heroes, too, known to Indians, Greeks, and Romans, point to one and the same origin, both by their name and by their history, is a fact by this time admitted by all whose admission is of real value. As heroes are in most cases gods in disguise, there is nothing very startling in the fact that nations, who had worshipped the same gods, should also have preserved some common legends of demi-gods or heroes, nay, even in a later phase of thought, of fairies and ghosts. The case, however, becomes much more problematical when we ask, whether stories also, fables told with a decided moral purpose, formed part of that earliest Aryan inheritance? This is still doubted by many who have no doubts whatever as to common Aryan myths and legends, and even those who, like myself, have tried to establish by tentative arguments the existence of common Aryan fables, dating from before the Aryan separation, have done so only by showing a possible connection between ancient popular saws and mythological ideas, capable of a moral application. To any one, for instance, who knows how in the poetical mythology of the Aryan tribes, the golden splendor of the rising sun leads to conceptions of the wealth of the Dawn in gold and jewels and her readiness to shower them upon her worshippers, the modern German proverb, *Morgenstunde hat Gold im Munde*, seems to have a kind of mythological ring, and the stories of benign fairies, changing everything into gold, sound likewise like an echo from the long-forgotten forest of our common Aryan home. If we know how the trick of dragging stolen cattle backwards into their place of hiding, so that their footprints might not lead to the discovery of the thief, appears again and again in the mythology of different Aryan nations, then the pointing of the same trick as a kind of proverb, intended to convey a moral lesson, and illustrated by fables of the same or a very similar character in India and Greece, makes one feel inclined to suspect that here too the roots of these fables may reach to a pro-ethnic period. *Vestigia nulla retrorsum* is clearly an ancient proverb, dating from a nomadic period, and when we see how Plato ("Alcibiades," i. 123) was perfectly familiar with the Æsopian myth or fable,—κατὰ τὸν Αἰσώπου μῦθον, he says—of the fox declining to enter the lion's cave, because all footsteps went into it and none came out, and how the Sanskrit Pañcatantra (III. 14) tells of a jackal hesitating to enter his own cave, because he sees the footsteps of a lion going in, but not coming out, we feel strongly inclined to admit a common origin for both fables. Here, however, the idea that the Greeks, like La Fontaine, had borrowed their fable from the Pañcatantra would be simply absurd, and it would be much more rational, if the process must be one of borrowing, to admit, as Benfey ("Pantschatantra," i. 381) does, that the Hindus, after Alexander's discovery of India, borrowed this story from the Greeks. But if we consider that each of the two fables has its own peculiar tendency, the one deriving its lesson from the absence of backward footprints of the victims, the other from the absence of backward footprints of the lion himself, the admission of a common Aryan proverb such as "*vestigia nulla retrorsum*" would far better explain the facts such as we find them. I am not ignorant of the difficulties of this explanation, and I would myself point to the fact that among the Hottentots, too, Dr. Bleek has found a fable of the jackal declining to visit the sick lion, "because the traces of the animals who went to see him did not turn back."8 Without, however, pronouncing any decided opinion on this vexed question, what I wish to place clearly before you is this, that the spreading of Aryan myths, legends, and fables, dating from a pro-ethnic period, has nothing whatever to do with the spreading of fables taking place in strictly historical times from India to Arabia, to Greece and the rest of Europe, not by means of oral tradition, but through more or less faithful translations of literary works. Those who like may doubt whether *Zeus* was *Dyaus*, whether *Daphne* was *Ahanâ*, whether *La Belle au Bois* was the mother of two children, called *L'Aurore* and *Le Jour*,9 but the fact that a collection of fables was, in the sixth century of our era, brought from India to Persia, and by means of various translations naturalized among Persians, Arabs, Greeks, Jews, and all the rest, admits of no doubt or cavil. Several thousand years have passed between those two migrations, and to mix them up together, to suppose that Comparative Mythology has anything to do with the migration of such fables as that of Perrette, would be an anachronism of a portentous character.

There is a third question, viz., whether besides the two channels just mentioned, there were others through which Eastern fables could have reached Europe, or Æsopian and other European fables have been transferred to the East. There are such channels, no doubt. Persian and Arab stories, of Indian origin, were through the crusaders brought back to Constantinople, Italy, and France; Buddhist fables were through Mongolian10 conquerors (13th century) carried to Russia and the eastern parts of Europe. Greek stories may have reached Persia and India at the time of Alexander's conquests and during the reigns of the Diadochi, and even Christian legends may have found their way to the East through missionaries, travellers, or slaves.

Lastly, there comes the question, how far our common human nature is sufficient to account for coincidences in beliefs, customs, proverbs, and fables, which, at first sight, seem to require an historical explanation. I shall mention but one instance. Professor Wilson ("Essays on Sanskrit Literature," i. p. 201) pointed out that the story of the Trojan horse occurs in a Hindu tale, only that instead of the horse we have an elephant. But he rightly remarked that the coincidence was accidental. In the one case, after a siege of nine years, the principal heroes of the Greek army are concealed in a wooden horse, dragged into Troy by a stratagem, and the story ends by their falling upon the Trojans and conquering the city of Priam. In the other story a king bent on securing a son-in-law, had an elephant constructed by able artists, and filled with armed men. The elephant was placed in a forest, and when the young prince came to hunt, the armed men sprang out, overpowered the prince and brought him to the king, whose daughter he was to marry. However striking the similarity may seem to one unaccustomed to deal with ancient legends, I doubt whether any comparative mythologist has postulated a common Aryan origin for these two stories. They feel that, as far as the mere construction of a wooden animal is concerned, all that was necessary to explain the origin of the idea in one place was present also in the other, and that while the Trojan horse forms an essential part of a mythological cycle, there is nothing truly mythological or legendary in the Indian story. The idea of a hunter disguising himself in the skin of an animal, or even of one animal assuming the disguise of another,[11] are familiar in every part of the world, and if that is so, then the step from hiding under the skin of a large animal to that of hiding in a wooden animal is not very great.

Every one of these questions, as I said before, must be treated on its own merits, and while the traces of the first migration of Aryan fables can be rediscovered only by the most minute and complex inductive processes, the documents of the latter are to be found in the library of every intelligent collector of books. Thus, to return to Perrette and the fables of Pilpay, Huet, the learned bishop of Avranches, the friend of La Fontaine, had only to examine the prefaces of the principal translations of the Indian fables in order to track their wanderings, as he did in his famous "Traite de l'Origine des Romans," published at Paris in 1670, two years after the appearance of the first collection of La Fontaine's fables. Since his time the evidence has become more plentiful, and the whole subject has been more fully and more profoundly treated by Sylvestre de Sacy,[12] Loiseleur Deslongchamps,[13] and Professor Benfey.[14] But though we have a more accurate knowledge of the stations by which the Eastern fables reached their last home in the West, Bishop Huet knew as well as we do that they came originally from India through Persia by way of Bagdad and Constantinople.

In order to gain a commanding view of the countries traversed by these fables, let us take our position at Bagdad in the middle of the eighth century, and watch from that central point the movements of our literary caravan in its progress from the far East to the far West. In the middle of the eighth century, during the reign of the great Khalif Almansur, Abdallah ibn Almokaffa wrote his famous collection of fables, the "Kalila and Dimnah," which we still possess. The Arabic of these fables has been published by Sylvestre de Sacy, and there is an English translation of it by Mr. Knatchbull, formerly Professor of Arabic at Oxford. Abdallah ibn Almokaffa was a Persian by birth, who after the fall of the Omeyyades became a convert to Mohammedanism, and rose to high office at the court of the Khalifs. Being in possession of important secrets of state, he became dangerous in the eyes of the Khalif Almansur, and was foully murdered.[15] In the preface, Abdallah ibn Almokaffa tells us that he translated these fables from Pehlevi, the ancient language of Persia; and that they had been translated into Pehlevi (about two hundred years before his time) by Barzûyeh, the physician of Khosru Nushirvan, the King of Persia, the contemporary of the Emperor Justinian. The King of Persia had heard that there existed in India a book full of wisdom, and he had commanded his Vezier, Buzurjmihr, to find a man acquainted with the languages both of Persia and India. The man chosen was Barzûyeh. He travelled to India, got possession of the book, translated it into Persian, and brought it back to the court of Khosru. Declining all rewards beyond a dress of honor, he only stipulated that an account of his own life and opinions should be added to the book. This account, probably written by himself, is extremely curious. It is a kind of *Religio Medici* of the sixth century, and shows us a soul dissatisfied with traditions and formularies, striving after truth, and finding rest only where many other seekers after truth have found rest before and after him, in a life devoted to alleviating the sufferings of mankind.

There is another account of the journey of this Persian physician to India. It has the sanction of Firdúsi, in the great Persian epic, the Shah Nâmeh, and it is considered by some16 as more original than the one just quoted. According to it, the Persian physician read in a book that there existed in India trees or herbs supplying a medicine with which the dead could be restored to life. At the command of the king he went to India in search of those trees and herbs; but, after spending a year in vain researches, he consulted some wise people on the subject. They told him that the medicine of which he had read as having the power of restoring men to life had to be understood in a higher and more spiritual sense, and that what was really meant by it were ancient books of wisdom preserved in India, which imparted life to those who were dead in their folly and sins.17 Thereupon the physician translated these books, and one of them was the collection of fables, the "Kalila and Dimnah."

It is possible that both these stories were later inventions; the preface also by Ali, the son of Alshah Farési, in which the names of Bidpai and King Dabshelim are mentioned for the first time, is of later date. But the fact remains that Abdallah ibn Almokaffa, the author of the oldest Arabic collection of our fables, translated them from Pehlevi, the language of Persia at the time of Khosru Nushirvan, and that the Pehlevi which he translated was believed to be a translation of a book brought from India in the middle of the sixth century. That Indian book could not have been the Pañcatantra, as we now possess it, but must have been a much larger collection of fables, for the Arabic translation, the "Kalilah and Dimnah," contains eighteen chapters instead of the five of the Pañcatantra, and it is only in the fifth, the seventh, the eighth, the ninth, and the tenth chapters that we find the same stories which form the five books of the Pañkatantra in the *us ornatior*. Even in these chapters the Arabic translator omits stories which we find in the Sanskrit , and adds others which are not to be found there.

In this Arabic translation the story of the Brahman and the pot of rice runs as follows:—

"A religious man was in the habit of receiving every day from the house of a merchant a certain quantity of butter (oil) and honey, of which, having eaten as much as he wanted, he put the rest into a jar, which he hung on a nail in a corner of the room, hoping that the jar would in time be filled. Now, as he was leaning back one day on his couch, with a stick in his hand, and the jar suspended over his head, he thought of the high price of butter and honey, and said to himself, 'I will sell what is in the jar, and buy with the money which I obtain for it ten goats, which, producing each of them a young one every five months, in addition to the produce of the kids as soon as they begin to bear, it will not be long before there is a large flock.' He continued to make his calculations, and found that he should at this rate, in the course of two years, have more than four hundred goats. 'At the expiration of this term I will buy,' said he, 'a hundred black cattle, in the proportion of a bull or a cow for every four goats. I will then purchase land, and hire workmen to plough it with the beasts, and put it into tillage, so that before five years are over I shall, no doubt, have realized a great fortune by the sale of the milk which the cows will give, and of the produce of my land. My next business will be to build a magnificent house, and engage a number of servants, both male and female; and, when my establishment is completed, I will marry the handsomest woman I can find, who, in due time becoming a mother, will present me with an heir to my possessions, who, as he advances in age, shall receive the best masters that can be procured; and, if the progress which he makes in learning is equal to my reasonable expectations, I shall be amply repaid for the pains and expense which I have bestowed upon him; but if, on the other hand, he disappoints my hopes, the rod which I have here shall be the instrument with which I will make him feel the displeasure of a justly-offended parent.' At these words he suddenly raised the hand which held the stick towards the jar, and broke it, and the contents ran down upon his head and face."[18] . . . .

You will have observed the coincidences between the Arabic and the Sanskrit versions, but also a considerable divergence, particularly in the winding up of the story. The Brahman and the holy man both build their castles in the air; but, while the former kicks his wife, the latter only chastises his son. How this change came to pass we cannot tell. One might suppose that, at the time when the book was translated from Sanskrit into Pehlevi, or from Pehlevi into Arabic, the Sanskrit story was exactly like the Arabic story, and that it was changed afterwards. But another explanation is equally admissible, viz., that the Pehlevi or the Arabic translator wished to avoid the offensive behavior of the husband kicking his wife, and therefore substituted the son as a more deserving object of castigation.

We have thus traced our story from Sanskrit to Pehlevi, and from Pehlevi to Arabic; we have followed it in its migrations from the hermitages of Indian sages to the court of the kings of Persia, and from thence to the residence of the powerful Khalifs at Bagdad. Let us recollect that the Khalif Almansur, for whom the Arabic translation was made, was the contemporary of Abderrhaman, who ruled in Spain, and that both were but little anterior to Harun al Rashid and Charlemagne. At that time, therefore, the way was perfectly open for these Eastern fables, after they had once reached Bagdad, to penetrate into the seats of Western learning, and to spread to every part of the new empire of Charlemagne. They may have done so, for all we know; but nearly three hundred years pass before these fables meet us again in the literature of Europe. The Carlovingian empire had fallen to pieces, Spain had been rescued from the Mohammedans, William the Conqueror had landed in England, and the Crusades had begun to turn the thoughts of Europe towards the East, when, about the year 1080, we hear of a Jew of the name of Symeon, the son of Seth, who translated these fables from Arabic into Greek. He states in his preface that the book came originally from India, that it was brought to the King Chosroes of Persia, and then translated into Arabic. His own translation into Greek must have been made from an Arabic MS. of the "Kalila and Dimna," in some places more perfect, in others less perfect, than the one published by De Sacy. The Greek has been published, though very imperfectly, under the title of "Stephanites and Ichnelates."[19] Here our fable is told as follows (p. 337):—

"It is said that a beggar kept some honey and butter in a jar close to where he slept. One night he thus thought within himself: 'I shall sell this honey and butter for however small a sum; with it I shall buy ten goats, and these in five months will produce as many again. In five years they will become four hundred. With them I shall buy one hundred cows, and with them I shall cultivate some land. And what with their calves and the harvests, I shall become rich in five years, and build a house with four wings,[20] ornamented with gold, and buy all kinds of servants, and marry a wife. She will give me a child, and I shall call him Beauty. It will be a boy, and I shall educate him properly; and if I see him lazy, I shall give him such a flogging with this stick. . . . .' With these words he took a stick that was near him, struck the jar, and broke it, so that the honey and milk ran down on his beard."

This Greek translation might, no doubt, have reached La Fontaine; but as the French poet was not a great scholar, least of all a reader of Greek MSS., and as the fables of Symeon Seth were not published till 1697, we must look for other channels through which the old fable was carried along from East to West.

There is, first of all, an Italian translation of the "Stephanites and Ichnelates," which was published at Ferrara in 1583.21,B The title is, "Del Governo de' Regni. Sotto morali essempi di animali ragionanti tra loro. Tratti prima di lingua Indiana in Agarena da Lelo Demno Saraceno. Et poi dall' Agarena nella Greca da Simeone Setto, philosopho Antiocheno. Et hora tradotti di Greco in Italiano." This translation was probably the work of Giulio Nuti.

There is, besides, a Latin translation, or rather a free rendering of the Greek translation by the learned Jesuit, Petrus Possinus, which was published at Rome in 1666.22,C This may have been, and, according to some authorities, has really been one of the sources from which La Fontaine drew his inspirations. But though La Fontaine may have consulted this work for other fables, I do not think that he took from it the fable of Perrette and the milk-pail.

The fact is, these fables had found several other channels through which, as early as the thirteenth century, they reached the literary market of Europe, and became familiar as household words, at least among the higher and educated classes. We shall follow the course of some of these channels. First, then, a learned Jew, whose name seems to have been Joel, translated our fables from Arabic into Hebrew (1250?). His work has been preserved in one MS. at Paris, but has not yet been published, except the tenth book, which was communicated by Dr. Neubauer to Benfey's journal, "Orient und Occident" (vol. i. p. 658). This Hebrew translation was translated by another converted Jew, Johannes of Capua, into Latin. His translation was finished between 1263–1278, and, under the title of "Directorium Humanæ Vitæ," it became very soon a popular work with the select reading public of the thirteenth century.23,D In the "Directorium," and in Joel's translation, the name of Sendebar is substituted for that of Bidpay. The "Directorium" was translated into German at the command of Eberhard, the great Duke of Würtemberg,24,E and both the Latin and the German translation occur, in repeated editions, among the rare books printed between 1480 and the end of the fifteenth century.25 A Spanish translation, founded both on the German and the Latin s, appeared at Burgos in 1493;26 and from these different sources flowed in the sixteenth century the Italian renderings of Firenzuola (1548)27 and Doni (1552).28 As these Italian translations were repeated in French29 and English, before the end of the sixteenth century, they might no doubt have supplied La Fontaine with subjects for his fables.

But, as far as we know, it was a third channel that really brought the Indian fables to the immediate notice of the French poet. A Persian poet, of the name of Nasr Allah, translated the work of Abdallah ibn Almokaffa into Persian about 1150. This Persian translation was enlarged in the fifteenth century by another Persian poet, Husain ben Ali called el Vaez, under the title of "Anvári Suhaili."30 This name will be familiar to many members of the Indian Civil Service, as being one of the old Haileybury class-books which had to be construed by all who wished to gain high honors in Persia. This work, or at least the first books of it, were translated into French by David Sahid of Ispahan, and published at Paris in 1644, under the title of "Livre des Lumières, ou, la Conduite des Rois, composé par le Sage Pilpay, Indien." This translation, we know, fell into the hands of La Fontaine, and a number of his most charming fables were certainly borrowed from it.

But Perrette with the milk-pail has not yet arrived at the end of her journey, for if we look at the "Livre des Lumières," as published at Paris, we find neither the milkmaid nor her prototype, the Brahman who kicks his wife, or the religious man who flogs his boy. That story occurs in the later chapters, which were left out in the French translation; and La Fontaine, therefore, must have met with his model elsewhere.

Remember that in all our wanderings we have not yet found the milkmaid, but only the Brahman or the religious man. What we want to know is who first brought about this metamorphosis.

No doubt La Fontaine was quite the man to seize on any jewel which was contained in the Oriental fables, to remove the cumbersome and foreign-looking setting, and then to place the principal figure in that pretty frame in which most of us have first become acquainted with it. But in this case the charmer's wand did not belong to La Fontaine, but to some forgotten worthy, whose very name it will be difficult to fix upon with certainty.

We have, as yet, traced three streams only, all starting from the Arabic translation of Abdallah ibn Almokaffa, one in the eleventh, another in the twelfth, a third in the thirteenth century, all reaching Europe, some touching the very steps of the throne of Louis XIV., yet none of them carrying the leaf which contained the story of "Perrette," or of the "Brahman," to the threshold of La Fontaine's home. We must, therefore, try again.

After the conquest of Spain by the Mohammedans, Arabic literature had found a new home in Western Europe, and among the numerous works translated from Arabic into Latin or Spanish, we find towards the end of the thirteenth century (1289) a Spanish translation of our fables, called "Calila é Dymna."31,F In this the name of the philosopher is changed from Bidpai to Bundobel. This, or another translation from Arabic, was turned into Latin verse by Raimond de Béziers in 1313 (not published).

Lastly, we find in the same century another translation from Arabic straight into Latin verse, by Baldo, which became known under the name of "Æsopus alter."32,G

From these frequent translations, and translations of translations, in the eleventh, twelfth, and thirteenth centuries, we see quite clearly that these

Indian fables were extremely popular, and were, in fact, more widely read in Europe than the Bible, or any other book. They were not only read in translations, but having been introduced into sermons,33,H homilies, and works on morality, they were improved upon, acclimatized, localized, moralized, till at last it is almost impossible to recognize their Oriental features under their homely disguises.

I shall give you one instance only.

Rabelais, in his "Gargantua," gives a long description how a man might conquer the whole world. At the end of this dialogue, which was meant as a satire on Charles V., we read:—

"There was there present at that time an old gentleman well experienced in the wars, a stern soldier, and who had been in many great hazards, named Echephron, who, hearing this discourse, said: 'J'ay grand peur que toute ceste entreprise sera semblable à la farce *du pot au laict* duquel un cordavanier se faisoit riche par resverie, puis le pot cassé, n'eut de quoy disner.'"

This is clearly our story, only the Brahman has, as yet, been changed into a shoemaker only, and the pot of rice or the jar of butter and honey into a pitcher of milk. Now it is perfectly true that if a writer of the fifteenth century changed the Brahman into a shoemaker, La Fontaine might, with the same right, have replaced the Brahman by his milkmaid. Knowing that the story was current, was, in fact, common property in the fifteenth century, nay, even at a much earlier date, we might really be satisfied after having brought the germs of "Perrette" within easy reach of La Fontaine. But, fortunately, we can make at least one step further, a step of about two centuries. This step backwards brings us to the thirteenth century, and there we find our old Indian friend again, and this time really changed into a milkmaid. The book I refer to is written in Latin, and is called, "Dialogus Creaturarum optime moralizatus;" in English, the "Dialogue of Creatures moralized." It was a book intended to teach the principles of Christian morality by examples taken from ancient fables. It was evidently a most successful book, and was translated into several modern languages. There is an old translation of it in English, first printed by Rastell,34 and afterwards repeated in 1816. I shall read you from it the fable in which, as far as I can find, the milkmaid appears for the first time on the stage, surrounded already by much of that scenery which, four hundred years later, received its last touches at the hand of La Fontaine.

"DIALOGO C. (p. ccxxiii.) For as it is but madnesse to trust to moche in surete, so it is but foly to hope to moche of vanyteys, for vayne be all erthly thinges longynge to men, as sayth Davyd, Psal. xciiii: Wher of it is tolde in fablys that a lady uppon a tyme delyvered to her mayden a *galon of mylke* to sell at a cite, and by the way, as she sate and restid her by a dyche side, she began to thinke that with the money of the mylke she wold bye an henne, the which shulde bringe forth chekyns, and when they were growyn to hennys she wolde sell them and by piggis, and eschaunge them in to shepe, and the shepe in to oxen, and so whan she was come to richesse she sholde be maried right worshipfully unto some worthy man, and thus she reioycid. And whan she was thus mervelously comfortid and ravisshed inwardly in her secrete solace, thinkynge with howe great ioye she shuld be ledde towarde the chirche with her husbond on horsebacke, she sayde to her self: 'Goo we, goo we.' Sodaynlye she smote the ground with her fote, myndynge to spurre the horse, but her fote slypped, and she fell in the dyche, and there lay all her mylke, and so she was farre from her purpose, and never had that she hopid to have."35

Here we have arrived at the end of our journey. It has been a long journey across fifteen or twenty centuries, and I am afraid our following Perrette from country to country, and from language to language, may have tired some of my hearers. I shall, therefore, not attempt to fill the gap that divides the fable of the thirteenth century from La Fontaine. Suffice it to say, that the milkmaid, having once taken the place of the Brahman, maintained it against all comers. We find her as Dona Truhana, in the famous "Conde Lucanor," the work of the Infante Don Juan Manuel,36,I who died in 1347, the grandson of St. Ferdinand, the nephew of Alfonso the Wise, though himself not a king, yet more powerful than a king; renowned both by his sword and by his pen, and possibly not ignorant of Arabic, the language of his enemies. We find her again in the "Contes et Nouvelles" of Bonaventure des Periers,K published in the sixteenth century, a book which we know that La Fontaine was well acquainted with. We find her after La Fontaine in all the languages of Europe.37

	OLD COLLECTION OF INDIAN FABLES.
A.D.	
500– 600	531–579. Khosru Nushirvan, King of Persia; his physician, Barzûyeh, translates the Indian fables into *Pehlevi*, s. t. "Qalilag and Damnag" (lost). 570. Translation of the "Qualilag and Damnag," from Indian into *Syriac*, by Bud Periodeutes (Benfey and Socin).
700– 800	754–775. Khalif Almansur. Abdallah ibn Almokaffa (d. 760) translates the Pehlevi into *Arabic* (ed. de Sacy, 1816).

900–1000					
1000–1100				1080. Into *Greek*, by Simeon Seth, s. t. "Ichnelates et Stephanites," ed. Starkius, 1697.	
1100–1200		1118–53. Into *Persian*, by Abul Maali Nasr Allah (prose).			
1200–1300	Into *Latin* by Baldo, s. t. Alter Æsopus (ed. du Méril).	1289. Into *Spanish*, by order of the Infante Don Alfonso, s. t. "Calila é Dymna" (ed. de Gayangos)		1250. Into *Hebrew*, by Rabbi Joel.	
				1263–78. Into *Latin*, by Johannes of Capua, s. t. "Directorium humanæ vitæ" (print. 1480).	
1300–1400		1313. Into *Latin*, by Raimond de Beziers, s. t. "Calila et Dimna."			
				Into *German* under Eberhard, Duke of Würtemberg (d. 1325), printed before 1483.	
1400–1500		1494. Modernized in *Persian*, by Husain ben Ali, el Vaez, s. t. "Anvari Suhaili."		1493. Into *Spanish*, s. t. "Exemplario contra los Engaños."	

1500–1600	1590. New, by Abulfazl, for Akbar, "Ayari Danish."		1540. Into *Turkish*, by Ali Tchelebi, s. t. "Homayun Nameh."		1548. Into *Italian*, by Ange Firenzuola, s. t. "Discorsi degli Animali."				
	Translated into *Hindustani*, s. t. "Khirud Ufroz," the Illuminator of the Understanding.		1552. Into *Italian*, by Doni, s. t. "La Filosofia Morale."		1556. Into *French*, by Gabr. Cottier, s. t. "Le Plaisant Discours des Animaux."		1583. Into *Italian*, by G. Nuti, s. t. "Del Governo de' Regni."		
			1570. Into *English*, by North.		1579. Into *French*, by Pierre de La Rivey, s. t. "Deux Livres de Filosofie Fabuleuse."				
1600–1700	1644. Into *French*, by David Sahid d'Ispahan (Gaulmin), s. t. "Livre des Lumières, ou la Conduite des Rois, composé par le sage Pilpay, Indien" (4 cap. only).		—Into *Spanish*, by Brattuti, "Espejo politico," 1654.				1666. Into *Latin*, by Petrus Possinus.		
1700–1800			1724. Into *French*, by Galland, s. t. "Les Contes et Fables Indiennes de Bibpaï et de Lokman" (4 cap.						

| | | | only); finished in 1778 by Cardonne. | | |

You see now before your eyes the bridge on which our fables came to us from East to West. The same bridge which brought us Perrette brought us hundreds of fables, all originally sprung up in India, many of them carefully collected by Buddhist priests, and preserved in their sacred canon, afterwards handed on to the Brahminic writers of a later age, carried by Barzûyeh from India to the court of Persia, then to the courts of the Khalifs at Bagdad and Cordova, and of the emperors at Constantinople. Some of them, no doubt, perished on their journey, others were mixed up together, others were changed till we should hardly know them again. Still, if you once know the eventful journey of Perrette, you know the journey of all the other fables that belong to this Indian cycle. Few of them have gone through so many changes, few of them have found so many friends, whether in the courts of kings or in the huts of beggars. Few of them have been to places where Perrette has not also been. This is why I selected her and her passage through the world as the best illustration of a subject which otherwise would require a whole course of lectures to do it justice.

But though our fable represents one large class or cluster of fables, it does not represent all. There were several collections, besides the Pancatantra, which found their way from India to Europe. The most important among them is the "Book of the Seven Wise Masters, or the Book of Sindbad," the history of which has lately been written, with great learning and ingenuity, by Signor Comparetti.38

These large collections of fables and stories mark what may be called the high roads on which the literary products of the East were carried to the West. But there are, beside these high roads, some smaller, less trodden paths on which single fables, sometimes mere proverbs, similes, or metaphors, have come to us from India, from Persepolis, from Damascus and Bagdad. I have already alluded to the powerful influence which Arabic literature exercised on Western Europe through Spain. Again, a most active interchange of Eastern and Western ideas took place at a later time during the progress of the Crusades. Even the inroads of Mongolian tribes into Russia and the East of Europe kept up a literary bartering between Oriental and Occidental nations.

But few would have suspected a Father of the Church as an importer of Eastern fables. Yet so it is.

At the court of the same Khalif Almansur, where Abdallah ibn Almokaffa translated the fables of Calila and Dimna from Persian into Arabic, there lived a Christian of the name of Sergius, who for many years held the high office of treasurer to the Khalif. He had a son to whom he gave the best education that could then be given, his chief tutor being one Cosmas, an Italian monk, who had been taken prisoner by the Saracens, and sold as a slave at Bagdad. After the death of Sergius, his son succeeded him for some time as chief councillor (πρωτοσύμβουλος) to the Khalif Almansur. Such, however, had been the influence of the Italian monk on his pupil's mind, that he suddenly resolved to retire from the world, and to devote himself to study, meditation, and pious works. From the monastery of St. Saba, near Jerusalem, this former minister of the Khalif issued the most learned works on theology, particularly his "Exposition of the Orthodox Faith." He soon became the highest authority on matters of dogma in the Eastern Church, and he still holds his place among the saints both of the Eastern and Western Churches. His name was Joannes, and from being born at Damascus, the former capital of the Khalifs, he is best known in history as Joannes Damascenus, or St. John of Damascus. He must have known Arabic, and probably Persian; but his mastery of Greek earned him, later in life, the name of Chrysorrhoas, or Gold-flowing. He became famous as the defender of the sacred images, and as the determined opponent of the Emperor Leo the Isaurian, about 726. It is difficult in his life to distinguish between legend and history, but that he had held high office at the court of the Khalif Almansur, that he boldly opposed the iconoclastic policy of the Emperor Leo, and that he wrote the most learned theological works of his time, cannot be easily questioned.

Among the works ascribed to him is a story called "Barlaam and Joasaph."[39] There has been a fierce controversy as to whether he was the author of it or not. Though for our own immediate purposes it would be of little consequence whether the book was written by Joannes Damascenus or by some less distinguished ecclesiastic, I must confess that the arguments hitherto adduced against his authorship seem to me very weak.

The Jesuits did not like the book, because it was a religious novel. They pointed to a passage in which the Holy Ghost is represented as proceeding from the Father "and the Son," as incompatible with the creed of an Eastern ecclesiastic. That very passage, however, has now been proved to be spurious; and it should be borne in mind, besides, that the controversy on the procession of the Holy Ghost from the Father and the Son, or from the Father through the Son, dates a century later than Joannes. The fact, again, that the author does not mention Mohammedanism,[40] proves nothing against the authorship of Joannes, because, as he places Barlaam and Joasaph in the early centuries of Christianity, he would have ruined his story by any allusion to Mohammed's religion, then only a hundred years old. Besides, he had written a separate work, in which the relative merits of Christianity and

Mohammedanism are discussed. The prominence given to the question of the worship of images shows that the story could not have been written much before the time of Joannes Damascenus, and there is nothing in the style of our author that could be pointed out as incompatible with the style of the great theologian. On the contrary, the author of "Barlaam and Joasaph" quotes the same authors whom Joannes Damascenus quotes most frequently—*e.g.*, Basilius and Gregorius Nazianzenus. And no one but Joannes could have taken long passages from his own works without saying where he borrowed them.41

The story of "Barlaam and Joasaph"—or, as he is more commonly called, Josaphat—may be told in a few words: "A king in India, an enemy and persecutor of the Christians, has an only son. The astrologers have predicted that he would embrace the new doctrine. His father, therefore, tries by all means in his power to keep him ignorant of the miseries of the world, and to create in him a taste for pleasure and enjoyment. A Christian hermit, however, gains access to the prince, and instructs him in the doctrines of the Christian religion. The young prince is not only baptized, but resolves to give up all his earthly riches; and after having converted his own father and many of his subjects, he follows his teacher into the desert."

The real object of the book is to give a simple exposition of the principal doctrines of the Christian religion. It also contains a first attempt at comparative theology, for in the course of the story there is a disputation on the merits of the principal religions of the world—the Chaldæan, the Egyptian, the Greek, the Jewish, and the Christian. But one of the chief attractions of this manual of Christian theology consisted in a number of fables and parables with which it is enlivened. Most of them have been traced to an Indian source. I shall mention one only which has found its way into almost every literature of the world:42—

"A man was pursued by a unicorn, and while he tried to flee from it, he fell into a pit. In falling he stretched out both his arms, and laid hold of a small tree that was growing on one side of the pit. Having gained a firm footing, and holding to the tree, he fancied he was safe, when he saw two mice, a black and a white one, busy gnawing the root of the tree to which he was clinging. Looking down into the pit, he perceived a horrid dragon with his mouth wide open, ready to devour him, and when examining the place on which his feet rested, the heads of four serpents glared at him. Then he looked up, and observed drops of honey falling down from the tree to which he clung. Suddenly the unicorn, the dragon, the mice, and the serpents were all forgotten, and his mind was intent only on catching the drops of sweet honey trickling down from the tree."

An explanation is hardly required. The unicorn is Death, always chasing man; the pit is the world; the small tree is man's life, constantly gnawed by the black and the white mouse—*i.e.*, by night and day; the four serpents are the four elements which compose the human body; the dragon below is meant for the jaws of hell. Surrounded by all those horrors, man is yet able to forget them all, and to think only of the pleasures of life, which, like a few drops of honey, fall into his mouth from the tree of life.43

But what is still more curious is, that the author of "Barlaam and Josaphat" has evidently taken his very hero, the Indian Prince Josaphat, from an Indian source. In the "Lalita Vistara"—the life, though no doubt the legendary life, of Buddha—the father of Buddha is a king. When his son is born, the Brahman Asita predicts that he will rise to great glory, and become either a powerful king, or, renouncing the throne and embracing the life of a hermit become a Buddha.44 The great object of his father is to prevent this. He therefore keeps the young prince, when he grows up, in his garden and palaces, surrounded by all pleasures which might turn his mind from contemplation to enjoyment. More especially he is to know nothing of illness, old age, and death, which might open his eyes to the misery and unreality of life. After a time, however, the prince receives permission to drive out; and then follow the four drives,45 so famous in Buddhist history. The places where these drives took place were commemorated by towers still standing in the time of Fa Hian's visit to India, early in the fifth century after Christ, and even in the time of Hiouen Thsang, in the seventh century. I shall read you a short account of the three drives:46—

"One day when the prince with a large retinue was driving through the eastern gate of the city, on the way to one of his parks, he met on the road an old man, broken and decrepit. One could see the veins and muscles over the whole of his body, his teeth chattered, he was covered with wrinkles, bald, and hardly able to utter hollow and unmelodious sounds. He was bent on his stick, and all his limbs and joints trembled. 'Who is that man?' said the prince to his coachman. 'He is small and weak, his flesh and his blood are dried up, his muscles stick to his skin, his head is white, his teeth chatter, his body is wasted away; leaning on his stick, he is hardly able to walk, stumbling at every step. Is there something peculiar in his family, or is this the common lot of all created beings?'

"'Sir,' replied the coachman, 'that man is sinking under old age, his senses have become obtuse, suffering has destroyed his strength, and he is despised by his relations. He is without support and useless, and people have abandoned him, like a dead tree in a forest. But this is not peculiar to his family. In every creature youth is defeated by old age. Your father, your mother, all your relations, all your friends, will come to the same state; this is the appointed end of all creatures.'

"'Alas!' replied the prince, 'are creatures so ignorant, so weak and foolish as to be proud of the youth by which they are intoxicated, not seeing the old age which awaits them? As for me, I go away. Coachman, turn my chariot quickly. What have I, the future prey of old age—what have I to do with pleasure?' And the young prince returned to the city without going to the park.

"Another time the prince was driving through the southern gate to his pleasure-garden, when he perceived on the road a man suffering from illness, parched with fever, his body wasted, covered with mud, without a friend, without a home, hardly able to breathe, and frightened at the sight of himself, and the approach of death. Having questioned his coachman, and received from him the answer which he expected, the young prince said, 'Alas! health is but the sport of a dream, and the fear of suffering must take this frightful form. Where is the wise man who, after having seen what he is, could any longer think of joy and pleasure?' The prince turned his chariot, and returned to the city.

"A third time he was driving to his pleasure-garden through the western gate, when he saw a dead body on the road, lying on a bier and covered with a cloth. The friends stood about crying, sobbing, tearing their hair, covering their heads with dust, striking their breasts, and uttering wild cries. The prince, again, calling his coachman to witness this painful scene, exclaimed, 'Oh, woe to youth, which must be destroyed by old age! Woe to health, which must be destroyed by so many diseases! Woe to this life, where a man remains so short a time! If there were no old age, no disease, no death; if these could be made captive forever!' Then, betraying for the first time his intentions, the young prince said, 'Let us turn back, I must think how to accomplish deliverance.'

"A last meeting put an end to hesitation. He was driving through the northern gate on the way to his pleasure-gardens, when he saw a mendicant, who appeared outwardly calm, subdued, looking downwards, wearing with an air of dignity his religious vestment, and carrying an alms-bowl.

"'Who is that man?' asked the prince.

"'Sir,' replied the coachman, 'this man is one of those who are called Bhikshus, or mendicants. He has renounced all pleasures, all desires, and leads a life of austerity. He tries to conquer himself. He has become a devotee. Without passion, without envy, he walks about asking for alms.'

"'This is good and well said,' replied the prince. 'The life of a devotee has always been praised by the wise. It will be my refuge, and the refuge of other creatures; it will lead us to a real life, to happiness and immortality.'

"With these words the young prince turned his chariot, and returned to the city."

If we now compare the story of Joannes of Damascus, we find that the early life of Josaphat is exactly the same as that of Buddha. His father is a king, and after the birth of his son, an astrologer predicts that he will rise to glory; not, however, in his own kingdom, but in a higher and better one; in fact, that he will embrace the new and persecuted religion of the Christians. Everything is done to prevent this. He is kept in a beautiful palace, surrounded by all that is enjoyable; and great care is taken to keep him in ignorance of sickness, old age, and death. After a time, however, his father gives him leave to drive out. On one of his drives he sees two men, one maimed, the other blind. He asks what they are, and is told that they are suffering from disease. He then inquires whether all men are liable to disease, and whether it is known beforehand who will suffer from disease and who will be free; and when he hears the truth, he becomes sad, and returns home. Another time, when he drives out, he meets an old man with wrinkled face and shaking legs, bent down, with white hair, his teeth gone, and his voice faltering. He asks again what all this means, and is told that this is what happens to all men; and that no one can escape old age, and that in the end all men must die. Thereupon he returns home to meditate on death, till at last a hermit appears,47 and opens before his eyes a higher view of life, as contained in the Gospel of Christ.

No one, I believe, can read these two stories without feeling convinced that one was borrowed from the other; and as Fa Hian, three hundred years before John of Damascus, saw the towers which commemorated the three drives of Buddha still standing among the ruins of the royal city of Kapilavastu, it follows that the Greek father borrowed his subject from the Buddhist scriptures. Were it necessary, it would be easy to point out still more minute coincidences between the life of Josaphat and of Buddha, the founder of the Buddhist religion. Both in the end convert their royal fathers, both fight manfully against the assaults of the flesh and the devil, both are regarded as saints before they die. Possibly even a proper name may have been transferred from the sacred canon of the Buddhists to the pages of the Greek writer. The driver who conducts Buddha when he flees by night from his palace where he leaves his wife, his only son, and all his treasures, in order to devote himself to a contemplative life, is called Chandaka, in Burmese, Sanna.48 The friend and companion of Barlaam is called Zardan.49 Reinaud in his "Mémoire sur l'Inde," p. 91 (1849), was the first, it seems, to point out that Youdasf, mentioned by Massoudi as the founder of the Sabæan religion, and Youasaf, mentioned as the founder of Buddhism by the author of the "Kitáb-al-Fihrist," are both meant for Bodhisattva, a corruption quite intelligible with the system of transcribing that name with Persian letters.

Professor Benfey has identified Theudas, the sorcerer in "Barlaam and Joasaph," with the Devadatta of the Buddhist scriptures.50

How palpable these coincidences are between the two stories is best shown by the fact that they were pointed out, independently of each other, by scholars in France, Germany, and England. I place France first, because in point of time M. Laboulaye was the first who called attention to it in one of his charming articles in the "Debats."51 A more detailed comparison was given by Dr. Liebrecht.52 And, lastly, Mr. Beal, in his translation of the "Travels of Fa Hian,"53 called attention to the same fact—viz., that the story of Josaphat was borrowed from the "Life of Buddha." I could mention the names of two or three scholars besides who happened to read the two books, and who could not help seeing, what was as clear as daylight, that Joannes Damascenus took the principal character of his religious novel from the "Lalita Vistara," one of the sacred books of the Buddhists; but the merit of having been the first belongs to M. Laboulaye.

This fact is, no doubt, extremely curious in the history of literature; but there is another fact connected with it which is more than curious, and I wonder that it has never been pointed out before. It is well known that the story of "Barlaam and Josaphat" became a most popular book during the Middle Ages. In the East it was translated into Syriac(?), Arabic, Ethiopic, Armenian, and Hebrew; in the West it exists in Latin, French, Italian, German, English, Spanish, Bohemian, and Polish. As early as 1204, a King of Norway translated it into Icelandic, and at a later time it was translated by a Jesuit missionary into Tagala, the classical language of the Philippine Islands. But this is not all, Barlaam and Josaphat have actually risen to the rank of saints, both in the Eastern and in the Western churches. In the Eastern church the 26th of August is the saints' day of Barlaam and Josaphat; in the Roman Martyrologium, the 27th of November is assigned to them.

There have been from time to time misgivings about the historical character of these two saints. Leo Allatius, in his "Prolegomena," ventured to ask the question, whether the story of "Barlaam and Josaphat" was more real than the "Cyropædia" of Xenophon, or the "Utopia" of Thomas More; but, *en bon Catholique*, he replied, that as Barlaam and Josaphat were mentioned, not only in the Menæa of the Greek, but also in the Martyrologium of the Roman Church, he could not bring himself to believe that their history was imaginary. Billius thought that to doubt the concluding words of the author, who says that he received the story of "Barlaam and Josaphat" from men incapable of falsehood, would be to trust more in one's own suspicions than in Christian charity, which believeth all things. Bellarminus thought he could prove the truth of the story by the fact that, at the end of it, the author himself invokes the two saints Barlaam and Josaphat! Leo Allatius admitted, indeed, that some of the speeches and conversations occurring in the story might be the work of Joannes Damascenus, because Josaphat, having but recently been converted, could not have quoted so many passages from the Bible. But he implies that even this could be explained, because the Holy Ghost might have taught St. Josaphat what to say. At all events, Leo has no mercy for those "quibus omnia sub sanctorum nomine prodita male olent, quemadmodum de sanctis Georgio, Christophoro, Hippolyto, Catarina, aliisque nusquam eos in rerum natura extitisse impudentissime nugantur." The Bishop of Avranches had likewise his doubts; but he calmed them by saying: "Non pas que je veuille soustenir que tout en soit supposé: il y auroit de la témerité à desavouer qu'il y ait jamais eû de Barlaam ni de Josaphat. Le témoignage du Martyrologe, qui les met au nombre des Saints, et leur intercession que Saint Jean Damascene reclame à la fin de cette histoire ne permettent pas d'en douter."54

With us the question as to the historical or purely imaginary character of Josaphat has assumed a new and totally different aspect. We willingly accept the statement of Joannes Damascenus that the story of "Barlaam and Josaphat" was told him by men who came from India. We know that in India a story was current of a prince who lived in the sixth century B.C., a prince of whom it was predicted that he would resign the throne, and devote his life to meditation, in order to rise to the rank of a Buddha. The story tells us that his father did everything to prevent this; that he kept him in a palace secluded from the world, surrounded by all that makes life enjoyable; and that he tried to keep him in ignorance of sickness, old age, and death. We know from the same story that at last the young prince obtained permission to drive into the country, and that, by meeting an old man, a sick man, and a corpse, his eyes were opened to the unreality of life, and the vanity of this life's pleasures; that he escaped from his palace, and, after defeating the assaults of all adversaries, became the founder of a new religion. This is the story, it may be the legendary story, but at all events the recognized story of Gautama Śâkyamuni, best known to us under the name of Buddha.

If, then, Joannes Damascenus tells the same story, only putting the name of Joasaph or Josaphat, *i.e.*, Bodhisattva, in the place of Buddha; if all that is human and personal in the life of St. Josaphat is taken from the "Lalita Vistara"—what follows? It follows that, in the same sense in which La Fontaine's Perrette is the Brahman of the Pañcatantra, St. Josaphat is the Buddha of the Buddhist canon. It follows that Buddha has become a saint in the Roman Church; it follows that, though under a different name, the sage of Kapilavastu, the founder of a religion which, whatever we may think of its dogma, is, in the purity of its morals, nearer to Christianity than any other religion, and which counts even now, after an existence of 2,400 years, 455,000,000 of believers, has received the highest honors that the Christian Church can bestow. And whatever we may think of the sanctity of saints, let those who doubt the right of Buddha to a place among them read the story of his life as it is told in the Buddhist canon. If he lived the life which is there described, few saints have a better claim to the title than Buddha; and no one either in the Greek or in the Roman Church need be ashamed of having paid to Buddha's memory the honor that was intended for St. Josaphat, the prince, the hermit, and the saint.

History, here as elsewhere, is stranger than fiction; and a kind fairy, whom men call Chance, has here, as elsewhere, remedied the ingratitude and injustice of the world.

APPENDIX.

I AM enabled to add here a short account of an important discovery made by Professor Benfey with regard to the Syriac translation of our Collection of Fables. Doubts had been expressed by Sylvestre de Sacy and others, as to the existence of this translation, which was mentioned for the first time in Ebedjesu's catalogue of Syriac writers published by Abraham Ecchellensis, and again later by Assemani ("Biblioth. Orient.," tom. iii. part 1, p. 219). M. Renan, on the contrary, had shown that the title of this translation, as transmitted to us, "Kalilag and Damnag," was a guarantee of its historical authenticity. As a final k in Pehlevi becomes h in modern Persian, a title such as "Kalilag and Damnag," answering to "Kalilak and Damnak" in Pehlevi, in Sanskrit "Karaṭaka and Damanaka," could only have been borrowed from the Persian before the Mohammedan era. Now that the interesting researches of Professor Benfey on this subject have been rewarded by the happy discovery of a Syriac translation, there remains but one point to be cleared up, viz., whether this is really the translation made by Bud Periodeutes, and whether this same translation was made, as Ebedjesu affirms, from the Indian , or, as M. Renan supposes, from a Pehlevi version. I insert the account which Professor Benfey himself gave of his discovery in the Supplement to the "Allgemeine Zeitung" of July 12, 1871, and I may add that both and translation are nearly ready for publication (1875).

The oldest MS. of the Pantschatantra.

GÖTTINGEN, *July 6, 1871.*

The account I am about to give will recall the novel of our celebrated compatriot Freytag ("Die verlorene Handschrift," or "The Lost MS."), but with this essential difference, that we are not here treating of a creation of the imagination, but of a real fact; not of the MS. of a work of which many other copies exist, but of an unique specimen; in short, of the MS. of a work which, on the faith of one single mention, was believed to have been composed thirteen centuries ago. This mention, however, appeared to many critical scholars so untrustworthy, that they looked upon it as the mere result of confusion. Another most important difference is, that this search, which has lasted three years, has been followed by the happiest results: it has brought to light a MS. which, even in this century, rich in important discoveries, deserves to be ranked as of the highest value. We have acquired in this MS. the oldest specimen preserved to our days of a work, which, as translated into various languages, has been more widely disseminated and has had a greater influence on the development of civilization than any other work, excepting the Bible.

But to the point.

Through the researches, which I have published in my edition of the Pantschatantra,55 it is known that about the sixth century of our era, a work existed in India, which treated of deep political questions under the form of fables, in which the actors were animals. It contained various chapters, but these subdivisions were not, as had been hitherto believed, eleven to thirteen in number, but, as the MS. just found shows most clearly, there were at least twelve, perhaps thirteen or fourteen. This work was afterwards so entirely altered in India, that five of these divisions were separated from the other six or nine, and much enlarged, whilst the remaining ones were entirely set aside. This apparently curtailed, but really enlarged edition of the old work, is the Sanskrit book so well known as the Pantschatantra, "The Five Books." It soon took the place, on its native soil, of the old work, causing the irreparable loss of the latter in India.

But before this change of the old work had been effected in its own land, it had, in the first half of the sixth century, been carried to Persia, and translated into Pehlevi under King Chosru Nuschirvan (531–579). According to the researches which I have described in my book already quoted, the results of which are fully confirmed by the newly discovered MS., it cannot be doubted that, if this translation had been preserved, we should have in it a faithful reproduction of the original Indian work, from which, by various modifications, the Pantschatantra is derived. But unfortunately this Pehlevi translation, like its Indian original, is irretrievably lost.

But it is known to have been translated into Arabic in the eighth century by a native of Persia, by name Abdallah ibn Almokaffa (d. 760), who had embraced Islamism, and it acquired, partly in this language, partly in translations and retranslations from it (apart from the recensions in India, which penetrated to East, North, and South Asia,) that extensive circulation which has caused it to exercise the greatest influence on civilization in Western Asia, and throughout Europe.

Besides this translation into Pehlevi, there was, according to one account, another, also of the sixth century, in Syriac. This account we owe to a

Nestorian writer, who lived in the thirteenth century. He mentions in his catalogue of authors[56] a certain Bud Periodeutes, who probably about 570 had to inspect the Nestorian communities in Persia and India, and who says that, in addition to other books which he names, "he translated the book 'Qalîlag and Damnag' from the Indian."

Until three years ago, not the faintest trace of this old Syrian translation was to be found, and the celebrated Orientalist, Silvestre de Sacy, in the historical memoir which he prefixed to his edition of the Arabic translation, "Calila and Dimna" (Paris, 1816), thought himself justified in seeing in this mention a mere confusion between Barzûyeh, the Pehlevi translator, and a Nestorian Monk.

The first trace of this Syriac version was found in May, 1868. On the sixth of that month, Professor Bickell of Münster, the diligent promoter of Syrian philology, wrote to tell me that he had heard from a Syrian Archdeacon from Urumia, Jochannân bar Bâbisch, who had visited Münster in the spring to collect alms, and had returned there again in May, that, some time previously, several Chaldæan priests who had been visiting the Christians of St. Thomas in India, had brought back with them some copies of this Syriac translation, and had given them to the Catholic Patriarch in Elkosh (near Mossul). He had received one of these.

Though the news appeared so unbelievable and the character of the Syrian priest little calculated to inspire confidence in his statements, it still seemed to me of sufficient importance for me to ask my friends to make further inquiries in India, where other copies ought still to be in existence. Even were the result but a decided negative, it would be a gain to science. These inquiries had no effect in proving the truth of the archdeacon's assertions; but, at the same time, they did not disprove them. It would of course have been more natural to make inquiries among the Syrians. But from want of friends and from other causes, which I shall mention further on, I could hardly hope for any certain results, and least of all, that if the MS. really existed, I could obtain it, or a copy of it.

The track thus appeared to be lost, and not possible to be followed up, when, after the lapse of nearly two years, Professor Bickell, in a letter of February 22, 1870, drew my attention to the fact that the Chaldæan Patriarch, Jussuf Audo, who, according to Jochannân bar Bâbisch, was in possession of that translation, was now in Rome, as member of the Council summoned by the Pope.

Through Dr. Schöll of Weimar, then in Rome, and one Italian savant, Signor Ignazio Guidi, I was put into communication with the Patriarch, and with another Chaldæan priest, Bishop Qajjât, and received communications, the latest of June 11, 1870, which indeed proved the information of Jochannân bar Bâbisch to be entirely untrustworthy; but at the same time pointed to the probable existence of a MS. of the Syriac translation at Mardîn.

I did not wait for the last letters, which might have saved the discoverer much trouble, but might also have frustrated the whole inquiry; but, as soon as I had learnt the place where the MS. might be, I wrote; May 6, 1870, exactly two years after the first trace of the MS. had been brought to light, to my former pupil and friend, Dr. Albert Socin of Basle, who was then in Asia on a scientific expedition, begging him to make the most careful inquiries in Mardîn about this MS., and especially to satisfy himself whether it had been derived from the Arabian translation, or was independent of and older than the latter. We will let Dr. Socin, the discoverer of the MS., tell us himself of his efforts and their results.

"I received your letter of May 6, 1870, a few days ago, by Bagdad and Mossul, at Yacho on the Chabôras. You say that you had heard that the book was in the library at Mardîn. I must own that I doubted seriously the truth of the information, for Oriental Christians always say that they possess every possible book, whilst in reality they have but few. I found this on my journey through the 'Christian Mountain,' the Tûr el' 'Abedîn, where I visited many places and monasteries but little known. I only saw Bibles in Estrangelo character, which were of value, nowhere profane books; but the people are so fanatical, and watch their books so closely, that it is very difficult to get sight of anything; and one has to keep them in good humor. Unless after a long sojourn, and with the aid of bribery, there can never be any thought of buying anything from a monastic library. Arrived in Mardîn, I set myself to discover the book. I naturally passed by all Moslem libraries, as Syriac books only exist among the Christians. I settled at first that the library in question could only be the Jacobite Cloister, 'Der ez Zàferân,' the most important centre of the Christians of Mardîn. I therefore sent to the Patriarch of Diarbekir for most particular introductions, and started for 'Der ez Zàferân,' which lies in the mountains, 5½ hours from Mardîn. The recommendations opened the library to me. I looked through four hundred volumes, without finding anything; there was not much of any value. On my return to Mardîn, I questioned people right and left; no one knew anything about it. At length I summoned up courage one day, and went to the Chaldæan monastery. The different sects in Mardîn are most bitter against each other, and as I unfortunately lodged in the house of an American missionary, it was very difficult for me to gain access to these Catholics, who were unknown to me. Luckily my servant was a Catholic, and could state that I had no proselytizing schemes. After a time I asked about their books; Missals and Gospels were placed before me; I asked if they had any books of Fables. 'Yes, there was one there.' After a long search in the dust, it was found and brought to me. I opened it, and saw at the first glance, in red letters, 'Qalîlag and Damnag,' with the old termination g, which proved to me that the work was not translated from the Arabic 'Calila ve Dimnah.' You may be certain that I did not show what I felt. I soon laid the book quietly down. I had indeed before asked the monk specially for 'Kalila and Dimna,' and with some persistency, before I inquired generally for books of fables; but he had not the faintest suspicion that the book before him was the one so eagerly sought after. After about a week or ten days, in order to arouse no suspicion, I sent a trustworthy man to borrow the book; but he was asked at once if it were for the 'Frêngi den Prot' (Protestant), and my confidant was so good as to deny it, 'No, it was for himself.' I then examined the book more carefully. Having it safely in my possession, I was not alarmed at the idea of a little hubbub. I therefore made inquiries, but in all secret, whether they would sell it. 'No, never,' was the answer I expected and received, and the idea that I had borrowed it for myself was revived. I therefore began to have a copy made. But I was obliged to leave Mardîn and even the neighboring Diarbekir, before I received the copy. In Mardîn itself the return of the book was loudly demanded, as soon as they knew I was having it copied. I was indeed delighted when, through the kindness of friends, *post tot discrimina rerum* I received the book at Aleppo."

So far writes my friend, the fortunate discoverer, who, as early as the 19th of August, 1870, announced in a letter the happy recovery of the book. On April 20, 1871, he kindly sent it to me from Basle.

This is not the place to descant on the high importance of this discovery. It is only necessary to add that there is not the least doubt that it has put us in possession of the old Syriac translation, of which Ebedjesu speaks. There is only one question still to be settled, whether it is derived direct from the Indian, or through the Pehlevi translation? In either case it is the oldest preserved rendering of the original, now lost in India, and therefore of priceless value.

The fuller treatment of this and other questions, which spring from this discovery, will find a place in the edition of the , with translation and commentary, which Professor Bickell is preparing in concert with Dr. Hoffman and myself.

THEODOR BENFEY.

NOTES.

NOTE A.

IN modern times, too, each poet or fabulist tells the story as seems best to him. I give three recensions of the story of Perrette, copied from English schoolbooks.

THE MILKMAID.

A milkmaid who poised a full pail on her head,
Thus mused on her prospects in life, it is said:—
Let me see, I should think that this milk will procure
One hundred good eggs or fourscore, to be sure.
Well then, stop a bit, it must not be forgotten,
Some of these may be broken, and some may be rotten;
But if twenty for accident should be detached,
It will leave me just sixty sounds eggs to be hatched.
Well, sixty sound eggs—no, sound chickens I mean:
Of these some may die—we'll suppose seventeen;
Seventeen, not so many!—say ten at the most,
Which will leave fifty chickens to boil or to roast.
But then there's their barley, how much will they need?
Why, they take but one grain at a time when they feed,
So that's a mere trifle;—now then, let me see,
At a fair market-price how much money there'll be.
Six shillings a pair, five, four, three-and-six,
To prevent all mistakes that low price I will fix;
Now what will that make? Fifty chickens I said;
Fifty times three-and-six?—I'll ask brother Ned.
Oh! but stop, three-and-sixpence a pair I must sell them!
Well, a pair is a couple; now then let us tell them.
A couple in fifty will go (my poor brain),
Why just a score times, and five pairs will remain.

Twenty-five pairs of fowls, now how tiresome it is
That I can't reckon up such money as this.
Well there's no use in trying, so let's give a guess—

I'll say twenty pounds, and it can be no less.

Twenty pounds I am certain will buy me a cow,

Thirty geese and two turkeys, eight pigs and a sow;

Now if these turn out well, at the end of the year

I shall fill both my pockets with guineas, 'tis clear.

Forgetting her burden when this she had said,

The maid superciliously tossed up her head,

When, alas for her prospects! her milkpail descended,

And so all her schemes for the future were ended.

This moral, I think, may be safely attached—

"Reckon not on your chickens before they are hatched!"

JEFFREYS TAYLOR.

FABLE.

A country maid was walking with a pail of milk upon her head, when she fell into the following train of thoughts: "The money for which I shall sell this milk will enable me to increase my stock of eggs to three hundred. These eggs will bring at least two hundred and fifty chickens. The chickens will be fit to carry to market about Christmas, when poultry always bear a good price; so that by May-day I shall have money enough to buy me a new gown. Green?—let me consider—yes, green becomes my complexion best, and green it shall be. In this dress I will go to the fair, where all the young fellows will strive to have me for a partner; but I shall perhaps refuse every one of them, and with an air of distain toss from them." Charmed with this thought, she could not forbear acting with her head what thus passed in her mind, when down came the pail of milk, and with it all her fancied happiness.— *From Guy's "British Spelling Book."*

ALNASKER.

Alnasker was a very idle fellow, that would never set his hand to work during his father's life. When his father died he left him to the value of a hundred pounds in Persian money. In order to make the best of it he laid it out in glasses and bottles, and the finest china. These he piled up in a large open basket at his feet, and leaned his back upon the wall of his shop in the hope that many people would come in to buy. As he sat in this posture, with his eyes upon the basket, he fell into an amusing train of thought, and talked thus to himself: "This basket," says he, "cost me a hundred pounds, which is all I had in the world. I shall quickly make two hundred of it by selling in retail. These two hundred shall in course of trade rise to ten thousand, when I will lay aside my trade of a glass-man, and turn a dealer in pearls and diamonds, and all sorts of rich stones. When I have got as much wealth as I can desire, I will purchase the finest house I can find, with lands, slaves, and horses. Then I shall set myself on the footing of a prince, and will ask the grand Vizier's daughter to be my wife. As soon as I have married her, I will buy her ten black servants, the youngest and best that can be got for money. When I have brought this princess to my house, I shall take care to breed her in due respect for me. To this end I shall confine her to her own rooms, make her a short visit, and talk but little to her. Her mother will then come and bring her daughter to me, as I am seated on a sofa. The daughter, with tears in her eyes, will fling herself at my feet, and beg me to take her into my favor. Then will I, to impress her with a proper respect for my person, draw up my leg, and spurn her from me with my foot in such a manner that she shall fall down several paces from the sofa." Alnasker was entirely absorbed with his ideas, and could not forbear acting with his foot what he had in his thoughts; so that, striking his basket of brittle ware, which was the foundation of all his grand hopes, he kicked his glasses to a great distance into the street, and broke them into a thousand pieces.—"*Spectator.*" (From the "Sixth Book," published by the Scottish School Book Association, W. Collins & Co., Edinburgh).

NOTE B.

PERTSCH, in Benfey's "Orient und Occident," vol. ii. p. 261. Here the story is told as follows: "Perche si conta che un certo pouer huomo hauea uicino a doue dormiua, un mulino & del buturo, & una notte tra se pensando disse, io uenderò questo mulino, & questo butturo tanto per il meno, che io comprerò diece capre. Le quali mi figliaranno in cinque mesi altre tante, & in cinque anni multiplicheranno fino a quattro cento; Le quali barattero in cento buoi, & con essi seminarò una cãpagna, & insieme da figliuoli loro, & dal frutto della terra in altri cinque anni, sarò oltre modo ricco, & farò un palagio *quadro*, adorato, & comprerò schiaui una infinità, & prenderò moglie, la quale mi farà un figliuolo, & lo nominerò Pancalo, & lo farò ammaestrare come bisogna. Et se vedrò che non si curi con questa bacchetta cosí il percoterò. Con che prendendo la bacchetta che gli era uicina, & battendo di essa il vaso doue era il buturo, e lo ruppe, & fuse il buturo. Dopò gli partorì la moglie un figliuolo, e la moglie un dì gli disse, habbi un poco cura di questo fanciullo o marito, fino che io uo e torno da un seruigio. La quale essendo andata fu anco il marito chiamato dal Signore della terra, & tra tanto auuenne che una serpe salì sopra il fanciullo. Et vna donzella uicina, corsa là l'uccise. Tornato il marito uide insanguito l'vscio, & pensando che costei l'hauesse ucciso, auanti che il uedesse, le diede sul capo, di un bastone, e l'uccise. Entrato poi,

& sano trouando il figliuolo, & la serpe morta, si fu grandemente pentito, & piāse amaramente. Cosí adunque i frettolosi in molte cose errano." (Page 516.)

NOTE C.

THIS and some other extracts, from books not to be found at Oxford, were kindly copied for me by my late friend, E. Deutsch, of the British Museum.

"Georgii Pachymeris Michael Palæologus, sive Historia rerum a M. P. gestarum," ed. Petr. Possinus. Romæ, 1666.

Appendix ad observationes Pachymerianas, Specimen Sapientiæ Indorum veterum liber olim ex lingua Indica in Persicam a Perzoe Medico: ex Persica in Arabicam ab Anonymo: ex Arabica in Græcam a Symeone Seth, a Petro Possino Societ. Iesu, novissime e Græca in Latinam translatus.

"Huic talia serio nuganti haud paulo cordatior mulier. Mihi videris, Sponse, inquit, nostri cujusdam famuli egentissimi hominis similis ista inani provisione nimis remotarum et incerto eventu pendentrum rerum. Is diurnis mercedibus mellis ac butyri non magna copia collectâ duobus ista vasis e terra coctili condiderat. Mox secum ita ratiocinans nocte quadam dicebat: Mel ego istud ac butyrum quindecim minimum vendam denariis. Ex his decem Capras emam. Hæ mihi quinto mense totidem alias parient. Quinque annis gregem Caprarum facile quadringentarum confecero. Has commutare tunc placet cum bobus centum, quibus exarabo vim terræ magnam et numerum tritici maximum congeram. Ex fructibus hisce quinquennio multiplicatis, pecuniæ scilicet tantus existet modus, ut facile in locupletissimis numerer. Accedit dos uxoris quam istis opibus ditissiman nansciscar. Nascetur mihi filius quem jam nunc decerno nominare Panealum. Hunc educabo liberalissime, ut nobilium nulli concedat. Qui si ubi adoleverit, ut juventus solet, contumacem se mihi præbeat, haud feret impune. Baculo enim hoc illum hoc modo feriam. Arreptum inter hæc dicendum lecto vicinum baculum per tenebras jactavit, casuque incurrens in dolia mellis et butyri juxta posita, confregit utrumque, ita ut in ejus etiam os barbamque stillæ liquoris prosilirent; cætera effusa et mixta pulveri prorsus corrumperentur; ac fundamentum spei tantæ, inopem et multum gementem momento destitueret." (Page 602.)

NOTE D.

"DIRECTORIUM Humanæ Vitæ alias Parabolæ Antiquorum Sapientum," fol. s. l. e. a. k. 4 (circ. 1480?): "Dicitque olim quidam fuit heremita apud quendam regem. Cui rex providerat quolibet die pro sua vita. Scilicet provisionem de sua coquina et vasculum de melle. Ille vero comedebat decocta, et reservabat mel in quodam vase suspenso super suum caput donec esset plenum. Erat autem mel percarum in illis diebus. Quadam vero die: dum jaceret in suo lecto elevato capite, respexit vas mellis quod super caput ei pendebat. Et recordatus quoniam mel de die in diem vendebatur pluris solito seu carius, et dixit in corde suo. Quum fuerit hoc vas plenum: vendam ipsum uno talento auri: de quo mihi emam decem oves, et successu temporis he oves facient filios et filias, et erunt viginti. Postea vero ipsis multiplicatis cum filiis et filiabus in quatuor annis erunt quatuor centum. Tunc de quibuslibet quatuor ovibus emam vaccam et bovem et terram. Et vaccæ multiplicabuntur in filiis, quorum masculos accipiam mihi in culturam terre, præter id quod percipiam de eis de lacte et lana, donec non consummatis aliis quinque annis multiplicabuntur in tantum quod habebo mihi magnas substantias et divitias, et ero a cunctis reputatus dives et honestus. Et edificabo mihi tunc grandia et excellentia edificia pre omnibus meis vicinis et consanguinibus, itaque omnes de meis divitiis loquantur, nonne erit mihi illud jocundum, cum omnes homines mihi reverentiam in omnibus locis exhibeant. Accipiam postea uxorem de nobilibus terre. Cumque eam cognovero, concipiet et pariet mihi filium nobilem et delectabilem cum bona fortuna et dei beneplacito qui crescet in scientia virtute, et relinquam mihi per ipsum bonam memoriam post mei obitum et castigabo ipsum dietim: si mee recalcitraverit doctrine; ac mihi in omnibus erit obediens, et si non: percutiam eum isto baclo et erecto baculo ad percutiendum percussit vas mellis et fregit ipsum et defluxit mel super caput ejus."

NOTE E.

"DAS Buch der Weisheit der alter Weisen," Ulm, 1415. Here the story is given as follows:—

"Man sagt es wohnet eins mals ein brůder der dritten regel der got fast dienet, bei eins künigs hof, den versach der künig alle tag zů auff enthalt seines lebens ein kuchen speiss und ein fleschlein mit honig. diser ass alle tag die speiss von der kuchen und den honig behielt er in ein irden fleschlein das hieng ob seiner petstat so lang biss es voll ward. Nun kam bald eine grosse teür in den honig und eins morgens früe lag er in seinem pett und sach das honig in dem fleschlein ob seinem haubt hangen do fiel ym in sein gedanck die teüre des honigs und fieng an mit ihm selbs ze reden. wann diss fleschlein gantz vol honigs wirt so verkauff ich das umb fünff güldin, darum̄ kauff ich mir zehen gůter schaff und die machen alle des jahrs lember. und dann werden eins jahrs zweintzig und die und das von yn kummen mag in zehen jaren werden tausent. dann kauff ich umb fier schaff ein ku und kauff dobei ochsen und ertrich die meren sich mit iren früchten und do nimb ich dann die frücht zů arbeit der äcker. von den andern küen und schaffen nimb ich milich und woll ee das andre fünff jar fürkommen so wird es sich allso meren das ich ein grosse hab und reichtumb überkumen wird dann will ich mir selbs knecht und kellerin kauffen und hohe und hübsche bäw ton. und darnach so nimm ich mir ein hübsch weib von einem edeln geschlecht die beschlaff ich mit kurtzweiliger lieb. so enpfecht sie und gebirt mir ein schön glückseligten sun und gottförchtigen. und der wirt wachsen in lere und künsten und in weissheit. durch den lass ich mir einen gůten leümde nach meinem tod. aber wird er nit fölgig sein und meiner straff nit achten so wolt ich yn mit meinem stecken über sein rucken on erbermde gar hart schlahen. und nam sein stecken da mit man pflag das pet ze machen ym selbs ze zeigen wie frefelich er sein sun schlagen wölt. und schlůg das irden fass das ob seinem haubt hieng zů stücken dass ym das honig under sein antlit und in das pet troff und ward ym von allen sein gedencken nit dann das er sein antlit und pet weschen můst."

NOTE F.

THIS translation has lately been published by Don Pascual de Gayangos in the "Biblioteca de Autores Españoles," Madrid, 1860, vol. li. Here the story runs as follows (p. 57):—

"Del religioso que vertió la miel et la manteca sobre su cabeza.

"Dijo la mujer: 'Dicen que un religioso habia cada dia limosna de casa de un mercader rico, pan é manteca é miel e otras cosas, et comia el pan é lo ál condesaba, et ponia la miel é la manteca en un jarra, fasta quel a finchó, et tenia la jarra colgada á la cabecera de su cama. Et vino tiempo que encareció la miel é la manteca, et el religioso fabló un dia consigo mismo, estando asentado en su cama, et dijo así: Venderé cuanto está en esta jarra por tantos maravedís, é comparé con ellos diez cabras, et empreñarse-han, é parirán á cabo de cinco meses; et fizo cuenta de esta guisa, et falló que en cinco años montarian bien cuatrocientas cabras. Desí dijo: Venderlas-he todas, et con el precio dellas compraré cien vacas, por cada cuatro cabezas una vaca, é haberé simiente é sembraré con los bueyes, et aprovecharme-he de los becerros et de las fembras é de la leche é manteca, é de las mieses habré grant haber, et labraré muy nobles casas, é compraré siervos é siervas, et esto fecho casarme-he con una mujer muy rica, é fermosa, é de grant logar, é empreñarla-he de fijo varon, é nacerá complido de sus miembros, et criarlo-he como á fijo de rey, é castigarlo-he con esta vara, si non quisiere ser bueno é obediente'. E él deciendo esto, alzó la vara que tenia en la mano, et ferió en la olla que estaba colgada encima dél, é quebróla, é cayóle la miel é la manteca sobre su cabeza," etc.

NOTE G.

SEE "Poésies inédites du Moyen Âge," par M. Edélstand Du Méril. Paris, 1854. XVI. De Viro et Vase Olei (p. 239):—

All brackets and parentheses are in the original.

"Uxor ab antiquo fuit infecunda marito.

Mesticiam (l. mœstitiam) cujus cupiens lenire vix (l. vir) hujus,

His blandimentis solatur tristi[ti]a mentis:

Cur sic tristaris? Dolor est tuus omnis inanis:

Pulchræ prolis eris satis amodo munere felix.

Pro nihilo ducens conjunx hæc verbula prudens,

His verbis plane quod ait vir monstrat inane:

Rebus inops quidam . . . (bone vir, tibi dicam)

Vas oleo plenum, longum quod retro per ævum

Legerat orando, loca per diversa vagando,

Fune ligans ar(c)to, tecto[que] suspendit ab alto.

Sic præstolatur tempus quo pluris ematur[atur]

Qua locupletari se sperat et arte beari.

Talia dum captat, hæc stultus inania jactat:

Ecce potens factus, fuero cum talia nactus,

Vinciar uxori quantum queo nobiliori:

Tunc sobolem gignam, se meque per omnia dignam,

Cujus opus morum genus omne præibit avorum.

Cui nisi tot vitæ fuerint insignia rite,

Fustis hic absque mora feriet caput ejus et [h]ora.

Quod dum narraret, dextramque minando levaret,

Ut percussisset puerum quasi præsto fuisset

Vas in prædictum manus ejus dirigit ictum

Servatumque sibi vas il[l]ico fregit olivi."

I owe the following extract to the kindness of M. Paul Meyer:—

Apologi Phædrii ex ludicris I. Regnerii Belnensis doct. Medici, Divione, apud Petrum Palliot, 1643 in 12, 126 pages et de plus un index.

Le recueil se divise en deux partis, pars I., pars II. La fable en question est à la page 32, pars I. fab. xxv.

XXV.

Pagana et eius mercis emptor.

> Pagana mulier, lac in olla fictili,
> Ova in canistro, rustici mercem penus,
> Ad civitatem proximam ibat venditum.
> In eius aditu factus huic quidam obvius
>
> Quanti rogavit ista quæ fers vis emi?
> Et illa tanti. Tantin'? hoc fuerit nimis.
> Numerare num me vis quod est æquum? vide
> Hac merce quod sit nunc opus mihi plus dabo
> Quam præstet illam cede, et hos nummos cape,
> Ea quam superbe fœde rusticitas agit,
> Hominem reliquit additis conviciis,
> Quasi æstimasset vilius mercem optimam.
> Aversa primos inde vix tulerat gradus,
> Cum lubricato corruit strato viæ:
> Lac olla fundit quassa, gallinaceæ
> Testæ vitellos congerunt cœno suos
> Caput cruorem mittit impingens petræ
> Luxata nec fert coxa surgentem solo:
> Ridetur ejus non malum, sed mens procax,
> Qua merx et ipsa mercis et pretium perit;
> Seque illa deflens tot pati infortunia
> Nulli imputare quam sibi hanc sortem potest

Dolor sed omnis sæviter recruduit

Curationis danda cum merces fuit.

In re minori cum quis et fragili tumet

Hunc sortis ingens sternit indignatio.

NOTE H.

HULSBACH, "Sylva Sermonum," Basileæ, 1568, p. 28: "In sylva quadam morabatur heremicola jam satis provectæ ætatis, qui quaque die accedebat civitatem, afferens inde mensuram mellis, qua donabatur. Hoc recondebat in vase terreo, quod pependerat supra lectum suum. Uno dierum jacens in lecto, et habens bacalum in manu sua, hæc apud se dicebat: Quotidie mihi datur vasculum mellis, quod dum indies recondo, fiet tandem summa aliqua. Jam valet mensura staterem unum. Corraso autem ita floreno uno aut altero, emam mihi oves, quæ fœnerabunt mihi plures: quibus divenditis coëmam mihi elegantem uxorculam, cum qua transigam vitam meam lætanter: ex ea suscitabo mihi puellam, quam instituam honeste. Si vero mihi noluerit obedire, hoc baculo eam ita comminuam: atque levato baculo confregit suum vasculum, et effusum est mel, quare cassatum est suum propositum, et manendum adhuc in suo statu."

NOTE I.

"EL CONDE LUCANOR, compuesto por el excelentissimo Principe don Iuan Manuel, hijo del Infante don Manuel, y nieto del Santo Rey don Fernando," Madrid, 1642; cap. 29, p. 96. He tells the story as follows: "There was a woman called Dona Truhana (Gertrude), rather poor than rich. One day she went to the market carrying a pot of honey on her head. On her way she began to think that she would sell the pot of honey, and buy a quantity of eggs, that from those eggs she would have chickens, that she would sell them and buy sheep; that the sheep would give her lambs, and thus calculating all her gains, she began to think herself much richer than her neighbors. With the riches which she imagined she possessed, she thought how she would marry her sons and daughters, and how she would walk in the street surrounded by her sons and daughters-in-law; and how people would consider her happy for having amassed so large a fortune, though she had been so poor. While she was thinking over all this, she began to laugh for joy, and struck her head and forehead with her hand. The pot of honey fell down, was broken, and she shed hot tears because she had lost all that she would have possessed if the pot of honey had not been broken."

NOTE K.

BONAVENTURE des Periers, "Les Contes ou les Nouvelles." Amsterdam, 1735. Nouvelle XIV. (vol. i. p. 141). (First edition, Lyon, 1558): "Et ne les (les Alquemistes) sçauroiton mieux comparer qu'à une bonne femme qui portoit une potée de laict au marché, faisant son compte ainsi: qu'elle la vendroit deux liards: de ces deux liards elle en achepteroit une douzaine d'œufs, lesquelz elle mettroit couver, et en auroit une douzaine de poussins: ces poussins deviendroient grands, et les feroit chaponner: ces chapons vaudroient cinq solz la piece, ce seroit un escu et plus, dont elle achepteroit deux cochons, masle et femelle: qui deviendroient grands et en feroient une douzaine d'autres, qu'elle vendroit vingt solz la piece; apres les avoir nourris quelque temps, ce seroient douze francs, dont elle achepteroit une iument, qui porteroit un beau poulain, lequel croistroit et deviendroit tant gentil: il sauteroit et feroit *Hin*. Et en disant *Hin*, la bonne femme, de l'aise qu'elle avoit en son compte, se print à faire la ruade que feroit son poulain: et en ce faisant sa potée de laict va tomber, et se respandit toute. Et voila ses œufs, ses poussins, ses chappons, ses cochons, sa jument, et son poulain, tous par terre."

Footnotes to Chapter III:
On the Migration of Fables

1. La Fontaine, *Fables*, livre vii., fable 10.

2. Phædon, 61, 5: Μετὰ δὲ τὸν θεὸν, ἐννοήσας, ὅτι τὸν ποιητὴν δέοι, εἴπερ μέλλοι ποιητὴς εἶναι, ποιεῖν μύθους, ἀλλ' οὐ λόγους, καὶ αὐτὸς οὐκ ἦ μυθολογικὸς, διὰ ταῦτα δὴ οὓς προχείρους εἶχον καὶ ἠπιστάμην μύθους τοὺς Αἰσώπου, τούτων ἐποίησα οἷς πρώτοις ἐνέτυχον.

3. Robert, *Fables Inédites*, des XIIe, XIIIe, et XIVe Siècles; Paris, 1825; vol. i. p. ccxxvii.

4. *Pantschatantrum sive Quinquepartitum*, edidit I. G. L. Kosegarten. Bonnæ, 1848.

Pantschatantra, Fünf Bücher indischer Fabeln, aus dem Sanskrit übersetzt. Von Th. Benfey. Leipzig, 1859.

Hitopadesa, with interlinear translation, grammatical analysis, and English translation, in Max Müller's Handbooks for the study of Sanskrit. London, 1864.

Hitopadesa, eine alte indische Fabelsammlung aus dem Sanskrit zum ersten Mal in das Deutsche übersetzt. Von Max Müller. Leipzig, 1844.

5. *Pañcatantra*, v. 10.

6. *Hitopadeśa*, ed. Max Müller, p. 120; German translation, p. 159.

7. Note A, page 188.

8. *Hottentot Fables and Tales*, by Dr. W. H. I. Bleek, London, 1894, p. 19.

9. *Academy*, vol. v. p. 548.

10. *Die Märchen des Siddhi-kür*, or *Tales of an Enchanted Corpse*, translated from Kalmuk into German by B. Jülg, 1866. (This is based on the *Vetâlapañcaviṃśati.*) *Die Geschichte des Ardschi-Bordschi Chan*, translated from Mongolian by Dr. B. Jülg, 1868. (This is based on the *Siṃhâsanadvâtriṃśati.*) A Mongolian translation of the *Kalila and Dimnah*, is ascribed to Mélik Said Iftikhar eddin Mohammed ben Abou Nasr, who died A.D. 1280. See Barbier de Meynard, "Description de la Ville de Kazvin," *Journal Asiatique*, 1857, p. 284; Lancereau, *Pantchatantra*, p. xxv.

11. Plato's expression, "As I have put on the lion's skin" (*Kratylos*, 411), seems to show that he knew the fable of an animal or a man having assumed the lion's skin without the lion's courage. The proverb ὄνος παρὰ Κυμαίους seems to be applied to men boasting before people who have no means of judging. It presupposes the story of a donkey appearing in a lion's skin.

A similar idea is expressed in a fable of the Pañcatantra (IV. 8) where a dyer, not being rich enough to feed his donkey, puts a tiger's skin on him. In this disguise the donkey is allowed to roam through all the corn-fields without being molested, till one day he sees a female donkey, and begins to bray. Thereupon the owners of the field kill him.

In the Hitopadeśa (III. 3) the same fable occurs, only that there it is the keeper of the field who on purpose disguises himself as a she-donkey, and when he hears the tiger bray, kills him.

In the Chinese Avadânas, translated by Stanislas Julien (vol. ii. p. 59), the donkey takes a lion's skin and frightens everybody, till he begins to bray, and is recognized as a donkey.

In this case it is again quite clear that the Greeks did not borrow their fable and proverb from the Pañcatantra; but it is not so easy to determine positively whether the fable was carried from the

Greeks to the East, or whether it arose independently in two places.

12. *Calilah et Dimna, ou, Fables de Bidpai, en Arabe, précédées d'un Mémoire sur l'origine de ce livre.* Par Sylvestre de Sacy. Paris, 1816.

13. Loiseleur Deslongchamps, *Essai sur les Fables Indiennes, et sur leur Introduction en Europe.* Paris, 1838.

14. *Pantschatantra, Fünf Bucher indischer Fabeln, Märchen und Erzählungen, mit Einleitung.* Von. Th. Benfey. Leipzig, 1859.

15. See Weil, *Geschichte der Chalifen*, vol. ii. p. 84.

16. Benfey, p. 60.

17. Cf. *Barlaam et Joasaph*, ed. Boissonade, p. 37.

18. *Kalila and Dimna; or, the Fables of Bidpai, translated from the Arabic.* By the Rev. Wyndham Knatchbull, A.M. Oxford, 1819.

19. *Specimen Sapientiæ Indorum Veterum, id est Liber Ethico-Politicus pervetustus, dictus Arabice Kalilah ve Dimnah, Græce Stephanites et Ichnelates, nunc primum Græce ex MS. Cod. Holsteiniano prodit cum versione Latina, opera S. G. Starkii.* Berolini, 1697.

20. This expression, a four-winged house, occurs also in the Pañcatantra. As it does not occur in the Arabic, published by De Sacy, it is clear that Symeon must have followed another Arabic in which this adjective, belonging to the Sanskrit, and no doubt to the Pehlevi, also, had been preserved.

21. Note B, p. 190.

22. Note C, p. 191.

23. Note D, p. 192.

24. Note E, p. 193.

25. Benfey, *Orient und Occident*, vol. i. p. 138.

26. Ibid. vol. i. p. 501. Its title is: "Exemplario contra los engaños y peligros del mundo," ibid. pp. 167, 168.

27. *Discorsi degli animali, di Messer Agnolo Firenzuola, in prose di M. A. F.* (Fiorenza, 1548.)

28. *La Moral Filosophia del Doni, tratta da gli antichi scrittori.* Vinegia, 1552.

Trattati Diversi di Sendebar Indiano, filosopho morale. Vinegia, 1552.

P. 65. *Trattato Quarto.*

A woman tells her husband to wait till her son is born, and says:—

"Stava uno Romito domestico ne i monti di Brianza a far penitenza e teneva alcune cassette d' api per suo spasso, e di quelle a suoi tempi ne cavava il *Mele*, e di quello ne vendeva alcuna parte tal volta per i suoi besogni. Avenne che un' anno ne fu una gran carestia, e egli attendeva a conservarlo, e ogni giorno lo guardava mille volte, e gli pareva cent' anni ogni hora, che e gli indugiava a empierlo di Mele," etc.

29. *Le Plaisant et Facétieux Discours des Animaux, novellement traduict de Tuscan en François.* Lyon, 1556, par Gabriel Cottier.

Deux Livres de Filosofie Fabuleuse, le Premier Pris des Discours de M. Ange Firenzuola le Second Extraict des Traictez de Sandebar Indien, par Pierre de La Rivey. Lyon, 1579.

The second book is a translation of the second part of Doni's *Filosofia Morale.*

30. *The Anvar-i Suhaili, or the Lights of Canopus, being the Persian version of the Fables of Pilpay, or the Book, Kalilah and Damnah, rendered into Persian by Husain Vá'iz U'l-Káshifi, literally translated by E. B. Eastwick.* Hertford, 1854.

31. Note F, p. 194.

32. Note G, p. 194.

33. Note H, p. 196.

34. *Dialogues of Creatures moralysed*, sm. 4to, circ. 1517. It is generally attributed to the press of John Rastell, but the opinion of Mr. Haslewood, in his preface to the reprint of 1816, that the book was printed on the continent, is perhaps the correct one. (*Quaritch's Catalogue*, July, 1870.)

35. The Latin is more simple: "Unde cum quedam domina dedisset ancille sue lac ut venderet et lac portaret ad urbem juxta fossatum cogitare cepit quod de p̄cio lactis emerit gallinam quæ faceret pullos quos auctos in gallinas venderet et porcellos emeret eosque mutaret in oves et ipsas in boves. Sic que ditata contraheret cum aliquo nobili et sic gloriabatur. Et cum sic gloriaretur et cogitaret cum quanta gloria duceretur ad illum virum super equum dicendo gio gio cepit pede percutere terram quasi pungeret equum calcaribus. Sed tunc lubricatus est pes ejus et cecidit in fossatum effundendo lac. Sic enim non habuit quod

se adepturam sperabat." *Dialogus Creaturarum optime moralizatus* (ascribed to Nicolaus Pergaminus, supposed to have lived in the thirteenth century). He quotes Elynandus, in *Gestis Romanorum*. First edition, "per Gerardum leeu in oppido Goudensi inceptum; munere Dei finitus est, Anno Domini, 1480."

36. Note I, p. 197.

37. My learned German translator, Dr. Felix Liebrecht, says in a note: "Other books in which our story appears before La Fontaine are *Esopus*, by Burkhard Waldis, ed. H. Kurz, Leipzig, 1862, ii. 177; note to *Des Bettlers Kaufmannschaft*; and Oesterley, in Kirchoff's *Wendunmuth*, v. 44, note to i. 171, *Vergebene Anschleg reich zuwerden* (Bibl. des liter. Vereins zu Stuttg. No. 99)."

38. *Ricerche intorno al Libro di Sindibad.* Milano, 1869.

39. The Greek was first published in 1832 by Boissonade, in his *Anecdota Græca*, vol. iv. The title, as given in some MSS. is: Ἰστορία ψυχωφελὴς ἐκ τῆς ἐνδοτέρας τῶν Αἰθιόπων χώρας, τῆς Ἰνδῶν λεγομένης, πρὸς τὴν ἁγίαν πόλιν μετενεχθεῖσα διὰ Ἰωάννου τοῦ μοναχοῦ [other MSS. read, συγγράφεισα παρα τοῦ ἁγιου πατρος ἡμων Ἰωαννου τοῦ Δαμασκηνοῦ], ἀνδρὸς τιμίου καὶ ἐναρέτου μονῆς τοῦ ἁγίου Σάβα· ἐν ᾗ ὁ βίος Βαρλαὰμ καὶ Ἰωάσαφ τῶν ἀοιδίμων καὶ μακαρίων. Joannes Monachus occurs as the name of the author in other works of Joannes Damascenus. See Leo Allatius, Prolegomena, p. L., in *Damasceni Opera Omnia*. Ed. Lequien, 1748. Venice.

At the end the author says: Ἕως ὧδε τὸ πέρας τοῦ παρόντος λόγου, ὃν κατὰ δύναμιν ἐμὴν γεγράφηκα, καθὼς ἀκήκοα παρὰ τῶν ἀψευδῶς παραδεδωκότων μοι τιμίων ἀνδρῶν. Γένοιτο δὲ ἡμᾶς, τοὺς ἀναγινώκοντάς τε καὶ ἀκούοντας τὴν ψυχωφελῆ διήγησιν ταύτην, τῆς μερίδος ἀξιωθῆναι τῶν εὐαρεστησάντων τῷ κυρίῳ εὐχαῖς καὶ πρεσβείαις Βαρλαὰμ καὶ Ἰωάσαφ τῶν μακαρίων, περὶ ὧν ἡ διήγησις. See also Wiener, *Jahrbücher*, vol. lxiii. pp. 44–83; vol. lxxii. pp. 274–288; vol. lxxiii. pp. 176–202.

40. Littré, *Journal des Savants*, 1865, p. 337.

41. The *Martyrologium Romanum*, whatever its authority may be, states distinctly that the acts of Barlaam and Josaphat were written by Sanctus Joannes Damascenus. "Apud Indos Persis finitimos sanctorum Barlaam et Josaphat, quorum actus mirandos sanctus Joannes Damascenus conscripsit." See Leonis Allatii Prolegomena, in *Joannis Damasceni Opera*, ed. Lequien, vol. i.

p. xxvi. He adds: "Et Gennadius Patriarcha per Concil. Florent. cap. 5: οὐχ ἧττον δὲ καὶ ὁ Ἰωάννης ὁ μέγας τοῦ Δαμασκοῦ ὀφθαλμὸς ἐν τῷ βίῳ Βαρλαὰμ καὶ Ἰωσάφατ τῶν Ἰνδῶν μαρτυρεῖ λέγων."

42. The story of the caskets, well known from the *Merchant of Venice*, occurs in *Barlaam and Josaphat*, though it is used there for a different purpose.

43. Cf. Benfey, *Pantschatantra*, vol. i. p. 80; vol. ii. p. 528; *Les Avadanas, Contes et Apologues indiens*, par Stanislas Julien, i. pp. 132, 191; *Gesta Romanorum*, cap. 168; *Homáyun Nameh*, cap. iv.; Grimm, *Deutsche Mythologie*, pp. 758, 759; Liebrecht, *Jahrbücher für Rom. und Engl. Literatur*, 1860.

44. *Lalita Vistara*, ed. Calcutt., p. 126.

45. Ibid., p. 225.

46. See M. M.'s *Chips from a German Workshop*, Amer. ed., vol. i. p. 207.

47. Minayeff, *Mélanges Asiatiques*, vi. 5, p. 584, remarks: "According to a legend in the *Mahâvastu* of Yaśas or Yaśoda (in a less complete form to be found in Schiefner, *Eine tibetische Lebensbeschreibung Sâkyamunis*, p. 247; Hardy, *Manual of Buddhism*, p. 187; Bigandet, *The Life or Legend of Gaudama*, p. 113), a merchant appears in Yosoda's house, the night before he has the dream which induces him to leave his paternal house, and proclaims to him the true doctrine."

48. *Journal of the American Oriental Society*, vol. iii. p. 21.

49. In some places one might almost believe that Joannes Damascenus did not only hear the story of Buddha, as he says, from the mouth of people who had brought it to him from India, but that he had before him the very of the *Lalita Vistara*. Thus in the account of the three or four drives we find indeed that the Buddhist canon represents Buddha as seeing on three successive drives, first an old, then a sick, and at last a dying man, while Joannes makes Joasaph meet two men on his first drive, one maimed, the other blind, and an old man, who is nearly dying, on his second drive. So far there is a difference which might best be explained by admitting the account given by Joannes Damascenus himself, viz: that the story was brought from India, and that it was simply told him by worthy and truthful men. But, if it was so, we have here another instance of the tenacity with

which oral tradition is able to preserve the most minute points of the story. The old man is described by a long string of adjectives both in Greek and in Sanskrit, and many of them are strangely alike. The Greek γέρων, old, corresponds to the Sanskrit *jîrṇa*; πεπαλαιώμενος, aged, is Sanskrit *vṛddha*; ἐρρικνώμενος τὸ πρόσωπον, shriveled in his face, is *balînicitakâya*, the body covered with wrinkles; παρείμενος τὰς κνήμας, weak in his knees, is *pravedhayamânaḥ sarvângapratyangaiḥ*, trembling in all his limbs; συγκεκυφώς, bent, is *kubja*; πεπολιωμένος, gray, is *palitakeśa*; ἐστερημένος τοὺς ὀδόντας, toothless, is *khaṇḍadanta*; ἐγκεκομένα λαλῶν, stammering, is *khurakhurâvaśaktakaṇṭha*.

50. *Zeitschrift der Deutschen Morgenländischen Gesellschaft*, vol. xxiv p. 480.

51. *Débats*, 1859, 21 and 26 Juillet.

52. *Die Quellen des Barlaam und Josaphat, in Jahrbuch für roman. und engl. Litteratur*, vol. ii. p. 314, 1860.

53. *Travels of Fah-hian and Sung-yun, Buddhist Pilgrims from China to India.* (400 A.D. and 518 A.D.) Translated from the Chinese by Samuel Beal. London, Trübner & Co. 1869.

54. Littré, *Journal des Savants*, 1865, p. 337.

55. *Pantschatantra; Fünf. Bücher indischer Fabeln, Märchen und Erzählungen. Aus dem Sanskrit übersetzt mit Einleitung und Ammerkungen*, 2 Theile, Leipzig, 1859; and particularly in the first part, the introduction, called "Ueber das Indische Grundwerk, und dessen Ausflüsse, so wie über die Quellen und die Verbreitung des Inhalts derselben."

56. Cf. Assemani, *Biblioth. Orient.* iii. 1, 220, and Renan, in the *Journal Asiatique*, Cinq. Série, t. vii. 1856, p. 251.

IV.
ON THE RESULTS OF THE SCIENCE OF LANGUAGE. INAUGURAL LECTURE, DELIVERED IN THE IMPERIAL UNIVERSITY OF STRASSBURG, MAY 23, 1872.

YOU will easily understand that, in giving my first lecture in a German University, I feel some difficulty in mastering and repressing the feelings which stir within my heart. I wish to speak to you, as it becomes a teacher, with perfect calmness, thinking of nothing but of the subject which 1 have to treat. But here where we are gathered together to-day, in this old free imperial town, in this University, full of the brightest recollections of Alsatian history and German literature, even a somewhat gray-headed German professor may be pardoned if, for some moments at least, he gives free vent to the thoughts that are foremost in his mind. You will see, at least, that he feels and thinks as you all feel and think, and that in living away from Germany he has not forgotten his German language, or lost his German heart.

The times in which we live are great, so great, that we can hardly conceive them great enough; so great that we, old and young, cannot be great and good and brave and hardworking enough, if we do not wish to appear quite unworthy of the times in which our lot has been cast.

We older people have lived through darker times, when to a German, learning was the only refuge, the only comfort, the only pride; times when there was no Germany except in our recollection, and perhaps in our secret hopes. And those who have lived through those sadder days feel all the more deeply the blessings of the present. We have a Germany again, a united, great, and strong country; and I call this a blessing, not only in a material sense, as giving, at last, to our homes a real and lasting security against the inroads of our powerful neighbors, but also in a moral sense, as placing every German under a greater responsibility, as reminding us of our higher duties, as inspiring us with courage and energy for the battle of the mind even more than for the battle of the arm.

That blessing has cost us dear, fearfully dear, dearer than the friends of humanity had hoped; for, proud as we may be of our victories and our victors, let us not deceive ourselves in this, that there is in the history of humanity nothing so inhuman, nothing that makes us so entirely despair of the genius of mankind, nothing that bows us so low to the very dust, as war—

unless even war becomes ennobled and sanctified, as it was with us, by the sense of duty, duty towards our country, duty towards our town, duty towards our home, towards our fathers and mothers, our wives and children. Thus, and thus only, can even war become the highest and brightest of sacrifices; thus, and thus only, may we look history straight in the face, and ask, "Who would have acted differently?"

I do not speak here of politics in the ordinary sense of the word,—nay, I gladly leave the groping for the petty causes of the late war to the scrutiny of those foreign statesmen who have eyes only for the infinitesimally small, but cannot, or will not, see the powerful handiwork of Divine justice that reveals itself in the history of nations as in the lives of individuals. I speak of politics in their true and original meaning, as a branch of ethics, as Kant has proved them to be, and from this point of view, politics become a duty from which no one may shrink, be he young or old. Every nation must have a conscience, like every individual; a nation must be able to give to itself an account of the moral justification of a war in which it is to sacrifice everything that is most dear to man. And that is the greatest blessing of the late war, that every German, however deep he may delve in his heart, can say without a qualm or a quiver, "The German people did not wish for war, nor for conquest. We wanted peace and freedom in our internal development. Another nation or rather its rulers, claimed the right to draw for us lines of the Main, if not new frontiers of the Rhine; they wished to prevent the accomplishment of that German union for which our fathers had worked and suffered. The German nation would gladly have waited longer still, if thereby war could have been averted. We knew that the union of Germany was inevitable, and the inevitable is in no hurry. But when the gauntlet was thrown in our face, and, be it remembered, with the acclamation of the whole French nation, then we knew what, under Napoleonic sway, we might expect from our powerful neighbor, and the whole German people rose as one man for defense, not for defiance. The object of our war was peace, and a lasting peace, and therefore now, after peace has been won, after our often menaced, often violated, western frontier has been made secure forever by bastions, such as nature only can build, it becomes our duty to prove to the world that we Germans are the same after as before the war, that military glory has nothing intoxicating to us, that we want peace with all the world."

You know that the world at large does not prophesy well for us. We are told that the old and simple German manners will go, that the ideal interests of our life will be forgotten, that, as in other countries, so with us, our love for the True and the Beautiful will be replaced by love of pleasure, enjoyment, and vanities. It rests with us with all our might to confound such evil prophesies, and to carry the banner of the German mind higher than ever. Germany can remain great only by what has made her great—by simplicity of manners, contentment, industry, honesty, high ideals, contempt of luxury, of display, and of vain-glory. *"Non propter vitam vivendi perdere causas,"*— "Not for the sake of life to lose the real objects of life," this must be our watchword forever, and the *causæ vitæ*, the highest objects of life, are for us to-day, and will, I trust, remain for coming generations the same as they were in the days of Lessing, of Kant, of Schiller, and of Humboldt.

And nowhere, methinks, can this return to the work of peace be better inaugurated than here in this very place, in Strassburg. It was a bold conception to begin the building of the new temple of learning in the very midst of the old German frontier fortress. We are summoned here, as in the days of Nehemiah, when "the builders every one had his sword girded by his side and so builded." It rests with us, the young as well as the old, that this bold conception shall not fail. And therefore I could not resist the voice of my heart, or gainsay the wish of my friends who believed that I, too, might bring a stone, however small, to the building of this new temple of German science. And here I am among you to try and do my best. Though I have lived long abroad, and pitched my workshop for nearly twenty-five years on English soil, you know that I have always remained German in heart and mind. And this I must say for my English friends, that they esteem a German who remains German far more than one who wishes to pass himself off as English. An Englishman wishes every man to be what he is. I am, and I always have been, a German living and working in England. The work of my life, the edition of the Rig-Veda, the oldest book of the Indian, aye, of the whole Aryan world, could be carried out satisfactorily nowhere but in England, where the rich collections of Oriental MSS., and the easy communications with India, offer to an Oriental scholar advantages such as no other country can offer. That by living and working in England I have made some sacrifices, that I have lost many advantages which the free intercourse with German scholars in a German university so richly offers, no one knows better than myself. Whatever I have seen of life, I know of no life more perfect than that of a German professor in a German school or university. You know what Niebuhr thought of such a life, even though he was a Prussian minister and ambassador at Rome. I must read you some of his words, they sound so honest and sincere: "There is no more grateful, more serene life than that of a German teacher or professor, none that, through the nature of its duties and its work, secures so well the peace of our heart and our conscience. How many times have I deplored it with a sad heart, that I should ever have left that path of life to enter upon a life of trouble which, even at the approach of old age, will probably never give me lasting peace. The office of a schoolmaster, in particular, is one of the most honorable, and despite of all the evils which now and then disturb its ideal beauty, it is for a truly noble heart the happiest path of life. It was the path which I had once chosen for myself, and how I wish I had been allowed to follow it!"

I could quote to you the words of another Prussian ambassador, Bunsen. He, too, often complained with sadness that he had missed his true path in life. He too, would gladly have exchanged the noisy hotel of the ambassador for the quiet home of a German professor.

From my earliest youth it has been the goal of my life to act as a professor in a German university, and if this dream of my youth was not to be fulfilled in its entirety, I feel all the more grateful that, through the kindness of my friends and German colleagues, I have been allowed, at least once in my life, to act during the present spring and summer as a real German professor in a German university.

This was in my heart, and I wanted to say it, in order that you might know with what purpose I have come, and with what real joy I begin the work which has brought us together to-day.

I shall lecture during the present term on "The Results of the Science of Language;" but you will easily understand that to sum up in one course of lectures the results of researches which have been carried on with unflagging industry by three generations of scholars, would be a sheer impossibility. Besides, a mere detailing of results, though it is possible, is hardly calculated to subserve the real objects of academic teaching. You would not be satisfied with mere results: you want to know and to understand the method by which they have been obtained. You want to follow step by step that glorious progress of discovery which has led us to where we stand now. What is the use of knowing the Pythagorean problem, if we cannot prove it? What would be the use of knowing that the French *larme* is the same as the German *Zähre* (tear), if we could not with mathematical exactness trace every step by which these two words have diverged till they became what they are?

The results of the Science of Language are enormous. There is no sphere of intellectual activity which has not felt more or less the influence of this new science. Nor is this to be wondered at. Language is the organ of all knowledge, and though we flatter ourselves that we are the lords of language, that we use it as a useful tool, and no more, believe me there are but few who can maintain their complete independence with respect to language, few who can say of her, Ἔχω Λαΐδα, οὐκ ἔχομαι. To know language historically and genetically, to be able more particularly to follow up the growth of our technical terms to their very roots, this is in every science the best means to keep up a living connection between the past and the present, the only way to make us feel the ground on which we stand.

Let us begin with what is nearest to us, *Philology*. Its whole character has been changed as if by magic. The two classical languages, Greek and Latin, which looked as if they had fallen from the sky or been found behind the hedge, have now recovered their title-deeds, and have taken their legitimate place in that old and noble family which we call the Indo-European, the Indo-Germanic, or by a shorter, if not a better name, the Aryan. In this way not only have their antecedents been cleared up, but their mutual relationship, too, has for the first time been placed in its proper light. The idea that Latin was derived from Greek, an idea excusable in scholars of the Scipionic period, or that Latin was a language made up of Italic, Greek, and Pelasgic elements, a view that had maintained itself to the time of Niebuhr, all this has now been shown to be a physical impossibility. Greek and Latin stand together on terms of perfect equality; they are sisters, like French and Italian:—

"Facies non omnibus una,

Nec diversa tamen qualem decet esse sororum."

If it could be a scientific question which of the two is the elder sister, Greek or Latin, Latin, I believe, could produce better claims of seniority than Greek. Now, as in the modern history of language we are able to explain many things that are obscure in French and Italian by calling in the Provençal, the Spanish, the Portuguese, nay, even the Wallachian and the Churwälsch, we can do the same in the ancient history of language, and get light for many things which are difficult and unintelligible in Greek and Latin, by consulting Sanskrit, Zend, Gothic, Irish, and even Old Bulgarian. We can hardly form an idea of the surprise which was occasioned among the scholars of Europe by the discovery of the Aryan family of languages, reaching with its branches from the Himalayan mountains to the Pyrenees. Not that scholars of any eminence believed at the end of the last century that Greek and Latin were derived from Hebrew: that prejudice had been disposed of once for all, in Germany at least, by Leibniz. But after that theory had been given up, no new truly scientific theory had taken its place. The languages of the world, with the exception of the Semitic, the family type of which was not to be mistaken, lay scattered about as *disjecta membra poëtæ*, and no one thought of uniting them again into one organic whole. It was the discovery of Sanskrit which led to the reunion of the Aryan languages, and if Sanskrit had taught us nothing else, this alone would establish its claim to a place among the academic sciences of our century.

When Greek and Latin had once been restored to their true place in the natural system of the Aryan languages, their special treatment, too, became necessarily a different one. In grammar, for instance, scholars were no longer satisfied to give forms and rules, and to place what was irregular by the side of what was regular. They wished to know the reasons of the rules as well as of the exceptions; they asked why the forms were such as they were, and not otherwise; they required not only a logical, but also an historical foundation of grammar. People asked themselves for the first time, why so small a change as *mensa* and *mensæ* could express the difference between one and many tables; why a single letter, like *r*, could possess the charm of changing I love, *amo*, into I am loved, *amor*. Instead of indulging in general speculations on the logic of grammar, the riddles of grammar received their solution from a study of the historical development of language. For every language there was to be a historical grammar, and in this way a revolution was produced in philological studies to be compared only to the revolution produced in chemistry by the discoveries of Lavoisier, or in geology by the theories of Lyell. For instance, instead of attempting an explanation why the genitive singular and the ablative plural of the first and second declensions could express rest in a place—*Romæ*, at Rome; *Tarenti*, at Tarentum; *Athenis*, at Athens; *Gabiis*, at Gabii—one glance at the past history of these languages showed that these so-called genitives were not and never had been genitives, but corresponded to the old locatives in *i* and *su* in Sanskrit. No doubt, a pupil can be made to learn anything that stands in a grammar; but I do not believe that it can conduce to a sound development of his intellectual powers if he first learns at school the real meaning of the genitive and ablative, and then has to accept on trust that, somehow or other, the same cases may express rest in a place. A well-known English divine, opposed to reform in spelling, as in everything else, once declared that the fearful orthography of English formed the best psychological foundation of English orthodoxy, because a child that had once been brought to believe that t-h-r-o-u-g-h sounded like "through," t-h-o-u-g-h like "though," r-o-u-g-h like "rough," would afterwards believe anything. Be that as it may, I do not consider that grammatical rules like those just quoted on the genitive and ablative, assuming the power of the locative, are likely to strengthen the reasoning powers of any schoolboy.

Even more pernicious to the growth of sound ideas was the study of etymology, as formerly carried on in schools and universities. Everything here was left to chance or to authority, and it was not unusual that two or three etymologies of the same word had to be learnt, as if the same word might have had more than one parent. Yet it is many years since Otfried Müller told classical scholars that they must either surrender the whole subject of the historical growth of language, etymology, and grammatical morphology, or trust in these matters entirely to the guidance of Comparative Philology. As a student at Leipzig, I lived to see old Gottfried Hermann quoting the paradigms of Sanskrit grammar in one of his last *Programs*; and

Boeckh declared in 1850, at the eleventh meeting of German philologists, that, in the present state of the science of language, the grammar of the classical languages cannot dispense with the coöperation of comparative grammar. And yet there are scholars even now who would exclude the Science of Language from schools and universities. What gigantic steps truly scientific etymology has made in Greek and Latin, every scholar may see in the excellent works of Curtius and Corssen. The essential difference between the old and the new systems consists here, too, in this, that while formerly people were satisfied if they knew, or imagined they knew, from what source a certain word was derived, little value is now attached to the mere etymology of a word, unless at the same time it is possible to account, according to fixed phonetic laws, for all the changes which a word has undergone in its passage through Latin, Greek, and Sanskrit. How far this conscientiousness may be carried is shown by the fact that the best comparative philologists decline to admit, on phonetic grounds, the identity of such words as the Latin *Deus*, and the Greek Θεός, although the strongest internal arguments may be urged in favor of the identity of these words.[1,A]

Let us go on to *Mythology*. If mythology is an old dialect, outliving itself, and, on the strength of its sacred character, carried on to a new period of language, it is easy to perceive that the historical method of the Science of Language would naturally lead here to most important results. Take only the one fact, which no one at present would dare to question, that the name of the highest deity among the Greeks and Romans, Ζεύς, and *Jupiter*, is the same as the Vedic *Dyaus*, the sky, and the old German *Zio*, Old Norse *Tyr*, whose name survives in the modern names of *Dienstag* or *Tuesday*. Does not this one word prove the union of those ancient races? Does it not show us, at the earliest dawn of history, the fathers of the Aryan race, the fathers of our own race, gathered together in the great temple of nature, like brothers of the same house, and looking up in adoration to the sky as the emblem of what they yearned for, a father and a God. Nay, can we not hear in that old name of *Jupiter*, i.e., Heaven-Father, the true key-note which still sounds on in our own prayer, "Our Father which art in heaven," and which imparts to these words their deepest tone, and their fullest import? By an accurate study of these words we are able to draw the bonds of language and belief even more closely together. You know that the nom. sing. of Ζεύς has the acute, and so has the nom. sing. of *Dyaus*; but the vocative of Ζεύς has the circumflex, and so has likewise the vocative of *Dyaus* in the Veda.[2,B] Formerly the accent might have been considered as something late, artificial, and purely grammatical: the Science of Language has shown that it is as old as language itself, and it has rightly called it the very soul of words. Thus even in these faint pulsations of language, in the changes of accent in Greek and Sanskrit, may we feel the common blood that runs in the veins of the old Aryan dialects.

History, too, particularly the most ancient history, has received new light and life from a comparative study of languages. Nations and languages were in ancient times almost synonymous, and what constitutes the ideal unity of a nation lies far more in the intellectual factors, in religion and language, than in common descent and common blood. But for that very reason we must here be most cautious. It is but too easily forgotten that if we speak of Aryan and Semitic families, the ground of classification is language, and language only. There are Aryan and Semitic languages, but it is against all rules of logic to speak, without an expressed or implied qualification, of an Aryan race, of Aryan blood, of Aryan skulls, and to attempt ethnological classification on purely linguistic grounds. These two sciences, the Science of Language and the Science of Man, cannot, at least for the present, be kept too much asunder; and many misunderstandings, many controversies, would have been avoided, if scholars had not attempted to draw conclusions from language to blood, or from blood to language. When each of these sciences shall have carried out independently its own classification of men and of languages, then, and then only, will it be time to compare their results; but even then, I must repeat, what I have said many times before, it would be as wrong to speak of Aryan blood as of dolichocephalic grammar.3

We have all accustomed ourselves to look for the cradle of the Aryan languages in Asia, and to imagine these dialects flowing like streams from the centre of Asia to the South, the West, and the North. I must confess that Professor Benfey's protest against this theory seems to me very opportune, and his arguments in favor of a more northern, if not European, origin of the whole Aryan family of speech, deserve, at all events, far more attention than they have hitherto received.

For the same reasons it seems to me at least a premature undertaking to use the greater or smaller number of coincidences between two or more of the Aryan languages as arguments in support of an earlier or later separation of the people who spoke them. First of all, there are few points on which the opinions of competent judges differ more decidedly than when the exact degrees of relationship between the single Aryan languages have to be settled. There is agreement on one point only, viz., that Sanskrit and Zend are more closely united than any other languages. But though on this point there can hardly be any doubt, no satisfactory explanation of this extraordinary agreement has as yet been given. In fact, it has been doubted whether what I called the "Southern Division" of the Aryan family could properly be called a division at all, as it consisted only of varieties of one and the same type of Aryan speech. As soon as we go beyond Sanskrit and Zend, the best authorities are found to be in open conflict. Bopp maintained that the Slavonic languages were most closely allied to Sanskrit, an opinion shared by Pott. Grimm, on the contrary, maintained a closer relationship between

Slavonic and German. In this view he was supported by Lottner, Schleicher, and others, while Bopp to the last opposed it. After this, Schleicher (as, before him, Newman in England) endeavored to prove a closer contact between Celtic and Latin, and, accepting Greek as most closely united with Latin, he proceeded to establish a Southwestern European division, consisting of Celtic, Latin, and Greek, and running parallel with the Northwestern division, consisting of Teutonic and Slavonic; or, according to Ebel, of Celtic, Teutonic, and Slavonic.

But while these scholars classed Greek with Latin, others, such as Grassmann and Sonne, pointed out striking peculiarities which Greek shares with Sanskrit, and with Sanskrit only, as, for instance, the augment, the voiceless aspirates, the *alpha privativum* (a, not an), the *mâ* and μή *prohibitivum*, the *tara* and τερο as the suffix of the comparative, and some others. A most decided divergence of opinion manifested itself as touching the real relation of Greek and Latin. While some regarded these languages not only as sisters, but as twins, others were not inclined to concede to them any closer relationship than that which unites all the members of the Aryan family. While this conflict of opinions lasts (and they are not mere assertions, but opinions supported by arguments), it is clear that it would be premature to establish any historical conclusions, such, for instance, as that the Slaves remained longer united with the Indians and Persians than the Greeks, Romans, Germans, and Celts; or, if we follow Professor Sonne, that the Greeks remained longer united with the Indians than the other Aryan nations. I must confess that I doubt whether the whole problem admits of a scientific solution. If in a large family of languages we discover closer coincidences between some languages than between others, this is no more than we should expect, according to the working of what I call the Dialectic Process. All these languages sprang up and grew and diverged, before they were finally separated; some retained one form, others another, so that even the apparently most distant members of the same family might, on certain points, preserve relics in common which were lost in all the other dialects, and *vice versâ*. No two languages, not even Lithuanian and Old Slavonic, are so closely united as Sanskrit and Zend, which share together even technical terms, connected with a complicated sacrificial ceremonial. Yet there are words occurring in Zend, and absent in Sanskrit, which crop up again sometimes in Greek, sometimes in Latin, sometimes in German.4,C As soon as we attempt to draw from such coincidences and divergences historical conclusions as to the earlier or later separation of the nations who developed these languages, we fall into contradictions like those which I pointed out just now between Bopp, Grimm, Schleicher, Ebel, Grassmann, Sonne, and others. Much depends, in all scientific researches, on seeing that the question is properly put. To me the question, whether the closer relations between certain independent dialects furnish evidence as to the successive times of their separation, seems, by its very nature, fruitless. Nor have the answers been at all satisfactory. After a number of coincidences between the various members of the Aryan family have been carefully collected, we know no more in the end than what we knew at first, viz., that all the Aryan dialects are closely connected with each other. We know—

1. That Slavonic is most closely united with German (Grimm, Schleicher);

2. That German is most closely united with Celtic (Ebel, Lottner);

3. That Celtic is most closely united with Latin (Newman, Schleicher);

4. That Latin is most closely united with Greek (Mommsen, Curtius);

5. That Greek is most closely united with Sanskrit (Grassmann, Sonne, Kern);

6. That Sanskrit is most closely united with Zend (Burnouf).

Let a mathematician draw out the result, and it will be seen that we know in the end no more than we knew at the beginning. Far be it for me to use a mere trick in arguing, and to say that none of these conclusions can be right, because each is contradicted by others. Quite the contrary. I admit that there is some truth in every one of these conclusions, and I maintain, for that very reason, that the only way to reconcile them all is to admit that the single dialects of the Aryan family did not break off in regular succession, but that, after a long-continued community, they separated slowly, and, in some cases, contemporaneously, from their family-circle, till they established at last, under varying circumstances, their complete national independence. This seems to me all that at present one may say with a good conscience, and what is in keeping with the law of development in all dialects.

If now we turn away from the purely philological results of the Science of Language, in order to glance at the advantages which other sciences have derived from it, we shall find that they consist mostly in the light that has been shed on obscure words and old customs. This advantage is greater than, at first sight, it might seem to be. Every word has its history, and the beginning of this history, which is brought to light by etymology, leads us back far beyond its first historical appearance. Every word, as we know, had originally a predicative meaning, and that predicative meaning differs often very considerably from the later traditional or technical meaning. This predicative meaning, however, being the most original meaning of the word, allows us an insight into the most primitive ideas of a nation.

Let us take an instance from jurisprudence. *Pœna*, in classical Latin, means simply punishment, particularly what is either paid or suffered in order to atone for an injury. (*Si injuriam faxit alteri, viginti quinque æris pœnæ sunto, fragm. xii. tab.*) The word agrees so remarkably, both in form and meaning, with the

Greek ποινή, that Mommsen assigned to it a place in what he calls Græco-Italic ideas.5 We might suppose, therefore, that the ancient Italians took *pœna* originally in the sense of ransom, simply as a civil act, by which he who had inflicted injury on another was, as far as he and the injured person were concerned, restored *in integrum*. The etymology of the word, however, leads us back into a far more distant past, and shows us that when the word *pœna* was first framed, punishment was conceived from a higher moral and religious point of view, as a purification from sin; for *pœna*, as first shown by Professor Pott (and what has he not been the first to show?) is closely connected with the root pu, to purify. Thus we read in the "Atharva-veda," xix. 33, 3:—

"Tvám bhúmim átyeshi ójasâ

Tvám védyâm sîdasi cấrur adhvaré

Tvám pavítram ṛshayo bhárantas

Tvám puníhi duritā́ni asmát."

"Thou, O God of Fire, goest mightily across the earth; thou sittest brilliantly on the altar at the sacrifice. The prophets carry Thee as the Purifier; purify us from all misdeeds."

From this root *pu* we have, in Latin, *pūrus*, and *pŭtus*, as in *argentum purum putum*, fine silver, or in *purus putus est ipse*, Plaut. Ps. 4, 2, 31. From it we also have the verb *purgare*, for *purigare*, to purge, used particularly with reference to purification from crime by means of religious observances. If this transition from the idea of purging to that of punishing should seem strange, we have only to think of *castigare*, meaning originally to purify, but afterwards in such expressions as *verbis et verberibus castigare*, to chide and to chasten.

I cannot convince myself that the Latin *crimen* has anything in common with κρίνειν. The Greek κρίνειν is no doubt connected with Latin *cer-no*, from which *cribrum*, sieve. It means to separate, to sift, so that κρῖμα may well signify a judgment, but not a crime or misdeed. *Crīmen*, as every scholar knows or ought to know, meant originally an accusation, not a crime, and, in spite of all appearances to the contrary, has nothing whatever in common with *discrīmen*, which means what separates two things, a difference, a critical point. *In crimen venire* means to get into bad repute, to be calumniated; *in discrimine esse* means to be in a critical and dangerous position.

It is one of the fundamental laws of etymology that in tracing words back to their roots, we have to show that their primary, not their secondary meanings agree with the meaning of the root. Therefore, even if *crīmen* had assumed in later times the meaning of judgment, yet its derivation from the Greek κρίνειν would have to be rejected, because it would explain the secondary only, but not the primary meaning of *crīmen*. Nothing is clearer than the historical development of the meanings of *crīmen*, beginning with accusation, and ending with guilt.

I believe I have proved that *crīmen* is really and truly the same word as the German *Verleumdung*, calumny.6 *Verleumdung* comes from *Leumund*, the Old High-German *hliumunt*, and this *hliumunt* is the exact representative of the Vedic *śromata*, derived from the root *śru*, to hear, *cluere*, and signifying good report, glory, the Greek κλέος, the Old High-German *hruom*. The German word *Leumund* can be used in a good and a bad sense, as good or evil report, while the Latin *crī-men*, for *croe-men* (like *liber* for *loeber*), is used only *in malam partem*. It meant originally what is heard, report, *on dit*, gossip, accusation; lastly, the object of an accusation, a crime, but never judgment, in the technical sense of the word.

The only important objection that could be raised against tracing *crīmen* back to the root *śru*, is that this root has in the Northwestern branch of the Aryan family assumed the form *clu*, instead of *cru*, as in κλέος, *cliens*, *gloria*, O.Sl. *slovo*, A.S. *hlûd*, loud, *inclutus*. I myself hesitated for a long time on account of this phonetic difficulty, nor do I think it is quite removed by the fact that Bopp ("Comp. Gr." § 20) identified the German *scrir-u-mês*, we cry (instead of *scriw-u-mês*), with Sk. *śrâv-ayâ-mas*, we make hear; nor by the *r* in *in-cre-p-are*, in κράζω, as compared with κλάζω, nor even by the *r* in ἀ-κρο-ά-ομαι, which Curtius seems inclined to derive from *śru*. The question is whether this phonetic difficulty is such as to force us to surrender the common origin of *śromata*, *hliumunt*, and *crīmen*; but even if this should be the case, the derivation of *crīmen* from *cerno* or κρίνειν would remain as impossible as ever.

This will give you an idea in what manner the Science of Language can open before our eyes a period in the history of law, customs, and manners, which hitherto was either entirely closed, or reached only by devious paths. Formerly, for instance, it was supposed that the Latin word *lex*, law, was connected with the Greek λόγος. This is wrong, for λόγος never means law in the sense in which *lex* does. λόγος, from λέγειν, to collect, to gather, signifies, like κατάλογος, a gathering, a collection, an ordering, be it of words or thoughts. The idea that there is a λόγος, an order or law, for instance, in nature, is not classical, but purely modern. It is not improbable that *lex* is connected with the English word *law*, only not by way of the Norman *loi*. English *law* is A.S. *lagu* (as *saw* corresponds both to the German *Sage* and *Säge*), and it meant originally what was laid down or settled, with exactly the same conception as the German *Gesetz*. It has been attempted to derive the Latin *lex*, too, from the same root, though there is this difficulty, that the root of *liegen* and *legen* does not elsewhere occur in Latin. The mere disappearance of the aspiration would be no serious obstacle. If, however, the Latin *lex* cannot be derived from that root, we must, with Corssen, refer it to the same cluster of words to which *ligare*, to bind, *obligatio*, binding, and the Oscan ablative *lig-ud* belong, and assign to it the original meaning of *bond*. On no account can it be derived from *legere*, to read, as if it meant a bill first read before the people, and afterwards receiving legal sanction by their approval.

From these considerations we gain at least this negative result, that, before their separation, the Aryan languages had no settled word for law; and even such negative results have their importance. The Sanskrit word for law is *dharma*, derived from *dhar*, to hold fast. The Greek word is νόμος, derived from νέμειν, to dispense, from which *Nemesis*, the dispensing deity, and perhaps even *Numa*, the name of the fabulous king and lawgiver of Rome.

Other words might easily be added which, by the disclosure of their original meaning, give us interesting hints as to the development of legal conceptions and customs, such as marriage, inheritance, ordeals, and the like. But it is time to cast a glance at theology, which, more even than jurisprudence, has experienced the influence of the Science of Language. What was said with regard to mythology, applies with equal force to theology. Here, too, words harden, and remain unchanged longer even than in other spheres of intellectual life; nay, their influence often becomes greater the more they harden, and the more their original meaning is forgotten. Here it is most important that an intelligent theologian should be able to follow up the historical development of the *termini technici* and *sacrosancti* of his science. Not only words like *priest, bishop, sacrament,* or *testament*, have to be correctly apprehended in that meaning which they had in the first century, but expressions like λόγος, πνεῦμα ἅγιον, δικαιοσύνη have to be traced historically to the beginnings of Christianity, and beyond, if we wish to gain a conception of their full purport.

In addition to this, the Philosophy of Religion, which must always form the true foundation of theological science, owes it to the Science of Language that the deepest germs of the consciousness of God among the different nations of the world have for the first time been laid open. We know now with perfect certainty that the names, that is, the most original conceptions, of the Deity among the Aryan nations, are as widely removed from coarse fetichism as from abstract idealism. The Aryans, as far as the annals of their language allow us to see, recognized the presence of the Divine in the bright and sunny aspects of nature, and they, therefore, called the blue sky, the fertile earth, the genial fire, the bright day, the golden dawn their *Devas*, that is, their bright ones. The same word, *Deva* in Sanskrit, *Deus* in Latin, remained unchanged in all their prayers, their rites, their superstitions, their philosophies, and even to-day it rises up to heaven from thousands of churches and cathedrals,—a word which, before there were Brahmans or Germans, had been framed in the dark workshop of the Aryan mind.

That the natural sciences, too, should have felt the electric shock of our new science is not surprising, considering that man is the crown of nature, the apex to which all other forces of nature point and tend. But that which makes man man, is language. *Homo animal rationale, quia orationale*, as Hobbes said. Buffon called the plant a sleeping animal; living philosophers speak of the animal as a dumb man. Both, however, forget that the plant would cease to be a plant if it awoke, and that the brute would cease to be a brute the moment it began to speak. There is, no doubt, in language a transition from the material to the spiritual: the raw material of language belongs to nature, but the form of language, that which really makes language, belongs to the spirit. Were it possible to trace human language *directly* back to natural sounds, to interjections or imitations, the question whether the Science of Language belongs to the sphere of the natural or the historical sciences would at once be solved. But I doubt whether this crude view of the origin of language counts one single supporter in Germany. With one foot language stands, no doubt, in the realm of nature, but with the other in the realm of the spirit. Some years ago, when I thought it necessary to bring out as clearly as possible the much neglected natural element in language, I tried to explain in what sense the Science of Language had a right to be called the last and the highest of the natural sciences. But I need hardly say that I did not lose sight, therefore, of the intellectual and historical character of language; and I may here express my conviction that the Science of Language will yet enable us to withstand the extreme theories of the evolutionists, and to draw a hard and fast line between spirit and matter, between man and brute.

This short survey must suffice to show you how omnipresent the Science of Language has become in all spheres of human knowledge, and how far its limits have been extended, so that it often seems impossible for one man to embrace the whole of its vast domain. From this I wish, in conclusion, to draw some necessary advice.

Whoever devotes himself to the study of so comprehensive a science must try never to lose sight of two virtues: conscientiousness and modesty. The older we grow, the more we feel the limits of human knowledge. "Good care is taken," as Goethe said, "that trees should not grow into the sky." Every one of us can make himself real master of a small field of knowledge only, and what we gain in extent, we inevitably lose in depth. It was impossible that Bopp should know Sanskrit like Colebrooke, Zend like Burnouf, Greek like Hermann, Latin like Lachmann, German like Grimm, Slavonic like Miklosich, Celtic like Zeuss. That drawback lies in the nature of all comparative studies. But it follows by no means that, as the French proverb says, *qui trop embrasse, mal étreint*. Bopp's "Comparative Grammar" will always mark an epoch in linguistic studies, and no one has accused the old master of superficiality. There are, in fact, two kinds of knowledge; the one which we take in as real nourishment, which we convert *in succum et sanguinem*, which is always present, which we can never lose; the other which, if I may say so, we put into our pockets, in order to find it there whenever it is wanted. For comparative studies the second kind of knowledge is as important as the first, but in order to use it properly, the greatest conscientiousness is required. Not only ought we, whenever we have to use it, to go back to the original sources, to accept nothing on trust, to quote nothing at second-hand, and to verify every single point before we rely on it for comparative purposes, but, even after we have done everything to guard against error, we ought to proceed with the greatest caution and modesty. I consider, for instance, that an accurate knowledge of Sanskrit is a *conditio sine quâ non* in the study of Comparative Philology. According to my conviction, though I know it is not shared by others, Sanskrit must forever remain the central point of our studies. But it is clearly impossible for us, while engaged in a scholarlike study of Sanskrit, to follow at the same time the gigantic strides of Latin, Greek, German, Slavonic, and Celtic philology. Here we must learn to be satisfied with what is possible, and apply for advice whenever we want it, to those who are masters in these different departments of philology. Much has of late been said of the antagonism between comparative and classical philology. To me it seems that these two depend so much on each other for help and advice that their representatives ought to be united by the closest ties of fellowship. We must work on side by side, and accept counsel as readily as we give it. Without the help of Comparative Philology, for instance, Greek scholars would never have arrived at a correct understanding of the Digamma—nay, a freer intercourse with his colleague, Bopp, would have preserved Bekker from several mistakes in his restoration of the Digamma in Homer. Latin scholars would have felt far more hesitation in introducing the old *d* of the ablative in Plautus, if the analogy of Sanskrit had not so clearly proved its legitimacy.

On the other hand, we, comparative philologists, should readily ask and gladly accept the advice and help of our classical colleagues. Without their guidance, we can never advance securely; their warnings are to us of the greatest advantage, their approval our best reward. We are often too bold, we do not see all the difficulties that stand in the way of our speculations, we are too apt to forget that, in addition to its general Aryan character, every language has its peculiar genius. Let us all be on our guard against omniscience and infallibility. Only through a frank, honest, and truly brotherly coöperation can we hope for a true advancement of knowledge. We all want the same thing; we all are *etymologists*—that is, lovers of truth. For this, before all things, the spirit of truth, which is the living spirit of all science, must dwell within us. Whoever cannot yield to the voice of truth, whoever cannot say, "I was wrong," knows little as yet of the true spirit of science.

Allow me, in conclusion, to recall to your remembrance another passage from Niebuhr. He belongs to the good old race of German scholars. "Above all things," he writes, "we must in all scientific pursuits preserve our truthfulness so pure that we thoroughly eschew every false appearance; that we represent not even the smallest thing as certain of which we are not completely convinced; that if we have to propose a conjecture, we spare no effort in representing the exact degree of its probability. If we do not ourselves, when it is possible, indicate our errors, even such as no one else is likely to discover; if, in laying down our pen, we cannot say in the sight of God, 'Upon strict examination, I have knowingly written nothing that is not true;' and if, without deceiving either ourselves or others, we have not presented even our most odious opponents in such a light only that we could justify it upon our death-beds—if we cannot do this, study and literature serve only to make us unrighteous and sinful."

Few, I fear, could add, with Niebuhr: "In this I am convinced that I do not require from others anything of which a higher spirit, if He could read my soul, could convict me of having done the contrary." But all of us, young as well as old, should keep these words before our eyes and in our hearts. Thus, and thus only, will our studies not miss their highest goal: thus, and thus only, may we hope to become true etymologists—*i.e.*, true lovers, seekers, and, I trust, finders of truth.

NOTES.

NOTE A.
Θεός AND Deus.

THAT Greek θ does not legitimately represent a Sanskrit, Latin, Slavonic, and Celtic *d* is a fact that ought never to have been overlooked by comparative philologists, and nothing could be more useful than the strong protest entered by Windischmann, Schleicher, Curtius, and others, against the favorite identification of Sk. *deva*, *deus*, and θεός. Considering it as one of the first duties, in all etymological researches, that we should pay implicit obedience to phonetic laws, I have never, so far as I remember, quoted θεός as identical with *deus*, together with the other derivatives of the root *div*, such as *Dyaus*, Ζεύς, *Jupiter*, *deva*, Lith. *deva-s*, Irish *día*.

But with all due respect for phonetic laws, I have never in my own heart doubted that θεός belonged to the same cluster of words which the early Aryans employed to express the brightness of the sky and of the day, and which helped them to utter their first conception of a god of the bright sky (*Dyaus*), of bright beings in heaven, as opposed to the powers of night and darkness and winter (*deva*), and, lastly, of deity in the abstract.7 I have never become an atheist; and though I did not undervalue the powerful arguments advanced against the identity of *deus* and θεός, I thought that other arguments also possessed their value, and could not be ignored with impunity. If, with our eyes shut, we submit to the dictates of phonetic laws, we are forced to believe that while the Greeks shared with the Hindus, the Italians, and Germans the name for the bright god of the sky Zeus, *Dyaus, Jovis, Zio*, and while they again shared with them such derivatives as δῖος, heavenly, Sk. *divyas*, they threw away the intermediate old Aryan word for god, *deva, deus*, and formed a new one from a different root, but agreeing with the word which they had rejected in all letters but one. I suppose that even the strongest supporters of the atheistic theory would have accepted δεός, if it existed in Greek, as a correlative of *deva* and *deus*; and I ask, would it not be an almost incredible coincidence, if the Greeks, after giving up the common Aryan word, which would have been δοιϝός or δειϝός or δεϝός, had coined a new word for god from a different root, yet coming so near to δεϝός as θεϝός? These internal difficulties seem to me nearly as great as the external: at all events it would not be right to attempt to extenuate either.

Now I think that, though much has been said against θεός for δεϝός, something may also be said in support of δεϝός assuming the form of θεός. Curtius is quite right in repelling all arguments derived from Sk. *duhitar* = θυγάτηρ, or Sk. *dvâr* = θύρ-α; but I think he does not do full justice to the argument derived from φιάλη and φιαρός. The Greek φιάλη has been explained as originally πιϝάλη, the lost digamma causing the aspiration of the initial π. Curtius says: "This etymology of φιάλη is wrecked on the fact that in Homer the word does not mean a vessel for drinking, but a kind of kettle." That is true, but the fact remains that in later Greek φιάλη means a drinking cup. Thus Pindar ("Isthm.," v. 58) says:—

Ἄνδωκε δ' αὐτῷ φέρτατος

οἰνοδόκον φιάλαν χρυσῷ πεφρικυῖαν Τελαμών,

which refers clearly to a golden goblet, and not a kettle. Besides, we have an exactly analogous case in the Sk. *pâtram*. This, too, is clearly derived from *pâ*, to drink, but it is used far more frequently in the sense of vessel in general, and its etymological meaning vanishes altogether when it comes to mean a vessel for something, a fit person. I see no etymology for φιάλη, except πιϝάλη, a drinking vessel.

Secondly, as to φιαρός, which is supposed to be the same as πιαρός, and to represent the Sanskrit *pívaras*, fat, Curtius says that it occurs in Alexandrian poets only, that it there means bright, resplendent, and is used as an adjective of the dawn, while πιαρός means fat, and fat only. Against this I venture to remark, first, that there are passages where φιαρός means sleek, as in Theocr. ii. 21, φιαρωτέρα ὄμφακος ὠμᾶς, said of a young plump girl, who in Sanskrit would be called *pívarî*; secondly, that while πῖαρ is used for cream, φιαρός is used as an adjective of cream; and, thirdly, that the application of φιαρός to the dawn is hardly surprising, if we remember the change of meaning in λιπαρός in Greek, and the application in the Veda of such words as *ghṛta pratîka*, to the dawn. Lastly, as in φιάλη, I see no etymology for φιαρός, except πιϝαρός.

I think it is but fair therefore to admit that θεός for δεϝός would find some support by the analogy of φιάλη for πιϝάλη, and of φιαρός for πιϝαρός. There still remain difficulties enough to make us cautious in asserting the identity of θεός and *deus*; but in forming our own opinion these difficulties should be weighed impartially against the internal difficulties involved in placing θεός as a totally independent word, by the side of *deva* and *deus*. And, as in φιάλη and φιαρός, may we not say of θεός also that there is no etymology for it, if we separate it from Ζεύς and δῖος, from *Dyaus* and *divyas*? Curtius himself rejects Plato's and Schleicher's derivation of θεός from θέω, to run: likewise C. Hoffmann's from *dhava*, man; likewise Bühler's from a root *dhi*, to think or to shine; likewise that of Herodotus and A. Göbel from θες, a secondary form of θε, to settle. Ascoli's analysis is highly sagacious, but it is too artificial. Ascoli[8] identifies θεός, not with *deva*, but with *divyá-s*. *Divyás* becoming διϝεός (like *satya*, ἐτεός), the accent on the last syllable would produce the change to δϝεό-ς, ϝ would cause aspiration in the preceding consonant and then disappear, leaving θεός = *divyás*. All these changes are just possible phonetically, but, as Curtius observes, the point for which the theists contend is not gained, for we should still have to admit that the Greeks lost the common word for god, *deva* and *deus*, and that they alone replaced it by a derivative *divya*, meaning heavenly, not bright.

Curtius himself seems in favor of deriving θεός from θες, to implore, which we have in θεσ-σάμενοι, θέσσαντο, πολύθεστος, etc. Θεός, taken as a passive derivative, might, he thinks, have the meaning of ἀρητός in πολυάρητος, and mean the implored being. I cannot think that this is a satisfactory derivation. It might be defended phonetically and etymologically, though I cannot think of any analogous passive derivatives of a root ending in *s*. Where it fails to carry conviction is in leaving unexplained the loss of the common Aryan word for deity, and in putting in its place a name that savors of very modern thought.

I think the strongest argument against the supposed aspirating power of medial *v*, and its subsequent disappearance, lies in the fact that there are so many words having medial *v*, which show no trace of this phonetic process (Curtius, p. 507). On the other hand, it should be borne in mind, that the Greeks might have felt a natural objection to the forms which would have rendered *deva* with real exactness, I mean δοιός or δέος, the former conveying the meaning of double, the latter of fear. A mere wish to keep the name for god distinct from these words might have produced the phonetic anomaly of which we complain; and, after all, though I do not like to use that excuse, there are exceptions to phonetic laws. No one can explain how ὄγδοος was derived from ὀκτώ or ἕβδομος from ἑπτά, yet the internal evidence is too strong to be shaken by phonetic objections. In the case of θεός and *deus* the internal evidence seems to me nearly as strong as in ὄγδοος and ἕβδομος, and though unwilling to give a final verdict, I think the question of the loss in Greek of the Aryan word for god and its replacement by another word nearly identical in form, but totally distinct in origin, should be left for the present an open question in Comparative Philology.

NOTE B.
THE VOCATIVE OF *Dyaús* AND Ζεύς.

THE vocative of *Dyaús*, having the circumflex, is one of those linguistic gems which one finds now and then in the Rig-Veda, and which by right ought to have a place of honor in a Museum of Antiquities. It is a unique form. It occurs but once in the Rig-Veda, never again, as far as we know at present, in the whole of Vedic literature, and yet it is exactly that form which a student of language would expect who is familiar with the working of the laws of accent in Sanskrit and in Greek. Without a thorough knowledge of these laws, the circumflexed vocative in Sanskrit, *Dyaús*, corresponding to Greek Ζεῦ, would seem a mere anomaly, possibly an accidental coincidence, whereas in reality it affords the most striking proof of the organic working of the laws of accent, and at the same time an unanswerable testimony in favor of the genuineness of the ancient of the Rig-Veda.

The laws of accent bearing on this circumflexed vocative are so simple that I thought they would have been understood by everybody. As this does not seem to have been the case, I add a few explanatory remarks.

It was Benfey who, as on so many other points, so on the accent of vocatives, was the first to point out (in 1845) that it was a fundamental law of the Aryan language to place the acute on the first syllable of all vocatives, both in the singular, and in the dual and plural.9 In Sanskrit this law admits of no exception; in Greek and Latin the rhythmic accent has prevailed to that extent that we only find a few traces left of the original Aryan accentuation. It is well known that in vocatives of nouns ending in *ius*, the ancient Romans preserved the accent on the first syllable, that they said *Vírgili*, *Váleri*, from *Virgílius* and *Valérius*. This statement of Nigidius Figulus, preserved by Gellius, though with the remark that in his time no one would say so, is the only evidence of the former existence of the Aryan law of accentuation in Latin. In Greek the evidence is more considerable, but the vocatives with the accent on the first syllable are, by the supreme law of the rhythmic accent in Greek, reduced to vocatives, drawing back their accent as far as they can, consistently with the law which restricts the accent to the last three syllables. Thus while in Sanskrit a word like Ἀγαμέμνων would in the vocative retract the accent on the first syllable Ἄγαμεμνον, the Greek could do no more than say Ἀγάμεμνον with the accent on the antepenultimate. In the same manner the vocative of Ἀριστοτέλης, can only be Ἀριστότελες, whereas in Sanskrit it would have been Ἄριστοτελες.

Here, however, the question arises, whether in words like Ἀγαμέμνων10 and Ἀριστοτέλης11 the accent was not originally on the antepenultimate, but drawn on the penultimate by the rhythmic law. This is certainly the case in ἥδιον, as the vocative of ἡδίων, for we know that both in Sanskrit and Greek, comparatives in ιων retract their accent as far as possible, and have it always on the first syllable in Sanskrit, always on the penultimate in Greek, if the last syllable is long. But, *cessante causâ cessat effectus*, and therefore the accent goes back on the antepenultimate, not only in the vocative, but likewise in the nom. neuter ἥδιον.

It is possible that the same process may explain the vocative δέσποτα from δεσπότης, if we compare Sanskrit compounds with *pati*, such as *dâsápati*, *gā́spati*, *dámpati*, which leave the accent on the first member of the compound. In Δημήτηρ also all becomes regular, if we admit the original accentuation to have been Δήμητηρ, changed in Δημήτηρ, but preserved in the genitive Δήμητρος, and the vocative Δήμητερ.12

But there are other words in which this cannot be the case, for instance, ἄδελφε, πόνηρε, μόχθερε from ἀδελφός, πονηρός, μοχθηρός. Here the accent is the old Aryan vocatival accent. Again, in πατήρ, πατέρα, Sk. *pitā́*, *pitáram*, in μήτηρ, μητέρα, Sk. *mâtā́*, *mâtáram*, in θυγάτηρ, θυγατέρα, Sk. *duhitā́*, *duhitáram*, the radical accent was throughout on the suffix *tár*, nor would the rules of the rhythmic accent in Greek prevent it from being on the antepenultimate in the accusative. The fact therefore that it is retracted on the penultimate and antepenultimate in the vocative, shows clearly that we have here, too, the last working of the original Aryan accentuation. The irregular accent in the nom. sing. of μήτηρ, instead of μητήρ, is probably due to the frequent use of the vocative (an explanation which I had adopted before I had seen Benfey's essay), and the same cause may explain the apparently irregular accentuation in θύγατρα, by the side of θυγατέρα, in θύγατρες, and θύγατρας. Similar vocatives with retracted accent are δᾶερ, nom. δαήρ, εἴνατερ, nom. εἰνάτηρ, γύναι, nom. γυνή, σῶτερ, nom. σωτήρ, ἄνερ, nom. ἀνήρ, Ἄπολλον, nom. Ἀπόλλων, Πόσειδον, nom. Ποσειδῶν, Ἥρακλες, nom. Ἡρακλῆς.

We have thus established the fact that one feature of the primitive Aryan accentuation, which consisted in the very natural process of placing the high accent on the first syllable of vocatives, was strictly preserved in Sanskrit, while in Greek and Latin it only left some scattered traces of its former existence. Without the light derived from Sanskrit, the changes in the accent of vocatives in Greek and Latin would be inexplicable, they would be, what they are in Greek grammar, mere anomalies; while, if placed by the side of Sanskrit, they are readily recognized as what they really are, remnants of a former age, preserved by frequent usage or by an agent whom we do not like to recognize, though we cannot altogether ignore him,—viz. chance.

Taking our position on the fact that change of accent in the vocative in Greek is due to the continued influence of an older system of Aryan accentuation, we now see how the change of nom. Ζεύς into voc. Ζεῦ, and of nom. *Dyaús*, into voc. *Dyaús*, rests on the same principle. In Sanskrit the change, though at first sight irregular, admits of explanation. What we call the circumflex in Sanskrit, is the combination of a rising and falling of the voice, or, as we should say in Greek, of an acute and grave accent. As *Dyaús* was originally *Diaús*, and is frequently used as two syllables in the Veda, the vocative would have been *Díaùs*, and this contracted would become *Dyaus*. Thus we have *paribhvé* from *paribhûs*. In Greek the facts are the same, but the explanation is more difficult. The general rule in Greek is that vocatives in ου, οι, and ευ, from oxytone or perispome nominatives, are perispome; as πλακοῦ, βοῦ, Λητοῖ, Πηλεῦ, βασιλεῦ, from πλακοῦς, οὖντος, placenta, βοῦς, Λητώ, Πηλεύς, βασιλεύς. The rationale of that rule has never been explained, as far as Greek is concerned. Under this rule the vocative of Ζεύς becomes Ζεῦ; but no Greek grammarian has attempted to explain the process by which Ζεύς becomes Ζεῦ, and nothing remains for the present but to admit that we have in it an ancient Aryan relic preserved in Greek long after the causes which had produced it had ceased to act. It would fall into the same category as εἶμι and ἴμεν. Here, too, the efficient cause of the length and shortness of the radical vowel *i*, viz., the change of accent, Sk. *émi*, but *imás*, has disappeared in Greek, while its effect has been preserved. But whatever explanation may hereafter be adopted, the simple fact which I had pointed out remains, the motive power which changed the nom. *dyaús* into the vocative *dyaús*, is the same which changed Ζεύς into Ζεῦ. Those who do not understand, or do not admit this, are bound to produce, from the resources of Greek itself, another motive power to account for the change of Ζεύς into Ζεῦ; but they must not imagine that a mere reference to a Greek elementary grammar suffices for explaining that process.

The passage in the Rig-Veda (VI. 51, 5) to which I referred is unique, and I therefore give it here, though it has in the meantime been most ably discussed by Benfey in his "Essay on the Vocative" (1872).

"Dyaúḥ pítaḥ pṛthivi mā́taḥ ádhruk

Ζεῦ πάτερ πλατεῖα μῆτερ ἀτρεκ(ές)

Ágne bhrā́taḥ vasavaḥ mṛláta naḥ13

Ignis φράτερ Ϝέσηϝες μέλδετε nos."

This passage is clearly one of great antiquity, for it still recognizes *Dyaús*, the father, as the supreme god, Earth, the mother, by his side, and Agni, fire, as the brother, not of Heaven and Earth, but of man, because living with men on the hearth of their houses. *Vasu*, as a general name of the bright gods, like *deva* in other hymns, corresponds, I believe, to the Greek adjective ἐΰς. The genitive plural ἐάων is likewise derived from ἐΰς or *vásus*, by Benfey (l.c. p. 57), and *dâtā́ vásûnâm* (Rv. VIII. 51, 5) comes certainly very near to δοτὴρ ἐάων. The only difficulty would be the ā instead of the η, as in ἐῆος, the gen. sing. of ἐΰς in Homer, a difficulty which might be removed by tracing the gen. plur. ἐάων back to a fem. ἐά, corresponding to a Sk. *vasavî* or *vasavyâ*. As to μέλδετε, it is phonetically the nearest approach to *mṛláta*, i.e., *mardata, though in Greek it means "make mild" rather than "be mild." Mild and *mollis* come from the same root.

What gives to this passage its special value is, that in all other passages when *dyaus* occurs as a vocative and as bisyllabic, it appears simply with the *udâtta*, thus showing at how early a time even the Hindus forgot the meaning of the circumflex on *dyaús*, and its legitimate appearance in that place. Thus in Rv. VIII. 100, 12, we read,—

"Sákhe Vishṇo vitarám ví kramasva,

Dyaúḥ dehí lokám vájrâya viskábhe

Hánâva vṛtrám riṇácâva síndhûn

Índrasya yantu prasavé vísṛshṭâḥ."

- 159 -

"Friend Vishṇu, stride further,

Dyaus give room for the lightning to leap,

Let us both kill Vṛtra and free the rivers,

Let them go, sent forth at the command of Indra."

Here, I have little doubt, the ancient Rishis pronounced *Dyaús*, but the later poets, and the still later *Âcâryas* were satisfied with the acute, and with the acute the word is written here in all the MSS. I know.

NOTE C.
ARYAN WORDS OCCURRING IN ZEND, BUT NOT IN SANSKRIT.

IT has been objected that the three instances which I had quoted of Zend words, not occurring in Sanskrit, but preserved in one or the other of the Indo-European languages, were not sufficient to establish the fact which I wished to establish, particularly as one of them, *kehrp*, existed in Sanskrit, or, at least, in Vedic Sanskrit, as *kṛp*. I admit that I ought to have mentioned the Vedic *kṛp*, rather than the later *kalpa*; but I doubt whether the conclusions which I wished to draw would have been at all affected by this. For what I remarked with regard to *kalpa*, applies with equal force to *kṛp*; it does not in Sanskrit mean body or flesh, like *kehrp*, and *corpus*, but simply form. But even if *kehrp* were not a case in point, nothing would have been easier than to replace it by other words, if at the time of printing my lecture I had had my collectanea at hand. I now subjoin a more complete list of words, present in Zend, absent in Sanskrit, but preserved in Greek, Latin, or German.

Zend *ana*, prep., upon; Greek ἀνά; Goth, *ana*, upon.

Zend *erezataêna*, adj., made of silver; Lat. *argentinus*. In Sk. we have *rajatam*, silver, but no corresponding adjective.

Zend *içi*, ice; O.N. *íss*; A.S. *îs*; O.H.S. *îs*.

Grimm compares the Irish *eirr*, snow, and he remarks that the other Aryan languages have each framed their own words for ice, Lith. *ledas*, O.S. *led*, and distantly connected with these, through the Russian *cholodnyi*, the Latin *glacies*, for *gelacies*, Greek κρύος, κρυμός, κρύσταλλος.

The root from which these Greek words for ice are derived has left several derivatives in other languages, such as Lat. *cru-s-ta*, and O.N. *hrí-m*, rime, hoar-frost, and in Zend *khrûta*, used as an adjective of *zim*, winter, originally the hard winter. In Zend *khrûma*, and *khrûra*, Sk. *krûra*, as in Greek κρυόεις, the meaning has changed to *crudus*, *crudelis*. In the English *raw*, O.H.G. *hrâo*, a similar change of meaning may be observed.

Another name connected with ice and winter is the Zend *zyâo*, frost, from the root *hi*, which has given us χι-ών, Sk. *hi-ma*, Lat. *hiem-s*, O.S. *zima*, but which in the simplest form has been preserved in Zend only and in the O.N. *gę*. Fick quotes *gę* with the doubtful meanings of cold and snow, Curtius with that of storm, identifying it with Norw. *gjö*, *nix autumni recens*.

There is still another name for snow, absent in Sanskrit, but fully represented in Zend and the other Aryan languages, viz., Zend *çnizh*, to snow, Lat. *nix*, Goth. *snaív-s*, Lith. *snig-ti*, to snow, Ir. *snechta*, snow, Gr. νίφ-α (acc).14

Zend *aêva*, one; Gr. οἶος.

Zend *kamara*, girdle, vault; Gr. καμάρα, vault, covered carriage; A.S. *himil*. Connected with this we find the Zend *kameredhe*, skull, vault of head, very nearly connected with κμέλεθρον, μέλαθρον.

Zend *kareta*, knife; Lith. *kalta-s*, knife; cf. *culter*, Sk. *kart-ari*, etc. The Slav. *korda*, O.N. *kordi*, Hung. *kard*, are treated by Justi as words borrowed from Persian.

Zend *cvant*, Lat. *quantus*. Sk. has *tâvat*, *tantus*, and *yâvat*, but not *kâvat*.

Zend *garaṇh*, reverence; Gr. γέρας.

Zend *thrâfaṇh*, food; Gr. -τρέφες.

Zend *da*, e.g. *vaêçmen-da*, towards the house; Gr. οἶκόν-δε; cf. Goth. *du*, to, O.S. *do*.

Zend *daiti*, gift; Gr. δόσις, Lat. *dôs*, *dôti-s*, Lith. *dúti-s*.

Zend *dâmi*, creation; Gr. θέμις, law.

Zend *naçu*, corpse; Gr. νέκυς; Goth. *nau-s*.

Zend *napo*, nom. sing.; A.S. *nefa*; O.H.G. *nefo*.

Zend *paithya* in *qaêpaithya*, own; Lat. *sua-pte*, *ipse*; Lith. *pati-s*, self.

Zend *peretu*, bridge; Lat. *portus*.

Zend *fraêsta*, most, best; Gr. πλεῖστος.

Zend *brvat*, brow; Gr. ἀβροῦτες (Macedon.); Lat. *frons*.

Zend *madh*, to cure; Lat. *mederi*.

Zend *man*, in *upa-man*, to wait; Lat. *manere*.

Zend *mîzhda*; Gr. μισθός; Goth. *mizd-ô*; O.S. *mîzda*.

Zend *yâre*, year; Goth. *jer*; O.S. *jarŭ*, spring.

Zend *yâoṇh, yâh*, to gird; *yâonha*, dress; Gr. ζωσ in ζώννυμι; O.S. *po-yasu*, girdle.

Zend *râçta*, straight; Lat. *rectus*; Goth. *raiht-s*.

Zend *rap*, to go; Lat. *repere*.

Zend *varez*, to work, *vareza*, work, *varstva*, work; Goth, *vaurkjan*, to work; Gr. ἔοργα, ῥέζω; Goth. *vaurstv*.

Zend *vaêti*, willow; Lith. *vȳti-s*, withy; Lat. *vîtis*.

Zend *çtaman*, mouth; Gr. στόμα.

Footnotes to Chapter IV: The Science of Language

1. Note A, p. 227.

2. Note B, p. 230.

3. See M. M.'s *Letter to Chevalier Bunsen, on the Turanian Languages*, 1854, second chapter, second section, "Ethnology versus Phonology."

4. Note C, p. 235.

5. "Judgment (*crimen*, κρίνειν), penance (*pœna*, ποινή), retribution (*talio*, ταλάω, τλῆναι, are Græco-Italic conceptions." Mommsen, *Röm. Geschichte*, vol. i. p. 25.

6. See my article in Kuhn's *Zeitschrift*, vol. xix. p. 46.

7. *Lectures on the Science of Language*, vol. ii. p. 467.

8. *Rendiconti del Reale Instituto Lombardo, classe de lettre*, iv. fasc. 6.

9. See Benfey, *Über die Enstehung des Indo-germanischen Vocativs*, Göttingen, 1872, p. 35.

10. The rule is that vocatives in ον from proper names in ων retract the accent, except Λακεδαῖμον, and those in φρον, as Λυκόφρον from Λυκόφρων.

11. Vocatives in ες from proper names in ης retract the accent, as Σώκρατες, except those in ωδες, ωλες, ωρες, ηρες, as Δειῶδες.

12. Benfey, l.c. p. 40.

- 162 -

13. See, also, M. M.'s *Lectures on the Science of Language*, vol. ii, p. 472.

14. See M. M.'s *Introduction to the Science of Religion*, p. 372, note.

V.
WESTMINSTER LECTURE.
ON MISSIONS.1

DELIVERED IN THE NAVE OF WESTMINSTER ABBEY,
ON THE EVENING OF DECEMBER 3, 1873.

THE number of religions which have attained stability and permanence in the history of the world is very small. If we leave out of consideration those vague and varying forms of faith and worship which we find among uncivilized and unsettled races, among races ignorant of reading and writing, who have neither a literature nor laws, nor even hymns and prayers handed down by oral teaching from father to son, from mother to daughter, we see that the number of the real historical religions of mankind amounts to no more than eight. The Semitic races have produced three—the Jewish, the Christian, the Mohammedan; the Aryan, or Indo-European races an equal number—the Brahman, the Buddhist, and the Parsi. Add to these the two religious systems of China, that of Confucius and Lao-tse, and you have before you what may be called the eight distinct languages or utterances of the faith of mankind from the beginning of the world to the present day; you have before you in broad outlines the religious map of the whole world.

All these religions, however, have a history, a history more deeply interesting than the history of language, or literature, or art, or politics. Religions are not unchangeable; on the contrary, they are always growing and changing; and if they cease to grow and cease to change, they cease to live. Some of these religions stand by themselves, totally independent of all the rest; others are closely united, or have influenced each other during various stages of their growth and decay. They must therefore be studied together, if we wish to understand their real character, their growth, their decay, and their resuscitations. Thus, Mohammedanism would be unintelligible without Christianity; Christianity without Judaism: and there are similar bonds that hold together the great religions of India and Persia—the faith of the Brahman, the Buddhist, and the Parsi. After a careful study of the origin and growth of these religions, and after a critical examination of the sacred books on which all of them profess to be founded, it has become possible to subject them all to a scientific classification, in the same manner as languages, apparently unconnected and mutually unintelligible, have been scientifically arranged and classified; and by a comparison of those points which all or some of them share in common, as well as by a determination of those which are peculiar to each, a new science has been called into life, a science which concerns us all, and in which all who truly care for religion must sooner or later take their part—*the Science of Religion*.

Among the various classifications2 which have been applied to the religions of the world, there is one that interests us more immediately to-night, I mean the division into Non-Missionary and Missionary religions. This is by no means, as might be supposed, a classification based on an unimportant or merely accidental characteristic; on the contrary, it rests on what is the very heart-blood in every system of human faith. Among the six religions of the Aryan and Semitic world, there are three that are opposed to all missionary enterprise—Judaism, Brahmanism, and Zoroastrianism; and three that have a missionary character from their very beginning—Buddhism, Mohammedanism, and Christianity.

The Jews, particularly in ancient times, never thought of spreading their religion. Their religion was to them a treasure, a privilege, a blessing, something to distinguish them, as the chosen people of God, from all the rest of the world. A Jew must be of the seed of Abraham: and when in later times, owing chiefly to political circumstances, the Jews had to admit strangers to some of the privileges of their theocracy, they looked upon them, not as souls that had been gained, saved, born again into a new brotherhood, but as strangers גֵרִים, as Proselytes (προσήλυτοι); which means men who have come to them as aliens, not to be trusted, as their saying was, until the twenty-fourth generation.3

A very similar feeling prevented the Brahmans from ever attempting to proselytize those who did not by birth belong to the spiritual aristocracy of their country. Their wish was rather to keep the light to themselves, to repel intruders; they went so far as to punish those who happened to be near enough to hear even the sound of their prayers, or to witness their sacrifices.4

The Parsi, too, does not wish for converts to his religion; he is proud of his faith, as of his blood; and though he believes in the final victory of truth and light, though he says to every man, "Be bright as the sun, pure as the moon," he himself does very little to drive away spiritual darkness from the face of the earth, by letting the light that is within him shine before the world.

But now let us look at the other cluster of religions, at Buddhism, Mohammedanism, and Christianity. However they may differ from each other in some of their most essential doctrines, this they share in common—they all have faith in themselves, they all have life and vigor, they want to convince, they mean to conquer. From the very earliest dawn of their existence these three religions were missionary; their very founders, or their first apostles, recognized the new duty of spreading the truth, of refuting error, of bringing the whole world to acknowledge the paramount, if not the divine, authority of their doctrines. This is what gives to them all a common expression, and lifts them high above the level of the other religions of the world.

Let us begin with Buddhism. We know, indeed, very little of its origin and earliest growth, for the earliest beginnings of all religions withdraw themselves by necessity from the eye of the historian. But we have something like contemporary evidence of the Great Council, held at Pâṭaliputra, 246 B.C., in which the sacred canon of the Buddhist scriptures was settled, and at the end of which missionaries were chosen and sent forth to preach the new doctrine, not only in India, but far beyond the frontiers of that vast country.5 We possess inscriptions containing the edicts of the king who was to Buddhism what Constantine was to Christianity, who broke with the traditions of the old religion of the Brahmans, and recognized the doctrines of Buddha as the state religion of India. We possess the description of the Council of Pâṭaliputra, which was to India what the Council of Nicæa, 570 years later, was to Europe; and we can still read there6 the simple story, how the chief elder who had presided over the Council, an old man, too weak to travel by land, and carried from his hermitage to the Council in a boat—how that man, when the Council was over, began to reflect on the future, and found that the time had come to establish the religion of Buddha in foreign countries. He therefore dispatched some of the most eminent priests to Cashmere, Cabul, and farther west, to the colonies founded by the Greeks in Bactria, to Alexandria on the Caucasus, and other cities. He sent others northward to Nepal, and to the inhabited portions of the Himalayan mountains. Another mission proceeded to the Dekhan, to the people of Mysore, to the Mahrattas, perhaps to Goa; nay, even Birma and Ceylon are mentioned as among the earliest missionary stations of Buddhist priests. We still possess accounts of their manner of preaching. When threatened by infuriated crowds, one of those Buddhist missionaries said calmly, "If the whole world, including the Deva heavens, were to come and terrify me, they would not be able to create in me fear and terror." And when he had brought the people to listen, he dismissed them with the simple prayer, "Do not hereafter give way to anger, as before; do not destroy the crops, for all men love happiness. Show mercy to all living beings, and let men dwell in peace."

No doubt, the accounts of the successes achieved by those early missionaries are exaggerated, and their fights with snakes and dragons and evil spirits remind us sometimes of the legendary accounts of the achievements of such men as St. Patrick in Ireland, or St. Boniface in Germany. But the fact that missionaries were sent out to convert the world seems beyond the reach of reasonable doubt;7 and this fact represents to us at that time a new thought, new, not only in the history of India, but in the history of the whole world. The recognition of a duty to preach the truth to every man, woman, and child, was an idea opposed to the deepest instincts of Brahmanism; and when, at the end of the chapter on the first missions, we read the simple words of the old chronicler, "who would demur, if the salvation of the world is at stake?" we feel at once that we move in a new world, we see the dawn of a new day, the opening of vaster horizons—we feel, for the first time in the history of the world, the beating of the great heart of humanity.8,A

The Koran breathes a different spirit; it does not invite, it rather compels the world to come in. Yet there are passages, particularly in the earlier portions, which show that Mohammed, too, had realized the idea of humanity, and of a religion of humanity; nay, that at first he wished to unite his own religion with that of the Jews and Christians, comprehending all under the common name of Islâm. Islâm meant originally humility or devotion; and all who humbled themselves before God, and were filled with real reverence, were called Moslim. "The Islâm," says Mohammed, "is the true worship of God. When men dispute with you, say, 'I am a Moslim.' Ask those who have sacred books, and ask the heathen; 'Are you Moslim?' If they are, they are on the right path; but if they turn away, then you have no other task but to deliver the message, to preach to them the Islâm."9

As to our own religion, its very soul is missionary, progressive, world-embracing; it would cease to exist, if it ceased to be missionary—if it disregarded the parting words of its Founder: "Go ye therefore and teach all nations, baptizing them in the name of the Father, and of the Son, and of the Holy Ghost; teaching them to observe all things I have commanded; and, lo, I am with you alway, even unto the end of the world."

It is this missionary character, peculiar to these three religions, Buddhism, Mohammedanism, and Christianity, which binds them together, and lifts them to a higher sphere. Their differences, no doubt, are great; on some points they are opposed to each other like day and night. But they could not be what they are, they could not have achieved what they have achieved, unless the spirit of truth and the spirit of love had been alive in the hearts of their founders, their first messengers, and missionaries.

The spirit of truth is the life-spring of all religion, and where it exists it must manifest itself, it must plead, it must persuade, it must convince and convert. Missionary work, however, in the usual sense of the word, is only one manifestation of that spirit; for the same spirit which fills the heart of the missionary with daring abroad, gives courage also to the preacher at home, bearing witness to the truth that is within him. The religions which can boast of missionaries who left the old home of their childhood, and parted with parents and friends—never to meet again in this life—who went into the wilderness, willing to spend a life of toil among strangers, ready, if need be, to lay down their life as witnesses to the truth, as martyrs for the glory of God—the same religions are rich also in those honest and intrepid inquirers who, at the bidding of the same spirit of truth, were ready to leave behind them the cherished creed of their childhood, to separate from the friends they loved best, to stand alone among men that shrug their shoulders, and ask, "What is truth?" and to bear in silence a martyrdom more galling often than death itself. There are men who say that, if they held the whole truth in their hand, they would not open one finger. Such men know little of the working of the spirit of truth, of the true missionary spirit. As long as there are doubt and darkness and anxiety in the soul of an inquirer, reticence may be his natural attitude. But when once doubt has yielded to certainty, darkness to light, anxiety to joy, the rays of truth will burst forth; and to close our hand or to shut our lips would be as impossible as for the petals of a flower to shut themselves against the summons of the sun of spring.

What is there in this short life that should seal our lips? What should we wait for, if we are not to speak *here* and *now*? There is missionary work at home as much as abroad; there are thousands waiting to listen if *one* man will but speak the truth, and nothing but the truth; there are thousands starving, because they cannot find that food which is convenient for them.

And even if the spirit of truth might be chained down by fear or prudence, the spirit of love would never yield. Once recognize the common brotherhood of mankind, not as a name or a theory, but as a real bond, as a bond more binding, more lasting than the bonds of family, caste, and race, and the questions, Why should I upon my hand? why should I open my heart? why should I speak to my brother? will never be asked again. Is it not far better to speak than to walk through life silent, unknown, unknowing? Has any one of us ever spoken to his friend, and opened to him his inmost soul, and been answered with harshness or repelled with scorn? Has any one of us, be he priest or layman, ever listened to the honest questionings of a truth-loving soul, without feeling his own soul filled with love? aye, without feeling humbled by the very honesty of a brother's confession?

If we would but confess, friend to friend, if we would be but honest, man to man, we should not want confessors or confessionals.

If our doubts and difficulties are self-made, if they can be removed by wiser and better men, why not give to our brother the opportunity of helping us? But if our difficulties are not self-made, if they are not due either to ignorance or presumption, is it not even then better for us to know that we are all carrying the same burden, the common burden of humanity, if haply we may find, that for the heavy laden there is but one who can give them rest?

There may be times when silence is gold, and speech silver: but there are times also when silence is death, and speech is life—the very life of Pentecost.

How can man be afraid of man? How can we be afraid of those whom we love?

Are the young afraid of the old? But nothing delights the older man more than to see that he is trusted by the young, and that they believe he will tell them the truth.

Are the old afraid of the young? But nothing sustains the young more than to know that they do not stand alone in their troubles, and that in many trials of the soul the father is as helpless as the child.

Are the women afraid of men? But men are not wiser in the things appertaining to God than women, and real love of God is theirs far more than ours.

Are men afraid of women? But though women may hide their troubles more carefully, their heart aches as much as ours, when they whisper to themselves, "Lord, I believe, help thou my unbelief."

Are the laity afraid of the clergy? But where is the clergyman who would not respect honest doubt more than unquestioning faith?

Are the clergy afraid of the laity? But surely we know, in this place at least, that the clear voice of honesty and humility draws more hearts than the harsh accents of dogmatic assurance or ecclesiastic exclusiveness.

> "There lives more faith in honest doubt,
>
> Believe me, than in half the creeds."

A missionary must know no fear; his heart must overflow with love—love of man, love of truth, love of God; and in this, the highest and truest sense of the word, every Christian is, or ought to be, a missionary.

And now, let us look again at the religions in which the missionary spirit has been at work, and compare them with those in which any attempt to convince others by argument, to save souls, to bear witness to the truth, is treated with pity or scorn. *The former are alive, the latter are dying or dead.*

The religion of Zoroaster—the religion of Cyrus, of Darius and Xerxes—which, but for the battles of Marathon and Salamis, might have become the religion of the civilized world, is now professed by only 100,000 souls—that is, by about a ten-thousandth part of the inhabitants of the world. During the last two centuries their number has steadily decreased from four to one hundred thousand, and another century will probably exhaust what is still left of the worshippers of the Wise Spirit, Ahura-mazda.

The Jews are about thirty times the number of the Parsis, and they therefore represent a more appreciable portion of mankind. Though it is not likely that they will ever increase in number, yet such is their physical vigor and their intellectual tenacity, such also their pride of race and their faith in Jehovah, that we can hardly imagine that their patriarchal religion and their ancient customs will soon vanish from the face of the earth.

But though the religions of the Parsis and Jews might justly seem to have paid the penalty of their anti-missionary spirit, how, it will be said, can the same be maintained with regard to the religion of the Brahmans? That religion is still professed by at least 110,000,000 of human souls, and, to judge from the last census, even that enormous number falls much short of the real truth. And yet I do not shrink from saying that their religion is dying or dead. And why? Because it cannot stand the light of day. The worship of Śiva, of Vishṇu, and the other popular deities, is of the same, nay, in many cases of a more degraded and savage character than the worship of Jupiter, Apollo, and Minerva; it belongs to a stratum of thought which is long buried beneath our feet: it may live on, like the lion and the tiger, but the mere air of free thought and civilized life will extinguish it. A religion may linger on for a long time, it may be accepted by the large masses of the people, because it is there, and there is nothing better. But when a religion has ceased to produce defenders of the faith, prophets, champions, martyrs, it has ceased to live, in the true sense of the word; and in that sense the old, orthodox Brahmanism has ceased to live for more than a thousand years.

It is true there are millions of children, women, and men in India who fall down before the stone image of Vishṇu, with his four arms, riding on a creature half bird, half man, or sleeping on the serpent; who worship Śiva, a monster with three eyes, riding naked on a bull, with a necklace of skulls for his ornament. There are human beings who still believe in a god of war, Kârtikêya, with six faces, riding on a peacock, and holding bow and arrow in his hands; and who invoke a god of success, Gaṇeśa, with four hands and an elephant's head, sitting on a rat. Nay, it is true that, in the broad daylight of the nineteenth century, the figure of the goddess Kali is carried through the streets of her own city, Calcutta,10 her wild disheveled hair reaching to her feet, with a necklace of human heads, her tongue protruded from her mouth, her girdle stained with blood. All this is true; but ask any Hindu who can read and write and think, whether these are the gods he believes in, and he will smile at your credulity. How long this living death of national religion in India may last, no one can tell: for our purposes, however, for gaining an idea of the issue of the great religious struggle of the future, that religion too is dead and gone.

The three religions which are alive, and between which the decisive battle for the dominion of the world will have to be fought, are the three missionary religions, *Buddhism, Mohammedanism, and Christianity*. Though religious statistics are perhaps the most uncertain of all, yet it is well to have a general conception of the forces of our enemies; and it is well to know that, though the number of Christians is double the number of Mohammedans, the Buddhist religion still occupies the first place in the religious census of mankind.11

Buddhism rules supreme in Central, Northern, Eastern, and Southern Asia, and it gradually absorbs whatever there is left of aboriginal heathenism in that vast and populous area.

Mohammedanism claims as its own Arabia, Persia, great parts of India, Asia Minor, Turkey, and Egypt; and its greatest conquests by missionary efforts are made among the heathen population of Africa.

Christianity reigns in Europe and America, and it is conquering the native races of Polynesia and Melanesia, while its missionary outposts are scattered all over the world.

Between these three powers, then, the religious battle of the future, the Holy War of mankind, will have to be fought, and is being fought at the present moment, though apparently with little effect. To convert a Mohammedan is difficult; to convert a Buddhist, more difficult still; to convert a Christian, let us hope, well nigh impossible.

What then, it may be asked, is the use of missionaries? Why should we spend millions on foreign missions, when there are children in our cities who are allowed to grow up in ignorance? Why should we deprive ourselves of some of the noblest, boldest, most ardent and devoted spirits and send them into the wilderness, while so many laborers are wanted in the vineyard at home.

It is right to ask these questions; and we ought not to blame those political economists who tell us that every convert costs us £200, and that at the present rate of progress it would take more than 200,000 years to evangelize the world. There is nothing at all startling in these figures. Every child born in Europe is as much a heathen as the child of a Melanesian cannibal; and it costs us more than £200 to turn a child into a Christian man. The other calculation is totally erroneous; for an intellectual harvest must not be calculated by adding simply grain to grain, but by counting each grain as a living seed, that will bring forth fruit a hundred and a thousand fold.

If we want to know what work there is for the missionary to do, what results we may expect from it, we must distinguish between two kinds of work: the one is *parental*, the other *controversial*. Among uncivilized races the work of the missionary is the work of a parent; whether his pupils are young in years or old, he has to treat them with a parent's love, to teach them with a parent's authority; he has to win them, not to argue with them. I know this kind of missionary work is often despised; it is called mere religious kidnapping; and it is said that missionary success obtained by such means proves nothing for the truth of Christianity; that the child handed over to a Mohammedan would grow up a Mohammedan, as much as a child taken by a Christian missionary becomes a Christian. All this is true; missionary success obtained by such means proves nothing for the truth of our creeds: but it proves, what is far more important, it proves Christian love. Read only the "Life of Patteson," the bishop of Melanesia; follow him in his vessel, sailing from island to island, begging for children, carrying them off as a mother her new-born child, nursing them, washing and combing them, clothing them, feeding them, teaching them in his Episcopal Palace, in which he himself is everything, nurse, and housemaid, and cook, schoolmaster, physician, and bishop—read there, how that man who tore himself away from his aged father, from his friends, from his favorite studies and pursuits, had the most loving of hearts for these children, how indignantly he repelled for them the name of savages, how he trusted them, respected them, honored them, and when they were formed and established, took them back to their island home, there to be a leaven for future ages. Yes, read the life, the work, the death of that man, a death in very truth, a ransom for the sins of others—and then say whether you would like to suppress a profession that can call forth such self-denial, such heroism, such sanctity, such love. It has been my privilege to have known some of the finest and noblest spirits which England has produced during this century, but there is none to whose memory I look up with greater reverence, none by whose friendship I feel more deeply humbled than by that of that true saint, that true martyr, that truly parental missionary.

The work of the parental missionary is clear, and its success undeniable, not only in Polynesia and Melanesia, but in many parts of India—(think only of the bright light of Tinnevelly)—in Africa, in China, in America, in Syria, in Turkey, aye, in the very heart of London.

The case is different with the controversial missionary, who has to attack the faith of men brought up in other religions, in religions which contain much truth, though mixed up with much error. Here the difficulties are immense, the results very discouraging. Nor need we wonder at this. We know, each of us, but too well, how little argument avails in theological discussion; how often it produces the very opposite result of what we expected; confirming rather than shaking opinions no less erroneous, no less indefensible, than many articles of the Mohammedan or Buddhist faith.

And even when argument proves successful, when it forces a verdict from an unwilling judge, how often has the result been disappointing; because in tearing up the rotten stem on which the tree rested, its tenderest fibres have been injured, its roots unsettled, its life destroyed.

We have little ground to expect that these controversial weapons will carry the day in the struggle between the three great religions of the world.

But there is a third kind of missionary activity, which has produced the most important results, and through which alone, I believe, the final victory will be gained. Whenever two religions are brought into contact, when members of each live together in peace, abstaining from all direct attempts at conversion, whether by force or by argument, though conscious all the time of the fact that they and their religion are on their trial, that they are being watched, that they are responsible for all they say and do—the effect has always been the greatest blessing to both. It calls out all the best elements in each, and at the same time keeps under all that is felt to be of doubtful value, of uncertain truth. Whenever this has happened in the history of the world, it has generally led either to the reform of both systems, or to the foundation of a new religion.

When after the conquest of India the violent measures for the conversion of the Hindus to Mohammedanism had ceased, and Mohammedans and Brahmans lived together in the enjoyment of perfect equality, the result was a purified Mohammedanism, and a purified Brahmanism.12 The worshippers of Vishṇu, Śiva, and other deities became ashamed of these mythological gods, and were led to admit that there was, either over and above these individual deities, or instead of them, a higher divine power (the Para-Brahma), the true source of all being, the only and almighty ruler of the world. That religious movement assumed its most important development at the beginning of the twelfth century, when Râmânuja founded the reformed sect of the worshippers of Vishṇu; and again, in the fourteenth century, when his fifth successor, Râmânanda, imparted a still more liberal character to that powerful sect. Not only did he abolish many of the restrictions of caste, many of the minute ceremonial observances in eating, drinking, and bathing, but he replaced the classical Sanskrit—which was unintelligible to the large masses of the people—by the living vernaculars, in which he preached a purer worship of God.

The most remarkable man of that time was a weaver, the pupil of Râmânanda, known by the name of Kabir. He indeed deserved the name which the members of the reformed sect claimed for themselves, Avadhûta, which means one who has shaken off the dust of superstition. He broke entirely with the popular mythology and the customs of the ceremonial law, and addressed himself alike to Hindu and Mohammedan. According to him, there is but one God, the creator of the world, without beginning and end, of inconceivable purity, and irresistible strength. The pure man is the image of God, and after death attains community with God. The commandments of Kabir are few: Not to injure anything that has life, for life is of God; to speak the truth; to keep aloof from the world; to obey the teacher. His poetry is most beautiful, hardly surpassed in any other language.

Still more important in the history of India was the reform of Nânak, the founder of the Sikh religion. He, too, worked entirely in the spirit of Kabir. Both labored to persuade the Hindus and Mohammedans that the truly essential parts of their creeds were the same, that they ought to discard the varieties of practical detail, and the corruptions of their teachers, for the worship of the *One Only Supreme*, whether he was termed Allah or Vishṇu.

The effect of these religious reforms has been highly beneficial; it has cut into the very roots of idolatry, and has spread throughout India an intelligent and spiritual worship, which may at any time develop into a higher national creed.

The same effect which Mohammedanism produced on Hinduism is now being produced, in a much higher degree, on the religious mind of India by the mere presence of Christianity. That silent influence began to tell many years ago, even at a time when no missionaries were allowed within the territory of the old East India Company. Its first representative was Ram Mohun Roy, born just one hundred years ago, in 1772, who died at Bristol in 1833, the founder of the Brahma-Samâj. A man so highly cultivated and so highly religious as he was, could not but feel humiliated at the spectacle which the popular religion of his country presented to his English friends. He drew their attention to the fact that there was a purer religion to be found in the old sacred writings of his people, the Vedas. He went so far as to claim for the Vedas a divine origin, and to attempt the foundation of a reformed faith on their authority. In this attempt he failed.

No doubt the Vedas and other works of the ancient poets and prophets of India, contain treasures of truth, which ought never to be forgotten, least of all by the sons of India. The late good Bishop Cotton, in his address to the students of a missionary institution at Calcutta, advised them to use a certain hymn of the Rig-Veda in their daily prayers.13 Nowhere do we find stronger arguments against idolatry, nowhere has the unity of the Deity been upheld more strenuously against the errors of polytheism than by some of the ancient sages of India. Even in the oldest of their sacred books, the Rig-Veda, composed three or four thousand years ago—where we find hymns addressed to the different deities of the sky, the air, the earth, the rivers—the protest of the human heart against many gods, breaks forth from time to time with no uncertain sound. One poet, after he has asked to whom sacrifice is due, answers, "to Him who is God above all gods."14 Another poet, after enumerating the names of many deities, affirms, without hesitation, that "these are all but names of Him who is One." And even when single deities are invoked, it is not difficult to see that, in the mind of the poet, each one of the names is meant to express the highest conception of deity of which the human mind was *then* capable. The god of the sky is called Father and Mother and Friend; he is the Creator, the Upholder of the Universe; he rewards virtue and punishes sin; he listens to the prayers of those who love him.

But granting all this, we may well understand why an attempt to claim for these books a divine origin, and thus to make them an artificial foundation for a new religion, failed. The successor of Ram Mohun Roy, the present head of the Brahma-Samâj, the wise and excellent Debendranâth Tagore, was for a time even more decided in holding to the Vedas as the sole foundation of the new faith. But this could not last. As soon as the true character of the Vedas,15 which but few people in India can understand, became known, partly through the efforts of native, partly of European scholars, the Indian reformers relinquished the claim of divine inspiration in favor of their Vedas, and were satisfied with a selection of passages from the works of the ancient sages of India, to express and embody the creed which the members of the Brahma-Samâj hold in common.16

The work which these religious reformers have been doing in India is excellent, and those only who know what it is, in religious matters, to break with the past, to forsake the established custom of a nation, to oppose the rush of public opinion, to brave adverse criticism, to submit to social persecution, can form any idea of what those men have suffered, in bearing witness to the truth that was within them.

They could not reckon on any sympathy on the part of Christian missionaries; nor did their work attract much attention in Europe till very lately, when a schism broke out in the Brahma-Samâj between the old conservative party and a new party, led by Keshub Chunder Sen. The former, though willing to surrender all that was clearly idolatrous in the ancient religion and customs of India, wished to retain all that might safely be retained: it did not wish to see the religion of India denationalized. The other party, inspired and led by Keshub Chunder Sen, went further in their zeal for religious purity. All that smacked of the old leaven was to be surrendered; not only caste, but even that sacred cord—the religious riband which makes and marks the Brahman, which is to remind him at every moment of his life, and whatever work he may be engaged in, of his God, of his ancestors, and of his children—even that was to be abandoned; and instead of founding their creed exclusively on the utterances of the ancient sages of their own country, all that was best in the sacred books of the whole world was selected and formed into a new sacred code.17,B

The schism between these two parties is deeply to be deplored; but it is a sign of life. It augurs success rather than failure for the future. It is the same schism which St. Paul had to heal in the Church of Corinth, and he healed it with the words, so often misunderstood, "Knowledge puffeth up, but charity edifieth."

In the eyes of our missionaries this religious reform in India has not found much favor: nor need we wonder at this. Their object is to transplant, if possible, Christianity in its full integrity from England to India, as we might wish to transplant a full-grown tree. They do not deny the moral worth, the noble aspirations, the self-sacrificing zeal of these native reformers; but they fear that all this will but increase their dangerous influence, and retard the progress of Christianity, by drawing some of the best minds of India, that might have been gained over to our religion, into a different current. They feel towards Keshub Chunder Sen18,C as Athanasius might have felt towards Ulfilas, the Arian Bishop of the Goths: and yet, what would have become of Christianity in Europe but for those Gothic races, but for those Arian heretics, who were considered more dangerous than downright pagans?

If we think of the future of India, and of the influence which that country has always exercised on the East, the movement of religious reform which is now going on appears to my mind the most momentous in this momentous century. If our missionaries feel constrained to repudiate it as their own work, history will be more just to them than they themselves.19 And if not as the work of Christian missionaries, it will be recognized hereafter as the work of those missionary Christians who have lived in India, as examples of a true Christian life, who have approached the natives in a truly missionary spirit, in the spirit of truth and in the spirit of love; whose bright presence has thawed the ice, and brought out beneath it the old soil, ready to blossom into new life. These Indian puritans are not against us; for all the highest purposes of life they are with us, and we, I trust, with them. What would the early Christians have said to men, outside the pale of Christianity, who spoke of Christ and his doctrine as some of these Indian reformers? Would they have said to them, "Unless you speak our language and think our thoughts, unless you accept our Creed and sign our Articles, we can have nothing in common with you."

O that Christians, and particularly missionaries, would lay to heart the words of a missionary Bishop!20 "I have for years thought," writes Bishop Patteson, "that we seek in our missions a great deal too much to make *English* Christians. . . . . Evidently the heathen man is not treated fairly, if we encumber our message with unnecessary requirements. The ancient Church had its 'selection of fundamentals.' . . . . Any one can see what mistakes we have made in India. . . . Few men think themselves into the state of the Eastern mind. . . . We seek to denationalize these races, as far as I can see; whereas we ought surely to change as little as possible—only what is clearly incompatible with the simplest form of Christian teaching and practice. I do not mean that we are to compromise truth . . . . but do we not overlay it a good deal with human traditions!"

If we had many such missionaries as Bishop Patteson and Bishop Cotton, if Christianity were not only preached, but lived in that spirit, it would then prove itself what it is—the religion of humanity at large, large enough itself to take in all shades and diversities of character and race.

And more than that—if this true missionary spirit, this spirit of truth and love, of forbearance, of trust, of toleration, of humility, were once to kindle the hearts of all those chivalrous ambassadors of Christ, the message of the Gospel which they have to deliver would then become as great a blessing to the giver as to the receiver. Even now, missionary work unites, both at home and abroad, those who are widely separated by the barriers of theological sects.21

It might do so far more still. When we stand before a common enemy, we soon forget our own small feuds. But why? Often, I fear, from motives of prudence only and selfishness. Can we not, then, if we stand in spirit before a common friend—can we not, before the face of God, forget our small feuds, for very shame? If missionaries admit to their fold converts who can hardly understand the equivocal abstractions of our creeds and formulas, is it necessary to exclude those who understand them but too well to submit the wings of their free spirit to such galling chains! When we try to think of the majesty of God, what are all those formulas but the stammerings of children, which only a loving father can interpret and understand! The fundamentals of our religion are not in these poor creeds; true Christianity lives, not in our belief, but in our love—*in our love of God, and in our love of man, founded on our love of God.*

That is the whole Law and the Prophets, that is the religion to be preached to the whole world, that is the Gospel which will conquer all other religions—even Buddhism and Mohammedanism—which will win the hearts of all men.

There can never be too much love, though there may be too much faith— particularly when it leads to the requirement of exactly the same measure of faith in others. Let those who wish for the true success of missionary work learn to throw in of the abundance of their faith; let them learn to demand less from others than from themselves. That is the best offering, the most valuable contribution which they can make to-day to the missionary cause.

Let missionaries preach the Gospel again as it was preached when it began the conquest of the Roman Empire and the Gothic nations; when it had to struggle with powers and principalities, with time-honored religions and triumphant philosophies, with pride of civilization and savagery of life—and yet came out victorious. At that time conversion was not a question to be settled by the acceptance or rejection of certain formulas or articles; a simple prayer was often enough: "God be merciful to me a sinner."

There is one kind of faith that revels in words, there is another that can hardly find utterance: the former is like riches that come to us by inheritance; the latter is like the daily bread, which each of us has to win in the sweat of his brow. We cannot expect the former from new converts; we ought not to expect it or to exact it, for fear that it might lead to hypocrisy or superstition. The mere believing of miracles, the mere repeating of formulas requires no effort in converts, brought up to believe in the Purânas of the Brahmans or the Buddhist Jâtakas. They find it much easier to accept a legend than to love God, to repeat a creed than to forgive their enemies. In this respect they are exactly like ourselves. Let missionaries remember that the Christian faith at home is no longer what it was, and that it is impossible to have one Creed to preach abroad, another to preach at home. Much that was formerly considered as essential is now neglected; much that was formerly neglected is now considered as essential. I think of the laity more than of the clergy; but what would the clergy be without the laity? There are many of our best men, men of the greatest power and influence in literature, science, art, politics, aye even in the Church itself, who are no longer Christian in the old sense of the word. Some imagine they have ceased to be Christians altogether, because they feel that they cannot believe as much as others profess to believe. We cannot afford to lose these men, nor shall we lose them if we learn to be satisfied with what satisfied Christ and the Apostles, with what satisfies many a hard-working missionary. If Christianity is to retain its hold on Europe and America, if it is to conquer in the Holy War of the future, it must throw off its heavy armor, the helmet of brass and the coat of mail, and face the world like David, with his staff, his stones, and his sling. We want less of creeds, but more of trust; less of ceremony, but more of work; less of solemnity, but more of genial honesty; less of doctrine, but more of love. There is a faith, as small as a grain of mustard-seed, but that grain alone can move mountains, and more than that, it can move hearts. Whatever the world may say of us, of us of little faith, let us remember that there was one who accepted the offering of the poor widow. She threw in but two mites, but that was all she had, even all her living.

NOTES.

NOTE A.

Mahâdayassâpi jinassa kaḍḍhanaṃ,

Vihâya pattaṃ amataṃ sukham pi te

Karimsu lokassa hitaṃ tahiṃ tahiṃ,

Bhaveyya ko lokahite pamâdavâ?

The first line is elliptical.

(Imitating) the resignation of the all-merciful Conqueror,

They also, resigning the deathless bliss within their reach,

Worked the welfare of mankind in various lands.

What man is there who would be remiss in doing good to mankind?

Hardy, in his "Manual of Buddhism" (p. 187), relates how fifty-four princes and a thousand fire-worshippers became the disciples of Buddha. "Whilst Buddha remained at Isipatana, Yasa, the son of Sujatá, who had been brought up in all delicacy, one night went secretly to him, was received with affection, became a priest, and entered the first path. The father, on discovering that he had fled, was disconsolate: but Buddha delivered to him a discourse, by which he became a rahat. The fifty-four companions of Yasa went to the monastery to induce him to return, and play with them as usual; but when they saw him, they were so struck with his manner and appearance, that they also resolved on becoming priests. When they went to Buddha, they were admitted, by the power of i r d h i received the p i r i k a r a requisites of the priesthood, and became rahats. Buddha had now sixty disciples who were rahats, and he commanded them to go by different ways, and proclaim to all that a supreme Buddha had appeared in the world."

Mr. Childers has kindly sent me the following extract from Fausböll's "Dhammapada" (p. 119), where the same story is told:—

.... Yasakulaputtassa upanissayasampattiṃ disvâ taṃ rattibhâge nibbijjitvâ gehaṃ pahâya nikkhantaṃ "ehi Yasati" pakkositvâ, tasmiñ ñeva rattibhâge sotâpattiphalaṃ punadivase arahattuṃ pâpesi. Apare pi tassa sahâyake catupaṇṇâsajane ehibhikkhupabbajjâya pabbâjetvâ arahattuṃ pâpesi. Evaṃ loke ekasaṭṭhiyâ arahantesu jâtesu vutthavasso pavâretva "caratha bhikkhave cârikan" ti saṭṭhiṃ bhikkhû disâsu pesetvâ..... "Seeing that the young nobleman Yasa was ripe for conversion, in the night, when weary with the vanities of the world he had left his home and embraced the ascetic life,—he called him, saying, 'Follow me, Yasa,' and that very night he caused him to obtain the fruition of the first path, and on the following day arhatship. And fifty-four other persons, who were friends of Yasa's, he ordained with the formula, 'Follow me, priest,' and caused them to attain arhatship. Thus when there were sixty-one arhats in the world, having passed the period of seclusion during the rains and resumed active duties, he sent forth the sixty priests in all directions, saying, 'Go forth, priests, on your rounds (or travels).'"

Another passage, too, showing Buddha's desire to see his doctrine preached in the whole world, was pointed out to me by Mr. Childers from the "Mahâparinibbâna Sutta," which has since been published by this indefatigable scholar in the "Journal of the Royal Asiatic Society," vol. vii., p. 77:—

"Three months before his death, when Gautama's health and strength is fast failing, he is tempted by Mâra, who comes to him and urges him to bring his life and mission at once to a close by attaining Nirvâṇa (dying). Buddha replies that he will not die until his disciples are perfect on all points, and able to maintain the Truth with power against all unbelievers. Mâra replies that this is already the case, whereupon Buddha uses these striking words: Na tâvâhaṃ pâpima parinibbayissâmi yâva me imaṃ brahmacariyaṃ na iddhañ c' eva bhavissati phîtañ ca vitthârikaṃ bâhujaññaṃ puthubhûtaṃ, yâvad eva manusschi suppakâsitan ti. 'O wicked one, I will not die until this my holy religion thrives and prospers, until it is widely spread, known to many peoples, and grown great, until it is completely published among men.' Mara again asserts that this is already the case, and Buddha replies, 'Strive no more, wicked one, the death of the Tathagata is at hand, at the end of three months from this time, the Tathâgata will attain Nirvâṇa.'"

NOTE B.
THE SCHISM IN THE BRAHMA-SAMÂJ.22,

THE present position of the two parties in the Brahma-Samâj is well described by Rajnarain Bose (the "Adi Brahmo Samaj," Calcutta, 1873, p. 11). "The particular opinions above referred to can be divided into two comprehensive classes—conservative and progressive. The conservative Brahmos are those who are unwilling to push religious and social reformation to any great extreme. They are of opinion that reformation should be gradual, the law of gradual progress being universally prevalent in nature. They also say that the principle of Brahmic harmony requires a harmonious discharge of all our duties, and that, as it is a duty to take a part in reformation, so there are other duties to perform, namely, those towards parents and society, and that we should harmonize all these duties as much as we can. However unsatisfactory such arguments may appear to a progressive Brahmo, they are such as could not be slighted at first sight. They are certainly such as to make the conservative Brahmo think sincerely that he is justified in not pushing religious and social reformation to any great extreme. The progressive Brahmo cannot therefore call him a hypocrite. A union of both the conservative and the progressive elements in the Brahmo church is necessary for its stability. The conservative element will prevent the progressive from spoiling the cause of reformation by taking premature and abortive measures for advancing that cause; the progressive element will prevent the conservative from proving a stolid obstruction to it. The conservative element will serve as a link between the progressive element and the orthodox community, and prevent the progressive Brahmo from being completely estranged from that community, as the native Christians are; while the progressive element will prevent the conservative from remaining inert and being absorbed by the orthodox community. The common interests of Brahmo Dharma should lead both classes to respect, and be on amicable terms with each other. It is true the progressive of the present half century will prove the conservative of the next; but there could never come a time when the two classes would cease to exist in the bosom of the church. She should, like a wise mother, make them live in peace with each other, and work harmoniously together for her benefit.

"As idolatry is intimately interwoven with our social fabric, conservative Brahmos, though discarding it in other respects, find it very difficult to do so on the occasion of such very important domestic ceremonies as marriage, s h r a d h (ancestral sacrifices), and u p a n a y a n a (spiritual apprenticing); but they should consider that Brahmoism is not so imperative on any other point as on the renunciation of idolatry. It can allow conservatism in other respects, but not on the point of idolatry. It can consider a man a Brahmo if he be conservative in other respects than idolatry; but it can never consider an idolater to be a Brahmo. The conservative Brahmo can do one thing, that is, observe the old ritual, leaving out only the idolatrous portion of it, if he do not choose to follow the positive Brahmo ritual laid down in the 'Anushthána Paddhati.' Liberty should be given by the progressive Brahmo to the conservative Brahmo in judging of the idolatrous character of the portions of the old ritual rejected by him. If a progressive Brahmo requires a conservative one to reject those portions which the former considers to be idolatrous, but the latter does not, he denies liberty of conscience to a fellow-Brahmo.

"The Adi Brahmo-Samaj is the national Hindu Theistic Church, whose principles of church reformation we have been describing above. Its demeanor towards the old religion of the country is friendly, but corrective and reformative. It is this circumstance which preëminently distinguishes it from the Brahmo-Samaj of India, whose attitude to that religion is antagonistic and offensive. The mission of the Adi Samaj is to fulfill the old religion, and not to destroy it. The attitude of the Adi Samaj to the old religion is friendly, but it is not at the same time opposed to progress. It is a mistake to call it a conservative church. It is rather a conservative-progressive church, or, more correctly, simply a church or religious body, leaving matters of social reformation to the judgments of individual members or bodies of such members. It contains both progressive and conservative members. As the ultra-progressive Brahmos, who wanted to eliminate the conservative element from it, were obliged to secede from it, so if a high conservative party arise in its bosom which would attempt to do violence to the progressive element and convert the church into a partly conservative one, that party also would be obliged to secede from it. Only men who can be tolerant of each others opinions, and can respect each others earnest convictions, progressive and conservative, can remain its members."

The strong national feeling of the Indian reformers finds expression in the following passage from "Brahmic Questions," p. 9:—

"A Samaj is accessible to all. The minds of the majority of our countrymen are not deeply saturated with Christian sentiments. What would they think of a Brahmo minister who would quote on the Vedi (altar) sayings from the Bible? Would they not from that time conceive an intolerable hatred towards Brahmoism and everything Brahmo? If quoting a sentence from the Bible or Koran offend our countrymen, we shall not do so. Truth is as catholic when taken from the Sâstras as from the Koran or the Bible. True liberality consists, not in quoting s from the religious Scriptures of other nations, but in bringing up, as we advance, the rear who are groveling in ignorance and superstition. We certainly do not act against the dictates of conscience, if we quote s from the Hindu Sâstras only, and not from all the religious Scriptures of all the countries on the face of the globe. Moreover, there is not a single saying in the Scriptures of other nations, which has not its counterpart in the Sâstras."

And again in "The Adi Brahma-Samaj, its Views and Principles," p. 1:—

"The members of the Adi Samaj, aiming to diffuse the truths of Theism among their own nation, the Hindus, have naturally adopted a Hindu mode of propagation, just as an Arab Theist would adopt an Arabian mode of propagation, and a Chinese Theist a Chinese one. Such differences in the aspect of Theism in different countries must naturally arise from the usual course of things, but they are adventitious, not essential, national, not sectarian. Although Brahmoism is universal religion, it is impossible to communicate a universal form to it. It must wear a particular form in a particular country. A so-called universal form would make it appear grotesque and ridiculous to the nation or religious denomination among whom it is intended to be propagated, and would not command their veneration. In conformity with such views, the Adi Samaj has adopted a Hindu form to propagate Theism among Hindus. It has therefore retained many innocent Hindu usages and customs, and has adopted a form of divine service containing passages extracted from the Hindu Sâstras only, a book of Theistic s containing selections from those sacred books only, and a ritual containing as much of the ancient form as could be kept consistently with the dictates of conscience."

NOTE C.
Extracts from Keshub Chunder Sen's Lecture on Christ and Christianity, 1870.

"Why have I cherished respect and reverence for Christ? . . . Why is it that, though I do not take the name of 'Christian,' I still persevere in offering my hearty thanksgivings to Jesus Christ? There must be something in the life and death of Christ,—there must be something in his great gospel which tends to bring comfort and light and strength to a heart heavy-laden with iniquity and wickedness. . . . I studied Christ ethically, nay spiritually,—and I studied the Bible also in the same spirit, and I must acknowledge candidly and sincerely that I owe a great deal to Christ and to the gospel of Christ. . . .

"My first inquiry was, What is the creed taught in the Bible? . . . Must I go through all the dogmas and doctrines which constitute Christianity in the eye of the various sects, or is there something simple which I can at once grasp and turn to account?

"I found Christ spoke one language, and Christianity another. I went to him prepared to hear what he had to say, and was immensely gratified when he told me: 'Love the Lord thy God with all thy heart, with all thy mind, with all thy soul, and with all thy strength, and love thy neighbor as thyself;' and then he added, 'This is the whole law and the prophets,' in other words, the whole philosophy, theology, and ethics of the law and the prophets are concentrated in these two great doctrines of love to God and love to man; and then elsewhere he said, 'This do and ye shall inherit everlasting life.' . . . If we love God and love man we become Christ-like, and so attain everlasting life.

"Christ never demanded from me worship or adoration that is due to God, the Creator of the Universe.... He places himself before me as the spirit I must imbibe in order to approach the Divine Father, as the great Teacher and guide who will lead me to God.

"There are some persons who believe that if we pass through the ceremony of baptism and sacrament, we shall be accepted by God, but if you accept baptism as an outward rite, you cannot thereby render your life acceptable to God, for Christ wants something internal, a complete conversion of the heart, a giving up the yoke of mammon and accepting the yoke of religion, and truth, and God. He wants us to baptize our hearts not with cold water, but with the fire of religious and spiritual enthusiasm; he calls upon us not to go through any outward rite, but to make baptism a ceremony of the heart, a spiritual enkindling of all our energies, of all our loftiest and most heavenly aspirations and activities. That is true baptism. So with regard to the doctrine of the sacrament. There are many who eat the bread and drink the wine at the sacramental table, and go through the ceremony in the most pious and fervent spirit; but, after all, what does the sacrament mean? If men simply adopt it as a tribute of respect and honor to Christ, shall he be satisfied? Shall they themselves be satisfied? Can we look upon them as Christians simply because they have gone through this rite regularly for twenty or fifty years of their lives? I think not. Christ demands of us absolute sanctification and purification of the heart. In this matter, also, I see Christ on one side, and Christian sects on the other.

"What is that bread which Christ asked his disciples to eat? what that wine which he asked them to taste? Any man who has simple intelligence in him, would at once come to the conclusion that all this was metaphorical, and highly and eminently spiritual. Now, are you prepared to accept Christ simply as an outward Christ, an outward teacher, an external atonement and propitiation, or will you prove true to Christ by accepting his solemn injunctions in their spiritual importance and weight? He distinctly says, every follower of his must eat his flesh and drink his blood. If we eat, bread is converted into strength and health, and becomes the means of prolonging our life; so, spiritually, if we take truth into our heart, if we put Christ into the soul, we assimilate the spirit of Christ to our spiritual being, and then we find Christ incorporated into our existence and converted into spiritual strength, and health, and joy, and blessedness. Christ wants something that will amount to self-sacrifice, a casting away of the old man, and a new growth in the heart. I thus draw a line of demarcation between the visible and outward Christ, and the invisible and inward Christ, between bodily Christ and spiritual Christ, between the Christ of images and pictures, and the Christ that grows in the heart, between dead Christ and living Christ, between Christ that lived and that was, and Christ that does live and that is. . . . .

"To be a Christian then is to be Christ-like. Christianity means becoming like Christ, not acceptance of Christ as a proposition or as an outward representation, but spiritual conformity with the life and character of Christ. And what is Christ? By Christ I understand one who said, 'Thy will be done;' and when I talk of Christ, I talk of that spirit of loyalty to God, that spirit of absolute determinedness and preparedness to say at all times and in all circumstances, 'Thy will be done, not mine.' . . . .

"This prayer about forgiving an enemy and loving an enemy, this transcendental doctrine of love of man, is really sweet to me, and when I think of that blessed Man of God, crucified on the cross, and uttering those blessed words, 'Father, forgive them, they know not what they do;' oh! I feel that I must love that being, I feel that there is something within me which is touched by these sweet and heavenly utterances, I feel that I must love Christ, let Christians say what they like against me; that Christ I must love, for he preached love for an enemy. . . . .

"When every individual man becomes Christian in spirit—repudiate the name, if you like—when every individual man becomes as prayerful as Christ was, as loving and forgiving towards enemies as Christ was, as self-sacrificing as Christ was, then these little units, these little individualities, will coalesce and combine together by the natural affinity of their hearts; and these new creatures, reformed, regenerated, in the child-like and Christ-like spirit of devotion and faith, will feel drawn towards each other, and they shall constitute a real Christian church, a real Christian nation. Allow me, friends, to say, England is not yet a Christian nation."

EXTRACTS FROM A CATECHISM ISSUED BY A MEMBER OF THE ADI BRAHMO-SAMAJ.

Q. Who is the deity of the Brahmos?

A. The One True God, one only without a second, whom all Hindu Śāstras proclaim.

Q. What is the divine worship of the Brahmos?

A. Loving God, and doing the works He loveth.

Q. What is the temple of the Brahmos?

A. The pure heart.

Q. What are the ceremonial observances of the Brahmos?

A. Good works.

Q. What is the sacrifice of the Brahmos?

A. Renunciation of selfishness.

Q. What are the austerities of the Brahmos?

A. Not committing sin. The Mahábhárata says, He who does not commit sin in mind, speech, action, or understanding, performs austerities; not he who drieth up his body.

Q. What is the place of pilgrimage of the Brahmos?

A. The company of the good.

Q. What is the Veda of the Brahmos?

A. Divine knowledge. It is superior to all Vedas. The Veda itself says: The inferior knowledge is the Rig Veda, the Yajur Veda, the Sama Veda, the Atharva Veda, etc.; the superior knowledge is that which treats of God.

Q. What is the most sacred formula of the Brahmos?

A. Be good and do good.

Q. Who is the true Brahman?

A. He who knows Brahma. The Brihadâraṇyaka-Upanishad says: He who departs from this world knowing God, is a Brahman. (See "Brahmic Questions of the Day," 1869.)

THE END AND THE MEANS
OF
CHRISTIAN MISSIONS.

A SERMON[23] PREACHED BY ARTHUR PENRHYN STANLEY, D.D., DEAN OF WESTMINSTER, ON THE DAY OF INTERCESSION FOR MISSIONS, WEDNESDAY, DECEMBER 3, 1873.

Then Agrippa said unto Paul, Almost thou persuadest me to be a Christian. And Paul said, I would to God, that, not only thou, but all that hear me this day, were both almost, and altogether such as I am, except these bonds.

Ὁ δὲ Ἀγρίππας πρὸς τὸν Παῦλον ἔφη· Ἐν ὀλίγῳ με πείθεις Χριστιανὸν γενέσθαι. Ὁ δὲ Παῦλος εἶπεν· Εὐξαίμην ἂν τῷ Θεῷ, καὶ ἐν ὀλίγῳ καὶ ἐν πολλῷ οὐ μόνον σε, ἀλλὰ καὶ πάντας τοὺς ἀκούοντάς μου σήμερον γενέσθαι τοιούτους, ὁποῖος κἀγώ εἰμι παρεκτὸς τῶν δεσμῶν τούτων. ACTS xxvi. 28, 29.

WHEN I preached on a like occasion last year, I spoke at some length of the prospects of Christian missions,[24] and I ventured to give seven grounds which the peculiar circumstances of our time afforded for greater confidence in the future. First, the better knowledge of the Divine nature acquired by the extinction of the once universal belief that all heathens were everlastingly lost; secondly, the increased acquaintance with the heathen religions themselves; thirdly, the instruction which Christian missionaries have gained or may gain from their actual experience in foreign parts; fourthly, the recognition of the fact that the main hindrance to the success of Christian missions arises from the vices and sins of Christendom; fifthly, an acknowledgment of the indirect influences of Christianity through legislation and civilization; sixthly, the newly awakened perception of the duty of making exact, unvarnished, impartial statements on this subject; seventhly, the testimony borne by missionary experience to the common elements and essential principles of the Christian religion.

On these—the peculiar grounds for hope and for exertion in this our generation—I content myself with referring to the observations which I then made, and which I will not now repeat.

I propose on this occasion to make a few remarks on the End and on the Means of Christian Missions; remarks which must of necessity be general in their import, but which for that reason are the more suitable to be offered by one who cannot speak from personal and special experience.

The is taken from a striking incident in the life of the greatest of apostolic missionaries. It was in the presence of Festus and Agrippa that Paul had poured forth those few burning utterances which to Festus seemed like madness, but which Paul himself declared to be words of truth and soberness. Then it was that the Jewish prince, Agrippa—far better instructed and seeing deeper into Paul's mind than the heathen Festus, yet still unconvinced—broke in upon the conversation with the words which in the English translation have well nigh passed into a proverb, "Almost thou persuadest me to be a Christian." The sense which they thus give would be in itself perfectly suitable to the halting, fickle character of the Herodian family, and would accurately describe the numerous half-converts throughout the world—"Almost," but not quite, "thou persuadest me to join the good cause." But the sense which, by the nearly universal consent of modern scholars, they really bear in the original is something still more instructive. The only meaning of which the Greek words are capable is an exclamation, half in jest and half in earnest, "It is but a very brief and simple argument that you offer to work so great a change;" or, if we may venture to bring out the sense more forcibly, "So few words, and such a vast conclusion!" "So slight a foundation, and so gigantic a superstructure!" "So scanty an outfit, and so perilous an enterprise!" The speech breathes something of the spirit of Naaman, when he was told to wash in the Jordan— "Are not Abana and Pharpar better than all the waters of Israel?" It is like the complaint of the popular prophets in the time of Hezekiah, whose taste demanded stronger flavor than the noble simplicity of Isaiah, "Thou givest us only line upon line, precept upon precept." It breathes the spirit of the Ephesian Christians who, when they heard St. John's repeated maxim of "Little children, love one another," said, "Is this all that he has to tell us?" It expresses the spirit of many an one since, who has stumbled at the threshold of the genuine Gospel—"So vague, so simple, so universal. Is this worth the sacrifice that you demand? Give us a demonstrative argument, a vast ceremonial, a complex system, a uniform government. Nothing else will satisfy us."

As Agrippa's objection, so is Paul's answer. It would have indeed borne a good sense had he meant what in our English version he is made to say, "I would that thou wert converted both 'almost and altogether.' Halfness or wholeness—I admire them both. Half a soul is better than none at all. To have come half way is better than never to have started at all; but half is only good, because it leads towards the whole." Nevertheless, following the real meaning of Agrippa's remark, St. Paul's retort, in fact, bears a yet deeper significance—"I would to God, that whether by little or by much, whether by brief arguments or by long arguments, somehow and somewhere, the change were wrought. The means to me are comparatively nothing, so long as the end is accomplished." It is the same spirit as that which dictated the noble expression in the Epistle to the Philippians: "Some preach Christ of envy and strife, some also of good will. The one preach Christ of contention, the other of love. What then? notwithstanding, every way, whether in pretence or in truth, Christ is preached."[25]

And then he proceeds to vindicate the end which makes him indifferent as to the means. Agrippa, in his brief taunt, had said, "Such are the arguments by which you would fain make me a *Christian*." It is one of the few, one of the only three occasions on which that glorious name is used in the New Testament. It is here charged not with the venerable meaning which we now attach to it, but with the novel and degrading associations which it bore in the mouth of every Jew and every Roman at that time—of Tacitus or Josephus, no less than of Festus or Agrippa. "Is it," so the king meant to say, "is it that you think to make me a *Christian*, a member of that despised, heretical, innovating sect, of which the very name is a sufficient condemnation?"

It is only by bearing this in mind that we see the force of St. Paul's answer. He does not insist on the word; he does not fight even for this sacred title; he does not take it up as a pugnacious champion might take up the glove which his adversary had thrown down; he does not say, "I would that thou wast a Christian." In his answer he bears his testimony to one of the gravest, the most fruitful, of all theological truths—that it is not the name but the thing, not the form but the reality, on which stress must be laid; and he gives the most lucid, heart-stirring illustration of what the reality is. "I would that not only thou, but all those who hear me were (I ask for no ambiguous catchword or byword, but) what you see before you; I would that you all were such as I am—such as I am, upheld by the hopes, filled with the affections, that sustain my charmed existence;" and then, with that exquisite courtesy which characterizes so many traits of the Apostle's history, glancing at the chains which bound him to the Roman guard—"'except these bonds.' This, whether you call it Christian or not, is what I desire to see you and all the world." "You see it before you in the life, the character, the spirit, of one who knows what Christianity is, and who wishes that all his fellow-creatures should partake of the happiness that he has gained, repose on the same principles that give him strength." This, then, is the statement of the greatest of missionaries, both as to the end which he sought to attain, and the means by which he and we should seek to attain it.

I. Let us first take the End: "Such as I am, except these bonds." That is the state to which St. Paul desired to bring all those who heard him. That, according to him, was the description of a Christian. No doubt if he had been pressed yet further, he would have said that he meant, "Such as Jesus Christ, my Lord." But he was satisfied with taking such a living, human, imperfect exemplification as he whom Festus and Agrippa saw in their presence. "Such as Paul was." Here is no ambiguous definition, no obsolete form. What manner of man he was we know even better than Festus or Agrippa knew. Look at him with all his characteristic peculiarities; a man passionately devoted to his own faithful friends, and clinging to the reminiscences of his race and country, yet with a heart open to embrace all mankind; a man combining the strongest convictions with an unbounded toleration of differences, and an unbounded confidence in truth; a man penetrated with the freedom of the Spirit, but with a profound appreciation of the value of great existing institutions, whether civil or religious—a thorough Roman citizen and a thorough Eastern gentleman; embarked on a career of daring fortitude and endurance, undertaken in the strength of the persuasion that in Jesus Christ of Nazareth he had seen the highest perfection of Divine and human goodness—a Master worth living for and worth dying for, whose Spirit was to be the regenerating power of the whole world. This character, this condition it was to which St. Paul desired that his hearers should be brought. One only reservation he makes; "except these bonds," except those limitations, those circumscriptions, those vexations, those irritations, which belonged to the suffering, toil-worn circumstances in which he was at that moment placed.

Such is the aim which, following the example of their most illustrious predecessor, all missionaries ought to have before their eyes. To create, to preach, to exhibit those elements of character, those apostolical graces, those

Divine intuitions, which even the hard Roman magistrate and the superficial Jewish prince recognized in Paul of Tarsus. Where these are, there is Christianity. In proportion as any of these are attained, in that proportion has a human being become a Christian. Wherever and in proportion as these are not, there the missionary's labor has failed—there the seed has been sown to no purpose—there the name of Christian may be, but the reality is not.

This preëminence of the object of Christian missions—namely, the formation of heroic, apostolic, and therefore Christian characters—has a wide practical importance. In these days—when there is so much temptation to dwell on the scaffolding, the apparatus, the organization of religion, as though it were religion itself—it is doubly necessary to bear in mind what true Religion is, wherein lies the essential superiority of Christianity to all the other forms of religion on the surface of the earth. It is not merely the baptism of thousands of infants, such as filled a large part of the aspirations even of so great a missionary as Francis Xavier; nor the adoption of the name of Christ, as was done on so vast a scale by the ferocious rebels of China; nor the repetition, with ever so much accuracy, of the Christian creed, as was done by the pretended converts from Mahommedanism or Judaism, under the terrible compulsion of the Catholic sovereigns of Spain. Nor is it the assurance ever so frequently repeated, that we are saved; nor is it the absolution, ever so solemnly pronounced by a priest; nor is it the shedding of floods of tears; nor is it the adoption of voluntary self-degradation or solitary seclusion. All these may be found in other religions in even greater force than in Christianity. That which alone, if anything, stamps Christianity as the supreme religion, is that its essence, its object, is in none of these things, valuable as some of them may be as signs and symptoms of the change which every mission is intended to effect. The change itself, the end itself, Christianity itself, is at once greater and simpler. It is to be such as Paul was; it is to produce characters, which in truthfulness, in independence, in mercy, in purity, in charity, may recall something of the great Apostle, even as he recalled something of the mind which was in Christ Jesus. It was this clear vision of what he desired to see as the fruits of his teaching that made St. Paul so ready to admire whatsoever things were lovely and of good report wherever he found them. In Gentile or in Jew, in heathen or in Christian, he recognized at once the spirits kindred to his own, and welcomed them accordingly. He felt that he could raise them yet higher; but he was eager to claim them as his brethren even from the first.26 Even in the legends which surround his history there has been preserved something of this genuine apostolic sympathy. It was a fine touch in the ancient Latin hymn which described how, when he landed at Puteoli, he turned aside to the hill of Pausilipo to shed a tear over the tomb of Virgil, and thought how much he might have made of that noble soul if he had found him still on earth:—

"Ad Maronis mausoleum

Ductus, fudit super eum

Piæ rorem lacrymæ—

'Quantum,' dixit, 'te fecissem

Si te vivum invenissem,

Poetarum maxime.'"

It was this which made him cling with such affectionate interest to his converts, to his friends, to his sons, as he calls them, in Christ Jesus. All that he sought, all that he looked for in them, was that they should show in their characters the seal of the spirit that animated himself. Whether they derived this character from himself or from Apollos or Cephas he cared not to ask. He was their pupil as much as their master. He disclaimed all dominion over their independent faith; he claimed only to be a helper in their joy.

This reproduction of Paul—this reproduction of all that is best in ourselves or better than ourselves—in the minds and hearts of mankind, is the true work of the Christian missionary; and, in order to do this, he must be himself that which he wishes to impress upon them in humility, goodness, courtesy, and holiness, except only the straitening bonds which cramp or confine each separate character, nation, and church. No disparager of Christian missions can dispute this *—no champion of Christian missions need go beyond this. When, in the last century, the Danish missionary, Schwarz, was pursuing his labors at Tanjore, and the Rajah Hyder Ali desired to treat with the English government, he said: "Do not send to me any of your agents, for I trust neither their words nor their treaties. But send to me the missionary of whose character I hear so much from every one; him will I receive and trust." That was the electrifying, vivifying effect of the apparition of such an one as Paul—"a man who had indeed done nothing worthy of bonds or of death"—a man in whose entire disinterestedness and in whose transparent honor the image and superscription of his Master was written so that no one could mistake it. "In every nation, he that feareth God and worketh righteousness" is the noblest work of God our Creator—the most precious result of human endeavor. If any such—by missionary efforts, either of convert or teacher, either direct or indirect—have been produced, then the prayers uttered, the labors inspired, the hopes expressed in these and like services have not been altogether in vain. One of the most striking facts to which our attention has been called as demanding our thankfulness on this day is the solemn testimony borne by the Government of India to the fruits of "the blameless lives and self-denying labors of its six hundred Protestant missionaries." And what are those fruits? Not merely the adoption of this or that outward form of Christianity by this or that section of the Indian community. It is something which is in appearance less, but in reality far greater than this. It is something less like the question of Agrippa, but more like the answer of Paul. It is that they have "infused new vigor into the stereotyped life of the vast populations placed under English rule;" it is that they are "preparing those populations to be in every way better men and better citizens of the great Empire under which they dwell." That is a verdict on which we can rest with the assurance that it is not likely to be reversed. Individual conversions may relapse—may be accounted for by special motives; but long-sustained, wide-reaching changes of the whole tenor and bent of a man or of a nation are beyond suspicion. When we see the immovable, and, as the official document says, "the stereotyped" forms of Indian life re-animated with a vigor unknown to the Oriental races in earlier days, this is a regeneration as surprising as that which, to a famous missionary of the past generation, seemed as impossible as the restoration of a mummy to life—namely, the conversion of a single Brahmin.

This, then, is the End of Christian missions, whether to heathens or to Christians, namely, to make better men and better citizens—to raise the whole of society by inspiring it with a higher view of duty, with a stronger sense of truth; with a more powerful conviction that only by goodness and truth can God be approached or Christ be served—that God is goodness and truth, and that Christ is the Image of God, because He is goodness and truth. If this be the legitimate result of Christianity, no further arguments are needed to prove that it contains a light which is worth imparting, and which, wherever it is imparted, vindicates its heavenly origin and its heavenly tendency.

II. This is the End; and now what are the Means? They are what we might expect in the view of so great an end. Anything (so the Apostle tells us), be it small or great, short or long, scanty or ample,—the manners of a Jew for Jews, the manners of a Gentile for Gentiles, "all things for all men,"[27]—are worth considering if "by any of these means he might save," that is, elevate, sanctify, purify any of those to whom he spoke. When we reflect upon the many various efforts to do good in this manifold world—the multitude of sermons, societies, agencies, excitements, which to some seem as futile and fruitless as to others they seem precious and important—it is a true consolation to bear in mind the Apostle's wise and generous maxim, "Whether by little or by much, whether in pretence or in truth, whether of strife or of good will, Christ is preached, and I therein do rejoice, yea, and will rejoice." It may be by a short, sudden, electric shock, or it may be by a long course of civilizing, humanizing tendencies. It may be by a single , such as that which awoke the conscience of Augustine; or a single interview like Justin's with the unknown philosopher; or it may be by a long systematic treatise—Butler's "Analogy," or Lardner's "Credibilia," or the "Institutes" of

Calvin, or the "Summa Theologiæ" of Aquinas. It may be by the sudden flush of victory in battle, such as convinced Clovis on the field of Tolbiac; or the argument of a peaceful conference, such as convinced our own Ethelbert. It may be by teachers steeped in what was by half the Christian world regarded as deadly heresy, such as the Arian Bishop Ulfilas, by whom were converted to the faith those mighty Gothic tribes which formed the first elements of European Christendom, and whose deeds Augustine regarded, notwithstanding their errors, as the glory of the Christian name.28 It may be by teachers immersed in superstitions as barbarous, as completely repudiated by the civilized world, as were those of the famous Roman Pontiff who sent the first missionaries to these shores. Sometimes the change has been effected by the sight of a single picture, as when Vladimir of Russia was shown the representation of the Last Judgment; sometimes by a dream or a sign, known only to those who were affected by it—such as the vision of the Cross which arrested Constantine on his way to Rome, or changed Colonel Gardiner's dissolute youth to a manhood of strict and sober piety. Sometimes it has been by the earnest preaching of missionaries, confessedly ill-educated and ill-prepared for the work which they had to accomplish; sometimes by the slow infiltration of Christian literature and Christian civilization; the grandeur, in old days, of Rome and Constantinople; in our days, the superiority of European genius, the spread of English commerce, the establishment of just laws, pure homes, merciful institutions.

We do not say that all these means are equally good or equally efficacious. St. Paul, in his argument with Agrippa, did not mean to say that "almost and altogether," that "much and little," were the same; he did not mean that it was equally good that Christ should be preached in strife or in good-will; he did not mean that a good end justified bad means, or that we may do evil that good may come; he did not mean to justify the falsehoods which are profanely called pious frauds, nor the persecutions which have been set on foot by those who thought to do God service, or the attempt to stimulate artificial excitement by undermining the moral strength and manly independence of the human spirit. God forbid! But what he meant, and what we mean with him, is this: In true Christian missions, in the conversion of human souls from dead works, from sin, from folly, from barbarism, from hardness, from selfishness, to goodness and purity, justice and truth, the field is so vast, the diversity of character in men and nations is so infinite, the enterprise so arduous, the aspects of Divine truth so various, that it is on the one hand a duty for each one to follow out that particular means of conversion which seems to him most efficacious, and on the other hand to acquiesce in the converging use of many means which cannot, by the nature of the case, appear equally efficacious to every one. Such a toleration, such an adoption of the different modes of carrying on what John Bunyan called "the Holy War," "the Siege of Man's Soul," must indeed be always controlled by the determination to keep the high, paramount, universal end always in view; by the vigilant endeavor to repress the exaggeration, to denounce the follies and the falsehoods which infect even the best attempts of narrow and fallible, though good and faithful, servants of their Lord. But, if once we have this principle fixed in our minds, it surely becomes a solace to remember that the soul of man is won by a thousand different approaches—that thus the instruments which often seem most unworthy may yet serve to produce a result far above themselves—that when "we have toiled all night and taken nothing" by keeping close to the shore, or by throwing out our nets always on one side, yet if we have courage "to launch out into the deep, and cast out our nets on the other side of the ship," we shall "enclose a great multitude of fishes, so that the net shall break."

He is a traitor to the cause who exalts the means above the end, or who seeks an end altogether different from that to which his allegiance binds him; but he is not a traitor, but a faithful soldier, who makes the best use of all the means that are placed in his hands. Long after the imperfect instruments have perished the results will endure, and in forms wholly unlike the insufficiency or the meagreness of the first propelling cause. The preaching of Henry Martyn may have been tinged by a zeal often not according to knowledge; but the savor of his holy and self-denying life has passed like a sweet-smelling incense through the whole framework of Indian society. "Even," so he said himself, "if I should never see a native converted, God may design by my patience and continuance in the work to encourage future missionaries."

The more profoundly we are impressed with the degradation of the heathen nations, with the corruption of the Christian churches, the more thankful should we be for any attempts, however slight and however various, to quicken the sluggish mass, and enlighten the blackness of the night, provided only that the mass is permanently quickened, and the darkness is in any measure dispelled. "I have lived too long," said Lord Macaulay on his return from India to England, "I have lived too long in a country where people worship cows, to think much of the differences which part Christians from Christians." And, in fact, as the official report to which I have referred testifies in strong terms, the presence of the great evils which Indian missionaries have to confront, has often produced in them a noble and truly Christian indifference to the trivial divergences between themselves. "Even a one-eyed man," says the proverb, "is a king amongst the blind." Even the shepherd's sling may perchance smite down the Goliath of Gath. The rough sledge-hammer of a rustic preacher may strike home, where the most polished scholar would plead in vain. The calm judgment of the wise and good, or the silent example, or the understanding sympathy, or the wide survey of the whole field of the religions of mankind, may awaken convictions which all the declamations of all the churches would fail to arouse.

The misery of the war on the coast of Africa, the terrible prospect of the Indian famine, may furnish the very opening which we most desire. They may be the very touchstones by which these suffering heathens will test the practical efficiency of a Christian government and a Christian nation, of Christian missionaries and Christian people, and, having so tested it, will judge.

When the first Napoleon suddenly found himself among the quicksands of the Red Sea he ordered his generals to ride out in so many opposite directions, and the first who arrived on firm ground to call on the rest to follow. This is what we may ask of all the various schemes and agencies—all the various inquiries after truth now at work in all the different branches and classes of Christendom—"Ride out amongst those quicksands! Ride out in the most opposite directions, and let him that first finds solid ground call out to us! It may perchance be the very ground in the midst of this quaking morass where we shall be able to stand firm and move the world."

There is one special variety of means which I would venture to name in conclusion. Ever since the close of the Apostolic age there have been two separate agencies in the Christian Church by which the work of conversion has been carried on. The chief, the recognized, the ordinary agency has been that of the clergy. Every presbyter, every bishop in the Church of the first ages, and again in the beginning of Christian Europe, was, in the strict sense of the word, a missionary; and although their functions have in these latter days been for the most part best fulfilled by following their stationary, fixed, pastoral charges, yet it is still from their ranks in all the different churches that the noble army of missionaries and martyrs in foreign lands has been, and is and must be recruited. Most unwise and unworthy would be any word which should underrate the importance of this mighty element in the work of renewing the face of the earth. But there has always been recognized, more or less distinctly, the agency of Christian laymen in this same work of evangelization. Not only in that more general sense in which I have already indicated the effect of the laws, and literature, and influence of Christian Europe—not only in that unquestionable sense in which the best of all missionaries is a high-minded governor, or an upright magistrate, or a devout and pure-minded soldier, who is always "trusting in God and doing his duty;" not only in these senses do we look for the coöperation of laymen, but also in the more direct forms of instruction, of intelligent and far-seeing interest in labors, which, though carried on mainly by the clergy, must, if they are to be good for anything, concern all mankind alike. In the early centuries of Christianity the aid of laymen was freely invoked and freely given in this great cause. Such was Origen, the most learned and the most gifted of the Fathers, who preached as a layman in the presence of presbyters and bishops. Such was one of the first evangelizers of India, Pantænus; such was the hermit Telemachus, whose earnest protest, aided by his heroic death, extinguished at Rome the horrors of the gladiatorial games; such was Antony, the mighty preacher in the wilds of the Thebaid and the streets of Alexandria; such, in later days, was Francis of Assisi, when first he began his career as the most famous preacher of the Middle Ages; such, just before the Reformation, was our own Sir Thomas More.29 In these instances, as in many others, the influence, the learning, the zeal of laymen, was directly imported into the work of Christianizing the nations of Europe. It is for this reason that we in our age also, so far as the law and order of our churches permit, have frequently received the assistance of laymen; who, by the weight of their character or their knowledge, can render a fresh testimony, or throw a fresh light on subjects where we, the clergy, should perhaps be heard less willingly. As their voices have been raised on this sacred subject of missions in many a humble parish church; as also on other sacred topics, such as Christian art and history, their words have often been heard within the consecrated walls of this and other great abbeys and cathedrals;—so, in the hope that a more systematic form may thus be given to our knowledge, and a more concentrated direction to our zeal, we shall have the privilege of listening this evening in the nave of this church to a scholar renowned throughout the world, whose knowledge of all heathen religions, ancient and modern, in their relation to the experience of Christian missions, probably exceeds that of any other single person in Europe.

I conclude by once more applying the Apostle's words to the Means and the End of Christian missions. We would to God that whether by little or by much, whether by sudden stroke or by elaborate reasoning, whether in a brief moment or by long process of years, whether by the fervor of active clergy, or by the learning of impartial laymen, whether by illiterate simplicity or by wide philosophy—not only those who hear me, but all on whom the services of this day, far and near, have any influence, may become, at least in some degree, such as was Paul the Apostle, such as have been the wisest and best of Christian missionaries, except only those bonds which belong to time and place, not to the Eternal Spirit and the Everlasting Gospel of Jesus Christ. We cannot wish a better wish, or pray a better prayer to God on this day than that amongst the missionaries who teach, amongst the heathens who hear, there should be raised up men who should exhibit that type of Christian truth and of Christian life which was seen by Festus and Agrippa in Paul of Tarsus. May the Giver of all good gifts give to us some portion of his cheerful and manly faith, of his fearless energy, of his horror of narrowness and superstition, of his love for God and for mankind, of his absolute faith in the triumph of his Redeemer's cause. May God our Father waken in us the sense that we are all his children; may the whole earth become more and more one fold under one Good Shepherd, Jesus Christ his Son; may the Holy Spirit of Heaven

> "Our souls inspire,
>
> And lighten with celestial fire."

ON THE VITALITY OF BRAHMANISM.

THE delivery of a lecture on Missions in Westminster Abbey by a layman, and that layman a German, caused great excitement at the time. While some persons of great experience and authority in Church and State expressed their full approval of the bold step which the Dean of Westminister had taken, and while some of the most devoted missionaries conveyed to me their hearty thanks for what I had said in my lecture, others could not find terms sufficiently violent to vent their displeasure against the Dean, and to proclaim their horror at the heretical opinions embodied in my address. I was publicly threatened with legal proceedings, and an eminent lawyer informed me in the "Times" of the exact length of imprisonment I should have to undergo.

I did not reply. I had lived long enough in England to know that no good cause can ever be served by a breach of the law, and neither the Dean nor I myself would have acted as we did unless it had been ascertained beforehand from the highest authorities that, with the sanction of the Dean, there was nothing illegal in a layman delivering such a lecture within the precincts of his Abbey. As to the opinions which I expressed on that occasion, I had expressed them before in my published "Lectures on the Science of Religion." Whether they are orthodox or heretical, others are more competent to determine than I am. I simply hold them to be true, and at my time of life, mere contradictions, abuse, or even threats are not likely to keep me from expressing opinions which, whether rightly or wrongly, seem to me founded in truth.

But while I refrained from replying to mere outbursts of anger, I gladly availed myself of the opportunity offered by an article published in the "Fortnightly Review" (July, 1874), by Mr. Lyall, a highly distinguished Indian civilian, in order to explain more fully some of the views expressed in my lecture which seemed liable to misapprehension. Unfortunately the writer of the article "On Missionary Religions" had not the whole of my lecture before him when writing his criticisms, but had to form his opinion of it from a condensed report which appeared in the "Times" of December 5th, 1873. The limits of a lecture are in themselves very narrow, and when so large a subject as that of which I had to treat in Westminster Abbey had to be condensed within sixty minutes, not only those who wish to misunderstand, but those also who try to judge fairly, may discover in what has been said, or what has not been said, a very different meaning from that which the lecturer wished to convey. And if a closely-packed lecture is compressed once more into one column of the "Times," it is hardly possible to avoid what has happened in this case. Mr. Lyall has blamed me for not quoting facts or statements which, as he will have seen by this time, I had quoted in my lecture. I am reminded by him, for instance, of the remarks made by Sir George Campbell in his report upon the government of Bengal in 1871–72, when he wrote, "It is a great mistake to suppose that the Hindu religion is not proselytizing; the system of castes gives room for the introduction of any number of outsiders; so long as people do not interfere with existing castes, they may form a new caste and call themselves Hindus; and the Brahmans are always ready to receive all who will submit to them and pay them. The process of manufacturing Rajputs from ambitious aborigines goes on before our eyes." "This," Mr. Lyall observes, "is one recently recorded observation out of many that might be quoted."

It is this very passage which I had quoted in my third note, only that in quoting it from the "Report on the Progress and Condition of India," laid before Parliament in 1873, I had added the caution of the reporter, that "this assertion must be taken with reserve."

With such small exceptions, however, I have really nothing to complain of in the line of argument adopted by Mr. Lyall. I believe that, after having read my paper, he would have modified some portions of what he has written, but I feel equally certain that it is well that what he has written should have been written, and should be carefully pondered both by those who have the interests of the natives, and by those who have the interests of Christian missions at heart. The few remarks which I take the liberty of making are made by way of explanation only; on all truly essential points I believe there is not much difference of opinion between Mr. Lyall and myself.

As my lecture in Westminister Abbey was delivered shortly after the publication of my "Introduction to the Science of Religion," I ventured to take certain points which I had fully treated there as generally known. One of them is the exact value to be ascribed to canonical books in a scientific treatment of religion. When Mr. Lyall observes *in limine*, that inferences as to the nature and tendency of various existing religions which are drawn from study and exegetic comparison of their scriptures, must be qualified by actual observation of these religions and their popular form and working effects, he expresses an opinion which I hold as strongly as he holds it himself. After enumerating the books which are recognized as sacred or authoritative by large religious communities in India, books of such bulk and such difficulty that it seems almost impossible for any single scholar to master them in their entirety, I added (p. 111), "And even then our eyes would not have reached many of the sacred recesses in which the Hindu mind has taken refuge, either to meditate on the great problems of life, or to free itself from the temptations and fetters of worldly existence by penances and mortifications of the most exquisite cruelty. India has always been teeming with religious sects, and its religious life has been broken up into countless local centres which it required all the ingenuity and perseverance of a priestly caste to hold together with a semblance of dogmatic uniformity."

We must take care, however, in all scientific studies, not to render a task impossible by attaching to it conditions which, humanly speaking, cannot be fulfilled. It is desirable, no doubt, to study some of the local varieties of faith and worship in every religion, but it is impossible to do this with anything like completeness. Were we to wait till we had examined every Christian sect before trusting ourselves to form a general judgment of Christianity, not one of us could honestly say that he knew his own religion. It seems to me that in studying religions we must expect to meet with the same difficulties which we have to encounter in the comparative study of languages. It may, no doubt, be argued with great force that no one knows English who is ignorant of the spoken dialects, of the jargon of sailors and miners, or of the slang of public-houses and prisons. It is perfectly true that what we call the literary and classical language is never the really living language of a people, and that a foreigner may know Shakespeare, Milton, and Byron, and yet fail to understand, if not the debates in Parliament, at all events the wrangling of sellers and buyers in the markets of the city. Nevertheless, when we learn English, or German, or French, or any of the dead languages, such as Latin and Greek, we must depend on grammars, which grammars are founded on a few classical writers; and when we speak of these languages in general, when we subject them to a scientific treatment, analyze them, and attempt to classify them, we avail ourselves for all such purposes almost exclusively of classical works, of literary productions of recognized authority. It is the same, and it can hardly be otherwise, when we approach the study of religions, whether for practical or for scientific purposes. Suppose a Hindu wished to know what the Christian religion really was, should we tell him to go first to Rome, then to Paris, then to St. Petersburg, then to Athens, then to Oxford, then to Berlin, that he might hear the sermons of Roman Catholics, Greeks, and Protestants, or read their so-called religious papers, in order to form out of these scattered impressions an idea of the real nature of the working effects of Christianity? Or should we not rather tell him to take the Bible, and the hymns of Christian Churches, and from them to form his ideal of true Christianity? A religion is much more likely to become "a mysterious thing," when it is sought for in the heart of each individual believer, where alone, no doubt, it truly lives, or in the endless shibboleths of parties, or in the often contradictory tenets of sects, than when it is studied in those sacred books which are recognized as authoritative by all believers, however much they may vary in their interpretations of certain passages, and still more in the practical application of the doctrines contained in their sacred codes to the ordering of their daily life. Let the dialects of languages or religions be studied by all means, let even the peculiarities in the utterances of each town, village, or family, be carefully noted; but let it be recognized at the same time that, for practical purposes, the immense variety of individual expression has to be merged in one general type, and that this alone supplies the chance of a truly scientific treatment.

So much in justification of the principle which I have followed throughout in my treatment of the so-called Book-religions, holding that they must be judged, first of all, out of their own mouths, *i.e.*, out of their sacred writings. Although each individual believer is responsible for his religion, no religion can be made responsible for each individual believer. Even if we adopt the theory of development in religion, and grant to every thinking man his right of private interpretation, there remains, and their must always remain, to the historian of religion, an appeal to the statutes of the original code with which each religion stands and falls, and by which alone it can justly be judged.

It may be, as Mr. Lyall says, an inveterate modern habit to assume all great historic names to represent something definite, symmetrical, and organized. It may be that Asiatic institutions, as he asserts, are incapable of being circumscribed by rules and formal definitions. But Mr. Lyall, if he directed his attention to European institutions, would meet with much the same difficulties there. Christianity, in the largest sense of the word, is as difficult to define as Brahmanism, the English constitution is as unsymmetrical as the system of caste. Yet, if we mean to speak and argue about them, we must attempt to define them, and with regard to any religion, whether Asiatic or European, no definition, it seems to me, can be fairer than that which we gain from its canonical books.

I now come to a more important point. I had divided the six great religions of the world into *Missionary* and *non-Missionary*, including Judaism, Brahmanism, and Zoroastrianism, under the latter; Buddhism, Christianity, and Mohammedanism, under the former category. If I had followed the good old rule of always giving a definition of technical terms, the objections raised by Mr. Lyall and others would probably never have been urged. I thought, however, that from the whole tenor of my lecture it would have been clear that by missionary religions I meant *those in which the spreading of the truth and the conversion of unbelievers are raised to the rank of a sacred duty by the founder or his immediate successors.* In explaining the meaning of the word proselyte, or προσήλυτος, I had shown that literally it means those who come to us, not those to whom we go, so that even a religion so exclusive as Judaism might admit proselytes, might possibly, if we insisted only on the etymological meaning of the word, be called proselytizing, without having any right to the name of a missionary religion. But I imagined that I had said enough to make such a misunderstanding impossible. We may say that the English nobility grows, but we should never say that it proselytizes, and it would be a mere playing with words if, because Brahmanism admits new-comers, we were to claim for it the title of a proselytizing religion. The Brahmanic Scriptures have not a word of welcome for converts, quite the contrary; and as long as these Scriptures are recognized as the highest authority by the Hindus themselves, we have no right to ascribe to Brahmanism what is in direct contradiction with their teaching. The burning of widows was not enjoined in the Vedas, and hence, in order to gain a sanction for it, a passage in the Veda was falsified. No such necessity was ever felt with regard to gaining converts for the Brahmanic faith, and this shows that, though admission to certain Brahmanic privileges may be easier at present than it was in the days of Viśvâmitra, conversion by persuasion has never become an integral portion of the Brahmanic law.

However, as Mr. Lyall does not stand alone in his opinions, and as others have claimed for Judaism and Zoroastrianism the same missionary character which he claims in the name of Brahmanism, a few explanations may not be out of place.

Till very lately, an orthodox Jew was rather proud of the fact that he and his people had never condescended to spread their religion among Christians by such means as Christians use for the conversion of Jews. The Parsi community, too, seemed to share with the Quakers a prudent reluctance in admitting outsiders to the advantages conferred by membership of so respectable and influential a community, while the Brahmans certainly were the very last to compass heaven and earth for the conversion of Mlecchas or outcasts. Suddenly, however, all this is changed. The Chief Rabbi in London, stung to the quick by the reproach of the absence of the missionary spirit in Judaism, has delivered a sermon to show that I had maligned his people, and that, though they never had missionaries, they had been the most proselytizing people in the world. Some strong arguments in support of the same view have been brought forward by the Rev. Charles Voysey, whose conception of Judaism, however, is founded rather on what the great prophets wished it should have been than on what history teaches us it was. As the facts and arguments advanced by the Jewish advocates did not modify my judgment of the historical character of Judaism, I did not think it necessary to reply, particularly as another eminent Rabbi, the editor of the "Jewish World," fully endorsed my views of Judaism, and expressed his surprise at the unorthodox theories advanced by so high an authority as Dr. Adler. I am informed, however, that the discussion thus originated will not remain without practical results, and that something like a Jewish Missionary Society is actually forming in London, to prove that, if missionary zeal is a test of life, the Jewish religion will not shrink from such a test. "We have done something," the Rev. Charles Voysey remarks, "to stir them up; but let us not forget that our reminder was answered, not by a repulse or expression of surprise, but by an assurance that many earnest Jews had already been thinking of this very work, and planning among themselves how they could revive some kind of missionary enterprise. Before long, I feel sure they will give practical evidence that the missionary spirit is still alive and striving in their religion." And again: "The Jews will soon show whether their religion is alive or dead, will soon meet the rival religions of the world on more than equal terms, and will once more take the lead in these days of enlightened belief, and in search after conceptions worthy of a God, just as of old Judaism stood on a lofty height, far above all the religions of mankind."

What has happened in London seems to have happened in Bombay also. The Zoroastrians, too, did not like to be told that their religion was dying, and that their gradual decay was due to the absence of the missionary spirit among them. We read in the "Oriental" of April, 1874, "There is a discussion as to whether it is contrary to the creed of Zoroaster to seek converts to the faith. While conceding that Zoroaster was himself opposed to proselytizing heathens, most of the Parsis hold that the great decrease in the number of his followers renders it absolutely necessary to attempt to augment the sect."

Lastly, Mr. Lyall stands up for Brahmanism, and maintains that in India Brahmanism had spread out during the last hundred years, while Islam and Christianity have contracted. "More persons in India," he says, "become every year Brahmanists, than all the converts to all the other religions in India, put together." "The number of converts," he maintains, "added to Brahmanism in the last few generations, especially in this country, must be immense; and *if the word proselyte may be used in the sense of one that has come, not necessarily being one that has been invited or persuaded to come*, then Brahmanism may lay claim to be by far the most successful proselytizing religion of modern times in India."

The words which I have ventured to put in italics, will show at once how little difference of opinion there is between Mr. Lyall and myself, as long as we use the same words in the same sense. If proselytizing could be used in the etymological sense, here assigned to it by Mr. Lyall, then, no doubt, Brahmanism would be a proselytizing or missionary religion. But this is mere playing with words. In English, proselytizing is never used in that sense. If I meant by missionary religions nothing more than religions which are capable of increase by admitting those that wish to be admitted, religions which say to the world at large, "Knock and it shall be opened unto you," but no more, then, no doubt, Brahmanism, or at least some phases of it, might be called by that name. But what, according to my explanation, constitutes a missionary religion is something totally different. It is the spirit of truth in the hearts of believers which cannot rest unless it manifests itself in thought, word, and deed, which is not satisfied till it has carried its message to every human soul, till what it believes to be the truth is accepted as the truth by all members of the human family.

That spirit imparts to certain religions a character of their own, a character which, if I am not mistaken, constitutes the vital principle of our own religion, and of the other two which, in that respect, stand nearest to Christianity—Buddhism and Mohammedanism. This is not a mere outward difference, depending on the willingness of others to join or not to join; it is an inward difference which stamped Christianity as a missionary religion, when as yet it counted no more than twelve apostles, and which lays on every one that calls himself a Christian the duty of avowing his convictions, whatever they may be, and gaining others to embrace the truth. In that sense every true Christian is a missionary. Mr. Lyall is evidently aware of all this, if we may judge by the expressions which he uses when speaking of the increase of Brahmanism. He speaks of the clans and races which inhabit the hill-tracts, the out-lying uplands, and the uncleared jungle districts of India, as *melting* into Hinduism. He represents the ethnical frontier, described by Mr. Hunter in the "Annals of Rural Bengal," as an ever-breaking shore of primitive beliefs, which *tumble* constantly into the ocean of Brahmanism. And even when he dwells on the fact that non-Aryans are invited by the Brahmans to enter in, he adds that this is done for the sake of profit and repute, not from a wish to eradicate error, to save souls, or to spread the truth. Such instances occurred even in the ancient history of India; and I had myself, in my "History of Ancient Sanskrit Literature," pointed out the case of the Rathakaras or carpenters who were admitted to the Vedic sacrifices, and who, probably from a mere similarity of name—their leader being called Bribu,— had the old Vedic Ribhus assigned to them as their peculiar deities. But these were exceptions, they were *concessions aux nègres*, deviations from traditional rules, entirely owing to the pressure of circumstances; not manifestations springing from religious impulses. If Mr. Lyall remarks himself, that a religion which thus, half involuntarily, enlarges its borders, is not, in the strict sense of the word, a missionary religion, he shows that he is fully aware of the profound difference between a religion that grows by mere agglomeration and a religion that grows by its own strength, by its irrepressible missionary zeal. In answer to his concluding remark, that this ground was *not* taken in my lecture, I can only say that it was, nay, that it formed the very foundation on which the whole argument of my lecture was meant to rest.

There is more force in the objections which Mr. Lyall raises against my calling Brahmanism already dead. The word was too strong; at all events, it was liable to be misunderstood. What I meant to say was that the popular worship of Śiva and Vishṇu belongs to the same intellectual stratum as the worship of Jupiter and Apollo, that it is an anachronism in the nineteenth century, and that, for our purposes, for prognosticating the issues of the religious struggles of the future, it may simply be set aside. For settling any of the questions that may be said to be pending between Christianity, Mohammedanism, and Buddhism, Brahmanism is dead. For converting any number of Christians, Mohammedans, and Buddhists back to idolworship, Brahmanism is dead. It may absorb Sonthals, and Gonds, and Bhils, and other half savage races, with their rough-hewn jungle deities, it may even raise them to a higher stage of civilization, and imbue them with the first principles of a truer faith and a purer worship, but for carrying any of the strong positions of Buddhism, Mohammedanism, and Christianity, Brahmanism is powerless and dead. In India itself, where it clings to the soil with a thousand roots, it was beaten by Buddhism, and, if it afterwards recovered its position, that was due to physical force, not to persuasion and conversion. The struggle between Mohammedanism and Brahmanism in India was on both sides a political rather than a religious struggle: still when a change of religion arose from conviction, we see Brahmanism yielding to the purer light of Islam, not Islam to Brahmanism.

I did not undervalue the actual power of Brahmanism, particularly its power of resistance; nor did I prophesy its speedy extinction. I said on the contrary that "a religion may linger on for a long time, and be accepted by the large masses of the people, because it is there, and there is nothing better." "It is true," I added, "there are millions of children, women, and men in India who fall down before the stone image of Vishṇu, with his four arms, riding on a creature, half-bird, half-man, or sleeping on the serpent; who worship Śiva, a monster with three eyes, riding naked on a bull, with a necklace of skulls for his ornament. There are human beings who still believe in a god of war, Kârtikeya, with six faces, riding on a peacock, and holding bow and arrow in his hands; and who invoke a god of success, Gaṇeśa, with four hands and an elephant's head, sitting on a rat. Nay, it is true that, in the broad daylight of the nineteenth century, the figure of the goddess Kali is carried through the streets of her own city, Calcutta, her wild disheveled hair reaching to her feet, with a necklace of human heads, her tongue protruded from her mouth, her girdle stained with blood. All this is true; but ask any Hindu who can read and write and think, whether these are the gods he believes in, and he will smile at your credulity. How long this living death of national religion in India may last, no one can tell: for our purposes, however, for gaining an idea of the issue of the great religious struggle of the future, that religion is dead and gone."

I ask Mr. Lyall, is this true or is it not? He says himself, "that Brahmanism may possibly melt away of a heap and break up, I would not absolutely deny." Would Mr. Lyall say the same of Buddhism, Mohammedanism, or Christianity? He points himself to the description which Gibbon gives of the ancient Roman religion in the second century of the Christian era, and shows how closely applicable it is to the present state of Brahmanism in India. "The tolerant superstition of the people, 'not confined by the claims of any speculative system,' the 'devout polytheist, whom fear, gratitude, and curiosity, a dream, or an omen, a singular disorder, or a distant journey, perpetually disposed to multiply the articles of his belief, and to enlarge the list of his protectors;' the 'ingenious youth alike instructed in every school to reject and despise the religion of the multitude;' the philosophic class who 'look with indulgence on the errors of the vulgar, diligently practice the ceremonies of their fathers, and devoutly frequent the temples of their gods;' the 'magistrates who know and value the advantages of religion as it is connected with civil government;'—all these scenes and feelings are represented in India at this moment, though by no means in all parts of India." If, then, in the second century a student of religious pathology had expressed his conviction that in spite of the number of its professors, in spite of its antiquity, in spite of its indigenous character, in spite of its political, civil, and social influences, in spite of its temples and priests, in spite of its schools and philosophers, the ancient religion of Jupiter had lost its vitality, was sick unto death, nay, for all real purposes was dead, would he have been far wrong? It may be replied, no doubt, that similar corruptions have crept into other religions also, that gaudy dolls are carried about in Christian cathedrals, that people are invited to see tears rolling down from the eyes of images, or to worship wine changed into blood, to say nothing of even more terrible hallucinations on the Eucharist propounded from so-called Protestant pulpits, and that, in spite of all this, we should not call the Christian religion dying or dead. This is true, and I thought that by my remarks on the different revivals of Hinduism from the twelfth to the nineteenth century, I had sufficiently indicated that new life may spring even from such apparently hopeless corruption. If it is Brahmanism that lives in the sects of Râmânuja and Râmânanda, in the poetry of Kabir and the wisdom of Nànak, in the honest purposes of Ram Mohun Roy and in the high aspirations of Keshub Chunder Sen, then I quite agree with Mr. Lyall that Brahmanism is not dead, but lives more intensely than ever.

But here, for some reason or other, Mr. Lyall seems to demur to my hopeful estimate of Brahmoism. He had expressed his own conviction that Brahmanism, though it might suddenly collapse and vanish, was more likely gradually to spiritualize and centralize its Pantheon, reduce its theology to a compact system, soften down its morals by symbolisms and interportations, discard "dogmatic extremes," and generally to bring itself into accordance with improved standards of science and intelligence. He had also quoted with implied approval the remark of qualified observers, "that we might at any time witness a great Brahmanic reforming revival in India, if some really gifted and singularly powerful prophet were to arise among the Hindus." But when I hinted that this prophet had actually arisen, and that in Brahmoism, as preached by Ram Mohun Roy, Debendranath Tagore, and Keshub Chunder Sen, we ought to recognize a transition from Brahmanism to a purer faith; when I pointed out that, though Christian missionaries might not wish to recognize Brahmoism as their work, it was the work of those missionary Christians who have lived in India as examples of a true Christian life, who have approached the natives in a truly missionary spirit, in the spirit of truth and in the spirit of love, Mr. Lyall replies that "Brahmoism, as propagated by Keshub Chunder Sen, seems to be Unitarianism of an European type, and, so far as one can understand its argument, appears to have no logical stability or *locus standi* between revelation and pure rationalism; that it propounds either too much or too little to its hearers." "A faith," he continues, "which contains mere fervent sentiments, and high conceptions of morality, does not partake of the complexion or nature of those religions which have encompassed the heart of great nations, nor is it generally supposed in India that Brahmoism is perceptibly on the increase."

Mutatis mutandis, this is very much what an orthodox Rabbi might have said of Christianity. Let us wait. I am not given to prophecy, but though I am no longer young, I still hold to a belief that a cause upheld with such honesty of purpose, purity, and unselfishness as Brahmoism has been, must and will meet with ultimate success. Does Mr. Lyall think that Unitarian Christianity is no Christianity? Does he find logical stability in Trinitarianism? Does he consider pure rationalism incompatible with revelation? Does he know of any teacher who might not be accused of saying either too little or too much? In A.D. 890 the Double Procession was as much a burning question as the Homoousia in 324,—are, therefore, both Channing and Dr. Döllinger to be anathematized now? Brahmoism may not be like the religions of old, but must the religions of the future be like the religions of the past? However, I do not wish to draw Mr. Lyall into a theological argument. His estimate of the real value and vitality of Brahmoism may be right, mine may be wrong. His presence in India, and his personal intercourse with the Brahmos, may have given him opportunities of judging which I have not. Only let us not forget that for watching the movements of a great struggle, and for judging of its successful issue, a certain distance from the field of battle has its advantages, and that judges in India have not always proved the best judges of India.

One point, however, I am quite willing to concede. If Brahmoism and similar movements may be considered as reforms and resuscitations of Brahmanism, then I withdraw my expression that Brahmanism is dead. Only let us remember that we are thus using Brahmanism in two very different senses, that we are again playing with words. In the one sense it is stark idolatry, in the other the loftiest spiritual worship. The former asserts the existence of many personal gods, the latter shrinks even from the attribute of personality as too human a conception of the Highest Spirit. The former makes the priest a kind of god on earth, the latter proclaims the priesthood of all men; the former is guided by scriptures which man calls sacred, the latter knows of no sacred oracles but the still small voice in the heart of every man. The two are like two opposite poles. What is negative on one side is positive on the other; what is regarded by the one as the most sacred truth is anathematized by the other as deadly error.

Mr. Lyall tells us of Ghási Dás, an inspired prophet, who sojourned in the wilderness for six months, and then issued forth preaching to the poor and ignorant the creed of the True Name (Satnám). He gathered about half a million people together before he died in 1850. He borrowed his doctrines from the well-known Hindu sect of the Satnâmis, and though he denounced Brahmanic abuses, he instituted caste rules of his own, and his successor was murdered, not for heresy, but because he aped Brahmanic insignia and privileges. Mr. Lyall thinks that this community, if left alone, will relapse into a modified Brahmanism. This may be so, but it can hardly be said, that a reform, the followers of which are murdered for aping Brahmanic insignia and privileges, represents Brahmanism which Mr. Lyall defines as "the broad denomination of what is recognized by all Hindus as the supreme theological faculty and the comprehensive scheme of authoritative tradition to which all minor beliefs are referred for sanction."

When I spoke of Brahmanism as dead, I meant the popular orthodox Brahmanism, which is openly patronized by the Brahmans, though scorned by them in secret; I did not, and could not, mean the worship of Bramah as the Supreme Spirit, which has existed in India from the time of the Upanishads to the present day, and has lately assumed the name of Brahmoism,—a worship so pure, so exalted, so deeply human, so truly divine, that every man can join in it without apostasy, whether he be born a Jew, a Gentile, or a Christian.

That many antagonistic forms of religious faith, some the most degraded, others the most exalted, should live on the same soil, among the same people, is indeed a disheartening truth, enough almost to shake one's belief in the common origin and the common destinies of the human race. And yet we must not shut our eyes to the fact that amongst ourselves, too, men who call themselves Christians are almost as widely separated from each other in their conceptions of the Divine and the Human, in their grounds of belief and in their sense of duty, as, in India, the worshippers of Gaṇeśa, the god of success, with four hands and an elephant's head, sitting on a rat, on one side, and the believers in the true Brahma on the other. There is a Christianity that is dead, though it may be professed by millions of people, but there is also, let us trust, a Christianity that is alive, though it may count but twelve apostles. As in India, so in Europe, many would call death what we call life, many would call life what we call death. Here, as elsewhere, it is high time that men should define the exact meaning of their words, trusting that definiteness, frankness, and honesty may offer a better chance of mutual understanding, and serve as a stronger bond of union between man and man, than vague formulas, faint-hearted reticence, and what is at the root of it all, want of true love of Man, and of true faith in God.

If Mr. Lyall imagined that the object of my Lecture was to discourage missionary efforts, he must have found out his mistake, when he came to read it, as I delivered it in Westminster Abbey. I know of no nobler life than that of a true missionary. I tried to defend the labors of the paternal missionary against disparaging criticisms. I tried to account for the small success of controversial missions, by showing how little is gained by mere argument and casuistry at home. And I pointed to the indirect missionary influence, exercised by every man who leads a Christian life in India or elsewhere, as the most encouraging sign of the final triumph of a pure and living Christianity. It is very possible, as Mr. Lyall says somewhat sarcastically, that "missionaries will even yet hardly agree that the essentials of their religion are not in the creeds, but in love; because they are sent forth to propound scriptures which say clearly that what we believe or disbelieve is literally a *burning* question." But those who, with Mr. Lyall, consider love of man founded on love of God, nothing but "flat morality," must have forgotten that a Higher One than they declared, that on these two hang all the law and the commandments. By placing abstruse tenets, the handiwork of Popes and Councils, in the place of Christ's teaching, and by making a belief in these positive articles a *burning* question, weak mortals have driven weak mortals to ask, "Are we Christians still?" Let them for once "by observation and experience" try the oldest and simplest and most positive article of Christianity, real love of man founded on real love of God, and I believe they will soon ask themselves, "When shall we be Christians at last?"

Footnotes to Chapter V:
On Missions

1. "NOTICE.

"Westminster Abbey. Day of Intercession for Missions, Wednesday, December 3d, 1873. Lecture in the Nave, at eight o'clock, p.m.

Hymn 25 (*Bp. Heber*)

Wittenberg (p. 50).

"From Greenland's icy mountains,

From India's coral strands,

Where Afric's sunny fountains,

Roll down their golden sands;

From many an ancient river,

From many a palmy plain,

They call us to deliver

Their land from error's chain.

"What though the spicy breezes

Blow soft o'er Ceylon's isle;

Though every prospect pleases,

And only man is vile!

In vain with lavish kindness

The gifts of God are strown;

The heathen in his blindness

Bows down to wood and stone.

"Can we whose souls are lighted

With wisdom from on high,

Can we to men benighted

The lamp of life deny?

Salvation, O Salvation!

The joyful sound proclaim,

Till earth's remotest nation

Has learnt Messiah's name.

"Waft, waft, ye winds, his story;

And you, ye waters, roll;

Till, like a sea of glory,

It spreads from pole to pole;

Till o'er our ransomed nature,

>   The Lamb for sinners slain,
>
>   Redeemer, King, Creator,
>
>   In bliss returns to reign. Amen.

"There will be a Lecture delivered in the Nave, on Missions, by Professor Max Müller, M.A.

Ps. 100 (*New Version*)

Old Hundredth (p. 21).

>   "With one consent let all the earth
>
>   To God their cheerful voices raise;
>
>   Glad homage pay with awful mirth,
>
>   And sing before Him songs of praise.
>
>   "Convinced that He is God alone,
>
>   From Whom both we and all proceed;
>
>   We whom He chooses for His own,
>
>   The flock that He vouchsafes to feed.
>
>   "O enter then His temple gate,
>
>   Thence to His courts devoutly press;
>
>   And still your grateful hymns repeat,
>
>   And still His Name with praises bless.
>
>   "For He's the Lord supremely good,
>
>   His mercy is forever sure;
>
>   His truth, which all times firmly stood,
>
>   To endless ages shall endure. Amen."

2. Different systems of classification applied to the religions of the world are discussed in my *Introduction to the Science of Religion*, pp. 122–143.

3. "Proselyto ne fidas usque ad vigesimam quartam generationem," Jalkut Ruth, f. 163. d; Danz, in Meuschen, *Nov. Test, ex Talm. illustr.*, p. 651.

4. *India, Progress and Condition*, Blue Book presented to Parliament, 1873, p. 99. "It is asserted (but the assertion must be taken with reserve) that it is a mistake to suppose that the Hindu religion is

not proselytizing. Any number of outsiders, so long as they do not interfere with established castes, can form a new caste, and call themselves Hindus, and the Brahmans are always ready to receive all who submit to and pay them." Can this be called proselytizing?

5. Cf. *Mahavanso*, cap. 5.

6. Cf. *Mahavanso*, cap. 12.

7. In some of the places mentioned by the *Chronicle* as among the earliest stations of Buddhist missions, relics have been discovered containing the names of the very missionaries mentioned by the *Chronicle*. See Koeppen, *Die Religion des Buddha*, p. 188.

8. Note A, p. 266.

9. "*Islâm* is the verbal noun, and *Moslim* the participle of the same root, which also yields *Salâm*, peace, and *salim* and *salym*, whole, honest. *Islâm* means, therefore, to satisfy or pacify by forbearance; it also means simply subjection." Sprenger, *Mohammad*, i. p. 69; iii. 486.

10. Lassen, *Indische Alterthumskunde*, vol. iv. p. 635. Cf. *Indian Antiquary*, 1873, p. 370. *Academy*, 1874, p. 61.

11. *Chips from a German Workshop*, vol. i.; *Essays on the Science of Religion*, pp. 161, 216.

12. Lassen, *Indische Alterthumskunde*, vol. iv. p. 606; Wilson, *Asiatic Researches*, xvi. p. 21.

13. See *Brahmic Questions of the Day*, 1869, p. 16.

14. *History of Ancient Sanskrit Literature*, by M. M. (2d ed.) p. 569.

15. *The Adi Brahma-Samaj, Its views and Principles*, Calcutta, 1870, p. 10.

16. *A Brief History of the Calcutta Brahma-Samâj*, 1868, p. 15.

17. See Note B, p. 269.

18. See Note C, p. 272.

19. The *Indian Mirror* (Sept. 10, 1869) constantly treats of missionary efforts of various kinds in a spirit which is not only friendly, but even desirous of reciprocal sympathy; and hopeful that whatever differences may exist between them (the missionaries) and the Brahmos, the two parties will heartily

combine as brethren to exterminate idolatry, and promote true morality in India.

Many of our ministers and leading men, says the *Indian Mirror*, are recruited from missionary schools, which, by affording religious education, prove more favorable to the growth and spread of Brahmoism than government schools with Comte and Secularism (*Indian Theism*, by S. D. Collet, 1870, p. 22).

20. *Life of John Coleridge Patteson*, by C. M. Yonge, ii. p. 167.

21. "The large body of European and American missionaries settled in India bring their various moral influences to bear upon the country with the greater force, because they act together with a compactness which is but little understood. Though belonging to various denominations of Christians, yet from the nature of their work, their isolated position, and their long experience, they have been led to think rather of the numerous questions on which they agree, than of those on which they differ, and they coöperate heartily together. Localities are divided among them by friendly arrangements, and, with a few exceptions, it is a fixed rule among them that they will not interfere with each other's converts and each other's spheres of duty. School books, translations of the Scriptures and religious works, prepared by various missions, are used in common; and help and improvements secured by one mission are freely placed at the command of all. The large body of missionaries resident in each of the presidency towns form missionary conferences, hold periodic meetings, and act together on public matters. They have frequently addressed the Indian government on important social questions involving the welfare of the native community, and have suggested valuable improvements in existing laws. During the past twenty years, on five occasions, general conferences have been held for mutual consultation respecting their missionary work; and in January last, at the latest of these gatherings, at Allahabad, 121 missionaries met together, belonging to twenty different societies, and including several men of long experience who have been twenty years in India." *India, Progress and Condition*, 1873, p. 134.

22. Brahma-Samâj, the Church of Brahma, is the general title. When the schism took place, the original Samâj was called Adi Brahma-Samâj, *i.e.*, the First Church of Brahma, while the progressive party, under Keshub Chunder Sen was distinguished by the name of the Brahma-Samâj of India. The vowels *u* and *o* are often the same in Bengali, and are sometimes used for *a*.

23. This sermon, which was preached by the Dean of Westminster in the forenoon of Wednesday, December 3d, 1873, and in which his reasons are stated for inviting a layman to speak on the subject of missions in the evening of the same day, and within the same sacred precincts, is here reprinted with his kind permission.

24. *Prospects of Christian Missions*, a sermon preached in Westminster Abbey on December 20, 1872. Strahan & Co., London.

25. Phil. i. 13–16.

26. Acts xiv. 16, 17; xvii. 23, 28; xix. 37; xxi. 26; xxii. 28; xxv. 11. Rom. ii. 6–15; xiii. 1–7; xiv. 9; 1 Cor. ix. 20–22; xx. 33. Phil. iv. 8.

27. 1 Cor. ix. 20–22.

28. In the well-known passage where, speaking of the moderation and humanity of these heretical Arians in the capture of Rome, he concludes: "Hoc Christi nomini, hoc Christiano tempori tribuendum quisquis non videt, cæcus; quisquis non laudat, ingratus; quisquis laudanti reluctatur, ingratus est." *De Civitate Dei*, i. c. 7. Compare Ibid. c. 1, and Sermon cv., *De. Ev. S. Luc.*

29. "Sir Thomas More, after he was called to the Bar in Lincoln's Inn, did, for a considerable time, read a public lecture out of S. Augustine, *De Civitate Dei*, in the Church of S. Lawrence in the Old Jewry to which the learneder sort of the City of London did resort." Wood's *Athenæ Oxonienses*, fol. ed. 1721, pp. 182, 183.

VII.
OPENING ADDRESS.

DELIVERED BY THE PRESIDENT OF THE ARYAN SECTION AT THE INTERNATIONAL CONGRESS OF ORIENTALISTS, HELD IN LONDON, SEPTEMBER 14–21, 1874.

NO one likes to be asked, what business he has to exist, and yet, whatever we do, whether singly or in concert with others, the first question which the world never fails to address to us, is *Dic cur hic?* Why are you here? or to put it into French, What is your *raison d'être?* We have had to submit to this examination even before we existed, and many a time have I been asked the question, both by friend and foe, What is the good of an International Congress of Orientalists?

I shall endeavor, as shortly as possible, to answer that question, and show that our Congress is not a mere fortuitous congeries of barren atoms or molecules, but that we are at least Leibnizian monads, each with his own self, and force and will, and each determined, within the limits of some preëstablished harmony, to help in working out some common purpose, and to achieve some real and lasting good.

It is generally thought that the chief object of a scientific Congress is social, and I am not one of those who are incapable of appreciating the delights and benefits of social intercourse with hard-working and honest-thinking men. Much as I detest what is commonly called society, I willingly give up glaciers and waterfalls, cathedrals and picture galleries, for one half hour of real society, of free, frank, fresh, and friendly intercourse, face to face, and mind to mind, with a great, and noble, and loving soul, such as was Bunsen; with a man intrepid in his thoughts, his words, and his deeds, such as was John Stuart Mill; or with a scholar who, whether he had been quarrying heavy blocks, or chiseling the most brittle filigree work, poured out all his treasures before you with the pride and pleasure of a child, such as was Eugéne Burnouf. A Congress therefore, and particularly an International Congress, would certainly seem to answer some worthy purpose, were it only by bringing together fellow workers of all countries and ages, by changing what were to us merely great names into pleasant companions, and by satisfying that very right and rational curiosity which we all feel, after having read a really good book, of seeing what the man looks like who could achieve such triumphs.

All this is perfectly true; yet, however pleasant to ourselves this social intercourse may appear, in the eyes of the world at large it will hardly be considered a sufficient excuse for our existence. In order therefore to satisfy that outer world that we are really doing something, we point of course to the papers which are read at our public meetings, and to the discussions which they elicit. Much as I value that feature also in a scientific congress, I confess I doubt, and I know that many share that doubt, whether the same result might not be obtained with much less trouble. A paper that contains something really new and valuable, the result, it may be, of years of toil and thought, requires to be read with care in a quiet corner of our own study, before the expression of our assent or dissent can be of any weight or value. There is too much hollow praise, and occasionally too much wrangling and ill-natured abuse at our scientific tournaments, and the world at large, which is never without a tinge of malice and a vein of quiet humor, has frequently expressed its concern at the waste of "oil and vinegar" which is occasioned by the frequent meetings of our British and Foreign Associations.

What then is the real use of a Congress, such as that which has brought us together this week from all parts of the world? What is the real excuse for our existence? Why are we here, and not in our workshops?

It seems to me that the real and permanent use of these scientific gatherings is twofold.

(1) They enable us to take stock, to compare notes, to see where we are, and to find out where we ought to be going.

(2) They give us an opportunity, from time to time, to tell the world where we are, what we have been doing for the world, and what, in return, we expect the world to do for us.

The danger of all scientific work at present, not only among Oriental scholars, but, as far as I can see, everywhere, is the tendency to extreme specialization. Our age shows in that respect a decided reaction against the spirit of a former age, which those with gray heads among us can still remember, an age represented in Germany by such names as Humboldt, Ritter, Böckh, Johannes, Müller, Bopp, Bunsen, and others; men who look to us like giants, carrying a weight of knowledge far too heavy for the shoulders of such mortals as now be; aye, men who *were* giants, but whose chief strength consisted in this, that they were never entirely absorbed or bewildered by special researches, but kept their eye steadily on the highest objects of all human knowledge; who could trace the vast outlines of the kosmos of nature or the kosmos of the mind with an unwavering hand, and to whose maps and guide books we must still recur, whenever we are in danger of losing our way in the mazes of minute research. At the present moment such works as Humboldt's "Kosmos," or Bopp's "Comparative Grammar," or Bunsen's "Christianity and Mankind," would be impossible. No one would dare to write them, for fear of not knowing the exact depth at which the *Protogenes Haeckelii* has lately been discovered or the lengthening of a vowel in the S a ṃ h i t a p â ṭ h a of the Rig-Veda. It is quite right that this should be so, at least, for a time; but all rivers, all brooks, all rills, are meant to flow into the ocean, and all special knowledge, to keep it from stagnation, must have an outlet into the general knowledge of the world. Knowledge for its own sake, as it is sometimes called, is the most dangerous idol that a student can worship. We despise the miser who amasses money for the sake of money, but still more contemptible is the intellectual miser who hoards up knowledge instead of spending it, though, with regard to most of our knowledge, we may be well assured and satisfied that, as we brought nothing into the world so we may carry nothing out.

Against this danger of mistaking the means for the end, of making bricks without making mortar, of working for ourselves instead of working for others, meetings such as our own, bringing together so large a number of the first Oriental scholars of Europe, seem to me a most excellent safeguard. They draw us out of our shell, away from our common routine, away from that small orbit of thought in which each of us moves day after day, and make us realize more fully, that there are other stars moving all around us in our little universe, that we all belong to one celestial system, or to one terrestrial commonwealth, and that, if we want to see real progress in that work with which we are more especially entrusted, the re-conquest of the Eastern world, we must work with one another, for one another, like members of one body, like soldiers of one army, guided by common principles, striving after common purposes, and sustained by common sympathies. Oriental literature is of such enormous dimensions that our small army of scholars can occupy certain prominent positions only; but those points, like the stations of a trigonometrical survey, ought to be carefully chosen, so as to be able to work in harmony together. I hope that in that respect our Congress may prove of special benefit. We shall hear, each of us, from others, what they wish us to do. "Why don't you finish this?" "Why don't you publish that?" are questions which we have already heard asked by many of our friends. We shall be able to avoid what happens so often, that two men collect materials for exactly the same work, and we may possibly hear of some combined effort to carry out great works, which can only be carried out *viribus unitis*, and of which I may at least mention one, a translation of the "Sacred Books of Mankind." Important progress has already been made for setting on foot this great undertaking, an undertaking which I think the world has a right to demand from Oriental scholars, but which can only be carried out by joint action. This Congress has helped us to lay the foundation-stone, and I trust that at our next Congress we shall be able to produce some tangible results.

I now come to the second point. A Congress enables us to tell the world what we have been doing. This, it seems to me, is particularly needful with regard to Oriental studies which, with the exception of Hebrew, still stand outside the pale of our schools and universities, and are cultivated by the very smallest number of students. And yet, I make bold to say, that during the last hundred, and still more during the last fifty years, Oriental studies have contributed more than any other branch of scientific research to change, to purify, to clear, and intensify the intellectual atmosphere of Europe, and to widen our horizon in all that pertains to the Science of Man, in history, philology, theology, and philosophy. We have not only conquered and annexed new worlds to the ancient empire of learning, but we have leavened the old world with ideas that are already fermenting even in the daily bread of our schools and universities. Most of those here present know that I am not exaggerating; but as the world is skeptical while listening to orations *pro domo*, I shall attempt to make good my assertions.

At first, the study of Oriental literature was a matter of curiosity only, and it is so still to a great extent, particularly in England. Sir William Jones, whose name is the only one among Oriental scholars that has ever obtained a real popularity in England, represents most worthily that phase of Oriental studies. Read only the two volumes of his life, and they will certainly leave on your mind the distinct impression that Sir William Jones was not only a man of extensive learning and refined taste, but undoubtedly a very great man—one in a million. He was a good classical scholar of the old school, a well-read historian, a thoughtful lawyer, a clear-headed politician, and a true gentleman, in the old sense of the word. He moved in the best, I mean the most cultivated society, the great writers and thinkers of the day listened to him with respect, and say what you like, we still live by his grace, we still draw on that stock of general interest which he excited in the English mind for Eastern subjects.

Yet the interest which Sir William Jones took in Oriental literature was purely æsthetic. He chose what was beautiful in Persian and translated it, as he would translate an ode of Horace. He was charmed with Kâlidâsa's play of "Sakuntala"—and who is not?—and he left us his classical reproduction of one of the finest of Eastern gems. Being a judge in India, he thought it his duty to acquaint himself with the native law-books in their original language, and he gave us his masterly translation of the "Laws of Manu." Sir William Jones was fully aware of the startling similarity between Sanskrit, Latin, and Greek. More than a hundred years ago, in a letter written to Prince Adam Czartoryski, in the year 1770, he says: "Many learned investigators of antiquity are fully persuaded, that a very old and almost primeval language was in use among the northern nations, from which not only the Celtic dialect, but even Greek and Latin are derived; in fact, we find πατήρ and μήτηρ in Persian, nor is θυγάτηρ so far removed from *dockter*, or even ὄνομα and *nomen* from Persian *nâm*, as to make it ridiculous to suppose that they sprang from the same root. We must confess," he adds, "that these researches are very obscure and uncertain, and you will allow, not so agreeable as an ode of Hafez, or an elegy of Amr'alkeis." In a letter, dated 1787, he says: "You will be surprised at the resemblance between Sanskrit and both Greek and Latin."

Colebrooke also, the great successor of Sir William Jones, was fully aware of the relationship between Sanskrit, Greek, Latin, German, and even Slavonic. I possess some curious MS. notes of his, of the year 1801 or 1802, containing long lists of words, expressive of the most essential ideas of primitive life, and which he proved to be identical in Sanskrit, Greek, Latin, German, and Slavonic.1

Yet neither Colebrooke nor Sir William Jones perceived the full import of these facts. Sir William Jones died young; Colebrooke's energies, marvelous as they were, were partly absorbed by official work, so that it was left to German and French scholars to bring to light the full wealth of the mine which those great English scholars had been the first to open. We know now that in language, and in all that is implied by language, India and Europe are one; but to prove this, against the incredulity of all the greatest scholars of the day, was no easy matter. It could be done effectually in one way only, viz., by giving to Oriental studies a strictly scientific character, by requiring from Oriental students not only the devotion of an *amateur*, but the same thoroughness, minuteness, and critical accuracy which were long considered the exclusive property of Greek and Latin scholars. I could not think of giving here a history of the work done during the last fifty years. It has been admirably described in Benfey's "History of the Science of Language."2 Even if I attempted to give merely the names of those who have been most distinguished by really original discoveries—the names of Bopp, Pott, Grimm, Burnouf, Rawlinson, Miklosich, Benfey, Kuhn, Zeuss, Whitley, Stokes—I am afraid my list would be considered very incomplete.

But let us look at what has been achieved by these men, and many others who followed their banners! The East, formerly a land of dreams, of fables, and fairies, has become to us a land of unmistakable reality; the curtain between the West and the East has been lifted, and our old forgotten home stands before us again in bright colors and definite outlines. Two worlds, separated for thousands of years, have been reunited as by a magic spell, and we feel rich in a past that may well be the pride of our noble Aryan family. We say no longer vaguely and poetically *Ex Oriente Lux*, but we know that all the most vital elements of our knowledge and civilization,—our languages, our alphabets, our figures, our weights and measures, our art, our religion, our traditions, our very nursery stories, come to us from the East; and we must confess that but for the rays of Eastern light, whether Aryan or Semitic or Hamitic, that called forth the hidden germs of the dark and dreary West, Europe, now the very light of the world, might have remained forever a barren and forgotten promontory of the primeval Asiatic continent. We live indeed in a new world; the barrier between the West and the East, that seemed insurmountable, has vanished. The East is ours, we are its heirs, and claim by right our share in its inheritance.

We know what it was for the Northern nations, the old barbarians of Europe, to be brought into spiritual contact with Rome and Greece, and to learn that beyond the small, poor world in which they had moved, there was an older, richer, brighter world, the ancient world of Rome and Athens, with its arts and laws, its poetry and philosophy, all of which they might call their own and make their own by claiming the heritage of the past. We know how, from that time, the Classical and Teutonic spirits mingled together and formed that stream of modern thought on whose shores we ourselves live and move. A new stream is now being brought into the same bed, the stream of Oriental thought, and already the colors of the old stream show very clearly the influence of that new tributary. Look at any of the important works published during the last twenty years, not only on language, but on literature, mythology, law, religion, and philosophy, and you will see on every page the working of a new spirit. I do not say that the East can ever teach us new things, but it can place before us old things, and leave us to draw from them lessons more strange and startling than anything dreamt of in our philosophy.

Before all, a study of the East has taught us the same lesson which the Northern nations once learnt in Rome and Athens, that there are other worlds beside our own, that there are other religions, other mythologies, other laws, and that the history of philosophy from Thales to Hegel is not the whole history of human thought. In all these subjects the East has supplied us with parallels, and with all that is implied in parallels, viz., the possibility of comparing, measuring, and understanding. The *comparative spirit* is the truly scientific spirit of our age, nay of all ages. An empirical acquaintance with single facts does not constitute knowledge in the true sense of the word. All human knowledge begins with the Two or the Dyad, the comprehension of two single things as one. If in these days we may still quote Aristotle, we may boldly say that "there is no science of that which is unique." A single event may be purely accidental, it comes and goes, it is inexplicable, it does not call for an explanation. But as soon as the same fact is repeated, the work of comparison begins, and the first step is made in that wonderful process which we call generalization, and which is at the root of all intellectual knowledge and of all intellectual language. This primitive process of comparison is repeated again and again, and when we now give the title of *Comparative* to the highest kind of knowledge in every branch of science, we have only replaced the old word *intelligent* (*i.e.*, interligent) or intertwining, by a new and more expressive term, *comparative*. I shall say nothing about the complete revolution of the study of languages by means of the comparative method, for here I can appeal to such names as Mommsen and Curtius, to show that the best among classical scholars are themselves the most ready to acknowledge the importance of the results obtained by the intertwining of Eastern and Western philology.

But take mythology. As long as we had only the mythology of the classical nations to deal with, we looked upon it simply as strange, anomalous, and irrational. When, however, the same strange stories, the same hallucinations, turned up in the most ancient mythology of India, when not only the character and achievements, but the very names of some of the gods and heroes were found to be the same, then every thoughtful observer saw that there must be a system in that ancient madness, that there must be some order in that strange mob of gods and heroes, and that it must be the task of comparative mythology to find out, what reason there is in all that mass of unreason.

The same comparative method has been applied to the study of religion also. All religions are Oriental, and with the exception of the Christian, their sacred books are all written in Oriental languages. The materials, therefore, for a comparative study of the religious systems of the world had all to be supplied by Oriental scholars. But far more important than those materials, is the spirit in which they have been treated. The sacred books of the principal religions of mankind had to be placed side by side with perfect impartiality, in order to discern the points which they share in common as well as those that are peculiar to each. The results already obtained by this simple juxtaposition are full of important lessons, and the fact that the truths on which all religions agree far exceed those on which they differ, has hardly been sufficiently appreciated. I feel convinced, however, that the time will come when those who at present profess to be most disquieted by our studies, will be the most grateful for our support,—for having shown by evidence which cannot be controverted, that all religions spring from the same sacred soil, the human heart; that all are quickened by the same divine spirit, the still small voice; and that, though the outward forms of religion may change, may wither and decay, yet, as long as man is what he is and what he has been, he will postulate again and again the Infinite as the very condition of the Finite, he will yearn for something which the world cannot give, he will feel his weakness and dependence, and in that weakness and dependence discover the deepest sources of his hope, and trust, and strength.

A patient study of the sacred scriptures of the world is what is wanted at present more than anything else, in order to clear our own ideas of the origin, the nature, the purposes of religion. There can be no science of one religion, but there can be a science of many. We have learnt already one lesson, that behind the helpless expressions which language has devised, whether in the East or in the West, for uttering the unutterable, be it *Dyaushpitâ* or *Ahuramazda*, be it *Jehovah* or *Allah*, be it the All or the Nothing, be it the First Cause or Our Father in heaven, there is the same intention, the same striving, the same stammering, the same faith. Other lessons will follow, till in the end we shall be able to restore that ancient bond which unites not only the East with the West, but all the members of the human family, and may learn to understand what a Persian poet meant when he wrote many centuries ago (I quote from Mr. Conway's "Sacred Anthology"), "Diversity of worship has divided the human race into seventy-two nations. From among all their dogmas I have selected one—the Love of God."

Nor is this comparative spirit restricted to the treatment of language, mythology, and religion. While hitherto we knew the origin and spreading of most of the ancient arts and sciences in one channel only, and had to be satisfied with tracing their sources to Greece and Rome, and thence down the main stream of European civilization, we have now for many of them one or two parallel histories in India and in China. The history of geometry, for instance,—the first formation of geometrical conceptions or technical terms—was hitherto known to us from Greece only: now we can compare the gradual elaboration of geometrical principles both in Greece and India, and thus arrive at some idea of what is natural or inevitable, and what is accidental or purely personal in each. It was known, for instance, that in Greece the calculation of solid figures began with the building of altars, and you will hear to-day from Dr. Thibaut, that in India also the first impulse to geometric science was given, not by the measuring of fields, as the name implies, but by the minute observances in building altars.

Similar coincidences and divergences have been brought to light by a comparative study of the history of astronomy, of music, of grammar, but, most of all, by a comparative study of philosophic thought. There are indeed few problems in philosophy which have not occupied the Indian mind, and nothing can exceed the interest of watching the Hindu and the Greek, working on the same problems, each in his own way, yet both in the end arriving at much the same results. Such are the coincidences between the two, that but lately an eminent German professor,[3] published a treatise to show that the Greeks had borrowed their philosophy from India, while others lean to the opinion that in philosophy the Hindus are the pupils of the Greeks. This is the same feeling which impelled Dugald Stewart, when he saw the striking similarity between Greek and Sanskrit, to maintain that Sanskrit must have been put together after the model of Greek and Latin by those arch-forgers and liars, the Brahmans, and that the whole of Sanskrit literature was an imposition. The comparative method has put an end to such violent theories. It teaches us that what is possible in one country is possible also in another; it shows us that, as there are antecedents for Plato and Aristotle in Greece, there are antecedents for the Vedânta and Sânkhya philosophies in India, and that each had its own independent growth. It is true, that when we first meet in Indian philosophy with our old friends, the four or five elements, the atoms, our metaphysics, our logic, our syllogism, we are startled; but we soon discover that, given the human mind and human language, and the world by which we are surrounded, the different systems of philosophy of Thales and Hegel, of Vyâsa and Kapila, are inevitable solutions. They all come and go, they are maintained and refuted, till at last all philosophy ends where it ought to begin, with an inquiry into the necessary conditions and the inevitable forms of knowledge, represented by a criticism of Pure Reason and, what is more important still, by a criticism of Language.

Much has been done of late for Indian philosophy, particularly by Ballantyne and Hall, by Cowell and Gough, by the editors of the "Bibliotheca Indica," and the "Pandit." Yet it is much to be desired, that some young scholars, well versed in the history of European philosophy, should devote themselves more ardently to this promising branch of Indian literature. No doubt they would find it a great help, if they were able to spend some years in India, in order to learn from the last and fast disappearing representatives of some of the old schools of Indian philosophy what they alone can teach. What can be done by such a combination of Eastern and Western knowledge, has lately been shown by the excellent work done by Dr. Kielhorn, the Professor of Sanskrit at the Deccan College in Punah. But there is now so much of published materials, and Sanskrit MSS. also are so easily obtained from India, that much might be done in England, or in France, or in Germany—much that would be of interest not only to Oriental scholars, but to all philosophers whose powers of independent appreciation are not entirely blunted by their study of Plato and Aristotle, of Berkeley, Hume, and Kant.

I have so far dwelt chiefly on the powerful influence which the East, and more particularly India, has exercised on the intellectual life and work of the West. But the progress of Oriental scholarship in Europe, and the discovery of that spiritual relationship which binds India and England together, have likewise produced practical effects of the greatest moment in the East. The Hindus, in their first intercourse with English scholars, placed before them the treasures of their native literature with all the natural pride of a nation that considered itself the oldest, the wisest, the most enlightened nation in the world. For a time, but for a short time only, the claims of their literature to a fabulous antiquity were admitted, and dazzled by the unexpected discovery of a new classical literature, people raved about the beauty of Sanskrit poetry in truly Oriental strains. Then followed a sudden reaction, and the natives themselves, on becoming more and more acquainted with

European history and literature, began to feel the childishness of their claims, and to be almost ashamed of their own classics. This was a national misfortune. A people that can feel no pride in the past, in its history and literature, loses the mainstay of its national character. When Germany was in the very depth of its political degradation, it turned to its ancient literature, and drew hope for the future from the study of the past. Something of the same kind is now passing in India. A new taste, not without some political ingredients, has sprung up for the ancient literature of the country; a more intelligent appreciation of their real merits has taken the place of the extravagant admiration for the masterworks of their old poets; there is a revival in the study of Sanskrit, a surprising activity in the republication of Sanskrit s, and there are traces among the Hindus of a growing feeling, not very different from that which Tacitus described, when he said of the Germans: "Who would go to Germany, a country without natural beauty, with a wretched climate, miserable to cultivate or to look at—*unless it be his fatherland?*"

Even the discovery that Sanskrit, English, Greek, and Latin are cognate languages, has not been without its influence on the scholars and thinkers, or the leaders of public opinion, in India. They, more than others, had felt for a time most keenly the intellectual superiority of the West, and they rose again in their own estimation by learning that, physically, or at all events, intellectually, they had been and might be again, the peers of Greeks and Romans and Saxons. These silent influences often escape the eye of the politician and the historian, but at critical moments they decide the fate of whole nations and empires.4,A

The intellectual life of India at the present moment is full of interesting problems. It is too much the fashion to look only at its darker sides, and to forget that such intellectual regenerations as we are witnessing in India, are impossible without convulsions and failures. A new race of men is growing up in India, who have stepped, as it were, over a thousand years, and have entered at once on the intellectual inheritance of Europe. They carry off prizes at English schools, take their degrees in English universities, and are in every respect our equals. They have temptations which we have not, and now and then they succumb; but we, too, have temptations of our own, and we do not always resist. One can hardly trust one's eyes in reading their writings, whether in English or Bengali, many of which would reflect credit on our own Quarterlies. With regard to what is of the greatest interest to us, their scholarship, it is true that the old school of Sanskrit scholars is dying out, and much will die with it which we shall never recover; but a new and most promising school of Sanskrit students, educated by European professors, is springing up, and they will, nay, to judge from recent controversies, they have already become most formidable rivals to our own scholars. The essays of Dr. Bhao Daji, whom, I regret to say, we have lately lost by death, on disputed points in Indian archæology and literature, are most valuable. The indefatigable Rajendra Lal Mitra is rendering most excellent service in the publications of the Asiatic Society at Calcutta, and he discusses the theories of European Orientalists with all the ease and grace of an English reviewer. The Râjah of Besmah, Giriprasâda-sinha, has just finished his magnificent edition of the "White Yajurveda." The Sanskrit books published at Calcutta by Târânâtha, and others, form a complete library, and Târânâtha's new "Dictionary of the Sanskrit Language" will prove most useful and valuable. The editions of Sanskrit s published at Bombay by Professor Bhâṇḍârkar, Shankar Pandurang Pandit, and others, need not fear comparison with the best work of European scholars. There is a school of native students at Benares whose publications, under the auspices of Mr. Griffith, have made their journal, the "Pandit," indispensable to every Sanskrit scholar. Râjârâmasâstrî's and Bâlaśâstrî's edition of the "Mahâbhâshya" has received the highest praise from European students. In the "Antiquary," a paper very ably conducted by Mr. Burgess, we meet with contributions from several learned natives, among them from his Highness the Prince of Travancore, from Ram Dass Sen, the Zemindar of Berhampore, from Kâshinâth Trimbak Telang, from Sashagiriśâstrî, and others, which are read with the greatest interest and advantage by European scholars. The collected essays of Ram Dass Sen well deserve a translation into English, and Rajanîkânta's "Life of the Poet Jajadeva," just published, bears witness to the same revival of literary tastes and patriotic feelings.

Besides this purely literary movement, there is a religious movement going on in India, the Brahmo-Samâj, which, both in its origin and its later development, is mainly the result of European influences. It began with an attempt to bring the modern corrupt forms of worship back to the purity and simplicity of the Vedas; and by ascribing to the Veda the authority of a Divine Revelation, it was hoped to secure that infallible authority without which no religion was supposed to be possible. How was that movement stopped, and turned into a new channel? Simply by the publication of the Veda, and by the works of European scholars, such as Stevenson, Mill, Rosen, Wilson, and others, who showed to the natives what the Veda really was, and made them see the folly of their way.5,B Thus the religion, the literature, the whole character of the people of India are becoming more and more Indo-European. They work for us, as we work for them. Many a letter have I received from native scholars in which they express their admiration for the wonderful achievements of European ingenuity, for railways, and telegraphs, and all the rest; and yet what, according to their own confession, has startled them and delighted them most, is the interest we have taken in their literature, and the new life which we have imparted to their ancient history. I know these matters seem small, when we are near to them, when we are in the very midst of them. Like the tangled threads hanging on a loom, they look worthless, purposeless. But history weaves her woof out of all of them, and after a time, when we see the full and finished design, we perceive that no color, however quiet, could have been dropped, no shade, however slight, could have been missed, without spoiling the whole.

And now, after having given this account of our stewardship, let me say in conclusion a few words on the claims which Oriental studies have on public sympathy and support.

Let me begin with the Universities—I mean, of course the English Universities—and more particularly that University which has been to me for many years an *Alma Mater*, Oxford. While we have there, or are founding there, professorships for every branch of Theology, Jurisprudence, and Physical Science, we have hardly any provision for the study of Oriental languages. We have a chair of Hebrew, rendered illustrious by the greatest living theologian of England, and we have a chair of Sanskrit, which has left its mark in the history of Sanskrit literature; but for the modern languages of India, whether Aryan or Dravidian, for the language and literature of Persia, both ancient and modern, for the language and antiquities of Egypt and Babylon, for Chinese, for Turkish, nay even for Arabic, there is nothing deserving the name of a chair. When in a Report on University Reform, I ventured to point out these gaps, and to remark that in the smallest of German Universities most of these subjects were represented by professors, I was asked whether I was in earnest in maintaining that Oxford, the first University in what has rightly been called the greatest Oriental Empire, ought really to support the study of Oriental languages.

The second claim we prefer is on the Missionary Societies. I have lately incurred very severe obloquy for my supposed hostility to missionary enterprise. All I can say is, I wish that there were ten missionaries for every one we have now. I have always counted missionaries among my best friends; I have again and again acknowledged how much Oriental studies and linguistic studies in general, owe to them, and I am proud to say that, even now, while missionaries at home have abused me in unmeasured language, missionaries abroad, devoted, hard-working missionaries, have thanked me for what I said of them and their work in my lay-sermon in Westminster Abbey last December.

Now it seems to me that, first of all, our Universities, and I think again chiefly of Oxford, might do much more for missions than they do at present. If we had a sufficient staff of professors for Eastern languages, we could prepare young missionaries for their work, and should be able to send out from time to time such men as Patteson, the Bishop of Melanesia, who was every inch an Oxford man. And in these missionaries we might have not only apostles of religion and civilization, but at the same time, the most valuable pioneers of scientific research. I know there are some authorities at home who declare that such a combination is impossible, or at least undesirable; that a man cannot serve two masters, and that a missionary must do his own work and nothing else. Nothing, I believe, can be more mistaken. First of all, some of our most efficient missionaries have been those who have done also the most excellent work as scholars, and whenever I have conversed on this subject with missionaries who have seen active service, they all agree that they cannot be converting all day long, and that nothing is more refreshing and invigorating to them than some literary or scientific work. Now what I should like to see is this: I should like to see ten or twenty of our non-resident fellowships, which at present are doing more harm than good, assigned to missionary work, to be given to young men who have taken their degree, and who, whether laymen or clergymen, are willing to work as assistant missionaries on distant stations, with the distinct understanding that they should devote some of their time to scientific work, whether the study of languages, or flowers, or stars, and that they should send home every year some account of their labors. These men would be like scientific consuls, to whom students at home might apply for information and help. They would have opportunities of distinguishing themselves by really useful work, far more than in London, and after ten years, they might either return to Europe with a well-established reputation, or if they find that they have a real call for missionary work, devote all their life to it. Though to my own mind there is no nobler work than that of a missionary, yet I believe that some such connection with the Universities and men of science would raise their position, and would call out more general interest, and secure to the missionary cause the good-will of those whose will is apt to become law.

Thirdly, I think that Oriental studies have a claim on the colonies and the colonial governments. The English colonies are scattered all over the globe, and many of them in localities where an immense deal of useful scientific work might be done, and would be done with the slightest encouragement from the local authorities, and something like a systematic supervision on the part of the Colonial Office at home. Some years ago I ventured to address the Colonial Secretary of State on this subject, and a letter was sent out in consequence to all the English colonies, inviting information on the languages, monuments, customs, and traditions of the native races. Some most valuable reports have been sent home during the last five or six years, but when it was suggested that these reports should be published in a permanent form, the expense that would have been required for printing every year a volume of Colonial Reports, and which would not have amounted to more than a few hundred pounds for all the colonies of the

British Empire, part of it to be recovered by the sale of the book, was considered too large.

Now we should bear in mind that at the present moment some of the tribes living in or near the English colonies in Australia, Polynesia, Africa, and America, are actually dying out, their languages are disappearing, their customs, traditions, and religions will soon be completely swept away. To the student of language, the dialect of a savage tribe is as valuable as Sanskrit or Hebrew, nay, for the solution of certain problems, more so; every one of these languages is the growth of thousands and thousands of years, the workmanship of millions and millions of human beings. If they were now preserved, they might hereafter fill the most critical gaps in the history of the human race. At Rome at the time of the Scipios, hundreds of people might have written down a grammar and dictionary of the Etruscan language, of Oscan, or Umbrian; but there were men then, as there are now, who shrugged their shoulders and said, What can be the use of preserving these barbarous, uncouth idioms?—What would we not give now for some such records?

And this is not all. The study of savage tribes has assumed a new interest of late, when the question of the exact relation of man to the rest of the animal kingdom has again roused the passions not only of scientific inquirers, but also of the public at large. Now what is wanted for the solution of this question, are more facts and fewer theories, and these facts can only be gained by a patient study of the lowest races of mankind. When religion was held to be the specific character of man, it was asserted by many travellers that they had seen races without any religious ideas; when language was seen to be the real frontier line between man and beast, it was maintained that there were human beings without language. Now all we want to know are facts, let the conclusions be whatever they may. It is by no means easy to decide whether savage tribes have a religion or not; at all events it requires the same discernment, and the same honesty of purpose as to find out whether men of the highest intellect among us have a religion or not. I call the Introduction to Spencer's "First Principles" deeply religious, but I can well understand that a missionary, reporting on a tribe of Spencerian savages, might declare that they had no idea whatsoever of religion. Looking at a report sent home lately by the indefatigable Governor of New South Wales, Sir Hercules Robinson, I find the following description of the religious ideas of the Kamilarois, one of the most degraded tribes in the Northwestern district of the colony:—

"Bhaiami is regarded by them as the maker of all things. The name signifies 'maker,' or 'cutter-out,' from the verb b h a i, b a i a l l i, b a i a. He is regarded as the rewarder and punisher of men according to their conduct. He sees all, and knows all, if not directly, through the subordinate deity

Turramûlan, who presides at the Bora. Bhaiami is said to have been once on the earth. Turramûlan is mediator in all the operations of Bhaiami upon man, and in all man's transactions with Bhaiami. Turramûlan means 'leg on one side only,' 'one-legged.'"

This description is given by the Rev. C. Greenway, and if there is any theological bias in it, let us make allowance for it. But there remains the fact that Bhaiami, their name for deity, comes from a root b h a i, to "make," to "cut out," and if we remember that hardly any of the names for deity, either among the Aryan or Semitic nations, comes from a root with so abstract a meaning, we shall admit, I think, that such reports as these should not be allowed to lie forgotten in the pigeon-holes of the Colonial Office, or in the pages of a monthly journal.

What applies to religion, applies to language. We have been told again and again that the Veddahs in Ceylon have no language. Sir Emerson Tennant wrote "that they mutually make themselves understood by signs, grimaces, and guttural sounds, which have little resemblance to definite words or language in general." When these statements were repeated, I tried to induce the Government of Ceylon to send a competent man to settle the question. I did not receive all I wanted, and therefore postponed the publication of what was sent me. But I may say so much, that more than half of the words used by the Veddahs, are, like Singhalese itself, mere corruption of Sanskrit; their very name is the Sanskrit word for hunter, v e d d h â, or, as Mr. Childers supposes, v y â d h a. There is a remnant of words in their language of which I can make nothing as yet. But so much is certain; either the Veddahs started with the common inheritance of Aryan words and ideas; or, at all events, they lived for a long time in contact with Aryan people, and adopted from them such words as were wanting in their language. If they now stand low in the scale of humanity, they once stood higher, nay they may possibly prove, in language, if not in blood, the distant cousins of Plato, and Newton, and Goethe.

It is most essential to keep *la carrière ouverte* for facts, even more than for theories, and for the supply of such facts the Colonial Government might render most useful service.

It is but right to state that whenever I have applied to the Governors of any of the Colonies, I have invariably met with the greatest kindness and readiness to help. Some of them take the warmest interest in these researches. Sir George Grey's services to the science of language have hardly been sufficiently appreciated as yet, and the Linguistic Library which he founded at the Cape, places him of right by the side of Sir Thomas Bodley. Sir Hercules Robinson, Mr. Musgrave in South Australia, Sir Henry Barkley at the Cape, and several others, are quite aware of the importance of linguistic and ethnological researches. What is wanted is encouragement from home, and some systematic guidance. Dr. Bleek, the excellent librarian of Sir George Grey's Library at the Cape, who has devoted the whole of his life to the study of savage dialects, and whose Comparative Grammar of the South African languages will hold its place by the side of Bopp's, Diez's, and Caldwell's Comparative Grammars, is most anxious that there should be a permanent linguistic and ethnological station established at the Cape; in fact, that there should be a linguist attached to every zoölogical station. At the Cape there are not only the Zulu dialects to be studied, but two most important languages, that of the Hottentots and that of the Bushmen. Dr. Bleek has lately been enabled to write down several volumes of traditional literature from the mouths of some Bushman prisoners, but he says, "my powers and my life are drawing to an end, and unless I have some young men to assist me, and carry on my work, much of what I have done will be lost." There is no time to be lost, and I trust therefore that my appeal will not be considered importunate by the present Colonial Minister.

Last of all, we turn to India, the very cradle of Oriental scholarship, and here, instead of being importunate and urging new claims for assistance, I think I am expressing the feelings of all Oriental scholars in publicly acknowledging the readiness with which the Indian Government, whether at home or in India, whether during the days of the old East India Company, or now under the auspices of the Secretary of State, has always assisted every enterprise tending to throw light on the literature, the religion, the laws and customs, the arts and manufactures of that ancient Oriental Empire.

Only last night I received the first volume of a work which will mark a new era in the history of Oriental typography. Three valuable MSS. of the Mahâbhâshya have been photolithographed at the expense of the Indian Government, and under the supervision of one whom many of us will miss here to-day, the late Professor Goldstücker. It is a magnificent publication, and as there are only fifty copies printed, it will soon become more valuable than a real MS.

There are two surveys carried on at the present moment in India, a literary and an archæological survey. Many years ago, when Lord Elgin went to India as Governor-general, I suggested to him the necessity of taking measures in order to rescue from destruction whatever could still be rescued of the ancient literature of the country. Lord Elgin died before any active measures could be taken, but the plan found a more powerful advocate in Mr. Whitley Stokes, who urged the Government to appoint some Sanskrit scholars to visit all places containing collections of Sanskrit MSS., and to publish lists of their titles, so that we might know, at all events, how much of a literature, that had been preserved for thousands of years, was still in existence at the present moment. This work was confided to Dr. Bühler, Dr. Kielhorn, Mr. Burnell, Rajendralal Mitra, and others. Several of their catalogues have been published, and there is but one feeling among all Sanskrit scholars as to the value of their work. But they also feel that the time has come for doing more. The mere titles of the MSS. whet our appetite, but do not satisfy it. There are, of course, hundreds of books where the title, the name of the author, the *locus et annus* are all we care to know. But of books which are scarce, and hitherto not known out of India, we want to know more. We want some information of the subject and its treatment, and if possible, of the date, of the author, and of the writers quoted by him. We want extracts, intelligently chosen, in fact, we want something like the excellent catalogue which Dr. Aufrecht has made for the Bodleian Library. In Mr. Burnell, Dr. Bühler, Dr. Kielhorn, the Government possesses scholars who could do that work admirably; what they want is more leisure, more funds, more assistance.

Contemporaneously with the Literary Survey, there is the Archæological Survey, carried on by that gallant and indefatigable scholar, General Cunningham. His published reports show the systematic progress of his work, and his occasional communications in the Journal of the Asiatic Society of Bengal tell us of his newest discoveries. The very last number of that journal brought us the news of the discovery of the wonderful ruins of the Buddhist temple of Bharahut,[6] which, with their representations of scenes from the early Buddhist literature, with their inscriptions and architectural style, may enable us to find a *terminus a quo* for the literary and religious history of India. We should not forget the services which Mr. Fergusson has rendered to the history of Indian architecture, both by awakening an interest in the subject, and by the magnificent publication of the drawings of the sculptures of Sanchi and Amravati, carried on under the authority of the Secretary of State for India. Let us hope that these new discoveries may supply him with materials for another volume, worthy of its companion.

It was supposed for a time that there was a third survey carried on in India, ethnological and linguistic, and the volume, published by Colonel Dalton, "Descriptive Ethnology of Bengal," with portraits from photographs, was a most excellent beginning. But the other India Governments have not hitherto followed the example of the Bengal Government, and nothing has of late come to my knowledge in this important line of research. Would not Dr. Hunter, who has done so much for a scientific study of the non-Aryan languages and races of India, take up this important branch of research, and give us, not only photographs and graphic description, but also, what is most wanted, scholarlike grammars of the principal races of India? Lists of words, if carefully chosen, like those in Colonel Dalton's work and in Sir George

Campbell's "Specimens," are, no doubt, most valuable for preliminary researches, but without grammars, none of the great questions which are still pending in Indian Ethnology will ever be satisfactorily and definitely settled. No real advance has been made in the classification of Indian dialects since the time when I endeavored, some twenty years ago, to sum up what was then known on that subject, in my letter to Bunsen "On the Turanian Languages." What I then for the first time ventured to maintain against the highest authorities in Indian linguistic ethnology, viz., that the dialects of the Mundas or the Koles constituted a third and totally independent class of languages in India, related neither to the Aryan nor to the Dravidian families, has since been fully confirmed by later researches, and is now, I believe, generally accepted. The fact also, on which I then strongly insisted, that the Uraon Koles, and Rajmahal Koles, might be Koles in blood, but certainly not in language, their language being, like that of the Gonds, Dravidian, is now no longer disputed. But beyond this, all is still as hypothetical as it was twenty years ago, simply because we can get no grammars of the Munda dialects. Why do not the German missionaries at Ranchi, who have done such excellent work among the Koles, publish a grammatical analysis of that interesting cluster of dialects? Only a week ago, one of them, Mr. Jellinghaus, gave me a grammatical sketch of the Mundári language, and even this, short as it is, was quite sufficient to show that the supposed relationship between the Munda dialects and the Khasia language, of which we have a grammar, is untenable. The similarities pointed out by Mason between the Munda dialects and the Talaing of Pegu, are certainly startling, but equally startling are the divergences; and here again no real result will be obtained without a comparison of the grammatical structure of the two languages. The other classes of Indian languages, the Taic, the Gangetic, subdivided into Trans-Himalayan and Sub-Himalayan, the Lohitic, and Tamulic, are still retained, though some of their names have been changed. Without wishing to defend the names which I had chosen for these classes, I must say that I look upon the constant introduction of new technical terms as an unmixed evil. Every classificatory term is imperfect. Aryan, Semitic, Hamitic, Turanian, all are imperfect, but, if they are but rightly defined, they can do no harm, whereas a new term, however superior at first sight, always makes confusion worse confounded. The chemists do not hesitate to call sugar an acid rather than part with an old established term; why should not we in the science of language follow their good example?

Dr. Leitner's labors in Dardistan should here be mentioned. They date from the year 1866. Considering the shortness of the time allotted to him for exploring that country, he has been most successful in collecting his linguistic materials. We owe him a vocabulary of two Shinâ dialects (the Ghilghiti and Astori), and of the Arnyia, the Khayuna, and the Kalâsha-Mânder. These vocabularies are so arranged as to give us a fair idea of the systems of conjugation and declension. Other vocabularies, arranged according to subjects, allow us an insight into the intellectual life of the Shinas, and we also receive most interesting information on the customs, legends, superstitions, and religion of the Dardus. Some of the important results, obtained by the same enterprising scholar in his excavations on the Takht-i-bahai hills will be laid before the Archæological Section of this Congress. It is impossible to look at the Buddhist sculptures which he has brought home without perceiving that there is in them a foreign element. They are Buddhist sculptures, but they differ both in treatment and expression from what was hitherto known of Buddhist art in various parts of the world. Dr. Leitner thinks that the foreign element came from Greece, from Greek or Macedonian workmen, the descendants of Alexander's companions; others think that local and individual influences are sufficient to account for apparent deviations from the common Buddhist type. On this point I feel totally incompetent to express an opinion, but whatever the judgment of our archæological colleagues may be, neither they nor we ourselves can have any doubt that Dr. Leitner deserves our sincere gratitude as an indefatigable explorer and successful discoverer.

Many of the most valuable treasures of every kind and sort, collected during these official surveys, and by private enterprise, are now deposited in the Indian Museum in London, a real mine of literary and archæological wealth, opened with the greatest liberality to all who are willing to work in it.

It is unfortunate, no doubt, that this meeting of Oriental scholars should have taken place at a time when the treasures of the Indian Museum are still in their temporary exile; yet, if they share in the regret felt by every friend of India, at the delay in the building of a new museum, worthy both of England and of India, they will also carry away the conviction, that such delay is simply due to a desire to do the best that can be done, in order to carry out in the end something little short of that magnificent scheme of an Indian Institute, drawn by the experienced hand of Mr. Forbes Watson.

And now, in conclusion, I have to express my own gratitude for the liberality both of the Directors of the old East India Company and of the present Secretary of State for India in Council, for having enabled me to publish that work the last sheet of which I am able to present to this Meeting to-day, the "Rig-Veda, with the Commentary of Sâyaṇâcârya." It is the oldest book of the Aryan world, but it is also one of the largest, and its publication would have been simply impossible without the enlightened liberality of the Indian Government. For twenty-five years I find, that taking the large and small editions of the Rig-Veda together, I have printed every year what would make a volume of about six hundred pages octavo. Such a publication would have ruined any bookseller, for it must be confessed, that there is little that is attractive in the Veda, nothing that could excite general interest. From an æsthetic point of view, no one would care for the hymns of the Rig-Veda, and I can well understand how, in the beginning of our century, even so discriminating a scholar as Colebrooke could express his opinion that, "The Vedas are too voluminous for a complete translation, and what they contain would hardly reward the labor of the reader, much less that of the translator. The ancient dialect in which they are composed, and specially that of the three first Vedas, is extremely difficult and obscure; and, though curious, as the parent of a more polished and refined language, its difficulties must long continue to prevent such an examination of the whole Vedas, as would be requisite for extracting all that is remarkable and important in those voluminous works. But they well deserve to be occasionally consulted by the Oriental scholar." Nothing shows the change from the purely æsthetic to the purely scientific interest in the language and literature of India more clearly than the fact that for the last twenty-five years the work of nearly all Sanskrit scholars has been concentrated on the Veda. When some thirty years ago I received my first lessons in Sanskrit from Professor Brockhaus, whom I am happy and proud to see to-day among us, there were but few students who ventured to dive into the depths of Vedic literature. To-day among the Sanskrit scholars whom Germany has sent to us—Professors Stenzler, Spiegel, Weber, Hang, Pertsch, Windisch—there is not one who has not won his laurels on the field of Vedic scholarship. In France also a new school of Sanskrit students has sprung up who have done most excellent work for the interpretation of the Veda, and who bid fair to rival the glorious school of French Orientalists at the beginning of this century, both by their persevering industry and by that "sweetness and light" which seems to be the birthright of their nation. But, I say again, there is little that is beautiful, in our sense of the word, to be found in the hymns of the Rig-Veda, and what little there is, has been so often dwelt on, that quite an erroneous impression as to the real nature of Vedic poetry has been produced in the mind of the public. My old friend, the Dean of St. Paul's, for instance, in some thoughtful lectures which he delivered this year on the "Sacred Poetry of Early Religions," has instituted a comparison between the Psalms and the hymns of the Veda, and he arrives at the conclusion that the Psalms are superior to the Vedic hymns. No doubt they are, from the point of view which he has chosen, but the chief value of these hymns lies in the fact that they are so different from the Psalms, or, if you like, that they are so inferior to the Psalms. They are Aryan, the Psalms Semitic; they belong to a primitive and rude state of society, the Psalms, at least most of them, are contemporaneous with or even later than the heydays of the Jewish monarchy. This strange misconception of the true character of the Vedic hymns seemed to me to become so general, that when some years ago I had to publish the first volume of my translation,

I intentionally selected a class of hymns which should in no way encourage such erroneous opinions. It was interesting to watch the disappointment. What, it was said, are these strange, savage, grotesque invocations of the Storm-gods, the inspired strains of the ancient sages of India? Is this the wisdom of the East? Is this the primeval revelation? Even scholars of high reputation joined in the outcry, and my friends hinted to me that they would not have wasted their life on such a book.

Now, suppose a geologist had brought to light the bones of a fossil animal, dating from a period anterior to any in which traces of animal life had been discovered before, would any young lady venture to say by way of criticism, "Yes, these bones are very curious, but they are not pretty!" Or suppose a new Egyptian statue had been discovered, belonging to a dynasty hitherto unrepresented by any statues, would even a school-boy dare to say, "Yes, it is very nice, but the Venus of Milo is nicer?" Or suppose an old MS. is brought to Europe, do we find fault with it, because it is not neatly printed? If a chemist discovers a new element, is he pitied because it is not gold? If a botanist writes on germs, has he to defend himself, because he does not write on flowers? Why, it is simply because the Veda is so different from what it was expected to be, because it is not like the Psalms, not like Pindar, not like the Bhagavadgîtâ, it is because it stands alone by itself, and reveals to us the earliest germs of religious thought, such as they really were; it is because it places before us a language, more primitive than any we knew before; it is because its poetry is what you may call savage, uncouth, rude, horrible, it is for that very reason that it was worth while to dig and dig till the old buried city was recovered, showing us what man was, what we were, before we had reached the level of David, the level of Homer, the level of Zoroaster, showing us the very cradle of our thoughts, our words, and our deeds. *I am not disappointed with the Veda*, and I shall conclude my address with the last verses of the last hymn, which you have now in your hands,—verses which thousands of years ago may have been addressed to a similar meeting of Aryan fellow-men, and which are not inappropriate to our own:—

Sám gacchadhvam sám vadadhvam sám vaḥ mánaṃsi jànatâm,

Devâh bhâgám yáthâ pū́rve7 saṃjânânā́ḥ upā́sate,

Samânáh mántraḥ sámitiḥ samánī́ samânám mánaḥ sahá cittám eshâm,

Samnám mántram abhí mantraye vaḥ samânéna vaḥ havíshâ juhomi.

Samânī́ vaḥ ā́kûtiḥ samânā́ hṛdayâni vaḥ,

Samânám astu vaḥ mánaḥ yáthâ vaḥ súsaha ásati.

"Come together! Speak together! Let your minds be concordant—the gods by being concordant receive their share, one after the other. Their word is the same, their counsel is the same, their mind is the same, their thoughts are at one; I address to you the same word, I worship you with the same sacrifice. Let your endeavor be the same! Let your hearts be the same! Let your mind be the same, that it may go well with you."

NOTES.

NOTE A.

IN the "Indian Mirror," published at Calcutta, 20 September, 1874, a native writer gave utterance almost at the same time to the same feelings:—

"When the dominion passed from the Mogul to the hands of Englishmen, the latter regarded the natives as little better than niggers, having a civilization perhaps a shade better than that of the barbarians.... The gulf was wide between the conquerors and the conquered.... There was no affection to lessen the distance between the two races.... The discovery of Sanskrit entirely revolutionized the course of thought and speculations. It served as the 'open sesame' to many hidden treasures. It was then that the position of India in the scale of civilization was distinctly apprehended. It was then that our relations with the advanced nations of the world were fully realized. We were niggers at one time. We now become brethren.... The advent of the English found us a nation low sunk in the mire of superstitions, ignorance, and political servitude. The advent of scholars like Sir William Jones found us fully established in a rank above that of every nation as that from which modern civilization could be distinctly traced. It would be interesting to contemplate what would have been our position if the science of philology had not been discovered.... It was only when the labor of scholars brought to light the treasures of our antiquity that they perceived how near we were to their races in almost all things that they held dear in their life. It was then that our claims on their affection and regard were first established. As Hindus we ought never to forget the labor of scholars. We owe them our life as a nation, our freedom as a recognized society, and our position in the scale of races. It is the fashion with many to decry the labors of those men as dry, unprofitable, and dreamy. We should know that it is to the study of the roots and inflections of the Sanskrit language that we owe our national salvation.... Within a very few years after the discovery of Sanskrit, a revolution took place in the history of comparative science. Never were so many discoveries made at once, and from the speculations of learned scholars like ——, the dawnings of many truths are even now visible to the world. . . . Comparative mythology and comparative religion are new terms altogether in the world. . . . We say again that India has no reason to forget the services of scholars."

NOTE B.

THE following letter addressed by me to the "Academy," October 17, 1874, p. 433, gives the reasons for this statement:—

"I was aware of the mission of the four young Brahmans sent to Benares in 1845, to copy out and study the four Vedas respectively. I had read of it last in the 'Historical Sketch of the Brahmo Samaj,' which Miss Collet had the kindness to send me. But what I said in my address before the Oriental Congress referred to earlier times. That mission in 1845 was, in fact, the last result of much previous discussion, which gradually weakened and destroyed in the mind of Ram Mohun Roy and his followers their traditional faith in the Divine origin of the Vedas. At first Ram Mohun Roy met the arguments of his English friends by simply saying, 'If you claim a Divine origin for your sacred books, so do we;' and when he was pressed by the argument derived from internal evidence, he appealed to a few hymns, such as the Gâyatrî, and to the Upanishads, as by no means inferior to passages in the Bible, and not unworthy of a divine author. The Veda with him was chiefly in the Upanishads, and he had hardly any knowledge of the hymns of the Rig-Veda. I state this on the authority of a conversation that passed between him and young Rosen, who was then working at the MSS. of the Rig-Veda-Sanhitâ in the British Museum, and to whom Ram Mohun Roy expressed his regret at not being able to read his own sacred books.

"There were other channels, too, through which, after Ram Mohun Roy's death in 1833, a knowledge of the studies of European scholars may have reached the still hesitating reformers of the Brahma Sabhá. Dvarka Náth Tagore paid a visit to Europe in the year 1845. I write from memory. Though not a man of deep religious feelings, he was an enlightened and shrewd observer of all that passed before his eyes. He was not a Sanskrit scholar; and I well recollect, when we paid a visit together to Eugène Burnouf, Dvarka Náth Tagore putting his dark delicate hand on one side of Burnouf's edition of the 'Bhagavat Purâna,' containing the French translation, and saying he could understand that, but not the Sanskrit original on the opposite page. I saw him frequently at Paris, where I was then engaged in collecting materials for a complete edition of the Vedas and the commentary of Sâyanâcârya. Many a morning did I pass in his rooms, smoking, accompanying him on the pianoforte, and discussing questions in which we took a common interest. I remember one morning, after he had been singing some Italian, French, and German music, I asked him to sing an Indian song. He declined at first, saying that he knew I should not like it; but at last he yielded, and sang, not one of the modern Persian songs, which commonly go by the name of Indian, but a genuine native piece of music. I listened quietly, but when it was over, I told him that it seemed strange to me, how one who could appreciate Italian and German music could find any pleasure in what sounded to me like mere noise, without melody, rhythm, or harmony. 'Oh,' he said, 'that is exactly like you Europeans! When I first heard your Italian and German music I disliked it; it was no music to me at all. But I persevered, I became accustomed to it, I found out what was good in it, and now I am able to enjoy it. But you despise whatever is strange to you, whether in music, or philosophy, or religion; you will not listen and learn, and we shall understand you much sooner than you will understand us.'

"In our conversations on the Vedas he never, as far as I recollect, defended the divine origin of his own sacred writings in the abstract, but he displayed great casuistic cleverness in maintaining that every argument that had ever been adduced in support of a supernatural origin of the Bible could be used with equal force in favor of a divine authorship of the Veda. His own ideas of the Veda were chiefly derived from the Upanishads, and he frequently assured me that there was much more of Vedic literature in India than we imagined. This Dvarka Náth Tagore was the father of Debendra Náth Tagore, the true founder of the Brahmo Samáj, who, in 1845, sent the four young Brahmans to Benares to copy out and study the four Vedas. Though Dvarka Náth Tagore was so far orthodox that he maintained a number of Brahmans, yet it was he also who continued the grant for the support of the Church, founded at Calcutta by Ram Mohun Roy. One letter written by Dvarka Náth Tagore from Paris to Calcutta in 1845, would supply the missing link between what was passing at that time in a room of a hotel on the Place Vendôme, and the resolution taken at Calcutta to find out, once for all, what the Vedas really are.

"In India itself the idea of a critical and historical study of the Veda originated certainly with English scholars. Dr. Mill once showed me the first attempt at printing the sacred Gâyatrî in Calcutta; and, if I am not mistaken, he added that unfortunately the gentleman who had printed it died soon after, thus confirming the prophecies of the Brahmans that such a sacrilege would not remain unavenged by the gods. Dr. Mill, Stevenson, Wilson, and others were the first to show to the educated natives in India that the Upanishads belonged to a later age than the hymns of the Rig-Veda, and likewise the first to exhibit to Ram Mohun Roy and his friends the real character of these ancient hymns. On a mind like Ram Mohun Roy's the effect was probably much more immediate than on his followers, so that it took several years before they decided on sending their commissioners to Benares to report on the Veda and its real character. Yet that mission was, I believe, the result of a slow process of attrition produced by the contact between native and European minds, and as such I wished to present it in my address at the Oriental Congress."

**Footnotes to Chapter VI (VII):
The Importance of Oriental Studies**

1. These lists of common Aryan words were published in the *Academy*, October 10, 1874, and are reprinted at the end of the next article "On the Life of Colebrooke."

2. *Geschichte der Sprachwissenschaft und Orientalischen Philologie in Deutschland*, von Theodor Benfey. München, 1869.

3. *Aristoteles' Metaphysik, eine Tochter der Sânkhya-Lehre des Kapila*, von Dr. C. B. Schlüter. 1874.

4. See Note A, p. 355.

5. See Note B, p. 356.

6. *Academy*, August 1, 1874.

7. I read y a t h â p û r v e as one word.

VIII.
LIFE OF COLEBROOKE.1

THE name and fame of Henry Thomas Colebrooke are better known in India, France, Germany, Italy—nay, even in Russia—than in his own country. He was born in London on the 15th of June, 1765; he died in London on the 10th of March, 1837; and if now, after waiting for thirty-six years, his only surviving son, Sir Edward Colebrooke, has at last given us a more complete account of his father's life, the impulse has come chiefly from Colebrooke's admirers abroad, who wished to know what the man had been whose works they know so well. If Colebrooke had simply been a distinguished, even a highly distinguished, servant of the East India Company, we could well understand that, where the historian has so many eminent services to record, those of Henry Thomas Colebrooke should have been allowed to pass almost unnoticed. The history of British India has still to be written, and it will be no easy task to write it. Macaulay's "Lives" of Clive and Warren Hastings are but two specimens to show how it ought to be, and yet how it cannot be, written. There is in the annals of the conquest and administrative tenure of India so much of the bold generalship of raw recruits, the statesmanship of common clerks, and the heroic devotion of mere adventurers, that even the largest canvas of the historian must dwarf the stature of heroes; and characters which, in the history of Greece or England, would stand out in bold relief, must vanish unnoticed in the crowd. The substance of the present memoir appeared in the "Journal" of the Royal Asiatic Society soon after Mr. Colebrooke's death. It consisted originally of a brief notice of his public and literary career, interspersed with extracts from his letters to his family during the first twenty years of residence in India. Being asked a few years since to allow this notice to appear in a new edition of his "Miscellaneous Essays," which Mr. Fitz-Edward Hall desired to republish, Sir Edward thought it incumbent on him to render it more worthy of his father's reputation. The letters in the present volume are, for the most part, given in full; and some additional correspondence is included in it, besides a few papers of literary interest, and a journal kept by him during his residence at Nagpur, which was left incomplete. Two addresses delivered to the Royal Asiatic and Astronomical Societies, and the narrative of a journey to and from the capital of Berar, are given in an appendix and complete the volume, which is now on the eve of publication.

Although, as we shall see, the career of Mr. Colebrooke, as a servant of the East India Company, was highly distinguished, and in its vicissitudes, as here told by his son, both interesting and instructive, yet his most lasting fame will not be that of the able administrator, the learned lawyer, the thoughtful financier and politician, but that of the founder and father of true Sanskrit scholarship in Europe. In that character Colebrooke has secured his place in the history of the world, a place which neither envy nor ignorance can ever take from him. Had he lived in Germany, we should long ago have seen his statue in his native place, his name written in letters of gold on the walls of academies; we should have heard of Colebrooke jubilees and Colebrooke scholarships. In England, if any notice is taken of the discovery of Sanskrit—a discovery in many respects equally important, in some even more important, than the revival of Greek scholarship in the fifteenth century—we may possibly hear the popular name of Sir William Jones and his classical translation of Sakuntala; but of the infinitely more important achievements of Colebrooke, not one word. The fact is, the time has not yet come when the full importance of the Sanskrit philology can be appreciated by the public at large. It was the same with Greek philology. When Greek began to be studied by some of the leading spirits in Europe, the subject seemed at first one of purely literary curiosity. When its claims were pressed on the public, they were met by opposition, and even ridicule; and those who knew least of Greek were most eloquent in their denunciations. Even when its study had become more general, and been introduced at universities and schools, it remained in the eyes of many a mere accomplishment—its true value for higher than scholastic purposes being scarcely suspected. At present we know that the revival of Greek scholarship affected the deepest interests of humanity, that it was in reality a revival of that consciousness which links large portions of mankind together, connects the living with the dead, and thus secures to each generation the full intellectual inheritance of our race. Without that historical consciousness the life of man would be ephemeral and vain. The more we can see backward, and place ourselves in real sympathy with the past, the more truly do we make the life of former generations our own, and are able to fulfill our own appointed duty in carrying on the work which was begun centuries ago in Athens and at Rome. But while the unbroken traditions of the Roman world, and the revival of Greek culture among us, restored to us the intellectual patrimony of Greece and Rome only, and made the Teutonic race in a certain sense Greek and Roman, the discovery of Sanskrit will have a much larger influence. Like a new intellectual spring, it is meant to revive the broken fibres that once united the Southeastern with the Northwestern branches of the Aryan family; and thus to reestablish the spiritual brotherhood, not only of the Teutonic, Greek, and Roman, but likewise of the Slavonic, Celtic, Indian, and Persian branches. It is to make the mind of man wider, his heart larger, his sympathies world-embracing; it is to make us truly *humaniores*, richer and prouder in the full perception of what humanity has been, and what it is meant to be. This is the real object of the more comprehensive studies of the nineteenth century, and though the full appreciation of this their true import may be reserved to the future, no one who follows the intellectual progress of mankind attentively can fail to see that, even now, the comparative study of languages, mythologies, and religions has widened our horizon; that much which was lost has been regained; and that a new world, if it has not yet been occupied, is certainly in sight. It is curious to observe that those to whom we chiefly owe the discovery of Sanskrit were as little conscious of the real importance of their discovery as Columbus was when he landed at St. Salvador. What Mr. Colebrooke did, was done from a sense of duty, rather than from literary curiosity; but there was also a tinge of enthusiasm in his character, like that which carries a traveller to the wastes of Africa or the icebound regions of the Pole. Whenever there was work ready for him, he was ready for the work. But he had no theories to substantiate, no preconceived objects to attain. Sobriety and thoroughness are the distinguishing features of all his works. There is in them no trace of haste or carelessness; but neither is there evidence of any extraordinary effort, or minute professional scholarship. In the same business-like spirit in which he collected the revenue of his province he collected his knowledge of Sanskrit literature; with the same judicial impartiality with which he delivered his judgments he delivered the results at which he had arrived after his extensive and careful reading; and with the same sense of confidence with which he quietly waited for the effects of his political and financial measures, in spite of the apathy or the opposition with which they met at first, he left his written works to the judgment of posterity, never wasting his time in the repeated assertion of his opinions, or in useless controversy, though he was by no means insensible to his own literary reputation. The biography of such a man deserves a careful study; and we think that Sir Edward Colebrooke has fulfilled more than a purely filial duty in giving to the world a full account of the private, public, and literary life of his great father.

Colebrooke was the son of a wealthy London banker, Sir George Colebrooke, a Member of Parliament, and a man in his time of some political importance. Having proved himself a successful advocate of the old privileges of the East India Company, he was invited to join the Court of Directors, and became in 1769 chairman of the Company. His chairmanship was distinguished in history by the appointment of Warren Hastings to the highest office in India, and there are in existence letters from that illustrious man to Sir George, written in the crisis of his Indian Administration, which show the intimate and confidential relations subsisting between them. But when, in later years, Sir George Colebrooke became involved in pecuniary difficulties, and Indian appointments were successively obtained for his two sons, James Edward and Henry Thomas, it does not appear that Warren Hastings took any active steps to advance them, beyond appointing the elder brother to an office of some importance on his secretariat. Henry, the younger brother, had been educated at home, and at the age of fifteen he had laid a solid foundation in Latin, Greek, French, and particularly in mathematics. As he never seems to have been urged on, he learned what he learned quietly and thoroughly, trying from the first to satisfy himself rather than others. Thus a love of knowledge for its own sake remained firmly engrained in his mind through life, and explains much of what would otherwise remain inexplicable in his literary career.

At the age of eighteen he started for India, and arrived at Madras in 1783, having narrowly escaped capture by French cruisers. The times were anxious times for India, and full of interest to an observer of political events. In his very first letter from India Colebrooke thus sketches the political situation:—

"The state of affairs in India seems to bear a far more favorable aspect than for a long time past. The peace with the Mahrattas and the death of Hyder Ally, the intended invasion of Tippoo's country by the Mahrattas, sufficiently removed all alarm from the country powers; but there are likewise accounts arrived, and which seem to be credited, of the defeat of Tippoo by Colonel Matthews, who commands on the other coast."

From Madras Colebrooke proceeded, in 1783, to Calcutta, where he met his elder brother, already established in the service. His own start in official life was delayed, and took place under circumstances by no means auspicious. The tone, both in political and private life, was at that time at its lowest ebb in India. Drinking, gambling, and extravagance of all kinds were tolerated even in the best society, and Colebrooke could not entirely escape the evil effects of the moral atmosphere in which he had to live. It is all the more remarkable that his taste for work never deserted him, and "that he would retire to his midnight Sanskrit studies unaffected by the excitement of the gambling-table." It was not till 1786—a year after Warren Hastings had left India—that he received his first official appointment, as Assistant Collector of Revenue in Tirhut. His father seems to have advised him from the first to be assiduous in acquiring the vernacular languages, and we find him at an early period of his Indian career thus writing on this subject: "The one, and that the most necessary, Moors (now called Hindustani), by not being written, bars all close application; the other, Persian, is too dry to entice, and is so seldom of any use, that I seek its acquisition very leisurely." He asked his father in turn to send him the Greek and Latin classics, evidently intending to carry on his old favorite studies, rather than begin a new career as an Oriental scholar. For a time he seemed, indeed, deeply disappointed with his life in India, and his prospects were anything but encouraging. But although he seriously thought of throwing up his position and returning to England, he was busy nevertheless in elaborating a scheme for the better regulation of the Indian service. His chief idea was, that the three functions of the civil service—the commercial, the revenue, and the diplomatic—

should be separated; that each branch should be presided over by an independent board, and that those who had qualified themselves for one branch should not be transferred to another. Curiously enough, he lived to prove by his own example the applicability of the old system, being himself transferred from the revenue department to a judgeship, then employed on an important diplomatic mission, and lastly raised to a seat in Council, and acquitting himself well in each of these different employments. After a time his discontent seems to have vanished. He quietly settled down to his work in collecting the revenue of Tirhut; and his official duties soon became so absorbing, that he found little time for projecting reforms of the Indian Civil Service.

Soon also his Oriental studies gave him a new interest in the country and the people. The first allusions to Oriental literature occur in a letter dated Patna, December 10, 1786. It is addressed to his father, who had desired some information concerning the religion of the Hindus. Colebrooke's own interest in Sanskrit literature was from the first scientific rather than literary. His love of mathematics and astronomy made him anxious to find out what the Brahmans had achieved in these branches of knowledge. It is surprising to see how correct is the first communication which he sends to his father on the four modes of reckoning time adopted by Hindu astronomers, and which he seems chiefly to have drawn from Persian sources. The passage (pp. 23–26) is too long to be given here, but we recommend it to the careful attention of Sanskrit scholars, who will find it more accurate than what has but lately been written on the same subject. Colebrooke treated, again, of the different measures of time in his essay "On Indian Weights and Measures," published in the "Asiatic Researches," 1798; and in stating the rule for finding the planets which preside over the day, called *Horâ*, he was the first to point out the coincidence between that expression and our name for the twenty-fourth part of the day. In one of the notes to his Dissertation on the Algebra of the Hindus he showed that this and other astrological terms were evidently borrowed by the Hindus from the Greeks, or other external sources; and in a manuscript note published for the first time by Sir E. Colebrooke, we find him following up the same subject, and calling attention to the fact that the word *Horâ* occurs in the Sanskrit vocabulary—the *Medinî-Kosha*, and bears there, among other significations, that of the rising of a sign of the zodiac, or half a sign. This, as he remarks, is in diurnal motion one *hour*, thus confirming the connection between the Indian and European significations of the word.

While he thus felt attracted towards the study of Oriental literature by his own scientific interests, it seems that Sanskrit literature and poetry by themselves had no charms for him. On the contrary, he declares himself repelled by the false taste of Oriental writers; and he speaks very slightingly of "the *amateurs* who do not seek the acquisition of useful knowledge, but would only wish to attract notice, without the labor of deserving it, which is readily accomplished by an ode from the Persian, an apologue from the Sanskrit, or a song from some unheard-of dialect of Hinduee, of which *amateur* favors the public with a *free* translation, without understanding the original, as you will immediately be convinced, if you peruse that repository of nonsense, the 'Asiatic Miscellany.'" He makes one exception, however, in favor of Wilkins. "I have never yet seen any book," he writes, "which can be depended on for information concerning the real opinions of the Hindus, except Wilkins's 'Bhagvat Geeta.' That gentleman was Sanskrit mad, and has more materials and more general knowledge respecting the Hindus than any other foreigner ever acquired since the days of Pythagoras." Arabic, too, did not then find much more favor in his eyes than Sanskrit. "Thus much," he writes, "I am induced to believe, that the Arabic language is of more difficult acquisition than Latin, or even than Greek; and, although it may be concise and nervous, it will not reward the labor of the student, since, in the works of science, he can find nothing new, and, in those of literature, he could not avoid feeling his judgment offended by the false taste in which they are written, and his imagination being heated by the glow of their imagery. A few dry facts might, however, reward the literary drudge....."

It may be doubted, indeed, whether Colebrooke would ever have overcome these prejudices, had it not been for his father's exhortations. In 1789, Colebrooke was transferred from Tirhut to Purneah; and such was his interest in his new and more responsible office, that, according to his own expression, he felt for it all the solicitude of a young author. Engrossed in his work, a ten years' settlement of some of the districts of his new collectorship, he writes to his father in July, 1790:—

"The religion, manners, natural history, traditions, and arts of this country may, certainly, furnish subjects on which my communications might, perhaps, be not uninteresting; but to offer anything deserving of attention would require a season of leisure to collect and digest information. Engaged in public and busy scenes, my mind is wholly engrossed by the cares and duties of my station; in vain I seek, for relaxation's sake, to direct my thoughts to other subjects; matters of business constantly recur. It is for this cause that I have occasionally apologized for a dearth of subjects, having no occurrences to relate, and the matters which occupy my attention being uninteresting as a subject of correspondence."

When, after a time, the hope of distinguishing himself impelled Colebrooke to new exertions, and he determined to become an author, the subject which he chose was not antiquarian or philosophical, but purely practical.

"Translations," he writes, in 1790, "are for those who rather need to fill their purses than gratify their ambition. For original compositions on Oriental history and sciences is required more reading in the literature of the East than I possess, or am likely to attain. My subject should be connected with those matters to which my attention is professionally led. One subject is, I believe, yet untouched—the agriculture of Bengal. On this I have been curious of information; and, having obtained some, I am now pursuing inquiries with some degree of regularity. I wish for your opinion, whether it would be worth while to reduce into form the information which may be obtained on a subject necessarily dry, and which (curious, perhaps) is, certainly, useless to English readers."

Among the subjects of which he wishes to treat in this work we find some of antiquarian interest, *e.g.*, what castes of Hindus are altogether forbid cultivating, and what castes have religious prejudices against the culture of particular articles. Others are purely technical; for instance, the question of the succession and mixture of crops. He states that the Hindus have some traditional maxims on the succession of crops to which they rigidly adhere; and with regard to mixture, he observes that two, three, or even four different articles are sown in the same field, and gathered successively, as they ripen; that they are sometimes all sown on the same day, sometimes at different periods, etc.

His letters now became more and more interesting, and they generally contain some fragments which show us how the sphere of his inquiries became more and more extended. We find (p. 39) observations on the Psylli of Egypt and the snake-charmers of India, on the Sikhs (p. 45), on human sacrifices in India (p. 46). The spirit of inquiry which had been kindled by Sir W. Jones, more particularly since the foundation of the Asiatic Society of Bengal in 1784, had evidently reached Colebrooke. It is difficult to fix the exact date when he began the study of Sanskrit. He seems to have taken it up and left it again in despair several times. In 1793 he was removed from Purneah to Nattore. From that place he sent to his father the first volumes of the "Asiatic Researches," published by the members of the Asiatic Society. He drew his father's attention to some articles in them, which would seem to prove that the ancient Hindus possessed a knowledge of Egypt and of the Jews, but he adds: "No historical light can be expected from Sanskrit literature; but it may, nevertheless, be curious, if not useful, to publish such of their legends as seem to resemble others known to European mythology." The first glimmering of comparative mythology in 1793!

Again he writes in 1793, "In my Sanskrit studies, I do not confine myself now to particular subjects, but skim the surface of all their sciences. I will subjoin, for your amusement, some remarks on subjects treated in the 'Researches.'"

What the results of that skimming were, and how far more philosophical his appreciation of Hindu literature had then become, may be seen from the end of the same letter, written from Rajshahi, December, 6, 1793:—

"Upon the whole, whatever may be the true antiquity of this nation, whether their mythology be a corruption of the pure deism we find in their books, or their deism a refinement from gross idolatry; whether their religious and moral precepts have been engrafted on the elegant philosophy of the Nyâya and Mimânsâ, or this philosophy been refined on the plainer of the Veda; the Hindu is the most ancient nation of which we have valuable remains, and has been surpassed by none in refinement and civilization; though the utmost pitch of refinement to which it ever arrived preceded, in time, the dawn of civilization in any other nation of which we have even the name in history. The further our literary inquiries are extended here, the more vast and stupendous is the scene which opens to us; at the same time, that the true and false, the sublime and the puerile, wisdom and absurdity, are so intermixed, that, at every step, we have to smile at folly, while we admire and acknowledge the philosophical truth, though couched in obscure allegory and puerile fable."

In 1794, Colebrooke presented to the Asiatic Society his first paper, "On the Duties of a Faithful Hindu Widow," and he told his father at the same time, that he meant to pursue his Sanskrit inquiries diligently, and in a spirit which seems to have guided all his work through life: "The only caution," he says, "which occurs to me is, not to hazard in publication anything crude or imperfect, which would injure my reputation as a man of letters; to avoid this, the precaution may be taken of submitting my manuscripts to private perusal."

Colebrooke might indeed from that time have become altogether devoted to the study of Sanskrit, had not his political feelings been strongly roused by the new Charter of the East India Company, which, instead of sanctioning reforms long demanded by political economists, confirmed nearly all the old privileges of their trade. Colebrooke was a free-trader by conviction, and because he had at heart the interests both of India and of England. It is quite gratifying to find a man, generally so cold and prudent as Colebrooke, warm with indignation at the folly and injustice of the policy carried out by England with regard to her Indian subjects. He knew very well that it was personally dangerous for a covenanted servant to discuss and attack the privileges of the Company, but he felt that he ought to think and act, not merely as the servant of a commercial company, but as the servant of the British Government. He wished, even at that early time, that India should become an integral portion of the British Empire, and cease to be, as soon as possible, a mere appendage, yielding a large commercial revenue. He was encouraged in these views by Mr. Anthony Lambert, and the two friends at last decided to embody their views in a work, which they privately printed, under the title of "Remarks on the Present State of the Husbandry and Commerce of Bengal." Colebrooke, as we know, had paid considerable attention to the subject of husbandry, and he now contributed much of the material which he had collected for a purely didactic work, to this controversial and political treatise. He is likewise responsible, and he never tried to shirk that responsibility, for most of the advanced financial theories which it contains. The volume was sent to England, and submitted to the Prime Minister of the day and several other persons of influence. It seems to have produced an impression in the quarters most concerned, but it was considered prudent to stop its further circulation on account of the dangerous free-trade principles, which it supported with powerful arguments. Colebrooke had left the discretion of publishing the work in England to his friends, and he cheerfully submitted to their decision. He himself, however, never ceased to advocate the most liberal financial opinions, and being considered by those in power in Leadenhall Street as a dangerous young man, his advancement in India became slower than it would otherwise have been.

A man of Colebrooke's power, however, was too useful to the Indian Government to be passed over altogether, and though his career was neither rapid nor brilliant, it was nevertheless most successful. Just at the time when Sir W. Jones had died suddenly, Colebrooke was removed from the revenue to the judicial branch of the Indian service, and there was no man in India, except Colebrooke, who could carry on the work which Sir W. Jones had left unfinished, viz.: "The Digest of Hindu and Mohammedan Laws." At the instance of Warren Hastings, a clause had been inserted in the Act of 1772, providing that "Maulavies and Pundits should attend the Courts, to expound the law and assist in passing the decrees." In all suits regarding inheritance, marriage, caste, and religious usages and institutions, the ancient laws of the Hindus were to be followed, and for that purpose a body of laws from their own books had to be compiled. Under the direction of Warren Hastings, nine Brahmans had been commissioned to draw up a code, which appeared in 1776, under the title of "Code of Gentoo Laws."[2] It had been originally compiled in Sanskrit, then translated into Persian, and from that into English. As that code, however, was very imperfect, Sir W. Jones had urged on the Government the necessity of a more complete and authentic compilation. s were to be collected, after the model of Justinian's Pandects, from law-books of approved authority, and to be digested according to a scientific analysis, with references to original authors. The task of arranging the -books and compiling the new code fell chiefly to a learned Pandit, Jagannâtha, and the task of translating it was now, after the death of Sir W. Jones, undertaken by Colebrooke. This task was no easy one, and could hardly be carried out without the help of really learned pandits. Fortunately Colebrooke was removed at the time when he undertook this work, to Mirzapur, close to

Benares, the seat of Brahmanical learning, in the north of India, and the seat of a Hindu College. Here Colebrooke found not only rich collections of Sanskrit MSS, but likewise a number of law pandits, who could solve many of the difficulties which he had to encounter in the translation of Jagannâtha's Digest. After two years of incessant labor, we find Colebrooke on January 3, 1797, announcing the completion of his task, which at once established his position as the best Sanskrit scholar of the day. Oriental studies were at that time in the ascendant in India. A dictionary was being compiled, and several grammars were in preparation. Types also had been cut, and for the first time Sanskrit s issued from the press in Devanâgarî letters. Native scholars, too, began to feel a pride in the revival of their ancient literature. The Brahmans, as Colebrooke writes, were by no means averse to instruct strangers; they did not even conceal from him the most sacred s of the Veda. Colebrooke's "Essays on the Religious Ceremonies of the Hindus," which appeared in the fifth volume of the "Asiatic Researches" in the same year as his translation of the "Digest," show very clearly that he had found excellent instructors, and had been initiated in the most sacred literature of the Brahmans. An important paper on the Hindu schools of law seems to date from the same period, and shows a familiarity, not only with the legal authorities of India, but with the whole structure of the traditional and sacred literature of the Brahmans, which but few Sanskrit scholars could lay claim to even at the present day. In the fifth volume of the "Asiatic Researches" appeared also his essay "On Indian Weights and Measures," and his "Enumeration of Indian Classes." A short, but thoughtful memorandum on the origin of caste, written during that period, and printed for the first time in his "Life," will be read with interest by all who are acquainted with the different views of living scholars on this important subject.

Colebrooke's idea was that the institution of caste was not artificial or conventional, but that it began with the simple division of freemen and slaves, which we find among all ancient nations. This division, as he supposes, existed among the Hindus before they settled in India. It became positive law after their emigration from the northern mountains into India, and was there adapted to the new state of the Hindus, settled among the aborigines. The class of slaves or S û d r a s consisted of those who came into India in that degraded state, and those of the aborigines who submitted and were spared. Menial offices and mechanical labor were deemed unworthy of freemen in other countries besides India, and it cannot therefore appear strange that the class of the Ś û d r a s comprehended in India both servants and mechanics, both Hindus and emancipated aborigines. The class of freemen included originally the priest, the soldier, the merchant, and the husbandman. It was divided into three orders, the B r â h m a ṇ a s , K s h a t r i y a s , and V a i ś y a s , the last comprehending merchants and husbandmen indiscriminately, being the yeomen of the country and the citizens of the town. According to Colebrooke's opinion, the Kshatriyas consisted originally of kings and their descendants. It was the order of princes, rather than of mere soldiers. The Brâhmaṇas comprehended no more than the descendants of a few religious men who, by superior knowledge and the austerity of their lives, had gained an ascendency over the people. Neither of these orders was originally very numerous, and their prominence gave no offense to the far more powerful body of the citizens and yeomen.

When legislators began to give their sanction to this social system, their chief object seems to have been to guard against too great a confusion of the four orders—the two orders of nobility, the sacerdotal and the princely, and the two orders of the people, the citizens and the slaves, by either prohibiting intermarriage, or by degrading the offspring of alliances between members of different orders. If men of superior married women of inferior, but next adjoining, rank, the offspring of their marriage sank to the rank of their mothers, or obtained a position intermediate between the two. The children of such marriages were distinguished by separate titles. Thus, the son of a Brâhmaṇa by a Kshatriya woman was called Mûrdhâbhishikta, which implies royalty. They formed a distinct tribe of princes or military nobility, and were by some reckoned superior to the Kshatriya. The son of a Brâhmaṇa by a Vaiśya woman was a Vaidya or Ambashṭha; the offspring of a Kshatriya by a Vaiśya was a Mahishya, forming two tribes of respectable citizens. But if a greater disproportion of rank existed between the parents—if, for instance, a Brâhmaṇa married a Śûdra, the offspring of their marriage, the Nishâda, suffered greater social penalties; he became impure, notwithstanding the nobility of his father. Marriages, again, between women of superior with men of inferior rank were considered more objectionable than marriages of men of superior with women of inferior rank, a sentiment which continues to the present day.

What is peculiar to the social system, as sanctioned by Hindu legislators, and gives it its artificial character, is their attempt to provide by minute regulations for the rank to be assigned to new tribes, and to point out professions suitable to that rank. The tribes had each an internal government, and professions naturally formed themselves into companies. From this source, while the corporations imitated the regulations of tribes, a multitude of new and arbitrary tribes sprang up, the origin of which, as assigned by Manu and other legislators, was probably, as Colebrooke admits, more or less fanciful.

In his "Remarks on the Husbandry and Internal Commerce of Bengal," the subject of caste in its bearing on the social improvement of the Indian nation was likewise treated by Colebrooke. In reply to the erroneous views then prevalent as to the supposed barriers which caste placed against the free development of the Hindus, he writes:—

"An erroneous doctrine has been started, as if the great population of these provinces could not avail to effect improvements, notwithstanding opportunities afforded by an increased demand for particular manufactures or for raw produce: because, 'professions are hereditary among the Hindus; the offspring of men of one calling do not intrude into any other; professions are confined to hereditary descent; and the produce of any particular manufacture cannot be extended according to the increase of the demand, but must depend upon the population of the caste, or tribe, which works on that manufacture; or, in other words, if the demand for any article should exceed the ability of the number of workmen who produce it, the deficiency cannot be supplied by calling in assistance from other tribes.'

"In opposition to this unfounded opinion, it is necessary that we not only show, as has been already done, that the population is actually sufficient for great improvement, but we must also prove, that professions are not separated by an impassable line, and that the population affords a sufficient number whose religions prejudices permit, and whose inclination leads them to engage in, those occupations through which the desired improvement may be effected.

"The Muselmans, to whom the argument above quoted cannot in any manner be applied, bear no inconsiderable proportion to the whole population. Other descriptions of people, not governed by Hindu institutions, are found among the inhabitants of these provinces; in regard to these, also, the objection is irrelevant. The Hindus themselves, to whom the doctrine which we combat is meant to be applied, cannot exceed nine tenths of the population; probably, they do not bear so great a proportion to the other tribes. They are, as is well known, divided into four grand classes; but the three first of them are much less numerous than the Śûdra. The aggregate of Brâhmaṇa, Kshatriya, and Vaiśya may amount, at the most, to a fifth of the population; and even these are not absolutely restricted to their own appointed occupations. Commerce and agriculture are universally permitted; and, under the designation of servants of the other three tribes, the Śûdras seem to be allowed to prosecute any manufacture.

"In this tribe are included not only the true Śûdras, but also the several castes whose origin is ascribed to the promiscuous intercourse of the four classes. To these, also, their several occupations were assigned; but neither are they restricted, by rigorous injunctions, to their own appointed occupations. For any person unable to procure a subsistence by the exercise of his own profession may earn a livelihood in the calling of a subordinate caste, within certain limits in the scale of relative precedence assigned to each; and no forfeiture is now incurred by his intruding into a superior profession. It was, indeed, the duty of the Hindu magistrate to restrain the encroachments of inferior tribes on the occupations of superior castes; but, under a foreign government, this restraint has no existence.

"In practice, little attention is paid to the limitations to which we have here alluded: daily observation shows even Brâhmanas exercising the menial profession of a Sûdra. We are aware that every caste forms itself into clubs, or lodges, consisting of the several individuals of that caste residing within a small distance; and that these clubs, or lodges, govern themselves by particular rules and customs, or by laws. But, though some restrictions and limitations, not founded on religious prejudices, are found among their by-laws, it may be received, as a general maxim, that the occupation appointed for each tribe is entitled merely to a preference. Every profession, with few exceptions, is open to every description of persons, and the discouragement arising from religious prejudices is not greater than what exists in Great Britain from the effects of municipal and corporation laws. In Bengal, the numbers of people actually willing to apply to any particular occupation are sufficient for the unlimited extension of any manufacture.

"If these facts and observations be not considered as a conclusive refutation of the unfounded assertion made on this subject, we must appeal to the experience of every gentleman who may have resided in the provinces of Bengal, whether a change of occupation and profession does not frequently and indefinitely occur? Whether Brâhmanas are not employed in the most servile offices? And whether the Sûdra is not seen elevated to situations of respectability and importance? In short, whether the assertion above quoted be not altogether destitute of foundation?"

It is much to be regretted that studies so auspiciously begun were suddenly interrupted by a diplomatic mission, which called Colebrooke away from Mirzapur, and retained him from 1798 to 1801 at Nagpur, the capital of Berar. Colebrooke himself had by this time discovered that, however distinguished his public career might be, his lasting fame must depend on his Sanskrit studies. We find him even at Nagpur continuing his literary work, particularly the compilation and translation of a Supplementary Digest. He also prepared, as far as this was possible in the midst of diplomatic avocations, some of his most important contributions to the "Asiatic Researches," one on Sanskrit prosody, which did not appear till 1808, and was then styled an essay on Sanskrit and Prakrit poetry; one on the Vedas, another on Indian Theogonies (not published), and a critical treatise on Indian plants. At last, in May, 1801, he left Nagpur to return to his post at

Mirzapur. Shortly afterwards he was summoned to Calcutta, and appointed a member of the newly constituted Court of Appeal. He at the same time accepted the honorary post of Professor of Sanskrit at the college recently established at Fort William, without, however, taking an active part in the teaching of pupils. He seems to have been a director of studies rather than an actual professor, but he rendered valuable service as examiner in Sanskrit, Bengali, Hindustani, and Persian. In 1801 appeared his essay on the Sanskrit and Prakrit languages, which shows how well he had qualified himself to act as professor of Sanskrit, and how well, in addition to the legal and sacred literature of the Brahmans, he had mastered the *belles lettres* of India also, which at first, as we saw, had rather repelled him by their extravagance and want of taste.

And here we have to take note of a fact which has never been mentioned in the history of the science of language, viz., that Colebrooke at that early time devoted considerable attention to the study of Comparative Philology. To judge from his papers, which have never been published, but which are still in the possession of Sir E. Colebrooke, the range of his comparisons was very wide, and embraced not only Sanskrit, Greek, and Latin, with their derivatives, but also the Germanic and Slavonic languages.3

The principal work, however, of this period of his life was his Sanskrit Grammar. Though it was never finished, it will always keep its place, like a classical *torso*, more admired in its unfinished state than other works which stand by its side; finished, yet less perfect. Sir E. Colebrooke has endeavored to convey to the general reader some idea of the difficulties which had to be overcome by those who, for the first time, approached the study of the native grammarians, particularly of Pâṇini. But this grammatical literature, the 3,996 grammatical *sûtras* or rules, which determine every possible form of the Sanskrit language in a manner unthought of by the grammarians of any other country, the glosses and commentaries, one piled upon the other, which are indispensable for a successful unraveling of Pâṇini's artful web, which start every objection, reasonable or unreasonable, that can be imagined, either against Pâṇini himself or against his interpreters, which establish general principles, register every exception, and defend all forms apparently anomalous of the ancient Vedic language; all this together is so completely *sui generis*, that those only who have themselves followed Colebrooke's footsteps can appreciate the boldness of the first adventurer, and the perseverance of the first explorer of that grammatical labyrinth. Colebrooke's own Grammar of the Sanskrit language, founded on works of native grammarians, has sometimes been accused of obscurity, nor can it be denied that for those who wish to acquire the elements of the language, it is almost useless. But those who know the materials which Colebrooke worked up in his grammar, will readily give him credit for what he has done in bringing the *indigesta moles* which he found before him into something like order. He made the first step, and a very considerable step it was, in translating the strange phraseology of Sanskrit grammarians into something at least intelligible to European scholars. How it could have been imagined that their extraordinary grammatical phraseology was borrowed by the Hindus from the Greeks, or that its formation was influenced by the grammatical schools established among the Greeks in Bactria, is difficult to understand, if one possesses but the slightest acquaintance with the character of either system, or with their respective historical developments. It would be far more accurate to say that the Indian and Greek systems of grammar represent two opposite poles, exhibiting the two starting-points from which alone the grammar of a language can be attacked, viz., the theoretical and the empirical. Greek grammar begins with philosophy, and forces language into the categories established by logic. Indian grammar begins with a mere collection of facts, systematizes them mechanically, and thus leads in the end to a system which, though marvelous for its completeness and perfection, is nevertheless, from a higher point of view, a mere triumph of scholastic pedantry.

Colebrooke's grammar, even in its unfinished state, will always be the best introduction to a study of the native grammarians—a study indispensable to every sound Sanskrit scholar. In accuracy of statement it still holds the first place among European grammars, and it is only to be regretted that the references to Pânini and other grammatical authorities, which existed in Colebrooke's manuscript, should have been left out when it came to be printed. The modern school of Sanskrit students has entirely reverted to Colebrooke's views on the importance of a study of the native grammarians. It is no longer considered sufficient to know the correct forms of Sanskrit declension or conjugation: if challenged, we must be prepared to substantiate their correctness by giving chapter and verse from Pâṇini, the fountain-head of Indian grammar. If Sir E. Colebrooke says that "Bopp also drew deeply from the fountain-head of Indian grammar in his subsequent labors," he has been misinformed. Bopp may have changed his opinion that "the student might arrive at a critical knowledge of Sanskrit by an attentive study of Foster and Wilkins, without referring to native authorities;" but he himself never went beyond, nor is there any evidence in his published works that he himself tried to work his way through the intricacies of Pâṇini.

In addition to his grammatical studies, Colebrooke was engaged in several other subjects. He worked at the Supplement to the "Digest of Laws," which assumed very large proportions; he devoted some of his time to the deciphering of ancient inscriptions, in the hope of finding some fixed points in the history of India; he undertook to supply the Oriental synonymes for Roxburgh's "Flora Indica"—a most laborious task, requiring a knowledge of botany as well as an intimate acquaintance with Oriental languages. In 1804 and 1805, while preparing his classical essay on the Vedas for the press, we find him approaching the study of the religion of Buddha. In all these varied researches, it is most interesting to observe the difference between him and all the other contributors to the "Asiatic Researches" at that time. They were all carried away by theories or enthusiasm; they were all betrayed into assertions or conjectures which proved unfounded. Colebrooke alone, the most hard-working and most comprehensive student, never allows one word to escape his pen for which he has not his authority; and when he speaks of the treatises of Sir W. Jones, Wilford, and others, he readily admits that they contain curious matter, but as he expresses himself, "very little conviction." When speaking of his own work, as for instance, what he had written on the Vedas, he says: "I imagine my treatise on the Vedas will be thought curious; but, like the rest of my publications, little interesting to the general reader."

In 1805, Colebrooke became President of the Court of Appeal—a high and, as it would seem, lucrative post, which made him unwilling to aspire to any other appointment. His leisure, though more limited than before, was devoted, as formerly, to his favorite studies; and in 1807 he accepted the presidency of the Asiatic Society—a post never before or after filled so worthily. He not only contributed himself several articles to the "Asiatic Researches," published by the Society, viz., "On the Sect of Jina," "On the Indian and Arabic Divisions of the Zodiack," and "On the Frankincense of the Ancients;" but he encouraged also many useful literary undertakings, and threw out, among other things, an idea which has but lately been carried out, viz., a *Catalogue raisonné* of all that is extant in Asiatic literature. His own studies became more and more concentrated on the most ancient literature of India, the Vedas, and the question of their real antiquity led him again to a more exhaustive examination of the astronomical literature of the Brahmans. In all these researches, which were necessarily of a somewhat conjectural character, Colebrooke was guided by his usual caution. Instead of attempting, for instance, a free and more or less divinatory translation of the hymns of the Rig-Veda, he began with the tedious but inevitable work of exploring the native commentaries. No one who has not seen his MSS., now preserved at the India Office, and the marginal notes with which the folios of Sâyaṇa's commentary are covered, can form any idea of the conscientiousness with which he collected the materials for his essay. He was by no means a blind follower of Sâyaṇa, or a believer in the infallibility of traditional interpretation. The question on which so much useless ingenuity has since been expended, whether in translating the Veda we should be guided by native authorities or by the rules of critical scholarship, must have seemed to him, as to every sensible person, answered as soon as it was asked. He answered it by setting to work patiently, in order to find out, first, all that could be learnt from native scholars, and afterwards to form his own opinion.

His experience as a practical man, his judicial frame of mind, his freedom from literary vanity, kept him, here as elsewhere, from falling into the pits of learned pedantry. It will seem almost incredible to later generations that German and English scholars should have wasted so much of their time in trying to prove, either that we should take no notice whatever of the traditional interpretation of the Veda, or that, in following it, we should entirely surrender our right of private judgment. Yet that is the controversy which has occupied of late years some of our best Sanskrit scholars, which has filled our journals with articles as full of learning as of acrimony, and has actually divided the students of the history of ancient religion into two hostile camps. Colebrooke knew that he had more useful work before him than to discuss the infallibility of fallible interpreters—a question handled with greater ingenuity by the Maimânsaka philosophers than by any living casuists. He wished to leave substantial work behind him; and though he claimed no freedom from error for himself, yet he felt conscious of having done all his work carefully and honestly, and was willing to leave it, such as it was, to the judgment of his contemporaries and of posterity. Once only during the whole of his life did he allow himself to be drawn into a literary controversy; and here, too, he must have felt what most men feel in the end—that it would have been better if he had not engaged in it. The subject of the controversy was the antiquity and originality of Hindu astronomy. Much had been written for and against it by various writers, but by most of them without a full command of the necessary evidence. Colebrooke himself maintained a doubtful attitude. He began, as usual, with a careful study of the sources at that time available, with translations of Sanskrit treatises, with astronomical calculations and verifications; but, being unable to satisfy himself, he abstained from giving a definite opinion. Bentley, who had published a paper in which the antiquity and originality of Hindu astronomy were totally denied, was probably aware that Colebrooke was not convinced by his arguments. When, therefore, an adverse criticism of his views appeared in the first number of our Review, Bentley jumped at the conclusion that it was written or inspired by Colebrooke. Hence arose his animosity, which lasted for many years, and vented itself from time to time in virulent abuse of Colebrooke, whom Bentley accused not only of unintentional error, but of willful misrepresentation and unfair suppression of the truth. Colebrooke ought to have known that in the republic of letters scholars are sometimes brought into strange society. Being what he was, he need not—nay, he ought not—to have noticed such literary rowdyism. But as the point at issue was of deep interest to him, and as he himself had a much higher opinion of Bentley's real merits than his reviewer, he at last vouchsafed an answer in the "Asiatic Journal" of March, 1826. With regard to Bentley's personalities, he says: "I never spoke nor wrote of Mr. Bentley with disrespect, and I gave no provocation for the tone of his attack on me." As to the question itself, he sums up his position with simplicity and dignity. "I have been no favorer," he writes, "no advocate of Indian astronomy. I have endeavored to lay before the public, in an intelligible form, the fruits of my researches concerning it. I have repeatedly noticed its imperfections, and have been ready to admit that it has been no scanty borrower as to theory."

Colebrooke's stay in India was a long one. He arrived there in 1782, when only seventeen years of age, and he left it in 1815, at the age of fifty. During all this time we see him uninterruptedly engaged in his official work, and devoting all his leisure to literary labor. The results which we have noticed so far, were already astonishing, and quite sufficient to form a solid basis of his literary fame. But we have by no means exhausted the roll of his works. We saw that a supplement to the "Digest of Laws" occupied him for several years. In it he proposed to recast the whole title of inheritance, so imperfectly treated in the "Digest" which he translated, and supplement it with a series of compilations on the several heads of Criminal Law, Pleading, and Evidence, as treated by Indian jurists. In a letter to Sir T. Strange he speaks of the Sanskrit as complete, and of the translation as considerably advanced; but it was not till 1810 that he published, as a first installment, his translation of two important treatises on inheritance, representing the views of different schools on this subject. Much of the material which he collected with a view of improving the administration of law in India, and bringing it into harmony with the legal traditions of the country, remained unpublished, partly because his labors were anticipated by timely reforms, partly because his official duties became too onerous to allow him to finish his work in a manner satisfactory to himself.

But although the bent of Colebrooke's mind was originally scientific, and the philological researches which have conferred the greatest lustre on his name grew insensibly beneath his pen, the services he rendered to Indian jurisprudence would deserve the highest praise and gratitude if he had no other title to fame. Among his earlier studies he had applied himself to the Roman law with a zeal uncommon among Englishmen of his standing, and he has left behind him a treatise on the Roman Law of Contracts. When he directed the same powers of investigation to the sources of Indian law he found everything in confusion. The s and glosses were various and confused. The local customs which abound in India had not been discriminated. Printing was of course unknown to these s; and as no supreme judicial intelligence and authority existed to give unity to the whole system, nothing could be more perplexing than the state of the law. From this chaos Colebrooke brought forth order and light. The publication of the "Dhayabhâga," as the cardinal exposition of the law of inheritance, which is the basis of Hindu society, laid the foundation of no less a work than the revival of Hindu jurisprudence, which had been overlaid by the Mohammedan conquest. On this foundation a superstructure has now been raised by the combined efforts of Indian and English lawyers: but the authority which is to this day most frequently invoked as one of conclusive weight and learning is that of Colebrooke. By the collection and revision of the ancient s which would probably have been lost without his intervention, he became in some degree the legislator of India.

In 1807 he had been promoted to a seat in Council—the highest honor to which a civilian, at the end of his career, could aspire. The five years' tenure of his office coincided very nearly with Lord Minto's Governor-generalship of India. During these five years the scholar became more and more merged in the statesman. His marriage also took place at the same time, which was destined to be happy, but short. Two months after his wife's death he sailed for England, determined to devote the rest of his life to the studies which had become dear to him, and which, as he now felt himself, were to secure to him the honorable place of the father and founder of true Sanskrit scholarship in Europe. Though his earliest tastes still attracted him strongly towards physical science, and though, after his return to England, he devoted more time than in India to astronomical, botanical, chemical, and geological researches, yet, as an author, he remained true to his vocation as a Sanskrit scholar, and he added some of the most important works to the long list of his Oriental publications. How high an estimate he enjoyed among the students of physical science is best shown by his election as President of the Astronomical Society, after the death of Sir John Herschel in 1822. Some of his published contributions to the scientific journals, chiefly on geological subjects, are said to be highly speculative, which is certainly not the character of his Oriental works. Nay, judging from the tenor of the works which he devoted to scholarship, we should think that everything he wrote on other subjects would deserve the most careful and unprejudiced attention, before it was allowed to be forgotten; and we should be glad to see a complete edition of all his writings, which have a character at once so varied and so profound.

We have still to mention some of his more important Oriental publications, which he either began or finished after his return to England. The first is his "Algebra, with Arithmetic and Mensuration, from the Sanskrit of Brahmagupta and Bhâskara, preceded by a Dissertation on the State of the Sciences as known to the Hindus," London, 1817. It is still the standard work on the subject, and likely to remain so, as an intimate knowledge of mathematics is but seldom combined with so complete a mastery of Sanskrit as Colebrooke possessed. He had been preceded by the labors of Burrow and E. Strachey; but it is entirely due to him that mathematicians are now enabled to form a clear idea of the progress which the Indians had made in this branch of knowledge, especially as regards indeterminate analysis. It became henceforth firmly established that the "Arabian Algebra had real points of resemblance to that of the Indians, and not to that of the Greeks; that the Diophantine analysis was only slightly cultivated by the Arabs; and that, finally, the Indian was more scientific and profound than either." Some of the links in his argument, which Colebrooke himself designated as weak, have since been subjected to renewed criticism; but it is interesting to observe how here, too, hardly anything really new has been added by subsequent scholars. The questions of the antiquity of Hindu mathematics—of its indigenous or foreign origin, as well as the dates to be assigned to the principal Sanskrit writers, such as Bhâskara, Brahmagupta, Aryabhaṭṭa, etc.,—are very much in the same state as he left them. And although some living scholars have tried to follow in his footsteps, as far as learning is concerned, they have never approached him in those qualities which are more essential to the discovery of truth than mere reading, viz., caution, fairness, and modesty.

Two events remain still to be noticed before we close the narrative of the quiet and useful years which Colebrooke spent in England. In 1818 he presented his extremely valuable collection of Sanskrit MSS. to the East India Company, and thus founded a treasury from which every student of Sanskrit has since drawn his best supplies. It may be truly said, that without the free access to this collection—granted to every scholar, English or foreign—few of the really important publications of Sanskrit s, which have appeared during the last fifty years, would have been possible; so that in this sense also, Colebrooke deserves the title of the founder of Sanskrit scholarship in Europe.

The last service which he rendered to Oriental literature was the foundation of the Royal Asiatic Society. He had spent a year at the Cape of Good Hope, in order to superintend some landed property which he had acquired there; and after his return to London, in 1822, he succeeded in creating a society which should do in England the work which the Asiatic Society of Bengal, founded in 1784 at Calcutta, by Sir W. Jones, had done in India. Though he declined to become the first president, he became the director of the new society. His object was not only to stimulate Oriental scholars living in England to greater exertions, but likewise to excite in the English public a more general interest in Oriental studies. There was at that time far more interest shown in France and Germany for the literature of the East than in England, though England alone possessed an Eastern Empire. Thus we find Colebrooke writing in one of his letters to Professor Wilson:—

"Schlegel, in what he said of some of us (English Orientalists) and of our labors, did not purpose to be uncandid, nor to undervalue what has been done. In your summary of what he said you set it to the right account. I am not personally acquainted with him, though in correspondence. I do think, with him, that as much has not been done by the English as might have been expected from us. Excepting you and me, and two or three more, who is there that has done anything! In England nobody cares about Oriental literature, or is likely to give the least attention to it."

And again:—

"I rejoice to learn that your great work on the Indian drama may be soon expected by us. I anticipate much gratification from a perusal. Careless and indifferent as our countrymen are, I think, nevertheless, you and I may derive some complacent feelings from the reflection that, following the footsteps of Sir W. Jones, we have, with so little aid of collaborators, and so little encouragement, opened nearly every avenue, and left it to foreigners, who are taking up the clue we have furnished, to complete the outline of what we have sketched. It is some gratification to national pride that the opportunity which the English have enjoyed has not been wholly unemployed."

Colebrooke's last contributions to Oriental learning, which appeared in the "Transactions" of the newly-founded Royal Asiatic Society, consist chiefly in his masterly treatises on Hindu philosophy. In 1823 he read his paper on the Sânkhya system; in 1824 his paper on the Nyâya and Vaiśeshika systems; in 1826 his papers on the Mîmânsâ; and, in 1827, his two papers on Indian Sectaries and on the Vedânta. These papers, too, still retain their value, unimpaired by later researches. They are dry, and to those not acquainted with the subject they may fail to give a living picture of the philosophical struggles of the Indian mind. But the statements which they contain can, with very few exceptions, still be quoted as authoritative, while those who have worked their way through the same materials which he used for the compilation of his essays, feel most struck by the conciseness with which he was able to give the results of his extensive reading in this, the most abstruse domain of Sanskrit literature. The publication of these papers on the schools of Indian metaphysics, which anticipated with entire fidelity the materialism and idealism of Greece and of modern thought, enabled Victor Cousin to introduce a brilliant survey of the philosophy of India into his Lectures on the History of Philosophy, first delivered, we think, in 1828. Cousin knew and thought of Colebrooke exclusively as a metaphysician. He probably cared nothing for his other labors. But as a metaphysician he placed him in the first rank, and never spoke of him without an expression of veneration, very unusual on the eloquent but somewhat imperious lips of the French philosopher.

The last years of Colebrooke's life were full of suffering, both bodily and mental. He died, after a lingering illness, on March 10, 1837.

To many even among those who follow the progress of Oriental scholarship with interest and attention, the estimate which we have given of Colebrooke's merits may seem too high; but we doubt whether from the inner circle of Sanskrit scholars, any dissentient voice will be raised against our awarding to him the first place among Sanskritists, both dead and living. The number of Sanskrit scholars has by this time become considerable, and there is hardly a country in Europe which may not be proud of some distinguished names. In India, too, a new and most useful school of Sanskrit students is rising, who are doing excellent work in bringing to light the forgotten treasures of their country's literature. But here we must, first of all, distinguish between two classes of scholars. There are those who have learnt enough of Sanskrit to be able to read s that have been published and translated, who can discuss their merits and defects, correct some mistakes, and even produce new and more correct editions. There are others who venture on new ground, who devote themselves to the study of MSS., and who by editions of new s, by translations of works hitherto untranslated, or by essays on branches of literature not yet explored, really add to the store of our knowledge. If we speak of Colebrooke as *facile princeps* among Sanskrit scholars, we are thinking of real scholars only, and we thus reduce the number of those who could compete with him to a much smaller compass.

Secondly, we must distinguish between those who came before Colebrooke and those who came after him, and who built on his foundations. That among the latter class there are some scholars who have carried on the work begun by Colebrooke beyond the point where he left it, is no more than natural. It would be disgraceful if it were otherwise, if we had not penetrated further into the intricacies of Pâṇini, if we had not a more complete knowledge of the Indian systems of philosophy, if we had not discovered in the literature of the Vedic period treasures of which Colebrooke had no idea, if we had not improved the standards of criticism which are to guide in the critical restoration of Sanskrit s. But in all these branches of Sanskrit scholarship those who have done the best work are exactly those who speak most highly of Colebrooke's labors, They are proud to call themselves his disciples. They would decline to be considered his rivals.

There remains, therefore, in reality, only one who could be considered a rival of Colebrooke, and whose name is certainly more widely known than his, viz., Sir William Jones. It is by no means necessary to be unjust to him in order to be just to Colebrooke. First of all, he came before Colebrooke, and had to scale some of the most forbidding outworks of Sanskrit scholarship. Secondly, Sir William Jones died young, Colebrooke lived to a good old age. Were we speaking only of the two men, and their personal qualities, we should readily admit that in some respects Sir W. Jones stood higher than Colebrooke. He was evidently a man possessed of great originality, of a highly cultivated taste, and of an exceptional power of assimilating the exotic beauty of Eastern poetry. We may go even further, and frankly admit that, possibly, without the impulse given to Oriental scholarship through Sir William Jones's influence and example, we should never have counted Colebrooke's name among the professors of Sanskrit. But we are here speaking not of the men, but of the works which they left behind; and here the difference between the two is enormous. The fact is, that Colebrooke was gifted with the critical conscience of a scholar—Sir W. Jones was not. Sir W. Jones could not wish for higher testimony in his favor than that of Colebrooke himself. Immediately after his death, Colebrooke wrote to his father, June, 1794:—

"Since I wrote to you the world has sustained an irreparable loss in the death of Sir W. Jones. As a judge, as a constitutional lawyer, and for his amiable qualities in private life, he must have been lost with heartfelt regret. But his loss as a literary character will be felt in a wider circle. It was his intention shortly to have returned to Europe, where the most valuable works might have been expected from his pen. His premature death leaves the results of his researches unarranged, and must lose to the world much that was only committed to memory, and much of which the notes must be unintelligible to those into whose hands his papers fall. It must be long before he is replaced in the same career of literature, if he is ever so. None of those who are now engaged in Oriental researches are so fully informed in the classical languages of the East; and I fear that, in the progress of their inquiries, none will be found to have such comprehensive views."

And again:—

"You ask how we are to supply his place? Indeed, but ill. Our present and future presidents may preside with dignity and propriety; but who can supply his place in diligent and ingenious researches? Not even the combined efforts of the whole Society; and the field is large, and few the cultivators."

Still later in life, when a reaction had set in, and the indiscriminate admiration of Sir W. Jones had given way to an equally indiscriminate depreciation of his merits, Colebrooke, who was then the most competent judge, writes to his father:—

"As for the other point you mention, the use of a translation by Wilkins, without acknowledgment, I can bear testimony that Sir W. Jones's own labors in Manu sufficed without the aid of a translation. He had carried an interlineary Latin version through all the difficult chapters; he had read the original three times through, and he had carefully studied the commentaries. This I know, because it appears clearly so from the copies of Manu and his commentators which Sir William used, and which I have seen. I must think that he paid a sufficient compliment to Wilkins, when he said, that without his aid he should never have learned Sanskrit. I observe with regret a growing disposition, here and in England, to depreciate Sir W. Jones's merits. It has not hitherto shown itself beyond private circles and conversation. Should the same disposition be manifested in print, I shall think myself bound to bear public testimony to his attainments in Sanskrit."

Such candid appreciation of the merits of Sir W. Jones, conveyed in a private letter, and coming from the pen of the only person then competent to judge both of the strong and the weak points in the scholarship of Sir William Jones, ought to caution us against any inconsiderate judgment. Yet we do not hesitate to declare that, as Sanskrit scholars, Sir William Jones and Colebrooke cannot be compared. Sir William had explored a few fields only, Colebrooke had surveyed almost the whole domain of Sanskrit literature. Sir William was able to read fragments of epic poetry, a play, and the laws of Manu. But the really difficult works, the grammatical treatises and commentaries, the philosophical systems, and, before all, the immense literature of the Vedic period, were never seriously approached by him. Sir William Jones reminds us sometimes of the dashing and impatient general who tries to take every fortress by bombardment or by storm, while Colebrooke never trusts to anything but a regular siege. They will both retain places of honor in our literary Walhallas. But ask any librarian, and he will say that at the present day the collected works of Sir W. Jones are hardly ever consulted by Sanskrit scholars, while Colebrooke's essays are even now passing through a new edition, and we hope Sir Edward Colebrooke will one day give the world a complete edition of his father's works.

APPENDIX.

COMPARATIVE VIEW OF SANSKRIT AND OTHER LANGUAGES,

By T. H. COLEBROOKE.

Oxford, September, 1874.

I MENTIONED in my Address before the Aryan section of the Oriental Congress that I possessed some MS. notes of Colebrooke's on Comparative Philology. They were sent to me some time ago by his son, Sir E. Colebrooke, who gave me leave to publish them, if I thought them of sufficient importance. They were written down, as far as we know, about the years 1801 or 1802, and contain long lists of words expressive of some of the most important elements of early civilization, in Sanskrit, Greek, Latin, Teutonic, Celtic, and Slavonic. Like everything that Colebrooke wrote, these lists are prepared with great care. They exist in rough notes, in a first, and in a second copy. I give them from the second copy, in which many words from less important languages are omitted, and several doubtful comparisons suppressed. I have purposely altered nothing, for the interest of these lists is chiefly historical, showing how, long before the days of Bopp and Grimm, Colebrooke had clearly perceived the relationship of all the principal branches of the Aryan family, and, what is more important, how he had anticipated the historical conclusions which a comparison of the principal words of the great dialects of the Aryan family enables us to draw with regard to the state of civilization anterior to the first separation of the Aryan race. No one acquainted with the progress which Comparative Philology has made during the last seventy years would think of quoting some of the comparisons here suggested by Colebrooke as authoritative. The restraints which phonetic laws have since imposed on the comparison of words were unknown in his days. But with all that, it is most surprising to see how careful Colebrooke was, even when he had to guess, and how well he succeeded in collecting those words which form the earliest common dictionary of our ancestors, and supply the only trustworthy materials for a history of the very beginnings of the Aryan race.

Max Muller.

The transliteration system in this section is different from Müller's. Note in particular:

c, c'h, ch, j : k, kh, c, j (Müller's k, kh, *k*, *g*)
rĭ : ṛ (Müller's *ri*)
ä ï ö ü : dots represent dieresis, not umlaut

The letter ṭ was shown as t́ (t with acute). This has been regularized because Colebrooke's form may not display reliably. The form ń for ṇ has been retained; ḍ does not occur.

Father.

Sans. Pitrĭ (-tá). *Beng. Hind.* Pitá. *Pers.* Pider.

Sans. Janayitrĭ (-tá). *Gr.* Geneter, Gennetor. *Lat.* Genitor.

Sans. Táta. *Beng.* Tát. *Arm.* Tat. *Wal. Corn.* Tad. *Ang.* Dad.

Sans. Vaptrĭ (-tá). *Beng.* Bápá. *Hind.* Bábá, Báp. *Germ.* Vater. *Belg.* Vader. *Isl.* Bader. *Gr. Lat.* Pater.

Mother.

Sans. Janayitrĭ, Jananí. *Gr.* Gennêteira. *Lat.* Genitrix.

Sans. Mátrĭ (-tá). *Beng.* Mátá. *Lat.* Mater. *Gr.* Meter. *Sclav.* Mati. *Ir.* Mat'hair. *Germ.* Mutter. *Sax.* Moder. *Belg. Isl.* Mooder.

N.B. The roots *jan* and *jani* (the past tense of which last is *jajnyé*, pronounced *jagyé* in Bengal, Tirhut, etc.) are evidently analogous to the Latin *gigno*, and Greek *gennao*.

Son.

Sans. Putra. *Hind.* Putr, Pút. *Támil.* Putren. *Ori.* Púá.

Sans. Súnu. *Hind.* Sún, Suän. *Goth.* Sunus. *Sax.* Suna. *Belg.* Soen, Sone. *Sue.* Son. *Dalm.* Szun. *Pol. Boh.* Syn. *Scl.* Sin, Syn.

Grandson.

Sans. Naptrĭ (-tá). *Lat.* Nepos. *Hind.* Nátí. *Mahr.* Nátú.

Granddaughter.

Sans. Naptrí. *Lat.* Neptis. *Hind.* Natní. *Beng.* Nátní. *Ori.* Nátuni.

Daughter's Son.

Sans. Dauhitra. *Beng.* Dauhitro. *Hind.* Dóhtá. *Gr.* Thugatridous.

Son's Son.

Sans. Pautra. *Hind.* Pótá. *Beng.* Pautro.

Daughter.

Sans. Duhitrĭ (-tá). *Beng.* Duhitá. *Hind.* Dóhitá. *Goth.* Dauhter. *Sax.* Dohter. *Pers.* Dokhter. *Belg.* Dochtere. *Germ.* Tochter. *Gr.* Thygater. *Sue.* Dotter. *Isl.* Dooter. *Dan.* Daater.

Sans. Tócá. *Russ.* Doke. *Hind.* Dhíya, Dhí. *Or.* Jhíä. *Scl.* Hzhi. *Dalm.* Hchii. *Boh.* Dey, Deera. *Ir.* Dear.

Brother.

Sans. Bhrátrĭ (-tá). *Hind.* Bhrátá, Bhaï, Bhayá, Bír, Bíran. *Pers.* Birádar. *Corn.* Bredar. *Wal.* Braud. *Ir.* Brathair. *Arm.* Breur. *Mona.* Breyr. *Scl.* Brat. *Russ.* Brate. *Dalm.* Brath. *Boh.* Bradr. *Germ.* Bruder. *Ang.-Sax.* Brother. *Sax.* Brother. *Lat.* Frater. *Gall.* Frère.

Sister.

Sans. Bhaginí. *Hind.* Bhagní, Bahin, Bhainá. *Beng.* Bhoginí, Boïn. *Mahr.* Bahin. *Or.* Bhauní.

Sans. Swasrĭ (-sá). *Ir.* Shiur. *Gall.* Soeur. *Mona.* Sywr. *Sicil.* Suora. *Lat.* Soror. *Germ.* Schwester. *Sax.* Sweoster. *Goth.* Swister. *Holl.* Zuster. *Wal.* C'huaer.

Father-in-law.

Sans. Śwaśura. *Beng.* Sósur. *Mahr.* Sasará. *Hind.* Susar, Súsrá, Sasúr. *Lat.* Sócer, Socerus. *Gr.* Hecyros.

Mother-in-law.

Sans. Śwaśrú. *Beng.* Sosru, Sásuri. *Hind.* Sás. *Mahr.* Sású. *Lat.* Socrus. *Gr.* Hecyra.

Wife's Brother.

Sans. Syála. *Beng.* Syáloc. *Hind.* Sálá. *Or.* Salá.

Husband's Brother.

Sans. Dévrĭ (-vá), Dévara. *Hind.* Déwar. *Guj.* Díyar. *Mahr.* Dír. *Gr.* Daêr. *Lat.* Levir (*olim* Devir).

Son-in-law.

Sans. Jámátrĭ (-tá). *Hind.* Jamáí, Jawáí. *Pers.* Dámád.

Widow.

Sans. Vidhavá. *Lat.* Vidua. *Sax.* Widwa. *Holl.* Weduwe.

Daughter-in-law.

Sans. Badhú. *Hind.* Bahú. *Beng.* Bäú. *Gall.* Bru.

Sans. Snushá. *Cashm.* Nus. *Penj.* Nuh. *Gr.* Nyos. *Lat.* Nurus.

Sun.

Sans. Heli (-lis). *Gr.* Helios. *Arm.* Heol. *Wal.* Hayl, Heyluen.

Sans. Mitra. *Pehl.* Mithra.

Sans. Mihara, Mahira. *Pers.* Mihr.

Sans. Súra, Súrya. *Hind.* Súrej. *Mahr.* Súrj, Súrya. *Ori.* Suruy.

Moon.

Sans. Chandra. *Hind.* Chánd, Chandr, Chandramá.

Sans. Más (máh). *Pers.* Máh. *Boh.* Mesyc. *Pol.* Miesyac. *Dalm.* Miszecz.

Star.

Sans. Tárá. *Hind.* Tárá. *Pers.* Sitareh. *Gr.* Aster. *Belg.* Sterre. *Sax.* Steorra. *Germ.* Stern. *Corn. Arm.* Steren.

Month.

Sans. Mása (-sas). *Hind.* Mahiná, Más. *Pers.* Máh. *Scl.* Messcz. *Dalm.* Miszecz. *Wal.* Misguaith. *Gr.* Mene. *Lat.* Mensis. *Gall.* Mois.

Day.

Sans. Diva. *Mahr.* Diwas. *Lat.* Dies. *Sax.* Dæg.

Sans. Dina. *Hind.* Din. *Boh.* Den. *Scl.* Dan. *Dalm.* Daan. *Pol.* Dzien. *Ang.* (Ant.) Den.

Night.

Sans. Rátri. *Hind.* Rát. *Penj.* Rátter.

Sans. Niś, Niśá. *Wal. Arm.* Nos.

Sans. Nactá. *Lat.* Nox. *Gr.* Nyx. *Goth.* Nahts, Nauts. *Sax.* Niht. *Isl.* Natt. *Boh.* Noc. *Gall.* Nuit.

By Night.

Sans. (adv.) Nactam. *Lat.* Noctu. *Gr.* Nyctor.

Sky, Heaven.

Sans. Div, Diva. *Beng.* Dibi. *Liv.* Debbes.

Sans. Swar, Swarga. *Hind.* Swarag. *Guz.* Sarag. *Cant.* Cerua.

Sans. Nabhas. *Beng.* Nebho. *Russ.* Nebo. *Scl.* Nebu. *Boh.* Nebe. *Pol.* Niebo.

God.

Sans. Déva (-vas), Dévatá. *Hind.* Déwatá. *Penj.* Déú. *Tamil.* Taivam. *Lat.* Deus. *Gr.* Theos. *Wal.* Diju. *Ir.* Diu.

Sans. Bhagaván. *Dalm.* Bogh. *Croat.* Bog.

Fire.

Sans. Agni. *Casm.* Agin. *Beng.* Águn. *Hind.* Ag. *Scl.* Ogein. *Croat.* Ogayn. *Pol.* Ogien. *Dalm.* Ogany. *Lat.* Ignis.

Sans. Vahni. *Boh.* Ohen.

Sans. Anala. *Beng.* Onol. *Mona.* Aul.

Sans. Śushman (má). *Cant.* Sua.

Sans. Tanúnapát. *Wal.* Tân. *Ir.* Teene.

Sans. Varhis. *Sax.* Vür. *Belg.* Vier.

Water.

Sans. Áp. *Pers.* Áb.

Sans. Pániya. *Hind.* Páni.

Sans. Udaca. *Russ.* Ouode. *Scl.* Voda. *Boh.* Woda.

Sans. Níra, Nára. *Beng.* Nír. *Carn.* Níra. *Tel.* Níllu. *Vulg. Gr.* Nero.

Sans. Jala. *Hind.* Jal. *Ir.* Gil.

Sans. Arńa. *Ir.* An.

Sans. Vár, Vári. *Beng.* Bár. *Ir.* Bir. *Cant.* Vra.

Cloud.

Sans. Abhra. *Penj.* Abhar. *Casm.* Abar. *Pers.* Abr. *Gr.* Ombros. *Lat.* Imber.

Man.

Sans. Nara. *Pers.* Nar. *Gr.* Aner.

Sans. Mánava, Mánusha. *Guz.* Mánas. *Beng.* Mánus. *Dan.* Mand. *Sax.* Man, Men.

Mind.

Sans. Manas. *Gr.* Menos. *Lat.* Mens.

Bone.

Sans. Had´d´a. *Hind.* Hadí.

Sans. Asthi. *Lat.* Os. *Gr.* Osteon.

Hand.

Sans. Hasta. *Hind.* Hát'h. *Penj.* Hatt'h. *Beng.* Hát. *Pers.* Dest.

Sans. Cara. *Gr.* Cheir. *Vulg. Gr.* Chere.

Sans. Páni. *Wal.* Pawen. *Ang.* Paw.

Knee.

Sans. Jánu. *Penj.* Jáhnu. *Pers.* Zánu. *Hind.* Gutaná. *Gr.* Gonu. *Lat.* Genu. *Gall.* Genou. *Sax.* Cneow.

Foot.

Sans. Páda, Pad. *Or.* Pád. *Beng.* Pod, Pá. *Hind.* Páú, Payar. *Lat.* Pes (pedis). *Gr.* Pous (podos). *Vulg. Gr.* Podare. *Gall.* Pied. *Goth.* Fotus. *Sax.* Fot, Vot. *Sue.* Foot.

Sans. Anghri. *Beng.* Onghri. *Scl.* Noga. *Pol.* Nogi.

Breast.

Sans. Stana. *Beng.* Stan. (*Ang.* Pap.) *Gr.* Sternon. *Lat.* Sternum. (*Ang.* Chest.)

Navel.

Sans. Nábhi. *Hind.* Nábh. *Beng.* Náï. *Or.* Nahi. *Pers.* Náf. *Gr.* Omphalos. *Sax.* Nafela, Navela.

Ear.

Sans. Carńa. *Hind.* Cán. *Arm.* Skuarn. *Corn.* Skevam.

Nose.

Sans. Nasicá, Násá, Nasya. *Hind.* Nác. *Penj.* Nacca. *Casm.* Nast. *Lat.* Nasus. *Germ.* Nase. *Belg.* Nuese. *Sax.* Noese, Nosa. *Sue.* Nasa. *Boh.* Nos. *Scl.* Nus. *Dalm.* Nooss.

Tooth.

Sans. Danta. *Hind.* Dánt. *Penj.* Dand. *Pers.* Dendan. *Wal.* Dant. *Lat.* Dens. *Gall.* Dent. *Gr.* Odous (-ontos). *Belg.* Tant, Tand. *Sax.* Toth.

Mouth.

Sans. Muc'ha. *Hind.* Muc'h, Muh, Munh, Múnh. *Penj.* Múh. *Guz.* Móh. *Sax.* Muth.

Elbow.

Sans. Anka, flank; Anga, membrum. *Gr.* Agkōn.

Voice.

Sans. Vách (vác). *Lat.* Vox. *Gr.* Ossa.

Name.

Sans. Náman (-ma). *Hind.* Nám, Náoṅ. *Pers.* Nám. *Gr.* Onoma. *Lat.* Nomen. *Gall.* Nom. *Sax.* Nama.

King.

Sans. Ráj (-t´, -d´), Rájan (-já). *Hind.* Rájá. *Lat.* Rex. *Gall.* Roy. *Wal.* Rhuy, Rhiydh. *Ir.* Righ, Rak.

Kingdom.

Sans. Rájnya (-am). *Lat.* Regnum.

Town.

Sans. C'héta. *Hind.* C'hérá. *Wal.* Kaer. *Arm.* Koer.

House.

Sans. Ócas. *Gr.* Oicos.

Sans. Grĭha. *Hind.* Ghar. *Casm.* Gar.

Ship *or* Boat.

Sans. Nau (naus). *Gr.* Naus. *Lat.* Navis. *Pers.* Nau. *Hind.* Nau, Naú. *Or.* Ná. *Carn.* Náviya.

A Small Boat.

Sans. Plava. *Mah.* Plav. *Gr.* Ploion.

Thing, Wealth.

Sans. Rai (rás). *Lat.* Res.

Mountain.

Sans. Parvata. *Hind.* Parbat, Pahár. *Penj.* Parabat. *Carn.* Parbatavu.

Sans. Adri. *Penj.* Adari. *Ir.* Ard.

Sans. Naga, Aga. *Ir.* Aigh.

Sans. Grávan (-vá), Giri. *Lus.* Grib. *Scl.* Hrib.

Rock *or* Stone.

Sans. Prastara. *Hind.* Patt'har. *Guz.* Pat'har. *Beng.* Pat'har. *Gr.* Petra. *Lat.* Petra.

Sans. Grávan (-vâ). *Penj.* Garáv.

Tree.

Sans. Dru (drus), Druma (-mas). *Gr.* Drys (Drymos, a wood). *Epir.* Druu. *Russ.* Dreous. *Scl.* Drevu.

Sans. Taru. *Goth.* Triu, Trie. *Sax.* Treo, Treow. *Dan.* Tree.

Pomegranate.

Sans. Róhita. *Gr.* Rhoa, Rhoia.

Horse.

Sans. Ghóṭaca. *Hind.* Ghórá. *Guz.* Ghóró. *Casm.* Guru. *Wal.* Goruydh, Govar.

Sans. Haya (-yas). *Ant. Sans.* Arusha. *Isl.* Hors, Hestur. *Dan.* Hest. *Sue.* Hast. *Sax.* Hors.

Sans. Aśva. *Penj.* Aswa. *Pers.* Asp.

Ass.

Sans. C'hara. *Penj.* C'har. *Pers.* Khar.

Sans. Gardabha. *Hind.* Gadhá. *Tirh.* Gadahá.

Mule.

Sans. Aświatara. *Pers.* Astar.

Camel.

Sans. Ushṭra. *Hind.* Unt. *Guz.* Ut. *Penj.* Ustar. *Pers.* Ushtur, Shutur.

Ox, Cow, Bull.

Sans. Gó (gaus). *Hind.* Gau, Gáí. *Beng.* Goru. *Pers.* Gau. *Sax.* Cu. *Sue.* Koo. *Belg.* Koe. *Germ.* Kue. *Sans.* Ucshan (-shá). *Sax.* Oxa. *Dan.* Oxe. *Isl.* Uxe. *Boh.* Ochse. *Germ.* Ochs. *Wai.* Ychs.

Sans. Vrĭsha, Vrĭshan (-shá). *Tirh.* Brikh. *Boh.* Byk. *Pol.* Beik. *Dalm.* Bak. *Lus.* Bik. *Hung.* Bika. *Wal.* Byuch. *Arm.* Biych. *Corn.* Byuh.

Goat.

Sans. Bucca, Barcara. *Hind.* Bacrá. *Mahr.* Bócar. *Guz.* Bócaró. *Beng.* Bócá. *Arm.* Buch. *Corn.* Byk. *Sax.* Bucca. *Gall.* Bouc. *Sue.* Bock. *Belg.* Bocke. *Ital.* Becco.

Ewe.

Sans. Avi (-vis). *Gr.* Ois. *Lat.* Ovis. *Sax.* Eowe.

Wool.

Sans. Urṅá. *Hind.* Un. *Scl.* Volna. *Pol.* Welna. *Boh.* Wlna. *Dalm.* Vuna. *Sue.* Ull. *Isl.* Ull. *Belg.* Wul. *Germ.* Wolle. *A.-Sax.* Wulle. *Wal.* Gulan. *Corn.* Gluan. *Arm.* Gloan. *Ir.* Olann.

Hair of the Body.

Sans. Lava. *Ir.* Lo.

Sans. Lóman (-ma), Róman (-ma). *Hind.* Róán. *Beng.* Lóm, Róm. *Casm.* Rúm. *Mah.* Rómé.

Hair of the Head.

Sans. Césa. *Hind.* Cés. *Casm.* Cís. *Lat.* Crinis.

Sans. Bála. *Hind.* Bál.

Hog.

Sans. Súcara (fem -rî). *Penj.* Súr. *Hind.* Súär, Súwar, Sú, Suén.
Beng. Shúcar, Shúór. *Mahr.* Dúcar. *Tirh.* Súgar. *Nepal.* Surún. *Dan.* Suin.
Sue. Swiin. *Lus.* Swina. *Carn.* Swynia, Swine. *Ang.* Swine. *Sax.* Sugn.
Holl. Soeg, Sauwe. *Germ.* Sauw. *Ang.* Sow. *Belg.* Soch. *Lat.* Sus. *Gr.* Hys, Sys.
Lacon. Sika. *Pers.* Khuc. *Wal.* Húkh. *Corn.* Hoch, Hoh.

Boar.

Sans. Varáha. *Hind.* Baráh. *Oris.* Barahá. *Beng.* Boráhó, Borá.
Corn. Bora, Baedh. *Belg.* Beer. *Sax.* Bar. *Ang.* Boar. *Span.* Berraco.
Gall. Verrat. *Ital.* Verro.

Mouse.

Sans. Múshaca, Múshá. *Hind.* Mus, Musá, Musí, Músrí, Músná. *Penj.* Múshá.
Tirh. Mús. *Lat.* Mus. *Gr.* Mûs. *Sax.* Mus.

Bear.

Sans. Ricsha. *Hind.* Rích'h. *Penj.* Richh. *Guz.* Rénchh. *Tirh.* Rikh.

Sans. Bhalla, Bhallaca, Bhállúca. *Hind.* Bhál, Bhálú.

Sans. Ach'ha, Acsha. *Gr.* Arctos. *Wal.* Arth.

Wolf.

Sans. Vrĭca. *Dalm.* Vuuk. *Scl.* Vulk. *Pol.* Wulk.

Insect.

Sans. Crĭmi. *Pers.* Cirm. *Beng.* Crimi. *Tamil.* Crimi.

Serpent.

Sans. Ahi (ahis). *Gr.* Ophis. *Sans.* Sarpa. *Pers.* Serp. *Lat.* Serpens. *Hind.* Sárp.

Cuckoo.

Sans. Cocila. *Hind.* Coil. *Lat.* Cuculus. *Gr.* Kokkyx.

Sans. Pica. *Lat.* Picus.

Crab.

Sans. Carcata. *Beng.* Cáncrá, Céncrá. *Hind.* Céncrá, Cécrá. *Gr.* Carcinos.
Lat. Cancer. *Wal.* Krank. *Corn.* *Arm.* Kankr. *Gall.* Cancre. *Ir.* Kruban.
Sax. Crabbe. *Ang.* Crab.

Cucumber.

Sans. Carcatí. *Beng.* Cáncur. *Hind.* Cácrí. *Lat.* Cucumer, Cucumis. *Gall.* Concombre. *Ang.* Cucumber.

Sound.

Sans. Swana, Swána. *Lat.* Sonus. *Wal.* Sûn, Sôn, Sain. *Sax.* Sund.

Sleep.

Sans. Swapna, Śaya, Swápa. *Beng.* Shöön. *Hind.* (Supna) Sona [to sleep]. *Gr.* Hypnos. *Wal.* Heppian [to sleep]. *Sax.* Sleepan. *Ang.* Sleep.

New.

Sans. Nava (m. Navas, f. Navá, n. Navam), Navína. *Lat.* Novus. *Gr.* Neos, Nearos. *Pers.* Nó. *Hind.* Nayá, Nawén. *Beng.* Niara. *Wal. Corn.* Neuydh. *Ir.* Núadh. *Arm.* Nevedh, Noadh. *Gall.* Neuf. *Ang.* New. *Sax.* Neow.

Young.

Sans. Yuvan (Yuvâ). *Lat.* Juvenis.

Thin.

Sans. Tanus. *Lat.* Tenuis.

Great.

Sans. Mahâ. *Gr.* Megas. *Lat.* Magnus.

Broad.

Sans. Urus. *Gr.* Eurus.

Old.

Sans. Jírńas. *Gr.* Geron.

Other.

Sans. Itaras. *Gr.* Heteros.

Sans. Anyas. *Lat.* Alius.

Fool.

Sans. Múd'has, Múrchas. *Gr.* Moros.

Dry.

Sans. Csháras. *Gr.* Xeros.

Sin.

Sans. Agha. *Gr.* Hagos (veneratio, scelus).

One.

Sans. Eca. *Hind.* Beng. *etc.* Ec. *Pers.* Yéc.

Two.

Sans. Dwi (nom. du. Dwau). *Hind.* Do. *Pers.* Do. *Gr.* Dyo. *Lat.* Duo. *Gall.* Deux. *Corn.* Deau. *Arm.* Dou. *Ir.* Do. *Goth.* Twai. *Sax.* Twu. *Ang.* Two.

Three.

Sans. Tri (nom. pl. Trayas). *Lat.* Tres. *Gr.* Treis. *Gall.* Trois. *Germ.* Drei. *Holl.* Dry. *Sax.* Threo. *Ang.* Three. *Wal. Arm. Ir.* Tri. *Corn.* Tre.

Four.

Sans. Chatur (nom. pl. Chatwáras, fem. Chatasras). *Lat.* Quatuor. *Gall.* Quatre. *Gr.* Tessares. *Pers.* Chehár. *Hind.* Chehár.

And.

Sans. Cha. *Lat.* Que.

Five.

Sans. Pancha. *Hind.* Pánch. *Pers.* Penj. *Gr.* Pente. *Arm. Corn.* Pemp. *Wal.* Pymp.

Six.

Sans. Shash. *Pers.* Shesh. *Lat.* Sex. *Gr.* Hex. *Gall. Ang.* Six. *Wal.* Khuêkh. *Corn.* Huih. *Arm.* Huekh. *Ir.* She, Seishear.

Seven.

Sans. Sapta. *Lat.* Septem. *Gall.* Sept. *Germ.* Sieben. *Ang.* Seven. *Sax.* Seofon. *Gr.* Hepta. *Pers.* Heft. *Hind.* Sát. *Wal.* Saith. *Arm. Corn.* Seith. *Ir.* Sheakhd.

Eight.

Sans. Asht'a. *Pers.* Hasht. *Hind.* Áth. *Gall.* Huit. *Sax.* Eahta. *Ang.* Eight. *Ir.* Okht. *Lat.* Octo.

Nine.

Sans. Nava. *Hind.* Nó. *Lat.* Novem. *Wal. Corn.* Nau. *Arm.* Nâo. *Ir.* Nyi. *Pers.* Noh. *Gall.* Neuf. *Sax.* Nigon. *Ang.* Nine.

Ten.

Sans. Daśa. *Hind.* Das. *Pers.* Dah. *Lat.* Decem. *Ir.* Deikh. *Arm.* Dêk. *Corn.* Dêg.

PRONOUNS.

I.

Sans. Aham (acc. Má; poss. and dat. Mé; du. Nau; pl. Nas). *Lat. Gr.* Ego, etc. *Pers.* Men. *Hind.* Mai. *Ir.* Me. *Wal.* *Corn.* Mi. *Arm.* Ma.

Thou.

Sans. Twam (acc. Twá; poss. and dat. Té; du. Vám; pl. Vas). *Lat.* Tu, etc. *Gr.* Su, etc. *Hind.* Tú, Tain. *Beng.* Tumi, Tui. *Ir.* Tu. *Pers.* To. *Arm.* Te. *Corn.* Ta. *Wal.* Ti.

PREPOSITIONS, ETC.

Sans. Antar. *Lat.* Inter. *Sans.* Upari. *Gr.* Hyper. *Lat.* Super. *Sans.* Upa. *Gr.* Hypo. *Lat.* Sub. *Sans.* Apa. *Gr.* Apo. *Sans.* Pari. *Gr.* Peri. *Sans.* Pra. *Gr. Lat.* Pro. *Sans.* Pará. *Gr.* Pera. *Sans.* Abhi. *Gr.* Amphi. *Sans.* Ati. *Gr.* Anti. *Sans.* Ama. *Gr.* Amá. *Sans.* Anu. *Gr.* Ana.

TERMINATIONS.

Sans. (terminations of comparatives and superlatives) Taras, tamas. *Gr.* Teros, tatos. *Lat.* Terus, timus. *Sans.* Ishṭhas. *Gr.* Istos.

Sans. (termin. of nouns of agency) Trĭ. *Gr.* Tor, ter. *Lat.* Tor.

Sans. (termin. of participle) Tas. *Gr.* Tos. *Lat.* Tus.

Sans. (termin. of supine) Tum. *Lat.* Tum.

VERBS.

To Be, Root AS.

Sans. Asti, Asi, Asmi, Santi, Stha, Smas.

Gr. Esti, Eîs (Essi), Eimi (D. Emmi), Eisi (D. Enti), Este, Esmen (D. Eimes).

Lat. Est, Es, Sum, Sunt, Estis, Sumus.

To Go, Root I.

Sans. Éti, Ési. Émi, Yanti, Itha, Imas.

Lat. It, Is, Eo, Eunt, Itis, Imus.

Gr. Eîsi, Eîs, Eîmi, Eîsi, Ite, Imen (D. Imes).

To Eat, Root AD.

Sans. Atti, Atsi, Admi, Adanti, Attha, Admas. *Lat.* Edit, Edis, Edo, Edunt, Editis, Edimus. *Gr.* Esthiei. *Sax.* Etan.

To Give, Root DA.

Sans. Dadáti, Dadási, Dadámi. *Lat.* Dat, Das, Do. *Gr.* Didōsi, Didōs, Didōmi.

Hence, *Sans.* Dánam, *Lat.* Donum.

To Join, Root YUJ.

Sans. Yunacti, Yunjanti. *Lat.* Jungit, Jungunt. *Sans.* Yunajmi. *Gr.* Zeugnumi.

Hence, *Sans.* Yugam. *Lat.* Yugum. *Gr.* Zugos, Zugon. *Hind.* Juä. *Sax.* Geoc. *Ang.* Yoke. *Dutch.* Joek.

To Sit, Root SAD.

Sans. Sídati, Sídanti. *Lat.* Sedet, Sedent.

Hence, *Sans.* Sadas. *Lat.* Sedes.

To Subdue, Root DAM.

Sans. Dámayati. *Gr.* Damaei. *Lat.* Domat.

Hence, Damanam. Damnum.

To Drink, Root PA or PĪ

Sans. Pibati, Pibanti; Piyaté. *Lat.* Bibit, Bibunt. *Gr.* Pinei, Pinousi.

To Die, Root MRĬ.

Sans. Mrĭyaté, Mrĭyanté. *Lat.* Moritur, Moriuntur.

Hence, Mrĭtis, Mors, Mrĭtas, Mortuus.

To Know, Root JNYA.

Sans. Jánátí, Jánanti. *Gr.* Ginosco *or* Gignosco. *Lat.* Nosco.

Hence, Jnyátas. *Lat.* Nótus. *Gr.* Gnostos.

To Beget, Root JAN.

Sans. Jáyaté. Pret. Jajnyé (pronounced jagyé). *Gr.* Ginomai *vel* Gignomai. *Lat.* Gigno.

To Go, Root SRĬP.

Sans. Sarpati. *Lat.* Serpit. *Gr.* Herpei.

To See, Root DRĬS.

Gr. Derco. *Sans.* Dŕiś. *Hind.* Dék'h, to see.

To Procreate, Root SU.

Sans. Súyaté (rad. Sú).

Hence, *Sans.* Súta, son. *Hind.* Suän̈. *Gr.* Huios, Huieus.

To Know, Root VID.

Sans. Vid, to know. *Lat.* Video, to see.

To Delight, Root TRĬP.

Sans. Trip. *Gr.* Terpo.

To Strew, Root STRĬ.

Sans. Strĭ. *Lat.* Sterno. *Ang.* To strew. *Gr.* Stornumi, Stronnumi.

ADVERBS, ETC.

Sans. A. *Gr.* A *priv.* (before vowels An).

Sans. Su. *Gr.* Eû.

Sans. Dus. *Gr.* Dys.

Sans. Cha. *Gr.* Te. *Lat.* Que.

Sans. Na, No. *Lat.* Ne, Non. *Ang.* No.

Sans. Chit (in comp.). *Lat.* Quid. *Gr.* Ti.

Sans. Nanu. *Lat.* Nonne.

Sans. Prabháte. *Gr.* Proï.

Sans. Pura, Puratas. *Gr.* Pro, Proteros, etc.

Sans. Punar. *Gr.* Palin.

Sans. Pura. *Gr.* Palai.

Sans. Alam. *Gr.* Halis.

Sans. Hyas. *Gr.* Chthes.

Sans. Adya. *Hind.* Aj. *Lat.* Hodie.

Footnotes to Chapter VII (VIII): Life of Colebrooke

1. *Miscellaneous Essays.* By Henry Thomas Colebrooke. With a Life of the author by his son. In three volumes. London: 1872.

2. The word G e n t o o , which was commonly applied in the last century to the Hindus, is, according to Wilson, derived from the Portuguese word *gentio*, gentile or heathen. The word *caste*, too, comes from the same source.

3. See the list of words given at the end of this article, p. 400.

IX.
MY REPLY TO MR. DARWIN.

During the whole of the year that has just passed away, all my spare time has been required for the completion of my edition of the Rig-Veda and its Sanskrit commentary. I had to shut my eyes to everything else. Many a book which I felt tempted to read was put aside, and hardly a single Review could draw me away from my purpose. Thus it has come to pass that I did not know, till a few days ago, that some Lectures which I had delivered at the Royal Institution on "Mr. Darwin's Philosophy of Language," and which had been fully reported in "Fraser's Magazine" for May, June, and July, 1873, had elicited a reply emanating from one who writes if not in, at least with Mr. Darwin's name, and who himself would be, no doubt most proud to acknowledge the influence of "family bias." I could not have guessed from the title of the paper, "Professor Whitney on the Origin of Language: by George H. Darwin," that it was meant as an answer to the arguments which I had ventured to advance in my Lectures at the Royal Institution against Mr. Darwin's views on language. It was only when telling a friend that I soon hoped to find time to complete those Lectures, that I was asked whether I had seen Darwin's reply. I read it at once in the November number of the "Contemporary Review;" and, as it will take some time before I can hope to finish my book on "Language as the true barrier between Man and Beast," I determined, in the meantime, to publish a brief rejoinder to the defense of Mr. Darwin's philosophy, so ably and chivalrously conducted by his son.

With regard to the proximate cause of Mr. Darwin's defense of his father's views on language—viz. an article in the "Quarterly Review," I may say at once that I knew nothing about it till I saw Mr. G. Darwin's article; and if there should be any suspicion in Mr. Darwin's mind that the writer in the "Quarterly Review" is in any sense of the word my *alter ego* I can completely remove that impression.

It seems that the writer in the "Quarterly" expressed himself in the following terms with regard to Mr. Darwin's competency on linguistic problems:—

"Few recent intellectual phenomena are more astounding than the ignorance of these elementary yet fundamental distinctions and principles (*i.e.*, as to the essence of language) exhibited by conspicuous advocates of the monistic hypothesis. Mr. Darwin, for example, does not exhibit the faintest indication of having grasped them."

Mr. Darwin, I mean the father, if he has read my lectures, or anything else I have written, might easily have known that that is not the tone in which I write, least of all when speaking of men who have rendered such excellent service to the advancement of science as the author of the book "On the Origin of Species." To me, the few pages devoted to language by Mr. Darwin were full of interest, as showing the conclusions to which that school of philosophy which he so worthily represents is driven with regard to the nature and origin of language. If put into more becoming language, however, I do not think there would be anything offensive in stating that Mr. Darwin, Sr., knows the results of the Science of Language at second hand only, and that his opinions on the subject, however interesting as coming from him, cannot be accepted or quoted as authoritative. It has often done infinite mischief when men who have acquired a right to speak with authority on one subject, express opinions on other subjects with which they are but slightly acquainted. These opinions, though never intended for that purpose, are sure to be invested by others, particularly by interested persons, with an authority to which in themselves they have no right whatever. It is true it would be difficult to carry on any scientific work, without to some extent recognizing the authority of those who have established their claim to a certain amount of infallibility within their own special spheres of study. But when either the Pope expresses an opinion on astronomy, or the Duke of Wellington on a work of art, they certainly ought not to be offended if asked for their reasons, like any other mortals. No linguistic student, if he had ventured to express an opinion on the fertilization of orchids, differing from that of Mr. Darwin, would feel aggrieved by being told that his opinion, though showing intelligence, did not show that real grasp of the whole bearing of the problem which can be acquired by a life-long devotion only. If the linguistic student, who may be fond of orchids, cared only for a temporary triumph in the eyes of the world, he might easily find, among the numerous antagonists of Mr. Darwin, one who agreed with himself, and appeal to him as showing that he, though a mere layman in the Science of Botany, was supported in his opinions by other distinguished botanists. But no real advance in the discovery of truth can ever be achieved by such mere cleverness. How can the soundness and truth of Mr. Darwin's philosophy of language be established by an appeal like that with which Mr. Darwin, Jr., opens his defense of his father?

"Professor Whitney," he says, "is the first philologist of note who has professedly taken on himself to combat the views of Professor Max Müller; and as the opinions of the latter most properly command a vast deal of respect in England, we think it will be good service to direct the attention of English readers to this powerful attack, and, as we think, successful refutation of the somewhat dogmatic views of our Oxford linguist."

First of all, nothing would convey a more erroneous impression than to say that Professor Whitney was the first philologist of note who has combated my views. There is as much combat in the linguistic as in the physical camp, though Mr. Darwin may not be aware of it. Beginning with Professor Pott, I could give a long list of most illustrious scholars in Germany, France, Italy, and surely in England also, who have subjected my views on language to a far more searching criticism than Professor Whitney in America. But even if Professor Whitney were the only philologist who differed from me, or agreed with Mr. Darwin, how would that affect the soundness of Mr. Darwin's theories on language? Suppose I were to quote in return the opinion of M. Renouvier, the distinguished author of "Les Principes de la Nature," who, in his journal, "La Critique Philosophique," expresses his conviction that my criticism of Mr. Darwin's philosophy contains not a simple *polémique*, but has the character of a *redressement*; would that dishearten Mr. Darwin? I must confess that I had never before read Professor Whitney's "Lectures on Language," which were published in America in 1867; and I ought to thank Mr. Darwin for having obliged me to do so now, for I have seldom perused a book with greater interest and pleasure,—I might almost say, amusement. It was like walking through old familiar places, like listening to music which one knows one has heard before somewhere, and, for that very reason, enjoys all the more. Not unfrequently I was met by the *ipsissima verba* of my own lectures on the Science of Language, though immediately after they seemed to be changed into an inverted fugue. Often I saw how carefully the same books and pamphlets which I had waded through had been studied: and on almost every page there were the same doubts and difficulties, the same hopes and fears, the same hesitations and misgivings through which I myself well remembered having passed when preparing my two series of "Lectures on Language." Of course, we must not expect in Professor Whitney's Lectures, anything like a systematic or exhaustive treatment. They touch on points which were most likely to interest large audiences at Washington, and other towns in America. They were meant to be popular, and nothing would be more unfair than to blame an author for not giving what he did not mean to give. The only just complaint we have heard made about these Lectures is that they give sometimes too much of what is irreverently called "padding." Professor Whitney had read my own Lectures before writing his; and though he is quite right in saying the principal facts on which his reasonings are founded have been for some time past the commonplaces of Comparative Philology, and required no acknowledgment, he makes an honorable exception in my favor, and acknowledges most readily having borrowed here and there an illustration from my Lectures. As to my own views on the Science of Language, I am glad to find that on all really important points, he far more frequently indorses them—nay, corroborates them by new proofs and illustrations—than attempts to refute them; and even in the latter case he generally does so by simply pronouncing his decided preference for one out of two opinions, while I had been satisfied with stating what could be said on either side. He might here and there have tempered the wind to the shorn lamb, but I believe there is far more license allowed in America, in the expression of dissent, than in England; and it is both interesting and instructive in the study of Dialectic Growth, to see how words which would be considered offensive in England, have ceased to be so on the other side of the Atlantic, and are admitted into the most respectable of American Reviews.

With regard to the question, for instance, on which so much has lately been written, whether we ought to ascribe to language a natural growth or historical change, I see not one single argument produced on either side of the question in Professor Whitney's Second Lecture, beyond those which I had discussed in my Second Lecture. After stating all that could be said in support of extending the name of history to the gradual development of language, I tried to show that, after all, that name would not be quite accurate.

"The process," I said, "through which language is settled and unsettled combines in one the two opposite elements of necessity and free will. Though the individual seems to be the prime agent in producing new words and new grammatical forms, he is so only after his individuality has been merged in the common action of the family, tribe, or nation to which he belongs. He can do nothing by himself, and the first impulse to a new formation in language, though given by an individual, is mostly, if not always, given without premeditation, nay, unconsciously. The individual, as such, is powerless, and the results, apparently produced by him, depend on laws beyond his control, and on the coöperation of all those who form together with him one class, one body, one organic whole." (Page 43.)

After going through the whole argument, I summed up in the end by saying:—

"We cannot be careful enough in the use of our words. Strictly speaking, neither *history* nor *growth* is applicable to the changes of the shifting surface of the earth. *History* applies to the actions of free agents, *growth* to the natural unfolding of organic beings. We speak, however, of the growth of the crust of the earth,1 and we know what we mean by it; and it is in this sense, but not in the sense of growth as applied to a tree, that we have a right to speak of the growth of language."

What do we find in Professor Whitney's Second Lecture? He objects, like myself, to comparing the growth of language and the growth of a tree, and like myself, he admits of an excuse, viz., when the metaphor is employed for the sake of brevity or liveliness of delineation (p. 35). I had said:—

"Ever since Horace, it has been usual to compare the changes of language with the growth of trees. But comparisons are treacherous things; and though we cannot help using metaphorical expressions, we should always be on our guard," etc.

So far we are in perfect harmony. But immediately after, the wind begins to blow. One sentence is torn out from the con, where I had said:—

"That it is not in the power of man (not men) either to produce or to prevent change in language; that we might think as well of changing the laws which control the circulation of our blood, or of adding an inch to our height, as of altering the laws of speech, or inventing new words, *according to our pleasure.*"

In order to guard against every possible apprehension as to what I meant by *according to our pleasure*, I quoted the well-known anecdotes of the Emperor Tiberius and of the Emperor Sigismund, and referred to the attempts of Protagoras, and other purists, as equally futile. Here the Republican indignation of the American writer is roused; I, at least, can find no other motive. He tells me that what I really wanted to say was this:—

"If so high and mighty a personage as an emperor could not do so small a thing as alter the gender and termination of a single word—much less can any one of inferior consideration hope to accomplish such a change." . . .

He then exclaims:—

"The utter futility of deriving such a doctrine from such a pair of incidents, or a thousand like them, is almost too obvious to be worth the trouble of pointing out. . . . High political station does not confer the right to make or unmake language," etc.

Now every reader, even though looking only at these short extracts, will see that the real point of my argument is here entirely missed, though I do not mean to say that it was intentionally missed. The stress was laid by me on the words *according to our pleasure*; and in order to elucidate that point, I first quoted instances taken from those who in other matters have the right of saying *car tel est mon plaisir*, and then from others. I feel a little guilty in not having mentioned the anecdote about *carrosse*; but not being able to verify it, I thought I might leave it to my opponents. However, after having quoted the two Emperors, I quoted a more humble personage, Protagoras, and referred to other attempts at purism in language; but all that is, of course, passed over by my critic, as not answering his purpose.

Sometimes, amidst all the loud assertion of difference of opinion on Professor Whitney's part, not only the substantial, but strange to say, the verbal agreement between his and my own Second Lecture is startling. I had said: "The first impulse to a new formation in language, though given by an individual, is mostly, if not always, given *without premeditation*, nay, *unconsciously.*" My antagonist varies this very slightly and says: "The work of each individual is done *unpremeditately, or, as it were, unconsciously*" (p. 45). While I had said that we individually can no more change language, *selon notre plaisir*, than we can add an inch to our stature, Professor Whitney again adopts a slight alteration and expresses himself as follows: "They (the facts of language) are almost as little the work of man as is the form of his skull" (p. 52). What is the difference between us? What is the difference between changing our stature and changing our skull? Nor does he use the word growth as applied to language, less frequently than myself; nay, sometimes he uses it so entirely without the necessary limitations, that even I should have shrunk from adopting his phraseology. We read—"In this sense language is a growth" (p. 46); "a language, like an organic body, is no mere aggregate of similar particles—it is a complex of related and mutually helpful parts" (p. 46); "language is fitly comparable with an organized body" (p. 50); "compared with them, language is a real growth" (p. 51); etc., etc., etc.

In fact, after all has been said by Professor Whitney that had been said before, the only difference that remains is this—that he, after making all these concessions, prefers to class the Science of Language as an historical, not as a physical science. Why should he not? Everybody who is familiar with such questions, knows that all depends on a clear and accurate definition of the terms which we employ. The method of the Science of Language and the physical sciences is admitted, even by him, to be the same (p. 52). Everything therefore depends on the wider or narrower definition which we adopt of physical science. Enlarge the definition of the natural sciences, and the science of language will enter in freely; narrow it, and it will enter with difficulty, or not at all. The same with the historical sciences. Enlarge their definition, and the science of language will enter in freely; narrow it, and it will enter with difficulty, or not at all. There is hardly a word that is used in so many different meanings as nature, and that man in many of his apparently freest acts is under the sway of unsuspected laws of nature, cannot sound so very novel to a student of Kant's writings, to say nothing of later philosophers.[2] My principal object in claiming for the Science of Language the name of a physical science, was to make it quite clear, once for all, that Comparative Philology was totally distinct from ordinary Philology, that it treats language not as a vehicle of literature, but for its own sake; that it wants to explain the origin and development far more than the idiomatic use of words, and that for all these purposes it must adopt a strictly inductive method. Many of these views which, when I delivered my first lectures, met with very determined opposition, are now generally accepted, and I can well understand, that younger readers should be surprised at the elaborate and minute arguments by which I tried to show in what sense the Science of Language may be counted as one of the physical sciences. Let them but read other books of the same period, and they will see with how much zeal these questions were then being discussed, particularly in England. Writing in

England, and chiefly for English readers, I tried as much as possible to adapt myself to the intellectual atmosphere of that country, and as to the classification of the inductive sciences, I started from that which was then most widely known, that of Whewell in his "History of the Inductive Sciences." He classes the Science of Language as one of the palaitiological sciences, but makes a distinction between palaitiological sciences treating of material things—for instance, geology, and others respecting the products which result from man's imaginative and social endowments—for instance, Comparative Philology. He still excludes the latter from the circle of the physical sciences,3 properly so called, but he adds:—

"We have seen that biology leads us to psychology, if we choose to follow the path; and thus the passage from the material to the immaterial has already unfolded itself at one point; and we now perceive that there are several large provinces of speculation which concern subjects belonging to man's immaterial nature, and which are governed by the same laws as sciences altogether physical. It is not our business to dwell on the prospects which our philosophy thus opens to our contemplation: but we may allow ourselves, in this last stage of our pilgrimage among the foundations of the physical sciences, to be cheered and animated by the ray that thus beams upon us, however dimly, from a higher and brighter region."

Considering the high position which Dr. Whewell held among the conflicting parties of philosophic and religious thought in England, we should hardly have expected that the hope which he expressed of a possible transition from the material to the immaterial, and the place which he tentatively, and I more decidedly, assigned to the Science of Language, could have roused any orthodox animosities. Yet here is the secret spring of Professor Whitney's efforts to claim for the Science of Language, in spite of his own admissions as a scholar, a place among the moral and historical, as distinct from the physical sciences. The theological bias, long kept back, breaks through at last, and we are treated to the following sermon:—

"There is a school of modern philosophers who are trying to materialize all science, to eliminate the distinction between the physical and the intellectual and moral, to declare for nought the free action of the human will, and to resolve the whole story of the fates of mankind into a series of purely material effects, produced by assignable physical causes, and explainable in the past, or determinable in the future, by an intimate knowledge of those causes, by a recognition of the action of compulsory motives upon the passively obedient nature of man. With such, language will naturally pass, along with the rest, for a physical product, and its study for physical science; and, however we may dissent from their general classification, we cannot quarrel with its application in the particular instance. But by those who still hold to the grand distinction," etc., etc., etc.

At the end of this arguing *pro* and *con.*, the matter itself remains exactly where it was before. The Science of Language is a physical science, if we extend the meaning of nature so far as to include human nature, in those manifestations at least where the individual does not act freely, but under reciprocal restraint. The Science of Language is an historical, or, as Professor Whitney prefers to call it, a moral science, if we comprehend under history the acts performed by men "unpremeditately, or, as it were, unconsciously," and therefore beyond the reach of moral considerations.

I may seem to have entered more fully into this question than its real importance requires, but I was anxious, before replying to Mr. Darwin's objections, to show to him the general style of argument that pervades Professor Whitney's writings, and the character of the armory from which he has borrowed his weapons against me. I have not been able to get access to Professor Whitney's last article, and shall therefore confine myself here to those arguments only which Mr. Darwin has adopted as his own, though, even if I had seen the whole of the American article, I should have preferred not to enter into any personal controversy with Professor Whitney. I have expressed my sincere appreciation of the industry and acumen which that scholar displays in his lectures on the Science of Language. There are some portions, particularly those on the Semitic and American languages, where he has left me far behind. There are some illustrations extremely well chosen, and worked out with a touch of poetic genius; there are whole chapters where by keeping more on the surface of his subject, he has succeeded in making it far more attractive and popular than I could have hoped to do. That treatment, however, entails its dangers, unless an author remembers, at every moment, that in addressing a popular audience he is in honor bound to be far more careful than if he writes for his own professional colleagues only. The comparative portion, I mean particularly the Seventh Lecture, is hardly what one would have expected from so experienced a teacher, and it is strange to find (p. 219) the inscription on the Duilian column referred to about B.C. 263, after Ritschl and Mommsen had pointed out its affected archaisms; to see (p. 222) the name Ahura-Mazda rendered by "the mighty spirit;" to meet (p. 258) with "sarvanâman," the Sanskrit name for pronoun, translated by "name for everything, universal designation;" to hear the Phœnician alphabet still spoken of as the *ultimate* source of the world's alphabets, etc. Such mistakes, however, can be corrected, but what can never be corrected is the unfortunate tone which Professor Whitney has adopted throughout. His one object seems to be to show to his countrymen that he is the equal of Bopp, Renan, Schleicher, Steinthal, Bleek, Hang, and others— aye, their superior. In stating their opinions, in criticizing their work, in suggesting motives, he shrinks from nothing, evidently trusting to the old adage, *semper aliquid hæret*. I have often asked myself, why should Professor Whitney have assumed this exceptional position among Comparative

Philologists. It is not American to attack others, simply in order to acquire notoriety. America has possessed, and still possesses, some excellent scholars, whom every one of these German and French *savants* would be proud to acknowledge as his peers. Mr. Marsh's "Lectures on the English Language" are a recognized standard work in England; Professor's March's "Anglo-Saxon Grammar" has been praised by everybody. Why is there no trace of self-assertion or personal abuse in any of their works? It is curious to observe in Professor Whitney's works, that the less he has thought on certain subjects, the louder he speaks, and where arguments fail him, *epitheta ornantia*, such as *worthless, futile, absurd, ridiculous, superficial, unsound, high-flown, pretentious, disingenuous, false*, are poured out in abundance. I believe there is not one of these choice counters with which, at some time or other, he has not presented me; nay, he has even poured the soothing oil of praise over my bruised head. *Quand on se permet tout, on peut faire quelque chose.* But what has been the result? It has actually become a distinction to belong to the noble army of his martyrs, while, whenever one is praised by him, one feels inclined to say with Phocion, οὐ δὴ πού τι κακὸν λέγων ἐμαυτὸν λέληθα.

What such behavior may lead to, we have lately seen in an encounter between the same American *savant* and Professor Steinthal, of Berlin.4 In his earlier writings Professor Whitney spoke of Professor Steinthal as an eminent master in linguistic science, from whose writings he had derived the greatest instruction and enlightenment. Afterwards the friendly relations between the Yale and Berlin professors seem to have changed, and at last Professor Steinthal became so exasperated by the misrepresentations and the overbearing tone of the American linguist, that he, in a moment of irritation, forgot himself so far as to retaliate with the same missiles with which he had been assailed. What the missiles used in such encounters are, may be seen from a few specimens. One could hardly quote them all in an English Review. While dwelling on the system of bold misrepresentation adopted by Professor Whitney, Professor Steinthal calls him—"That vain man who only wants to be named and praised;" "that horrible humbug;" "that scolding flirt;" "that tricky attorney;" "wherever I read him, hollow vacuity yawns in my face; arrogant vanity grins at me." Surely, mere words can go no further—we must expect to hear of tomahawk and bowie-knife next. Scholars who object to the use of such weapons, whether for offensive or defensive purposes, can do nothing but what I have done for years—remain silent, select what is good in Professor Whitney's writings, and try to forget the rest.

Surely, students of language, of all people in the world, ought to know what words are made of, and how easy it is to pour out a whole dictionary of abuse without producing the slightest effect. A page of offensive language weighs nothing—it simply shows the gall of bitterness and the weakness of the cause; whereas real learning, real love of truth, real sympathy with our fellow-laborers, manifest themselves in a very different manner. There were philosophers of old who held that words must have been produced by nature, not by art, because curses produced such terrible effects. Professor Whitney holds that language was produced θέσει, not φύσει, and yet he shares the same superstitious faith in words. He bitterly complains that those whom he reviles, do not revile him again. He wonders that no one answers his strictures, and he is gradually becoming convinced that he is unanswerable. Whatever Mr. Darwin, Jr., may think of Professor Whitney as an ally, I feel certain that Mr. Darwin, Sr., would be the last to approve the spirit of his works, and that a few pages of his controversial writings would make him say: *Non tali auxilio.*

I now proceed to examine some of the extracts which Mr. Darwin, Jr., adopts from Professor Whitney's article, and even in them we shall see at once what I may call the spirit of the advocate, though others might call it by another name.

Instead of examining the facts on which my conclusions were founded, or showing, by one or two cases, at least, that I had made a mistake or offended against the strict rules of logic, there appears the following sweeping exordium, which has done service before in many an opening address of the counsel for the defendant:—

"It is never entirely easy to reduce to a skeleton of logical statement a discussion as carried on by Müller, because he is careless of logical sequence and connection, preferring to pour himself out, as it were, over his subject, in a gush of genial assertion and interesting illustration."

Where is the force of such a sentence? It is a mere pouring out of assertions, though without any interesting illustration, and not exactly genial. All we learn from it is, that Professor Whitney does not find it entirely easy to reduce what I have written to a skeleton of logical sequence, but whether the fault is mine or his, remains surely to be proved. There may be a very strong logical backbone in arguments which make the least display of Aldrich, while in others there is a kind of whited and sepulchral logic which seldom augurs well for what is behind and beneath.

There is a very simple rule of logic, sometimes called the Law of the Excluded Middle, according to which either a given proposition or its contradictory must be true. By selecting passages somewhat freely from different parts of Professor Whitney's lectures, nothing would be easier than to prove, and not simply to assert that he has violated again and again that fundamental principle. In his earlier Lectures we are told, that "to ascribe the differences of language and linguistic growth directly to physical causes, ... is wholly meaningless and futile" (p. 152). When we come to the great variety of the American languages, we are told that "their differentiation has been favored by the influence of the variety of climate and mode of life." On page 40, we read that a great genius "may now and then coin a new word!" On page 123, we are told "it is not true that a genius can impress a marked effect upon language." On page 177, M. Renan and myself are told that we have committed a serious error in admitting dialects as antecedent feeders of national or classical languages, and that it is hardly worth while to spend any effort in refuting such an opinion. On page 181, we read, "a certain degree of dialectic variety is inseparable from the being of any language," etc., etc., etc.

I should not call this a fair way of dealing with any book; I only give these few specimens to show that the task of changing Professor Whitney's Lecture into a logical skeleton would not always be an easy one.

The pleading is now carried on by Mr. G. Darwin:—

"In taking up the cudgels, Müller is *clearly* impelled by an overmastering fear lest man should lose 'his proud position in the creation' if his animal descent is proved."

I should in nowise be ashamed of the fear thus ascribed to me, but whether it was an overmastering fear, let those judge who have read such passages in my Lectures, as the following:—

"The question is not whether the belief that animals so distant as a man, a monkey, an elephant, and a humming bird, a snake, a frog, and a fish, could all have sprung from the same parents is monstrous, but simply and solely whether it is true. If it is true, we shall soon learn to digest it. Appeals to the pride or humility of man, to scientific courage, or religious piety, are all equally out of place."

If this and other passages in my Lectures are inspired by overmastering fear, then surely Talleyrand was right in saying that language was intended to disguise our thoughts. And may I not add, that if such charges can be made with impunity, we shall soon have to say, with a still more notorious diplomatist, "What is truth?" Such reckless charges may look heroic, but what applied to the famous charge of Balaclava, applies to them: *C'est magnifique, sans doute, mais ce n'est pas la guerre.*

I am next charged, I do not know whether by the senior or the junior counsel, with maintaining the extraordinary position that if an insensible graduation could be established between ape and man, their minds would be *identical.*

Here all depends on what is meant by *mind* and by *identical.* Does Mr. Darwin mean by "mind" something substantial—an agent that deals with the impressions received through the senses, as a builder deals with his bricks?

Then, according to his father's view, the one builder may build a mere hovel, the other may erect a cathedral, but through their descent they are substantially the same. Or does he mean by "mind," the mode and manner in which sensations are received and arranged, what one might call, in fact, the law of sensuous gravitation? Then I say again, according to his father's view, that law is substantially the same for animal and man. Nor is this a conclusion derived from Mr. Darwin's premises against his will. It is the opinion strongly advocated by him. He has collected the most interesting observations on the incipient germs, not only of language, but of æsthetics and ethics, among animals. If Mr. Darwin, Jr., holds that the mind of man is not substantially identical with the animal mind, if he admits a break somewhere in the ascending scale from the Protogenes to the first Man, then we should be driven to the old conclusion—viz., that man was formed of the dust of the ground, but that God breathed into his nostrils the breath of life, and man became a living soul. Does Mr. Darwin, Jr., accept this?

Next it is said, that by a similar argument the distinction between black and white, hot and cold, a high and a low note might be eliminated. This sounds no doubt formidable—it almost looks like a logical skeleton. But let us not be frightened by words. Black and white are no doubt as different as possible, so are hot and cold, a high and a low note. But what is the difference between a high and a low note? It is simply the smaller or larger number of vibrations in a given time. We can count these vibrations, and we also know that, from time to time, as the velocity of the vibrations increases, our dull senses can distinguish new tones. We have therefore here to deal with differences that used to be called differences of degree, as opposed to differences in kind. What applies to a low and a high note, applies to a low and high degree of heat, and to the various degrees of light which we call by the names of colors. In all these cases, what philosophers call the substance, remains the same, just as, according to evolutionists, the substance of man and animal is the same. Therefore, if man differs from an animal no more than a high note differs from a low, or, *vice versâ*, if a high note differs no more from a low than man differs from an ape, my argument would seem to stand in spite of the shower of words poured over it.

I myself referred to the difference between a high and a low note for a totally different purpose, viz., in order to call attention to those strange lines and limits in nature which, in spite of insensible graduation, enable us to distinguish broad degrees of sound which we call keys; broad degrees of light, which we call colors; broad degrees of heat, for which our language has a less perfect nomenclature. These lines and limits have never been explained, nor the higher limits which separate sound from light, and light from heat. Why we should derive pleasure from the exact number of vibrations which yield C, and then have painful sensations till we come to the exact number of vibrations which yield C sharp, remains as yet a mystery. But as showing that nature had drawn these sharp lines across the continuous stream of vibrations, whether of sound or light, seemed to me an important problem, particularly for evolutionist philosophers, who see in nature nothing but "insensible graduation."

The next charge brought against me is, that I overlook the undoubted and undisputed fact that species do actually vary in nature. This seems to me begging the whole question. If terms like *species* are fetched from the lumber-room of scholastic philosophy, they must be defined with logical exactness, particularly at present, when the very existence of such a thing as a *species* depends on the meaning which we assign to it. Nature gives us individuals only, and each individual differs from the other. But "species" is a thing of *human workmanship*,5 and it depends entirely on the disputed definition of the term, whether species vary or not. In one sense, Mr. Darwin's book, "On the Origin of Species," may be called an attempt to repeal the term "species," or, at all events, an attempt at giving a new definition to that word which it never had before. No one appreciates more than I do the service he has rendered in calling forth a new examination of that old and somewhat rusty instrument of thought.6 Only, do not let us take for granted what has to be proved.

The dust of words grows thicker and thicker as we go on, for I am next told that the same line of proof would show "that the stature of a man or boy was identical, because the boy passes through every gradation on attaining the one stature from the other. No one could maintain such a position who grasped the doctrines of continuity and of the differential calculus." It seems to me that even without the help of the differential calculus, we can, with the help of logic and grammar, put a stop to this argument. Boy is the subject, stature looks like a subject, but is merely a predicate, and should have been treated as such by Mr. Darwin. If a boy arrives by insensible graduation or growth at the stature of man, the man is substantially the same as the boy. His stature may be different, the color of his hair may be so likewise; but what philosophers used to call the substance, or the individuality, or the personality, or what we may call the man, remains the same. If evolutionists really maintain that the difference between man and beast is the same as between a grown-up man and a boy, the whole of my argument is granted, and granted with a completeness which I had no right to expect. Will Mr. Darwin, Senior, indorse the concessions thus made by Mr. Darwin, Junior?

In order to show how the simplest matters can be complicated by a free use of scholastic terms, I quote the following sentence, which is meant as an answer to my argument:—

"According to what is called the Darwinian theory, organisms are in fact precisely the result of a multiple integration of a complex function of a very great number of variables; many of such variables being bound together by relationships amongst themselves, an example of one such relationship being afforded by the law, which has been called 'correlation of growth.'"

Next follows a rocket from Mr. Whitney's armory:—

"As a linguist," he says, "Professor Müller claims to have found in language an endowment which has no analogies, and no preparations in even the beings nearest to man, and of which, therefore, no process of transmutation could furnish an explanation. Here is the pivot on which his whole argument rests and revolves."

So far, the statement is correct, only that I expressed myself a little more cautiously. It is well known, that the animals which in other respects come nearest to man, possess very imperfect phonetic organs, and that it would be improper, therefore, to refer more particularly to them. But, however that may be, I expected at all events some proof that I had made a mistake, that my argument jars, or my pivot gives. But nothing of the kind. No facts, no arguments, but simply an assertion that I do not argue the case with moderation and acuteness, on strict scientific grounds, and by scientific methods in setting up language as the specific difference between man and animals. And why? Because many other writers have adduced other differences as *the* correct ones.

There is a good deal of purely explosive matter in these vague charges of want of moderation and acuteness. But what is the kernel? I represented language as the specific difference between man and animals, without mentioning other differences which others believe to be specific. It would seem to show moderation rather than the absence of it, if I confined myself to language, to the study of which I have devoted the whole of my life; and perhaps a certain acuteness, in not touching on questions which I do not pretend to have studied, as they ought to be. But there were other reasons, too, which made me look upon language as *the* specific difference. The so-called specific differences mentioned by others fall into two classes—those that are implied by language, as I defined the word, and those which have been proved untenable by Mr. Darwin and others. Let us read on now, to see what these specific differences are:—

"Man alone is capable of progressive improvement."	Partly denied by Mr. Darwin, partly shown to be the result of language, through which each successive generation profits by the experience of its predecessors.

"He alone makes use of tools or fire."	The former disproved by Mr. Darwin, the latter true.
"He alone domesticates other animals."	Denied, in the case of the ants.
"He alone possesses property."	Disproved by every dog in-the-manger.
"He alone employs language."	True.
"No other animal is self-conscious."	Either right or wrong, according to the definition of the word, and never capable of direct proof.
"He alone comprehends himself."	True, implied by language.
"He alone has the power of abstraction."	True, implied by language.
"He alone possesses general ideas."	True, implied by language.
"He alone has sense of beauty."	Disproved or rendered doubtful by sexual selection.
"He alone is liable to caprice."	Disproved by every horse, or monkey, or mule.
"He alone has the feeling of gratitude."	Disproved by every dog.
"He alone has the feeling of mystery."	*Cela me passe.*
"He alone believes in God."	True.

| "He alone is endowed with a conscience." | Denied by Mr. Darwin. |

Did it show then such want of moderation or acuteness if I confined myself to language, and what is implied by language, as the specific difference between man and beast? Really, one sometimes yearns for an adversary who can hit straight, instead of these random strokes page after page.

The next attack is so feeble that I should gladly pass it by, did I not know from past experience that the very opposite motive would be assigned to my doing so. I had stated that if there is a *terra incognita* which excludes all positive knowledge, it is the mind of animals. How, then, I am asked, do you know that no animal possesses the faintest germs of the faculty of abstracting and generalizing, and that animals receive their knowledge through the senses only? I still recollect the time when any philosopher who, even by way of illustration, ventured to appeal to the mind of animals, was simply tabooed, and I thought every student of the history of philosophy would have understood what I meant by saying that the whole subject was transcendent. However, here is my answer: I hold that animals receive their knowledge through the senses, because I can apply a crucial test, and show that if I shut their eyes, they cannot see. And I hold that they are without the faculty of abstracting and generalizing, because I have here nothing before me but mere assertions, I know of no crucial test to prove that these assertions are true. Those who have read my Lectures, and were able to reduce them to a skeleton of logical statement, might have seen that I had adduced another reason, viz., the fact that general conceptions are impossible without language (using language in the widest sense, so as to include hieroglyphic, numerical, and other signs), and that as no one has yet discovered any outward traces of language among animals, we are justified in not ascribing to them, as yet, the possession of abstract ideas. This seems to me to explain fully "why the same person (viz., my poor self) should be involved in such profound ignorance, and yet have so complete a knowledge of the limits of the animal mind." If I had said that man has five senses, and no more, would that be wrong? Yet having myself only five senses, I could not possibly prove that other men may not have a sixth sense, or at all events a disposition to develop it. But I am quite willing to carry my agnosticism, with regard to the inner life of animals, still further, and to say again what I wrote in my Lectures (p. 46):—

"I say again and again, that according to the strict rules of positive philosophy, we have no right either to assert or to deny anything with reference to the so-called mind of animals."

But there is another piece of Chinese artillery brought out by Mr. G. Darwin. As if not trusting it himself, he calls on Mr. Whitney to fire it off—"The minds of our fellow men, too," we are told, "are a *terra incognita* in exactly the same sense as are those of animals."

No student of psychology would deny that each individual has immediate knowledge of his own mind only, but even Mr. G. Darwin reminds Mr. Whitney that, after all, with man we have one additional source of evidence— viz., language; nay, he even doubts whether there may not be others, too. If Mr. Darwin, Jr., grants that, I willingly grant him that the horse's impression of green—nay, my friend's impression of green—may be totally different from my own, to say nothing of Daltonism, color-blindness, and all the rest.7

After this, I need hardly dwell on the old attempts at proving, by a number of anecdotes, that animals possess conceptual knowledge. The anecdotes are always amusing, and are sure to meet with a grateful public, but for our purpose they have long been ruled out of court. If Mr. Darwin, Jr., should ever pass through Oxford, I promise to show him in my own dog, Waldmann, far more startling instances of sagacity than any he has mentioned, though I am afraid he will be confirmed all the more in his anthropomorphic interpretation of canine intelligence.

Now comes a new appeal *ad populum*. I had ventured to say that in our days nothing was more strongly to be recommended to young and old philosophers than a study of the history of philosophy. There is a continuity, not only in Nature, but also in the progress of the human mind; and to ignore that continuity, to begin always like Thales or Democritus, is like having a special creation every day. Evolutionists seem to imagine that there is evolution for everything, except for evolutionism. What would chemists say, if every young student began again with the theory of a phlogiston, or every geologist with Vulcanism, or every astronomer with the Ptolemæic system? However, I did not go back very far; I only claimed a little consideration for the work done by such giants as Locke, Hume, Berkeley, and Kant. I expressed a hope that certain questions might be considered as closed, or, if they were to be re-opened, that at least the controversy should be taken up where it was left at the end of the last debate. Here, however, I failed to make any impression. My appeal is stigmatized as "an attempt to crush my adversaries by a reference to Kant, Hume, Berkeley, and Locke." And the popular tribune finishes with the following brave words: "Fortunately we live in an age, which (except for temporary relapses) does not pay any great attention to the pious founders, and which tries to judge for itself."

I never try to crush my adversaries by deputy. Kant, Hume, Berkeley, and Locke may all be antiquated for all I know; but I still hold it would be useful to read them, before we declare too emphatically that we have left them behind.

I cannot deny myself the satisfaction of quoting on this point the wise and weighty words of Huxley:—

"It is much easier to ask such questions than to answer them, especially if one desires to be on good terms with one's contemporaries: but, if I must give an answer, it is this: The growth of physical science is now so prodigiously rapid, that those who are actively engaged in keeping up with the present, have much ado to find time to look at the past, and even grow into the habit of neglecting it. But, natural as this result may be, it is none the less detrimental. The intellect loses, for there is assuredly no more effectual method of clearing up one's own mind on any subject than by talking it over, so to speak, with men of real power and grasp who have considered it from a totally different point of view. The parallax of time helps us to the true position of a conception, as the parallax of space helps us to that of a star. And the moral nature loses no less. It is well to turn aside from the fretful stir of the present, and to dwell with gratitude and respect upon the services of those mighty men of old who have gone down to the grave with their weapons of war, but who, while they yet lived, won splendid victories over ignorance."

Next follow some extraordinary efforts on Mr. Whitney's part to show that Locke, whose arguments I had simply re-stated, knew very little about human or animal understanding, and then the threadbare argument of the deaf and dumb is brushed up once more. Until something new is said on that old subject, I must be allowed to remain myself deaf and dumb.8

Then comes the final and decisive charge. I had said that "if the science of language has proved anything, it has proved that conceptual or discursive thought can be carried on in words only." Here again I had quoted a strong array of authorities—not, indeed, to kill free inquiry—I am not so bloodthirsty, as my friends imagine—but to direct it to those channels where it had been carried on before. I quoted Locke, I quoted Schelling, Hegel, Wilhelm von Humboldt, Schopenhauer, and Mansel—philosophers diametrically opposed to each other on many points, yet all agreeing in what seems to many so strange a doctrine, that conceptual thought is impossible without language (comprehending by language hieroglyphic, numerical, and similar symbols). I might have quoted many other thinkers and poets. Professor Huxley seems clearly to have seen the difference between trains of thought and trains of feelings. "Brutes," he says, "though, from the absence of language, they can have no trains of thoughts, but only trains of feelings, yet have a consciousness which, more or less distinctly, foreshadows our own." And who could express the right view of language more beautifully than Jean Paul?—

"Mich dünkt, der Mensch würde sich, so wie das spracblose Thier, das in der äussern Welt, wie in einem dunkeln, betäubenden Wellen-Meere schwimmt, ebenfalls in dem vollgestirnten Himmel der äussern Anschauung dumpf verlieren, wenn er das verworrene Leuchten nicht durch Sprache in Sternbilder abtheilte, und sich durch diese das Ganze in Theile für das Bewusstein auflösete."

Having discussed that question very fully in my Lectures, I shall attempt no more at present than to show that the objections raised by Mr. Darwin, Jr., entirely miss the point. Does he really think that those men could have spent all their lives in considering that question, and never have been struck by the palpable objections raised by him? Let us treat such neighbors, at least like ourselves. I shall, however, do my best to show Mr. Darwin that even I had not been ignorant of these objections. I shall follow him through every point, and, for fear of misrepresenting him, quote his own words:—

"(1) Concepts may be formed, and yet not put before the consciousness of the conceiver, so that he 'realizes' what he is doing."

Does that mean that the conceiver conceives concepts without conceiving them? Then, I ask, whom do these concepts belong to, where are they, and under what conditions were they realized? Is to conceive an active or a passive verb? May I once more quote Kant without incurring the suspicion of wishing to strangle free inquiry by authority? "Concepts," says the old veteran, "are founded on the spontaneity of thought, sensuous intuitions on the receptivity of impressions."

"(2) Complex thoughts are doubtless impossible without symbols, just as are the higher mathematics?"

Are lower mathematics possible without numerical symbols, and where is the line which separates complex from simple thought? Everything would seem to depend on that line which is so often spoken of by our critics. There ought to be something in that line which would at once remove the blunders committed by Humboldt and others. It would define the limit between inarticulate and articulate thought; it might possibly be the very frontier between the animal and the human mind, and yet that magic line is simply conceived, spoken of freely, but never realized, i.e., never traced with logical precision. Till that is done, that line, though it may exist, is to me as if it did not exist.

"(3) We know that dogs doubt and hesitate, and finally determine to act without any external determining circumstance."

How this argument fits in here, is not quite clear to me; but, whatever its drift may be, a perusal of Professor Huxley's excellent paper, "The Hypothesis that Animals are Automata," will supply a full answer.

"(4) Professor Whitney very happily illustrates the independence of thought from language, by calling up our state of mind when casting about, often in the most open manner, for new designations, for new forms of knowledge, or when drawing distinctions, and pointing conclusions, which words are then stretched or narrowed to cover."

Language with us has become so completely traditional, that we frequently learn words first and their meaning afterwards. The problem of the original relation between concepts and words, however, refers to periods when these words did not yet exist, but had to be framed for the first time. We are speaking of totally different things; he, of the geology, I, if I may say so, of the chemistry of speech. But even if we accepted the test from modern languages, does not the very form of the question supply the answer? If we want *new* designations, *new* forms of knowledge, do we not confess that we have old designations, though imperfect ones; old forms of knowledge which no longer answer our purpose? Our old words, then, become gradually stretched or narrowed, exactly as our knowledge becomes stretched or narrowed, or we at last throw away the old word, and borrow another from our own, or even from a foreign language.

"It is a proof," Mr. Darwin says, "that we realized and conceived the idea of the ure and nature of a musical sound before we had a word for it, that we had to borrow the expressive word *"timbre"* from the French."

But how did we realize and conceive the idea before we had a word for it? Surely, by old words. We called it quality, ure, nature—we knew it as the result of the presence and absence of various harmonics. In German, we stretched an old word, and called it *Farbe*; in English, *timbre* was borrowed from the French, just as we may call a pound *vingt-cinq francs*; but the French themselves got their word by the ordinary process—viz., by stretching the old word, *tympanum*.

"(5) If Müller had brought before him some wholly new animal he would find that he could shut his eyes, and call up the image of it readily enough without any accompanying name."

All this is far, far away from the real field of battle. No doubt, if I look at the sun and shut my eyes, the image remains for a time. By imagination I can also recall other sensuous impressions, and, in an attack of fever, I have had sensuous impressions resuscitated without my will. But how does that touch conceptual knowledge? As soon as I want to know what animal it is which I conjure up or imagine to myself, I must either have, for shortness' sake, its scientific name, or I must conceive and realize its ears, or its legs, or its tail, or something else, but always something for which there is a name.

I have thus, in spite of the old warning, *Ne Hercules contra duos*, gone through the whole string of charges brought against me by Mr. Darwin and Professor Whitney; and while trying to show them that I was not entirely unprepared for their combined attack, I hope I have not been wanting in that respect which is due even to a somewhat rancorous assailant. I have not returned evil for evil, nor have I noticed objections which I could not refute without seeming to be offensive. Is it not mere skirmishing with blank cartridge, when Professor Whitney assures me that I have never fathomed "the theory of the antecedency of the idea to the word in the minds of those who hold that theory?" Surely, that is the theory which everybody holds who forms his idea of the origin of language from the manner in which we acquire a traditional language ready made, or, later in life, learn foreign languages. It has been my object to show that our problem is not, how languages are learnt, but how language is developed. We might as well form our ideas of the origin of the alphabet from the manner in which we learn to write, and then smile when we are told that, in writing "F" we still draw in the two upper strokes, the two horns of the *cerastes*, and that the connecting line in the "H" is the last remnant of the lines dividing the sieve, both hieroglyphics occurring in the name of Chufu or Cheops.

Philosophy is a study as much as philology, and though common sense is, no doubt, very valuable within its proper limits, I do not hesitate to say, though I hear already the distant grumbling of *Jupiter tonans*, that it is generally the very opposite of philosophy. One of the most eminent and most learned of living German philosophers—Professor Carriere, of Munchen—says in a very friendly review of Professor Whitney's "Lectures on Language"—

"Philosophical depth and precision in psychological analysis are not his strong points, and in that respect the reader will hardly find anything new in his Lectures."

He goes on to say that—

"The American scholar did not see that language is meant first for forming, afterwards for communicating thought." "Wordmaking," he says with great truth, "is the first philosophy—the first poetry of mankind. We can have sensations, desires, intentions, but we cannot think, in the proper sense of the word, without language. Every word expresses the general. Mr. Whitney has not understood this, and his calling language a human institution is very shallow."

Against Professor Whitney's view that language is arbitrary and conventional, and against the opposite view that language is instinctive, Professor Carriere quotes the happy expression of M. Renan, "*La liaison du sens et du mot n'est jamais nécessaire, jamais arbitraire, toujours elle est motivée.*" Here the nail is hit on the head. Professor Carriero highly commends Professor Whitney's lectures, and he does by no means adopt all my own views; but he felt obliged to enter a protest against certain journalistic proceedings which in Germany have attracted general attention.

In conclusion, if I may judge from Professor Whitney's lectures, unless he has changed very much of late, I doubt whether he would prove a real ally of Mr. Darwin in his views on the origin of language. Towards the end of his article, even Mr. Darwin, Jr., becomes suspicious. Professor Whitney, he says, makes a dangerous assertion when he says that we shall never know anything of the transitional forms through which language has passed, and he advises his friend to read a book lately published by Count G. A. de Goddesand Liancourt and F. Pincott, called "Primitive and Universal Laws of Language," in which he would find much information and enlightenment on the real origin of roots. There is an unintentional irony in that advice which Professor Whitney will not fail to appreciate. How any one who cares for truth can speak of a dangerous assertion, I do not understand. The Pope may say so, or a barrister; a true friend of truth knows of no danger.

In his "Lectures on Language," Professor Whitney protests strongly against Darwinian materialism. But, as he confesses himself half a convert to the *Bow-wow* and *Pooh-pooh* theories, thus showing how wrong I was in supposing that those theories had no advocates among comparative philologists in the nineteenth century; nay, as now, after he has discovered at last that I am no believer in *Ding-dongism*, he seems inclined to say a kind word for the advocates of that theory—Heyse and Steinthal—who knows whether, after my Lectures on Darwin's "Philosophy of Language," he may not be converted by Bleek and Haeckel, the mad Darwinian, as he calls him?

All this, no doubt, has its humorous side, and I have tried to answer it good-humoredly. But it seems to me that it also has a very serious import. Why is there all this wrangling as to whether man is the descendant of a lower animal or not? Why cannot people examine the question in a temper more consonant with a real love of truth? Why look for artificial barriers between man and beast, if they are not there? Why try to remove real barriers, if they are there? Surely we shall remain what we are, whatever befall. When we throw the question back into a very distant antiquity, all seems to grow confused and out of focus. Yet time and space make little difference in the solution of these problems. Let us see what exists to-day. We see to-day that the lowest of savages—men whose language is said to be no better than the clucking of hens, or the twittering of birds, and who have been declared in many respects lower even than animals, possess this one specific characteristic, that if you take one of their babies, and bring it up in England, it will learn to speak as well as any English baby, while no amount of education will elicit any attempts at language from the highest animals, whether bipeds or quadrupeds. That disposition cannot have, been formed by definite nervous structures, congenitally framed, for we are told by the best Agriologists that both father and mother clucked like hens. This fact, therefore, unless disproved by experiment, remains, whatever the explanation may be.

Let us suppose, then, that myriads of years ago there was, out of myriads of animal beings, one, and one only, which made that step which in the end led to language, while the whole rest of the creation remained behind;—what would follow? That one being then, like the savage baby now, must have possessed something of his own—a germ very imperfect, it may be, yet found nowhere else, and that germ, that capacity, that disposition—call it what you like—is, and always will remain the specific difference of himself and all his descendants. It makes no difference whether we say it came of itself, or it was due to environment, or it was the gift of a Being in whom we live and move. All these are but different expressions for the Unknown. If that germ of the Logos had to pass through thousands of forms, from the Protogenes to Adam, before it was fit to fulfill its purpose, what is that to us? It was there *potentiâ* from the beginning; it manifested itself where it was, in the paulo-post-future man; it never manifested itself where it was not, in any of the creatures that were animals from the beginning, and remained so to the end.

Surely, even if all scholastic philosophy must now be swept away, if to be able to reduce all the wisdom of the past to a *tabula rasa* is henceforth to be the test of a true philosopher, a few landmarks may still be allowed to remain, and we may venture to quote, for instance, *Ex nihilo nihil fit*, without being accused of trying to crush free inquiry by an appeal to authority. Language is something, it pre-supposes something; and that which it pre-supposes, that from which it sprang, whatever its pre-historic, pre-mundane, pre-cosmic state may have been, must have been different from that from which it did not spring. People ask whether that germ of language was "slowly evolved," or "divinely implanted," but if they would but lay a firm grip on their words and thoughts, they would see that these two expressions, which have been made the watchwords of two hostile camps, differ from each other dialectically only.

That there is in us an animal—aye, a bestial nature—has never been denied; to deny it would take away the very foundation of Psychology and Ethics. We cannot be reminded too often that all the materials of our knowledge we share with animals; that, like them, we begin with sensuous impressions, and then, like ourselves, and like ourselves only, proceed to the General, the Ideal, the Eternal. We cannot be reminded too often that in many things we are like the beasts of the field, but that, like ourselves, and like ourselves only, we can rise superior to our bestial self, and strive after what is Unselfish, Good, and God-like. The wing by which we soar above the Sensuous, was called by wise men of old the *Logos*; the wing which lifts us above the Sensual, was called by good men of old the *Daimonion*. Let us take continual care, especially within the precincts of the Temple of Science, lest by abusing the gift of speech or doing violence to the voice of conscience, we soil the two wings of our soul, and fall back, through our own fault, to the dreaded level of the Gorilla.

Footnotes to Chapter VIII (IX):
Reply to Mr. Darwin

1. "The vast number of grammatical forms has had a stratified origin. As on the surface of the earth older and younger layers of stones are found one above the other, or one by the side of the other, We had similar appearances in language at any time of its existence." Curtius, *Zur Chronologie*, p. 14.

2. See *Academy*, 19 June, 1875.

3. As it has been objected that I had no right to claim Dr. Whewell's authority in support of my classification, I may here add a passage from a letter (Nov. 4, 1861) addressed to me by Dr. Whewell, in which he fully approves of my treating the Science of Language as one of the physical sciences. "You have more than once done me the honor, in your lectures, of referring to what I have written but it seems to me possible that you may not have remarked how completely I agree with you in classing the Science of Language among the physical sciences, as to its history and structure."

4. *Antikritik, Wie einer den Nagel auf den Kopf trifft*: Berl. 1874.

5. Cf. Sachs' *Botany*, p. 830.

6. See *Lectures on the Science of Language*, vol. ii.

7. Fiske, *Outlines of Cosmic Philosophy*, vol. i. p. 17.

8. See Kilian, *Uber die Racenfrage der Semitischen und Arischen Sprachbände*, 1874.

X.
IN SELF-DEFENSE.

PRESENT STATE OF SCIENTIFIC STUDIES.

It has been remarked by many observers that in all branches of physical as well as historical learning there is at the present moment a strongly pronounced tendency towards special researches. No one can hold his own among his fellow-workers who cannot point to some discovery, however small, to some observation, to some decipherings, to some edition of a hitherto unpublished, or, at least, to some conjectural readings which are, in the true sense of the word, his property. A man must now have served from the ranks before he is admitted to act as a general, and not even Darwin or Mommsen would have commanded general attention for their theories on the ancient history of Rome, or on the primitive development of animal life, unless they had been known for years as sturdy workers in their respective quarries.

On the whole, I believe that this state of public opinion has produced a salutary effect, but it has also its dangers. An army that means conquest, cannot always depend on its scouts and pioneers, nor must it be broken up altogether into single detachments of tirailleurs. From time to time, it has to make a combined movement in advance, and for that purpose it wants commanders who know the general outlines of the battle-field, and are familiar with the work that can best be done by each branch of the service.

EVOLUTIONISM.

If we look upon scholars, historians, students of physical science, and abstract philosophers, as so many branches of the great army of knowledge which has been fighting its way for centuries for the conquest of truth, it might be said, if we may follow up our comparison a little further, that the light cavalry of physical science had lately made a quick movement in advance, and detached itself too much from the support of the infantry and heavy artillery. The charge was made against the old impregnable fortress, the Origin of Life, and to judge from the victorious hurrahs of the assaulting squadron, we might have thought that a breach had at last been effected, and that the keys to the long hidden secrets of creation and development had been surrendered. As the general commanding this attack, we all recognize Mr. Darwin, supported by a brilliant staff of dashing officers, and if ever general was well chosen for victory, it was the author of the "Origin of Species."

There was indeed for a time a sanguine hope, shared by many a brave soldier, that the old warfare of the world would, in our time, be crowned with success, that we should know at last what we are, whence we came, and whither we go; that, beginning with the simplest elementary substances, we should be able to follow the process of combination and division, leading by numberless and imperceptible changes from the lowest Bathybios to the highest Hypsibios, and that we should succeed in establishing by incontrovertible facts what old sages had but guessed, viz., that there is nowhere anything hard and specific in nature, but all is flowing and growing, without an efficient cause or a determining purpose, under the sway of circumstances only, or of a self-created environment. Πάντα ῥεῖ.

But that hope is no longer so loudly and confidently expressed as it was some years ago. For a time all seemed clear and simple. We began with Protoplasm, which anybody might see at the bottom of the sea, developing into Moneres, and we ended with the bimanous mammal called *Homo*, whether *sapiens* or *insipiens*, everything between the two being matter of imperceptible development.

DIFFICULTIES IN EVOLUTIONISM.

The difficulties began where they generally begin, at the beginning and at the end. *Protoplasm* was a name that produced at first a soothing effect on the inquisitive mind, but when it was asked, whence that power of development, possessed by the Protoplasm which begins as a Moneres and ends as Homo, but entirely absent in other Protoplasm, which resists all mechanical manipulation, and never enters upon organic growth, it was seen that the problem of development had not been solved, but only shifted, and that, instead of simple Protoplasm, very peculiar kinds of Protoplasm were required, which under circumstances might become and remain a Moneres, and under circumstances might become and remain *Homo* forever. That which determined Protoplasm to enter upon its marvelous career, the first κινοῦν ἀκινητόν, remained as unknown as ever. It was open to call it an internal and unconscious, or an external and conscious power, or both together: physical, metaphysical, and religious mythology were left as free as ever. The best proof of this we find in the fact that Mr. Darwin himself retained his belief in a personal Creator, while Haeckel denies all necessity of admitting a conscious agent; and Von Hartmann[1] sees in what is called the philosophy of evolutionism the strongest confirmation of idealism, "all development being in truth but the realization of the unconscious reason of the creative idea."

GLOTTOLOGY AND EVOLUTIONISM.

While the difficulty at the beginning consists in this that, after all, nothing can be developed except what was enveloped, the difficulty at the end is this that something is supposed to be developed that was not enveloped. It was here where I thought it became my duty to draw Mr. Darwin's attention to difficulties which he had not suspected at all, or which, at all events, he had allowed himself to under-value. Mr. Darwin had tried to prove that there was nothing to prevent us from admitting a possible transition from the brute to man, as far as their physical structure was concerned, and it was natural that he should wish to believe that the same applied to their mental capacities. Now, whatever difference of opinion there might be among philosophers as to the classification and naming of these capacities, and as to any rudimentary traces of them to be discovered in animals, there had always been a universal consent that language was a distinguishing characteristic of man. Without inquiring what was implied by language, so much was certain, that language was something tangible, present in every man, absent in every brute. Nothing, therefore, was more natural than that Mr. Darwin should wish to show that this was an error: that language was nothing specific in man, but had its antecedents, however imperfect, in the signs of communication among animals. Influenced, no doubt, by the works of some of his friends and relatives on the origin of language, he thought that it had been proved that our words could be derived *directly* from imitative and interjectional sounds. If the Science of Language has proved anything, it has proved that this is not the case. We know that, with certain exceptions, about which there can be little controversy, all our words are derived from roots, and that every one of these roots is the expression of a general concept. "Without roots, no language; without concepts, no roots," these are the two pillars on which our philosophy of language stands, and with which it falls.

MR. WEDGWOOD'S DICTIONARY.

Any word taken from Mr. Wedgwood's Dictionary will show the difference between those who derive words *directly* from imitative and interjectional sounds, and those who do not. For instance, s.v. *to plunge*, we read:—

"Fr. *plonger* Du. *plotsen, plonssen, plonzen,* to fall into the water—Kil.; *plotsen,* also to fall suddenly on the ground. The origin, like that of *plump,* is a representation of the noise made by the fall. Swiss *bluntschen,* the sound of a thick heavy body falling into the water." Under *plump* we read, "that the radical image is the sound made by a compact body falling into the water, or of a mass of wet falling to the ground. *He smit den sten in't water, plump! seg dat,* 'He threw the stone into the water; it cried plump!' *Plumpen,* to make the noise represented by plump, to fall with such a noise, etc., etc., etc."

All this sounds extremely plausible, and to a man not specially conversant with linguistic studies, far more plausible than the real etymology of the word. To plunge is, no doubt, as Mr. Wedgwood says, the French *plonger* but the French *plonger* is *plumbicare,* while in Italian *piombare* is *cadere a piombo,* to fall straight like the plummet. To plunge, therefore, has nothing to do with the splashing sound of heavy bodies falling into the water, but with the concept of straightness, here symbolized by the plummet.

This case, however, would only show the disregard of historical facts with which the onomatopœic school has been so frequently and so justly charged. But as we cannot trace *plumbum*, or μόλυβος, or Old Slav. *olovo* with any certainty to a root such as *mal*, to be soft, let us take another word, such as *feather*. Here, again, we find that Mr. Wedgwood connects it with such words as Bav. *fledern*, Du. *vlederen*, to flap, flutter, the loss of the *l* being explained by such words as to splutter and to sputter. We have first to note the disregard of historical facts, for *feather* is O.H.G. *fedara*, Sk. pat-tra, Gr. πτερόν for πετερον, all derived from a root *pat*, to fly, from which we have also *penna*, old *pesna*, πέτ-ομαι, *peto*, *impetus*, etc. The root *pat* expresses violent motion, and it is specialized into upward motion, πέτομαι, I fly; downward motion, Sk. p a t a t i, he falls; and onward motion, as in Latin *peto*, *impetus*, etc. Feather, therefore, as derived from this root, was conceived as the instrument of flying, and was never intended to imitate the noise of Du. *vlederen*, to flutter, and to flap.

MY LECTURES ON MR. DARWIN'S PHILOSOPHY OF LANGUAGE.

As this want of historical treatment among onomatopœic philologists has frequently been dwelt on by myself and others, these instances may suffice to mark the difference between the school so ably and powerfully represented by Mr. Wedgwood, and the school of Bopp, to which I and most comparative philologists belong. It was in the name of that school that I ventured to address my protest to the school of evolutionists, reminding them of difficulties, which they had either ignored altogether, or, at all events, greatly undervalued, and putting our case before them in such a form that even philosophers, not conversant with the special researches of philologists, might gain a clear insight into the present state of our science, and form their opinion accordingly.

In doing this I thought I was simply performing a duty which, in the present state of divided and subdivided labor, has to be performed, if we wish to prevent a useless waste of life. However different our pursuits may be, we all belong, as I said before, to the same army, we all have the same interests at heart, we are bound together by what the French would call the strongest of all solidarities, the love of truth. If I had thought only of my own fellow-laborers in the field of the Science of Language, I should not have considered that there was any necessity for the three Lectures which I delivered in 1873 at the Royal Institution. In my first course of Lectures on the Science of Language (1861), delivered before Evolutionism had assumed its present dimensions, I had already expressed my conviction that language is the one great barrier between the brute and man.

"Man speaks," I said, "and no brute has ever uttered a word. Language is something more palpable than a fold of the brain or an angle of the skull. It admits of no caviling, and no process of natural selection will ever distill significant words out of the notes of birds or the cries of beasts."

No scholar, so far as I know, has ever controverted any of these statements. But when Evolutionism became, as it fully deserved, the absorbing interest of all students of nature, when it was supposed that, if a Moneres could develop into a Man, Bow-wow and Pooh-pooh might well have developed by imperceptible degrees into Greek and Latin, I thought it was time to state the case for the Science of Language and its bearing on some of the problems of Evolutionism more fully, and I gladly accepted the invitation to lecture once more on this subject at the Royal Institution in 1873. My object was no more than a statement of facts, showing that the results of the Science of Language did not at present tally with the results of Evolutionism, that words could no longer be derived directly from imitative and interjectional sounds, that between these sounds and the first beginnings of language, in the technical sense of the word, a barrier had been discovered, represented by what we call Roots, and that, as far as we know, no attempt, not even the faintest, has ever been made by any animal, except man, to approach or to cross that barrier. I went one step further. I showed that Roots were with man the embodiments of general concepts, and that the only way in which man realized general concepts, was by means of those roots, and words derived from roots. I therefore argued as follows: We do not know anything and cannot possibly know anything of the mind of animals: therefore, the proper attitude of the philosopher with regard to the mental capacities of animals is one of complete neutrality. For all we know, the mental capacities of animals may be of a higher order than our own, as their sensuous capacities certainly are in many cases. All this, however, is guesswork; one thing only is certain. If we are right that man realizes his conceptual thought by means of words, derived from roots, and that no animal possesses words derived from roots, it follows, not indeed, that animals have no conceptual thought (in saying this, I went too far), but that their conceptual thought is different in its realized shape from our own.

From public and private discussions which followed the delivery of my lectures at the Royal Institution (an abstract of them was published in "Fraser's Magazine," and republished, I believe, in America), it became clear to me that the object which I had in view had been fully attained. General attention had been roused to the fact that at all events the Science of

Language had something to say in the matter of Evolutionism, and I know that those whom it most concerned were turning their thoughts in good earnest to the difficulties which I had pointed out. I wanted no more, and I thought it best to let the matter ferment for a time.

MR. GEORGE DARWIN'S ARTICLE IN THE "CONTEMPORARY REVIEW."

But what was my surprise when I found that a gentleman who had acquired considerable notoriety, not indeed by any special and original researches in Comparative Philology, but by his repeated attempts at vilifying the works of other scholars, Professor Whitney, had sent a paper to Mr. Darwin, intended to throw discredit on the statements which I had recommended to his serious consideration. I did not know of that paper till an abstract of it appeared in the "Contemporary Review," signed George Darwin, and written with the avowed purpose of discrediting the statements which I had made in my Lecture at the Royal Institution. If Professor Whitney's appeal had been addressed to scholars only, I should gladly have left them to judge for themselves. But as Mr. Darwin, Jr., was prevailed upon to stand sponsor to Professor Whitney's last production, and to lend to it, if not the weight, at least the lustre of his name, I could not, without appearing uncourteous, let it pass in silence. I am not one of those who believe that truth is much advanced by public controversy, and I have carefully eschewed it during the whole of my literary career. But if I had left Professor Whitney's assertions unanswered, I could hardly have complained, if Mr. Darwin, Sr., and the many excellent *savants* who share his views, had imagined that I had represented the difficulties which the students of language feel with regard to animals developing a language, in a false light; that in fact, instead of wishing to assist, I had tried to impede the onward march of our brave army. I have that faith in οἱ περὶ Darwin, that I believe they want honest advice, from whatever quarter it may come, and I therefore was persuaded to deviate for once from my usual course, and, by answering *seriatim* every objection raised by Professor Whitney, to show that my advice had been tendered *bonâ fide*, that I had not spoken in the character of a special pleader, but simply and solely as a man of truth.

MY ANSWER TO MR. DARWIN.

My "Answer to Mr. Darwin" appeared in the "Contemporary Review" of November, 1874, and if it had only elicited the letter which I received from Mr. Darwin, Sr., I should have been amply repaid for the trouble I had taken in the matter.

It produced, however, a still more important result, for it elicited from the American assailant a hasty rejoinder, which opened the eyes even of his best friends to the utter weakness of his case. Professor Whitney, himself, had evidently not expected that I should notice his assault. He had challenged me so often before, and I had never answered him. Why, then, should I have replied now? My answer is, because, for the first time, his charges had been countersigned by another.

I had not even read his books before, and he blames me severely for that neglect, bluntly asking me, why I had not read them. That is indeed a question extremely difficult to answer without appearing to be rude. However, I may say this, that to know what books one must read, and what books one may safely leave unread, is an art which, in these days of literary fertility, every student has to learn. We know on the whole what each scholar is doing, we know those who are engaged in special and original work, and we are in duty bound to read whatever they write. This in the present state of Comparative Philology, when independent work is being done in every country of Europe, is as much as any man can do, nay, often more than I feel able to do. But then, on the other hand, we claim the liberty of leaving uncut other books in our science, which, however entertaining they may be in other respects, are not likely to contain any new facts. In doing this, we run a risk, but we cannot help it.

And let me ask Professor Whitney, if by chance he had opened a book and alighted on the following passage, would he have read much more?

"Take as instances *home* and *homely*, *scarce* and *scarcely*, *direct* and *directly*, *lust* and *lusty*, *naught* and *naughty*, *clerk* and *clergy*, a *forge* and a *forgery*, *candid* and *candidate*, *hospital* and *hospitality*, *idiom* and *idiocy*, *alight* and *delight*, etc."

Is there any philologist, comparative or otherwise, who does not know that *light*, the Gothic *liuhath*, is connected with the Latin *lucere*; that to *delight* is connected with Latin *delector*, Old French *deleiter*, and with Latin *de-lic-ere*; while to *alight* is of Teutonic origin, and connected with Gothic *leihts*, Latin *levis*, Sanskrit *laghus*?

But then, Professor Whitney continues, when at last he had forced me to read some of his writings, why did I not read them carefully? Why did I read Mr. Darwin's article in the "Contemporary Review" only, and not his own in an American journal?

Now here I feel somewhat guilty: still I can offer some excuse. I did not read Professor Whitney's reply in the American original, first, because I could not get it in time; secondly, because I only felt bound to answer the arguments which Mr. Darwin had adopted as his own. Looking at the original article afterwards, I found that I had not been entirely wrong. I see that Mr. Darwin has used a very wise discretion in his selection, and I may now tell Professor Whitney that he ought really to be extremely grateful that nothing except what Mr. Darwin had approved of, was placed before the English readers of the "Contemporary Review," and therefore answered by me in the same journal.

THE PHENICIAN ALPHABET.

Other charges, however, of neglect and carelessness on my part in reading Professor Whitney's writings, I can meet by a direct negative. Among the more glaring mistakes of his lectures which I had pointed out, was this, that fifteen years after Rougé's discovery, Professor Whitney still speaks of "the Phenician alphabet as the ultimate source of the world's alphabets." Professor Whitney answers: "If Professor Müller had read my twelfth lecture he would have found the derivative nature of the Phenician alphabet fully discussed." When I read this, I felt a pang, for it was quite true that I had not read that lecture. I saw a note to it, in which Professor Whitney states that the sketch of the history of writing contained in it was based on Steinthal's admirable essay on the "Development of Writing," and being acquainted with that, I thought I could dispense with lecture No. 12. However, as I thought it strange that there should be so glaring a contradiction between two lectures of the same course, that in one the Phenician alphabet should be represented as the ultimate source, in another as a derivative alphabet, I set to work and read lecture No. 12. Will it be believed that there is not one word in it about Rougé's discovery, published, as I said, fifteen years ago, that the old explanation that *Aleph* stood for an ox, *Beth* for a house, *Gimel* for camel, *Daleth* for door, is simply repeated, and that similarities are detected between the forms of the letters and the figures of the objects whose names they bear? Therefore of two things one, either Professor Whitney was totally ignorant of what has been published on this subject during the last fifteen years by Rougé, father and son, by Brugsch, Lenormant and others, or he thought he might safely charge me with having misrepresented him, because neither I nor any one else was likely to read lecture No. 12.

After this instance of what Professor Whitney considers permissible, I need hardly say more; but having been cited by him before a tribunal which hardly knows me, to substantiate what I had asserted in my "Answer to Mr. Darwin," it may be better to go manfully through a most distasteful task, to answer *seriatim* point after point, and thus to leave on record one of the most extraordinary cases of what I can only call Literary Daltonism.

LIKE AND UNLIKE.

I am accused by Professor Whitney of having read his lectures carelessly, because I had only been struck by what seemed to me repetitions from my own writings, without observing the deeper difference between his lectures and my own. He therefore advises me to read his lectures again. I am afraid I cannot do that, nor do I see any necessity for it, because though I was certainly staggered by a number of coincidences between his lectures and my own, I was perfectly aware that they differed from each other more than I cared to say. I imagined I had conveyed this as clearly as I could, without saying anything offensive, by observing that in many places his arguments seemed to me like an *inverted fugue* on a *motive* taken from my lectures. But if I was not sufficiently outspoken on that point, I am quite willing to make amends for it now.

AN INVERTED FUGUE.

I must give one instance at least of what I mean by an *inverted fugue*.

I had laid great stress on the fact that, though we are accustomed to speak of language as a thing by itself, language after all is not something independent and substantial, but, in the first instance, an act, and to be studied as such. Thus I said (p. 51):—

"To speak of language as a thing by itself, as living a life of its own, as growing to maturity, producing offspring, and dying away, is sheer mythology."

Again (p. 58):—

"Language exists in man, it lives in being spoken, it dies with each word that is pronounced, and is no longer heard."

When I came to Professor Whitney's Second Lecture, and read (p. 35):—

"Language has, in fact, no existence save in the minds and mouths of those who use it,"

I felt pleasantly reminded of what I knew I had said somewhere. But what was my surprise, when a few lines further on I read:—

"This truth is sometimes explicitly denied, and the opposite doctrine is set up, that language has a life and growth independent of its speakers, with which men cannot interfere. A recent popular writer (Professor Max Müller) asserts that, 'although there is a continuous change in language, it is not in the power of man either to produce or to prevent it. We might think as well of changing the laws which control the circulation of our blood, or of adding an inch to our height, as of altering the laws of speech, or inventing new words according to our own pleasure.'"

How is one to fight against such attacks? The very words which Professor Whitney had paraphrased before, only substituting "skull" for "height," and by which I had tried to prove "that languages are not the artful creations of individuals," are turned against me to show that, because I denied to any *single* individual the power of changing language *ad libitum*, I had set up the opposite doctrine, viz. that language has a life and growth independent of its speakers.

Does Professor Whitney believe that any attentive reader can be taken in by such artifices? Suppose I had said that in a well-organized republic no individual can change the laws according to his pleasure, would it follow that I held the opposite doctrine, that laws have a life and growth independent of the lawgiver? The simile is weak, because an individual may, under very peculiar circumstances, change a law according to his pleasure: but weak as it is, I hope it will convince Professor Whitney that Formal Logic is not altogether a useless study to a Professor of Linguistics. I only wonder what Professor Whitney would have said if he had been able to find in my Lectures a definition of language (p. 46), worthy of Friedrich Schlegel, viz.:—

"Language, like an organic body, is no mere aggregate of similar particles; it is a complex of related and mutually helpful parts."

And again:—

"The rise, development, decline, and extinction of language are like the birth, increase, decay, and death of a living creature."

In these poetical utterances of Professor Whitney's we have an outbreak of philological mythology of a very serious nature, and this many years after I had uttered my warning that "to speak of language as a thing by itself, as living a life of its own, as growing to maturity, producing offspring, and dying away, is sheer mythology" (I. p. 51).

REPETITIONS AND VARIATIONS.

It is, no doubt, quite natural that in reading Professor Whitney's lectures I should have been struck more forcibly than others by coincidences, which have reference not only to general arguments, but even to modes of expression and illustrations. I had pointed out some of these verbal or slightly disguised coincidences in my first article, but I could add many more. As we open the book, it begins by stating that the Science of Language is a modern science, that its growth was analogous to that of other sciences, that from a mere collection of facts it advanced to classification, and from thence to inductive reasoning on language. We are told that ancient nations considered the languages of their neighbors as merely barbarous, that Christianity changed that view, that a study of Greek, Latin, and Hebrew widened the horizon of scholars, and that at present no dialect, however rude, is without importance to the students of the Science of Language. Next comes the importance of the discovery of Sanskrit, and a challenge for a place among the recognized sciences in favor of our new science.

Now I ask any one who may have read my Lectures, whether it was not very natural that I should be struck with a certain similarity between my old course of lectures on the Science of Language, and the lectures delivered soon after on the Science of Language at Washington? But I was not blind to the differences, and I never wished to claim as my own what was original in the American book.

For instance, when the American Professor says that one of the most important problems is to find out "How we learn English," I said at once, "That's his ane;" and when after leading us from mother to grandmother, and great-grandmother, he ends with Adam, and says:—

"It is only the first man before whom every beast of the field and every fowl of the air must present itself, to see what he will call it; and whatever he calls any living creature, that is the name thereof, not to himself alone, but to his family and descendants, who are content to style each as their father had done before them."

I said again, "That's his ane."

When afterwards we read about the large and small number of words used by different ranks and classes, and by different writers, when we come to the changes in English, the phonetic changes, to phonetics in general, to changes of meaning, etc., few, I think, will fail to perceive what I naturally perceived most strongly, "the leaves of memory rustling in the dark." I perceived even such accidental reminiscences as:—

Old Prussian leaving behind a brief catechism (p. 215), and,

Old Prussian leaving behind an old catechism (p. 200);

Frisian having a literature of its own (p. 211), and the

Frisians having a literature of their own (p. 178),

though, of course, no other reader could possibly perceive such unimportant coincidences. These, no doubt, were mere accidents; but when we consider that there is perhaps no science which admits of more varied illustration than the Science of Language, then to find page after page the same instances which one had collected one's self, certainly left the impression that the soil from which these American lectures sprang, was chiefly alluvial. Of course, as Professor Whitney has acknowledged his indebtedness to me for these illustrations, I have no complaint to make, I only protest against his ingratitude in representing such illustrations as mere by-work. For the purpose of teaching and placing a difficult subject into its proper light, illustrations, I think, are hardly less important than arguments. In order to show, for instance, in what sense Chinese may be called a *parler enfantin*, I had said:—

"If a child says *up*, that *up* is to his mind, noun, verb, adjective, all in one. It means, I want to get up on my mother's lap."

What has Professor Whitney to say on the same subject?

"It is thus that, even at present, children begin to talk; a radical word or two means in their mouths a whole sentence; *up* signifies 'Take me up into your lap.'"

Enough of this, if not too much. Perhaps a thousand years hence, if any of our books survive so long, the question whether my lectures were written by myself, or by an American scholar settled in Germany, may exercise the critical acumen of the philologists of the future.

LECTURES PRINTED IN ENGLAND ALSO.

But I see there is one more charge of carelessness brought against me, and as I promised to answer every one, I must at least mention it.

"He has not even observed that my Lectures are printed and published in England, and not only in America."

Why I ought to have observed this, I do not understand. Would it have served as an advertisement? Should I have said that the author resided in Canada to secure his book against the imminent danger of piracy in England? Or does Professor Whitney suspect here too, one of those sinister influences which he thought had interfered with the sale of his books in England? However, whatever sin of omission I have committed, I am quite willing to apologize, in order to proceed to graver matters.

THE SCIENCE OF LANGUAGE AS ONE OF THE PHYSICAL SCIENCES.

I stand charged next not only with having read Professor Whitney's writings in too cursory a manner, but with actually having misrepresented his views on the question, so often discussed of late, whether the Science of Language should be reckoned one of the historical or one of the physical sciences. Let us look at the facts:—

I had tried to show in my very first Lecture in what sense the Science of Language might properly be called a physical, and in what sense it might be called an historical science. I had given full weight to the arguments on either side, because I felt that, owing to the twofold nature of man, much might be said with perfect truth for one or the other view. When I look back on what

I wrote many years ago, after having carefully weighed all that has been written on the subject during the last fifteen years, I am glad to find that I can repeat every word I then wrote, without a single change or qualification.

"The process" I said (p. 49), "through which language is settled and unsettled, combines in one the two opposite elements of necessity and freewill. Though the individual seems to be the prime mover in producing new words and new grammatical forms, he is so only after his individuality has been merged in the common action of the family, tribe, or nation to which he belongs. He can do nothing by himself, and the first impulse to a new formation in language, *though given by an individual*, is mostly, if not always, given without premeditation, nay, unconsciously. The individual, as such, is powerless, and the results apparently produced by him, depend on laws beyond his control, and on the coöperation of all those who form together with him one class, one body, or one organic whole. But though it is easy to show that language cannot be changed or moulded by the taste, the fancy, or genius of man, it is nevertheless through the instrumentality of man alone that language can be changed."

Now I ask any reader of Mr. Whitney's Lectures, whether he has found in them anything in addition to what I had said on this subject, anything materially or even in form, differing from it. He speaks indeed of the actual additions made by individuals to language, but he treats them, as I did, as rare exceptions (p. 32), and I cannot help thinking that when he wrote (p. 52):—

"Languages are almost as little the work of man as is the form of his skull, the outlines of his face, the construction of his arm and hand,"

he was simply paraphrasing what I had said, though, as will be seen, far more cautiously than my American colleague, because my remarks referred to the laws of language only, not to language as a whole (p. 47):—

"We might think as well of changing the laws which control the circulation of our blood, or of adding an inch to our height, as of altering the laws of speech, and inventing new words, *according to our own pleasure.*"

I cannot hope to convince Mr. Whitney, for after I had tried to explain to him, why I considered the question whether the Science of Language is to be classed as a physical or an historical science, as chiefly a question of technical definition, he replies:—

"That I should probably consider it as more than a matter of terminology or technical definition whether our science is an historical science, *because men make language*, or a physical science, *because men do not make language.*"

Everybody will see that to attempt a serious argument on such conditions, is simply impossible.

If Professor Whitney can produce one single passage in all my writings where I said that *men do not make language*, I promise to write no more on language at all. I see now that it is Schleicher who, according to Professor Whitney, at least, held these crude views, who called languages natural organisms, which, without being determinable by the will of man, arose, grew, and developed themselves, in accordance with fixed laws, and then again grow old and die out; who ascribed to language that succession of phenomena which is wont to be termed life, and who accordingly classed *Glottik*, the Science of Language, as a natural science. These are the very opinions which, with the exception of the last, are combated in my writings.

I understood perfectly well what Mr. Whitney meant, when he, like nearly all scholars before him, claimed the Science of Language as an historical or a moral science. Man is an amphibious creature, and all the sciences concerning man, will be more or less amphibious sciences. I did not rush into print, because he took the opposite side to the one I had taken. On the contrary, having myself laid great stress on the fact that language was not to be treated as an artful creation of the individual, I was glad that the artistic element in language, such as it is, should have found so eloquent an advocate. But I confess, I was disappointed when I saw that, with the exception of a few purely sentimental protests, there was nothing in Mr. Whitney's treatment of the subject that differed from my own. I proved this, if not to his satisfaction, at least to that of others, by giving *verbatim* extracts from his Lectures, and what is the consequence? As he can no longer deny his own words, he uses the only defense which remained, he now accuses me of garbling quotations and thus misrepresenting him. This, of course, may be said of all quotations, short of reprinting a whole chapter. Yet to my mind the charge is so serious, that I feel in duty bound to repel it, not by words, but by facts.

This is the way in which Professor Whitney tries to escape from the net in which he had entangled himself. In his reply to my argument he says:—

"He chooses even more than once a sentence, in order to prove that I maintain an opinion, directly from an argument in support of the opposite opinion; for instance, in quoting my words, 'that languages are almost as little the work of man as is the form of his skull,' he overlooks the preceding parts of the same sentence: '*as opposed* to the objects which he, the linguist, follows in his researches, and the results which he wishes to attain.' The whole is a part of a section which is to prove that the absence of reflection and conscious intent, takes away from the facts of language the subjective character which would otherwise belong to them as products of the voluntary action."

Very well. We now have what Professor Whitney says that he said. Let us now read what he really said (p. 51):—

"The linguistic student feels that he is not dealing with *the artful creations of individuals*. So far as concerns the purposes for which he examines them, and the results he would derive from them, they are almost as little the work of man as is the form of his skull."

To render "so far as concerns the purposes" by "Gegenüber den Zwecken, die er bei seinen Untersuchungen verfolgt," is a strong measure. But even thus, the facts remain as I, not as he, had stated them. There was no garbling on my part, but something worse than garbling on his, and all this for no purpose whatever, except for one which I do not like to suggest. As a linguistic student Professor Whitney feels what I had felt, 'that we are not dealing with the artful creations of individuals.' What Professor Whitney may feel besides about language, does not concern us, but it does concern us, and it does still more concern him, that he should not endeavor to impart to scientific language that character which, as he admits, it has not, viz., that of being the very artful creation of an individual.

I am quite willing to admit, and I have done so before on several occasions, that I may have laid too great stress on those characteristics of the Science of Language by which it belongs to the physical sciences. I have explained why I did so at the time. In fact these are not new questions. Because I had said, as Dr. Whewell had said before me,—

"That there are several large provinces of speculation which concern subjects belonging to man's immaterial nature, and which are governed by the same laws as sciences altogether physical,"

it did not follow, as Professor Whitney seems to think, that I regarded language as something like a cow or a potato. I cannot defend myself against such puerilities.

In reviewing Schleicher's essay, "On Darwinism tested by the Science of Language," I had said:—

"It is not very creditable to the students of the Science of Language that there should have been among them so much wrangling as to whether that science is to be treated as one of the natural or as one of the historical sciences. They, if any one, ought to have seen that they were playing with language, or rather that language was playing with them, and that unless a proper definition is first given of what is meant by nature and by natural science, the pleading for and against the admission of the Science of Language to the circle of the natural sciences, may be carried on *ad infinitum*. It is, of course, open to anybody so to define the meaning of nature as to exclude human nature, and so to narrow the sphere of the natural sciences, as to leave no place for the Science of Language. It is also possible so to interpret the meaning of growth that it becomes inapplicable alike to the gradual formation of the earth's crust, and to the slow accumulation of the *humus* of language. Let the definition of these terms be plainly laid down, and the controversy, if it will not cease at once, will at all events become more fruitful. It will then turn on the legitimate definition of such terms as nature and mind, necessity and free-will, and it will have to be determined by philosophers rather than by scholars. Unless appearances deceive us, it is not the tendency of modern philosophy to isolate human nature, and to separate it by impassable barriers from nature at large, but rather to discover the bridges which lead from one bank to the other, and to lay bare the hidden foundations which, deep beneath the surface, connect the two opposite shores. It is, in fact, easy to see that the old mediæval discussions on necessity and free-will are turning up again in our own time, though slightly disguised, in the discussions on the proper place which man holds in the realm of nature; nay, that the same antinomies have been at the root of the controversy from the days when Greek philosophers maintained that language existed φύσει or θέσει, to our own days, when scholars range themselves in two hostile camps, claiming for the Science of Language a place either among the physical or the historical branches of knowledge."

And again:—

"At all events we should never allow ourselves to forget that, if we speak of languages as natural productions, and of the Science of Language as one of the natural sciences, what we chiefly wish to say is, that languages are not produced by the free-will of individuals, and that, if they are works of art, they are works of what may be called a natural or unconscious art—an art in which the individual, though he is the agent, is not a free agent, but checked and governed from the very first breath of speech by the implied cooperation of those to whom his language is addressed, and without whose acceptance language, not being understood, would cease to be language."

In the first lecture which I delivered at Strassburg, I dwelt on the same problem, and said:—

"There is, no doubt, in language a transition from the material to the spiritual; the raw material of language belongs to nature, but the form of language, that which really makes language, belongs to the spirit. Were it possible to trace human language *directly* back to natural sounds, to interjections or imitations, the question whether the Science of Language belongs to the sphere of the natural or the historical sciences would at once be solved. But I doubt whether this crude view of the origin of language counts one single supporter in Germany. With one foot language stands, no doubt, in the realm of nature, but with the other in the realm of spirit. Some years ago, when I thought it necessary to bring out as clearly as possible the much neglected natural element in language, I tried to explain in what sense the Science of Language had a right to be called the last and the highest of the natural sciences. But I need hardly say that I did not lose sight, therefore, of the intellectual and historical character of language; and I may here express my conviction that the Science of Language will yet enable us to withstand the extreme theories of the evolutionists, and to draw a hard and fast line between spirit and matter, between man and brute."

Professor Whitney will see, therefore, that all that can be said, and be justly said, against treating the Science of Language as a purely physical science was not so new to me as he expected; nay, his friends might possibly tell him that the *pro's* and *con's* of this question had been far more fully and fairly weighed before his own lectures were published than afterwards. A writer on this subject, if he wishes to win new laurels, must do more than furbish up old weapons, and fight against monsters which owe their existence to nothing but his own heated imagination.

IS GLOTTOLOGY A SCIENCE?

His knowledge of the German language ought to have kept Professor Whitney from an insinuation that I had claimed for Glottology a place among the physical sciences, because I feared that otherwise the title of "science" would be altogether denied to my researches. Now whatever artificial restriction may have been forced on the term "science" in English and American, the corresponding term in German, *Wissenschaft*, has, as yet, resisted all such violence, and it was as a German that I ventured to call *Sprachwissenschaft* by its right name in English, and did not hesitate to speak even of a Science of Mythology, a Science of Religion, and a Science of Thought.

Finally, as to my wishing to smuggle in Glottology, and to secure for it at least some small corner in the circle of the Physical Sciences, I am afraid I cannot lay claim to such modesty. When at the meeting of the British Association at Oxford in 1847, Bunsen claimed the establishment of a separate section for Ethnology, he said:—

"If man is the apex of creation, it seems right on the one side, that a historical inquiry into his origin and development should never be allowed to sever itself from the general body of natural science, and, in particular, from physiology. But on the other hand, if man is the apex of creation, if he is the end to which all organic formations tend from the very beginning; if man is at once the mystery and the key of natural science; if that is the only view of natural science worthy of our age, then ethnologic philology, once established on principles as clear as the physiological are, is *the highest branch* of that science for the advancement of which this Association is instituted.

It is not an appendix to physiology or to anything else; but its object is, on the contrary, capable of becoming the end and goal of the labors and transactions of a scientific association."

These words of my departed friend express better than anything which I can say, what I meant by claiming for the Science of Language and the Science of Man, a place among the physical sciences. By enlarging the definition of physical science so as to make it comprehend both Anthropology and Glottology, I thought I was claiming a wider scope and a higher dignity for physical science. The idea of calling language a vegetable, in order to smuggle it through the toll-bar of the physical sciences, certainly never entered my mind.

When one remembers how since 1847, man has become the central point of the discussions of the British Association year after year, Bunsen's words sound almost prophetic, and it might have been guessed, even in America, that the friend and pupil of Bunsen was not likely to abate much in his claims for the recognition of the Science of Man, as the highest of all sciences.

Have I done? Yes, I believe I have answered all that required an answer in Mr. Darwin's article, in Professor Whitney's new attack in the "Contemporary Review," and in his Lectures. But alas! there is still a page bristling with challenges.

Have I read not only his lectures, but all his controversial articles? No. Then I ought.

Have I quoted any passage from his writings to prove that the less he has thought on a subject, the louder he speaks No. Then I ought.

Have I produced any proof that he wonders that no one answers his strictures? No. Then I ought.

He actually appeals to my honor. What can I do? I cannot say that I have since read all his controversial articles, but I have read a considerable number, and I frankly confess that on many points they have raised my opinion of Professor Whitney's acquirements. It is true, he is not an original worker, but he is a hard reader, and a very smart writer. The gall of bitterness that pervades all his writings, is certainly painful, but that concerns him far more than us.

LANGUAGE AND THOUGHT INSEPARABLE.

First then, I am asked to explain what I meant by saying that Professor Whitney speaks the loudest on subjects on which he has thought the least. I could best explain my meaning, if I were to collect all that Professor

Whitney has written on the relation of language to thought. He certainly grows most boisterous in these latitudes, and yet he evidently has never, as yet, read up that subject, nay, he seems convinced that what has been written on it by such dreamers as Locke, Schelling, Hegel, Humboldt, Schopenhauer, Mansel, and others, deserves no consideration whatever. To maintain, what every one of these philosophers maintains, that a conception cannot be entertained without the support of a word, would be, according to the Yale Professor, the sheerest folly (p. 125),—"part of that superficial and unsound philosophy which confounds and identifies speech, thought, and reason" (p. 439).

I can quite enter into these feelings, for I can still remember the mental effort that is required in order to surrender our usual view of language, as a mere sign or instrument of thought, and to recognize in it the realization of all conceptual thought. A mere dictionary would, no doubt, seem the best answer to those who hold that thought and language are inseparable, and to throw a stout Webster at our head might be considered by many as good a refutation of such sheer folly, as a slap in the face was supposed to be of Berkeley's idealism. However, Professor Whitney is an assiduous reader, and I do not at all despair that the time will come when he will see what these thinkers really mean by conceptual thought and by language, and I am quite prepared to hear him say that "he had known all that long ago, that any child knew it, that it was mere *bathos*, and that it was only due to a want of clear and definitive expression, or to a want of knowledge of English, excusable in a foreigner, if there had been so much darkening of counsel by words without thought." I shall then be told that:—

"I consulted excellent authorities, and I worked these up with a commendable degree of industry, but that I am wanting in the inner light ... and have never gained a comprehension of the movements that go on in my own mind, without which real insight into the relation of language to thought is impossible" (p. 268).

PROFESSOR PRANTL ON THE REFORM OF LOGIC.

In order to accelerate that event, may I advise Professor Whitney to read some articles lately published by Professor Prantl? Professor Prantl is *facile princeps* among German logicians, he is the author of the "History of Logic," and therefore perhaps even the American Professor will not consider him, as he does others who differ from him, as quite ignorant of the first rules of logic! At the meeting of the Royal Academy at Munich, March 6, 1875, Professor Prantl claimed permission, after having finished his "History of Logic," to lay some thoughts for the "Reform of Logic," before the members of that Academy, the very fundamental principle of that reform being

The essential unity of thought and language.

"Realized thought, or what others might call the realization of the faculty of thought, exists therefore in language only, and *vice versâ*, every element of language contains thought. Every kind of priority of real thought before its expression in language, is to be denied, as well as any separate existence of thought" (p. 181).

"In one sense I should not deny that there is something in animals which in a very high degree of elevation is called language in man. In recognition of the distance produced by this high degree of elevation, one can agree with Max Müller, that language is the true frontier between brute and man." (p. 168).

Or, if the Yale Professor wants a more popular treatment of the subject, he might read Dr. Loewe's essay on "The Simultaneity of the Genesis of Speech and Thought," also published this year. Dr. Loewe, too, avails himself gladly of the new results obtained by the Science of Language, and shows clearly that the origin of thought is the origin of language.

Every one who has to write on philosophical subjects in English, German, and French, or who has to superintend translations of what he has written into other languages, must know how difficult it is to guard always against being misunderstood, but a reader familiar with his subject at once makes allowance for this; he does not raise clouds of dust for nothing. Observe the difference between some criticisms passed on what I had said, by Dr. Loewe, and by others. I had said in my Lectures (ii. 82):—

"It is possible, without language, to see, to perceive, to stare at, to dream about things; but, without words, not even such simple *ideas* as white or black can be for a moment realized."

My German translator had rendered *ideas* by *Vorstellungen* while I used the word in the sense of concept, *Begriff*. Dr. Loewe in commenting on this passage says:—

"If M. M. maintains that *Vorstellungen*, such as white and black, cannot be realized for a moment without words, he is right, but only if by *Vorstellung* he means *Begriff*. And this is clearly his meaning, because shortly before he had insisted on the fact that it was conceptual thought which is impossible without words. Were we to take his words literally, then it would be wrong, for sensuous images (Sinnesbilder), such as white and black, do not require words for their realization. One glance at the psychical life of animals would suffice to prove that sensuous representation (Vorstellen) can be carried out without language, for it is equally certain that animals have sensuous images as that they have no words."

This is the language of a well-schooled philosopher, who cares for truth and not for controversy, *à tout prix*. Let us contrast it for a moment with the language of Professor Whitney (p. 249):—

"This may be taking a very high view of language; it certainly is taking a very low view of reason. If only that part of man's superior endowments which finds its manifestation in language is to receive the name of reason, what shall we style the rest? We had thought that the love and intelligence, the soul, that looks out of a child's eyes upon us to reward our care long before it begins to prattle, were also marks of reason," etc.

This is a pretty domestic idyl, but the marvelous confusion between conceptual thought and the inarticulate signs of the affections, will, I fear, remind logicians of infantine prattle with no mark of reason about it, rather than of scientific argument.

It is quite clear, therefore, from this single specimen, that it would be impossible to argue with Professor Whitney on this subject. He returns to it again and again, his language grows stronger and stronger every time, yet all the time he speaks like a man whom nothing shall convince that the earth does move. He does not even know that he might have quoted very great authorities on his side of the question, only that they, knowing the bearings of the whole problem, speak of their antagonists with the respect due say by Nyâya to a Sânkhya philosopher, not with the contempt which a Brahman feels for a [Mleccha](.).

GRAMMATICAL BLUNDERS.

But let us take a subject where, at all events, it is possible to argue with the Professor—I mean Sanskrit Grammar—and we shall see again that he is most apodictic when he is least informed. He has criticised the first volume of my translation of the Rig-Veda. He dislikes it very much, and gives me very excellent advice as to what I ought to have done and what I ought not. He thinks I ought to have thought of the large public who want to know something of the Veda, and not of mere scholars. He thinks that the hymns addressed to the Dawn would have pleased the young ladies better than the hymns to the Stormgods, and he broadly hints that all the *pièces justificatives* which I give in my commentary are *de trop*. A translation, such as Langlois', would, no doubt, have pleased him best. I do not object to his views, and I hope that he or his friends may some day give us a translation of the Rig-Veda, carried out in that spirit. I shall devote the remaining years of my life to carrying on what I ventured to call and still call the first *traduction raisonnée* of the Veda, on those principles which, after mature reflection, I adopted in the first volume, and which I still consider the only principles in accordance with the requirements of sound scholarship. The very reason why I chose the hymns to the Maruts was because I thought it was high time to put an end to the mere trifling with Vedic translation. They are, no doubt, the most difficult, the most rugged, and, it may be, the least attractive hymns, but they are on that very account an excellent introduction to a scholarlike study of the Veda. Mere guessing and skipping will not avail us here. There is no royal road to the discovery of the meaning of difficult words in the Veda. We must trace words of doubtful meaning through every passage where they occur, and we must give an account of their meaning by translating every passage that can be translated, marking the rest as, for the present, untranslatable. Boehtlingk and Roth's excellent Dictionary is the first step in that direction, and a most important step. But in it the passages have only undergone their first sifting and classifying; they are not translated, nor are they given with perfect completeness. Now if one single passage is left out of consideration in establishing the meaning of a word, the whole work has to be done again. It is only by adopting my own tedious, it may be, but exhaustive method that a scholar may feel that whatever work he has done, it is done once for all.

On such questions, however, it is easy to write a great deal in general terms; though it is difficult to say anything on which all competent scholars are not by this time fully agreed. It is not for me to gainsay my American critic that my renderings into English, being those of a foreigner, are tame and spiritless, but I doubt, whether in a new edition I shall change my translation, "the lights in heaven shine forth," for what the American Professor suggests: "a sheen shines out in the sky," or "gleams glimmer in the sky."

All this, however, anybody might have written after dinner. But once at least Professor Whitney, Professor of Sanskrit in Yale, attempts to come to close quarters, and ventures on a remark on Sanskrit grammar. It is the only passage in all his writings, as far as I remember, where, instead of indulging in mere sheet lightning, he comes down upon me with a crashing thunderbolt, and points out a real grammatical blunder. He says it is—

"An extremely violent and improbable grammatical process to render p a r i t a s t h u s h a s, as if the reading were p a r i t a s t h i v â ṃ s a s. The participial form t a s t h u s h a s has no right to be anything but an accusative plural, or a genitive or ablative singular; let us have the authority for making a nominative plural of it, and treating p a r i as its prefix, and better authority than the mere dictum of a Hindu grammarian."

Those who are acquainted with Vedic studies know that Professor Benfey has been for years preparing a grammar of the Vedic dialect, and, as there is plenty of work for all workers, I purposely left the grammatical questions to him, confining myself in my commentary to the most necessary grammatical remarks, and giving my chief attention to the meaning of words and the poetical conceptions of the ancient poets. If the use of the accusatival form t a s t h u s h a s , with the sense of a nominative, had been confined to the Veda, or had never been remarked on before, I ought, no doubt, to have called attention to it. But similar anomalous forms occur in Epic literature also, and more than that, attention had but lately been called to them by a very eminent Dutch scholar, Dr. Kern, who, in his translation of the Bṛhat-Saṃhitâ, remarks that the ungrammatical nom. plur. v i d u s h a s is by no means rare in the Mahâbhârata and kindred works. If Professor Whitney had only read as far as the eleventh hymn in the first book of the Rig-Veda, he would have met there in a b i b h y u s h a s an undoubted nom. plur. in u s h a s :—

tvā́m devā́ḥ ábibhyushaḥ tujyámânâsaḥ âvishuḥ,

The gods, stirred up, came to thee, not fearing.

Now, I ask, was I so far wrong when I said that Professor Whitney speaks loudest when he knows least, and that in charging me, for once at least, with a tangible blunder, he only betrayed his ignorance of Sanskrit grammar? In former times a scholar, after such a misfortune, would have taken a vow of silence or gone into a monastery. What will Professor Whitney do? He will take a vow of speech, and rush into a North American Review.

HARD AND SOFT.

There are other subjects to which Professor Whitney has of late paid much more attention than to Sanskrit Grammar, and we shall find that on them he argues in a much gentler tone.

It is well known that Professor Whitney held curious views about the relation of vowels to consonants, and I therefore was not surprised to hear from him that "my view of the essential difference between vowels and consonants will not bear examination." He mixes up what I call the substance (breath and voice) with the form (squeezes and checks), and forgets that *in rerum naturâ* there exist no consonants except as modifying the column of voice and breath, or as what Hindu grammarians call v y a n j a n a , *i.e.*, determinants; and no vowels except as modified by consonants. In order to support the second part of this statement, viz., that it is impossible to pronounce an initial vowel without a slight, and to many hardly perceptible, initial noise, the *coup de la glotte*, I had appealed to musicians who know how difficult it is, in playing on the flute or on the violin, to weaken or to avoid certain noises (*Ansatz*) arising from the first impulses imparted to the air, before it can produce really musical sensations. Professor Whitney, in quoting this paragraph, leaves out the sentence where I say that I want to explain the difficulty of pronouncing initial vowels without some *spiritus lenis*, and charges me with comparing all consonants with the unmusical noises of musical instruments. This was in 1866, whereas in 1854 I had said: "If we regard the human voice as a continuous stream of air, emitted as breath from the lungs and changed by the vibration of the *chordæ vocales* into vocal sound, as it leaves the larynx, this stream itself, as modified by certain positions of the mouth, would represent the vowels. In the consonants, on the contrary, we should have to recognize a number of stops opposing for a moment the free passage of this vocal air." I ask any scholar or lawyer, what is one to do against such misrepresentations? How is one to qualify them, when to call them unintentional would be nearly as offensive as to call them intentional?

The greatest offense, however, which I have committed in his eyes is that I revived the old names of *hard* and *soft*, instead of *surd* and *sonant*. Now I thought that one could only revive what is dead, but I believe there is not a single scholar alive who does not use always or occasionally the terms *hard* and *soft*. Even Professor Whitney can only call these technical terms obsolescent; but he thinks my influence is so omnipotent that, if I had struck a stroke against these obsolescent terms, they would have been well nigh or quite finished. I cannot accept that compliment. I have tried my strokes against much more objectionable things than *hard* and *soft*, and they have not yet vanished. I know of no living philologist who does not use the old terms *hard* and *soft*, though everybody knows that they are imperfect. I see that Professor Pott2 in one passage where he uses *sonant* thinks it necessary to explain it by *soft*. Why, then, am I singled out as the great criminal? I do not object to the use of *surd* or *sonant*. I have used these terms from the very beginning of my literary career, and as Professor Whitney evidently doubts my word, I may refer him to my *Proposals*, submitted to the Alphabetic Conferences in 1854. he will find that as early as that date, I already used *sonant*, though, like Pott, I explained this new term by the more familiar *soft*. If he will appeal to Professor Lepsius, he will hear how, even at that time, I had translated for him the chapters of the Prâtisâkhyas, which explain the true structure of a physiological alphabet, and ascribe the distinction between k and g to the absence and presence of voice. I purposely avoided these new terms, because I doubted, and I still doubt, whether we should gain much by their adoption. I do not exactly share the misgivings that a *surd mute* might be mistaken for a *deaf and dumb* letter, but I think the name is awkward. *Voiced* and *voiceless* would seem much better renderings of the excellent Sanskrit terms g h o s h a v a t and a g h o s h a , in order to indicate that it is the presence and absence of the voice which causes their difference. Frequent changes in technical terms are much to be deprecated,3 particularly if the new terms are themselves imperfect.

Every scholar knows by this time what is meant by *hard* and *soft*, viz., *voiceless* and *voiced*. The names *hard* and *soft*, though not perfect, have, like most imperfect names, some kind of excuse, as I tried to show by Czermak's experiments.4 But while a good deal may be said for *soft* and *hard*, what excuse can be pleaded for such a term as *media*, meaning originally a letter between the *Psila* and the *Dasea*? Yet, would it be believed that this very term is used by Professor Whitney on the page following immediately after his puritanical sermon against my backslidings!

This gentle sermon, however, which Professor Whitney preaches at me, as if I were the Pope of Comparative Philologists, is nothing compared with what follows later. When he saw that the difference between *voiced* and *voiceless* letters was not so novel to me as he had imagined, that it was known to me even before I published the Prâtisâkhya,—nay, when I had told him that, to quote the words of Professor Brücke, the founder of scientific phonetics,—

"The medias had been classed as *sonant* in all the systems elaborated by the students of language who have studied comparative phonology,"

he does not hesitate to write as follows:—

"Professor Müller, like some other students of philology (who except Professor Whitney himself?) finds himself unable longer to resist the force of the arguments against *hard* and *soft*, and is convinced that *surd* and *sonant* are the proper terms to use; but, instead of frankly abandoning the one, and accepting the other in their place, he would fain make his hearers believe that he has always held and taught as he now wishes he had done. It is either a case of disingenuousness or of remarkable self-deception: there appears to be no third alternative."

I call this a gentle reproof, as coming from Professor Whitney; but I must say at the same time that I seldom saw greater daring displayed, regardless of all consequences. The American captain sitting on the safety-valve to keep his vessel from blowing up, is nothing in comparison with our American Professor. I have shown that in 1854 the terms *surd* and *sonant* were no novelty to me. But as Professor Whitney had not yet joined our ranks at that time, he might very properly plead ignorance of a paper which I myself have declared antiquated by what I had written afterwards on the same subject. But will it be believed that in the very same lecture which he is criticising, there occurs the following passage (ii. p. 156):—

"What is it that changes k into g, t into d, p into b? B is called a media, a soft letter, a sonant, in opposition to P, which is called a tenuis, a hard letter, or a surd. But what is meant by these terms? A tenuis, we saw, was so called by the Greeks, in opposition to the aspirates, the Greek grammarians wishing to express that the aspirates had a rough or shaggy sound, whereas the tenues were bald, slight, or thin. This does not help us much. *Soft* and *hard* are terms which, no doubt, express an outward difference of b and p, but they do not explain the cause of that difference. *Surd* and *sonant* are apt to mislead; for if, according to the old system both p and b continue to be classed as mute, it is difficult to see how, taking words in their proper sense, a mute letter could be sonant. . . . . Both p and b are momentary negations of breath and voice; or, as the Hindu grammarians say, both are formed by complete contact. But b differs from p in so far as, in order to pronounce it, breath must have been changed by the glottis into voice, which voice, whether loud or whispered, partly precedes, partly follows the check."

And again:—

"But although the hardness and softness are secondary qualities of *tenues mediæ*, of surd and sonant letters, the true physiological difference between p and b, t and d, k and g, is that in the former the glottis is wide open, in the latter narrowed, so as to produce either whispered or loud voice."

In my introduction to the "Outline Dictionary for Missionaries," published in 1867, I wrote:—

"Unfortunately, everybody is so familiar with his alphabet, that it takes some time to convince people that they know next to nothing about the true nature of their letters. Take even a scholar, and ask him what is T, and he may possibly say, a dental tenuis; ask him what is D, and he may reply, a dental media. But ask him what he really means by a tenuis or media, or what he considers the true difference between T and D, and he may probably say that T is hard and D is soft; or that T is sharp and D is flat; or, on the contrary, as some writers have actually maintained, that the sound of D requires a stronger impulse of the tongue than the sound of T: but we shall never get an answer that goes to the root of the matter, and lays hold of the mainspring and prime cause of all these secondary distinctions between T and D. If we consult Professor Helmholtz on the same subject, he tells us that 'the series of so-called mediæ, b, d, g, differs from that of the tenues, p, t, k, by this, that for the former the glottis is, at the time of consonantal opening, sufficiently narrowed to enable it to sound, or at least to produce the noise of the *vox clandestina*, or whisper, while it is wide open with tenues, and therefore unable to sound. Mediæ are therefore accompanied by the tone of the voice, and this may even, where they begin a syllable, set in a moment before, and where they end a syllable, continue a moment after the opening of the mouth, because some air may be driven into the closed cavity of the mouth, and support the sound of the vocal chords of the larynx. Because of the narrowed glottis, the rush of the air is more moderate, the noise of the air less sharp than with the tenuis, so that a great mass of air may rush at once from the chest."

"This to many may seem strange and hardly intelligible. But if they find that, several centuries before our era, the Indian grammarians gave exactly the same definition of the difference between p, t, k, and b, d, g, such a coincidence may possibly startle them, and lead them to inquire for themselves into the working of that wonderful instrument by which we produce the various sounds of our alphabet."

If Professor Whitney asserts—

"That I *repeatedly* will not allow that the sonant letters *are* intonated, but only that they *may be* intonated,"

I have no answer but a direct negative. For me to say so, would be to run counter to all my own teaching, and if there is anywhere a passage that would admit of such a construction, Professor Whitney knows perfectly well that this could be due to nothing but an accidental want of precision in expressing myself. I know of no such passage.5

In order to leave no doubt as to the real distinction between k, t, p and g, d, b, I quoted, for the satisfaction of Sanskrit scholars, the technical terms by which native grammarians define so admirably the process of their formation, the vâhyaprayatna, viz., vivâraśvâsâghoshâḥ, and saṃvâranâdaghoshâḥ. Would it be believed that Professor Whitney accuses me of having invented these long Sanskrit terms, and to have appended them superfluously and pedantically, as he says, to each list of synonyms? "They are found in no Sanskrit grammarian," he says. Here again I have no answer but a direct negative. They are found in the native commentary on Pâṇini's Grammar, in Boehtlingk's edition, p. 4, and fully explained in the Mahâbhâshya.

If one has again and again to answer the assertions of a critic by direct negatives, is it to be wondered at that one rather shrinks from such encounters? I have for the last twenty years discussed these phonetic problems with the most competent authorities. Not trusting to my own knowledge of physiology and acoustics, I submitted everything that I had written on the alphabet, before it was published, to the approval of such men as Helmholtz, Alexander Ellis, Professor Rolleston, and I hold their *vu et approuvé*. I had no desire, therefore, to discuss these questions anew with Professor Whitney, or to try to remove the erroneous views which, till lately, he entertained on the structure of a physiological alphabet. I believe Professor Whitney has still much to learn on this subject, and as I never ask anybody to read what I myself have written, still less to read it a second time, might I suggest to him to read at all events the writings of Brücke, Helmholtz, Czermak, to say nothing of Wheatstone, Ellis, and Bell, before he again descends into this arena? If he had ever made an attempt to master that one short quotation from Brücke, which I gave on p. 159, or even that shorter one from Czermak, which I gave on p. 143:—

"Die Reibungslaute zerfallen genau so wie die Verschlusslaute in *weiche* oder *tönende*, bei denen das Stimmritzengeräusch oder der laute Stimmton mitlautet, und in *harte* oder *tonlose*, bei denen der Kehlkopf absolut still ist,"

the theory which I followed in the classification both of the Checks and the Breathings would not have sounded so unintelligible to him as he says it did; he would have received some rays of that inner light on phonetics which he misses in my Lectures, and would have seen that besides the disingenuousness or the self-deception which he imputes to me, in order to escape from the perplexity in which he found himself, there was after all a third alternative, though he denies it, viz., his being unwilling to confess his own ὀψιμαθία.

FIR, OAK, BEECH.

I now proceed to the next charge. I am told that I am in honor bound to produce a passage where Professor Whitney expressed his dissatisfaction at not being answered, or, as I had ventured to express it, considering the general style of his criticism, when he is angry that those whom he abuses, do not abuse him in turn. He is evidently conscious that there is some slight foundation for what I had said, for he says that if Steinthal thought he was angry, because "he (Mr. William Dwight Whitney) and his school" had not been refuted, instead of philosophers of the last century, he was mistaken. Yet what can be the meaning of this sentence, that "Professor Steinthal ought to have confronted *the living and aggressive* views of others," *i.e.*, of Mr. William Dwight Whitney and his school? (p. 365.)

However, I shall not appeal to that; I shall take a case which, in this tedious process of incrimination and recrimination, may perhaps revive for a moment the flagging interest of my readers.

I had in the second volume of my Lectures called attention to a curious parallelism in the changes of meaning in certain names of trees and in the changes of vegetation recorded in the strata of the earth. My facts were these. *Foraha* in Old High German, *Föhre* in modern German, *furh* in Anglo-Saxon, *fir* in English, signify the *pinus silvestris*. In the Lombard Laws the same word *fereha* means oak, and so does its corresponding word in Latin, *quercus*.

Secondly, φηγός in Greek means oak, the corresponding word in Latin, *fagus*, and in Gothic, *bôka*, means beech.

That is to say, in certain Aryan languages we find words meaning fir, assuming the meaning of oak; and words meaning oak, assuming the name of beech.

Now in the North of Europe geologists find that a vegetation of fir exists at the lowest depth of peat deposits; that this was succeeded by a vegetation of oak, and this by a vegetation of beech. Even in the lowest stratum a stone implement was found under a fir, showing the presence of human beings.

Putting these two sets of facts together, I said: Is it possible to explain the change of meaning in one word which meant fir and came to mean oak, and in another which meant oak and came to mean beech, by the change of vegetation which actually took place in early ages? I said it was an hypothesis, and an hypothesis only. I pointed out myself all that seemed doubtful in it, but I thought that the changes of meaning and the parallel changes of vegetation required an explanation, and until a better one could be given, I ventured to suggest that such changes of meaning were as the shadows cast on language by real, though prehistoric, events.

I asked for an impartial examination of the facts I had collected, and of the theory I had based on them. What do I receive from Professor Whitney? I must quote his *ipsissima verba*, to show the spirit that pervades his arguments:—

"It will not be difficult," he says, "to gratify our author by refuting his hypothesis. Not the very slightest shade of plausibility, that we can discover, belongs to it. Besides the serious minor objections to which it is liable, it involves at least three impossible suppositions, either one of which ought to be enough to insure its rejection.

"In the first place it assumes that the indications afforded by the peat-bogs of Denmark are conclusive as regards the condition of Europe—of all that part of it, at least, which is occupied by the Germanic and Italic races; that, throughout this whole region, firs, oaks, and beeches have supplanted and succeeded each other, notwithstanding that we find all of them, or two of them, still growing peaceably together in many countries."

Here Professor Whitney is, as usual, ploughing with my heifer. I said:—

"I must leave it to the geologist and botanist to determine whether the changes of vegetation as described above, took place in the same rotation over the whole of Europe, or in the North only,"

I had consulted several of my own geological friends, and they all told me that there was, as yet, no evidence in Central Europe and Italy of a succession of vegetation different from that in the North, and that, in the present state of geological science, they could say no more. In the absence of evidence to the contrary, I said, Let us wait and see; Professor Whitney says, Don't wait.

His second objection is his own, but hardly worthy of him.

"The hypothesis," he says, "assumes that the Germanic and Italic races, while they knew and named the fir-tree only, yet kept by them all the time, laid up in a napkin, the original term for oak, ready to be turned into an appellation for beech, when the oaks went out of fashion."

This is not so. The Aryan nations formed many new words, when the necessity for them arose. There, was no difficulty in framing ever so many names for the oak, and there can be little doubt that the name φηγός was derived from φάγω, the oak tree being called φηγός, because it supplied food or mast for the cattle. If there remained some consciousness of this meaning among the Greeks, and the Italians, and Germans, then the transference of the name from the oak to the beech would become still more easily intelligible, because both the beech-nuts and the acorns supplied the ordinary mast for cattle.

Professor Whitney probably had misgivings that these two objections were not likely to carry much weight, so he adds a third.

"The hypothesis," he says, "implies a method of transfer of names from one object to another which is totally inadmissible; this, namely—that, as the forest of firs gave way to that of oaks, the meaning of fir in the word *quercus* gave way to that of oak: and in like manner in the other case. Now if the Latins had gone to sleep some fine night under the shade of their majestic oaks, and had waked in the morning to find themselves *patulæ sub tegmine fagi*, they might naturally enough have been led, in their bewilderment, to give the old name to the new tree. But who does not see that, in the slow and gradual process by which, under the influence of a change of climatic conditions, one species of tree should come to prevail over another, the supplanter would not inherit the title of the supplanted, but would acquire one of its own, the two subsisting together during the period of the struggle, and that of the supplanted going out of use and memory as the species it designated disappeared?"

This objection was of course so obvious that I had thought it my duty to give a number of instances where old words have been transferred, not *per saltum*, but slowly and gradually, to new objects, such as *musket* originally a dappled sparrow-hawk, afterwards a gun. Other instances might have been added, such as θάπτω, the Sanskrit *dah*, the latter meaning to burn, the former to bury. But the best illustrations are unintentionally offered by Professor Whitney himself. On p. 303 he alludes to the fact that the names *robin* and *blackbird* have been applied in America, for the sake of convenience, and under the government of old associations, to birds essentially unlike, or only superficially like, those to which they belong in the mother country. Of course, every Englishman who settled in America knew that the bird he called *robin* was not the old Robin Redbreast he knew in England. Yet the two names co-existed for a time in literature, nay, they may still be said to co-exist in their twofold application, though, from a strictly American point of view, the supplanting American bird has inherited the title of the supplanted Cock-Robin of England.

Now, I ask, was there anything in these three cheap objections that required an answer? Two of them I had myself fully considered, the third was so flimsy that I thought no one would have dwelt on it. Anyhow, I felt convinced that every reader was competent to judge between Professor Whitney and myself, and it certainly never entered my mind that I was in honor bound, either to strike out my chapter on the Words for *Fir*, *Oak*, and *Beech*, or to fight.

Was I then so far wrong when I said that Professor Whitney cannot understand how anybody could leave what he is pleased to call his arguments, unheeded? Does he not express his surprise that in every new edition I adhere to my views on *Fir*, *Oak*, and *Beech*, though he himself had told me that I was wrong, and when he calls my expressed desire for real criticism a mere "rhetorical flourish," is this, according to the opinion of American gentlemen, or is it not, abuse?

EPITHETA ORNANTIA.

Professor Whitney's ideas of what is real criticism, and what is mere banter, personal abuse, or rudeness are indeed strange. He does not seem to be aware that his name has become a by-word, at least in Europe, and he defends himself against the charge of abusiveness with so much ardor that one sometimes feels doubtful whether it is all the mere rhetoric of a bad conscience, or a case of the most extraordinary self-deception. He declares in so many words that he was never personal (*Ich bestreite durchaus, dass was ich schrieb, im geringsten persönlich war*), and he immediately goes on to say that "Steinthal burst a two from anger and rancor, and his answer was a mere outpouring of abuse against his personality."

Now I am the last person or personality in the world to approve of the tone of Steinthal's answer, and if Professor Whitney asks why I had quoted it several times in public, it was because I thought it ought to be a warning to others. I think that all who are interested in maintaining certain civilized usages even in the midst of war, ought to protest against such a return to primitive savagery, and I am glad to find that my friend, Mr. Matthew Arnold, one of the highest authorities on the rules of literary warfare, entertains the same opinion, and has quoted what I had quoted from Professor Steinthal's pamphlet, together with other specimens of theological rancor, as extreme cases of bad taste.

I frankly admit, however, that, when I said that Steinthal had defended himself with the same weapons with which his American antagonist attacked him, I said too much. Professor Whitney does not proceed to such extremities as Professor Steinthal. But giving him full credit so far, I still cannot help thinking that it was a fight with poisoned arrows on one side, with clubs on the other. As Professor Whitney calls for proofs, here they are:—

Page 332. Why does he call Professor Steinthal, *Hajjim Steinthal?* Is that personal or not?

Page 335. "Professor Steinthal startles and rebuffs a commonsense inquirer with a reply from a wholly different and unexpected point of view; as when you ask a physician, 'Well, Doctor, how does your patient promise this morning?' and he answers, with a wise look and an oracular shake of the head, 'It is not given to humanity to look into futurity.' The effect is not destitute of the element of *bathos*." Is that personal?

Page 337. Steinthal's mode of arguing is "more easy and convenient than fair and ingenuous." Is that personal?

Page 338. "A mere verbal quibble."

Page 346. "The eminent psychologist may show himself a mere blunderer."

Page 356. "To our unpsychological apprehension, there is something monstrous in the very suggestion that a word is an act of the mind."

Page 357. "Prodigious .... Chaotic nebulosity .... We should not have supposed any man, at this age of the world, capable of penning the sentences we have quoted."

Page 359. "We are heartily tired of these comparisons that go limping along on one foot, or even on hardly the decent stump of a foot."

Page 363. "Can there be more utter mockery than this? We ask for bread, and a stone is thrown us."

Page 365. "He does not take the slightest notice of the *living* and *aggressive* views of others."

Page 366. "All this, again, is in our opinion very verbiage, mere turbid talk."

Page. 367. "The statement is either a truism or falsity."

Page 372. "We must pronounce Professor Steinthal's attempt .... a complete failure, a mere continuation of the same delusive reasonings by which he originally arrived at it."

Page 374. "We have found in his book nothing but mistaken facts and erroneous deductions."

If that is the language in which Professor Whitney speaks of one whom he calls—

"An eminent master in linguistic science, from whom he has derived great instruction and enlightenment," and "whose books he has constantly had upon his table,"

what can other poor mortals like myself expect? It is true he has avoided actionable expressions, while Professor Steinthal has not, at least, according to German and English law. But suppose that hereafter, when certain small animals have crossed what he calls "the impervious distance," and acquired the power of language, they were to say, "We have only stung you, and you have killed us," would they obtain much commiseration?

I had collected a number of *epitheta ornantia* which I had gathered at random from Mr. Whitney's writings, such as *worthless, futile, absurd, ridiculous, superficial, unsound, high-flown, pretentious, disingenuous, false*, and I claimed the honor of every one of them having been presented to me as well as to other scholars by our American assailant. Here, for the first time, Professor Whitney seems staggered at his own vocabulary. However, he is never at a loss how to escape. "As the epithets are translated into German," he says, "he is quite unable to find the passages to which I may refer." This is feeble. However, without taxing his memory further, he says that he feels certain it must be a mistake, because he never could have used such language. He never in his life said anything personal, but criticised opinions only. This is "the language of simple-minded consciousness of rectitude."

What can I do? Professor Whitney ought to know his own writings better than I do, and nothing remains to me, in order to repel the gravest of all accusations, but to publish in the smallest type the following Spicilegium. I must add that in order to do this work once for all, I have complied with Professor Whitney's request, and read nearly all the articles with which he has honored every one of my writings, and in doing so I believe I have at last found the key to much that seemed to me before almost inexplicable.

Formerly I had simply acquiesced in the statement made by one of his best friends, Professor Weber,[6] who, some ten years ago, when reproving Professor Whitney for the acrimony of his language, said:—

"I believe I am not wrong when I trace it to two causes: first, Professor Whitney found himself forced to acknowledge as erroneous and to withdraw several of his former views and assertions, which he had defended with great assurance, and this disturbed his equanimity; secondly, and still more, there were the miserable political circumstances of North America, which could not but exercise an irritating and galling effect on so warm a patriot as Whitney, an effect which was transferred unconsciously to his literary criticisms and polemics, whenever he felt inclined to it."

These two scholars were then discussing the question, whether the Nakshatras or the Lunar Zodiac of the Hindus, should be considered as the natural discovery of the Brahmans, or as derived by them, one knows not how, from China, from Chaldæa, or from some other unknown country. They both made great efforts, Professor Weber chiefly in Sanskrit, Professor Whitney in astronomy, in order to substantiate their respective opinions. Professor Weber showed that Professor Whitney was not very strong in Sanskrit, Professor Whitney retaliated by showing that Professor Weber, as a philologue, had attempted to prove that the precession of the equinox was from West to East, and not from East to West. All this, at the time, was amusing to bystanders, but by this time both combatants have probably found out, that the hypothesis of a foreign origin of the Nakshatras, whether Chinese or Babylonian, was uncalled for, or, at all events, is as uncertain to-day as it was ten years ago. I myself, not being an astronomer, had been content to place the evidence from Sanskrit sources before a friend of mine, an excellent astronomer at Oxford, and after discussing the question again and again with him, had arrived at the conviction that there was no excuse for so violent a theory as postulating a foreign origin of the simple triseinadic division of the Nakshatra Zodiac. I quite admit that my practical knowledge of astronomy is very small,[7] but I do believe that my astronomical ignorance was an advantage rather than a disadvantage to me in rightly understanding the first glimmerings of astronomical ideas among the Hindus. Be that as it may, I believe that at the present moment few scholars of repute doubt the native origin of the Nakshatras, and hardly one admits an early influence of Babylonian or Chinese science on India. I stated my case in the preface to the fourth volume of my edition of the Rig-Veda, and if anybody wishes to see what can be done by misrepresentation, let him read what is written there, and what Professor Whitney made of it in his articles in the "Journal of the American Oriental Society." His misunderstandings are so desperate, that he himself at times feels uneasy, and admits that a more charitable interpretation of what I wanted to say would be possible. When I saw this style of arguing, the utter absence of any regard for what was, or what might charitably be supposed to have been, my meaning, I made up my mind once for all, that that American gentleman should never have an answer from me, and in spite of strong temptation I kept my resolve till now. A man who could say of

Lassen that his statements were "wholly and reprehensibly incorrect," because he said that Colebrooke had shown that the Arabs received their lunar mansions from the Hindus, was not likely to show mercy to any other German professor.

I find, however, by reading one of his Essays, that there is a more special reason why, in his repeated onslaughts on me, both before and after the Rebellion, "he thinks he may dispense with the ordinary courtesies of literary warfare." I may tell it in his own words:—

"Some one (I may add the name, now, it was the late Professor Goldstücker) falls fiercely upon the work of a company of collaborators; they unite in its defense; thereupon the aggressor reviles them as a mutual admiration society; and Müller repeats the accusation, giving it his own indorsement, and volunteering in addition that of another scholar."

I might possibly represent the case in a different light, but I am willing to accept the *acte d'accusation* as it comes from the hand of my accuser; nay more, I am quite ready to plead guilty to it. Only let me explain how I came to commit this great offense. What is here referred to must have happened more than ten years ago. Professor Goldstücker had criticised the Sanskrit Dictionary published by Professors Boehtlingk and Roth, and "the company of collaborators" had united in its defense, only, as Professor Whitney is authorized to assure us, "without any apparent or known concert." Professor Goldstücker was an old friend of mine, to whom in the beginning of my literary career at Berlin and in Paris, I was indebted for much personal kindness. He helped me when no one else did, and many a day, and many a night too, we had worked together at the same table, he encouraging me to persevere when I was on the point of giving up the study of Sanskrit altogether. When Professor Goldstücker came to England, he undertook a new edition of Wilson's "Sanskrit Dictionary," and he very soon became entangled in a controversy with "the company of collaborators" of another Sanskrit dictionary, published at the expense of the Russian Academy. I do not defend him, far from it. He had a weakness very common among scholars;—he could not bear to see a work praised beyond its real merits, and he thought it was his duty to set everything right that seemed to him wrong. He was very angry with me, because I would not join in his condemnation of the St. Petersburg dictionary. I could not do that, because, without being blind to its defects, I considered it a most valuable performance, highly creditable to all its collaborators; nay, I felt bound to say so publicly in England, because it was in England that this excellent work had been unduly condemned. This embittered my relations with Professor Goldstücker, and when the attacks by the company of collaborators on him grew thicker and thicker, while I was treated by them with the greatest civility, he persuaded himself that I had taken part against him, that I had in fact become a sleeping partner in what was then called the "International Praise Insurance Society." To show him once for all that this was not the case, and that I was perfectly independent of any company of collaborators, I wrote what I wrote at the time. Nor did I do so without having had placed before me several reviews, which certainly seemed to give to the old saying *laudari a viro laudato* a novel meaning. Having done what I thought I was bound to do for an old friend, I was perfectly prepared to take the consequences of what might seem a rash act, and when I was twitted with having done so anonymously, I, of course, thought it my duty to reprint the article, at the first opportunity, with my name. Now let it be borne in mind that one of the chief culprits, nay, as appeared afterwards, the most eager mischief-maker, was Professor Whitney himself, and let us now hear what he has to say. As if he himself were entirely unconcerned in the matter, instead of having been the chief culprit, he speaks of "cool effrontery;" "magisterial assumption, towards a parcel of naughty boys caught in their naughtiness;" "most discreditable;" "the epithet outrageous is hardly too strong." Here his breath fails him, and, fortunately for me, the climax ends. And this, we are asked to believe, is not loud and boisterous but gentle and calm: it is in fact "the language of simple-minded consciousness of rectitude!"

These gentle onslaughts were written and published by Professor Whitney ten years ago. I happen to know that a kind of *colportage* was established to send his articles to gentlemen whom they would not otherwise have reached. I was told again and again, that I ought to put an end to these maneuvers, and yet, during all these years, I thought I could perfectly well afford to take no notice of them. But when after such proceedings Professor Whitney turns round, and challenges me before a public which is not acquainted with these matters, to produce any of the *epitheta ornantia* I had mentioned as having been applied by him to me, to Renan, to Schleicher, to Oppert, to Bleek, nay, even to Bopp and Burnouf and Lassen, when with all "the simple-minded consciousness of rectitude" he declares, that he was never personal, then I ask, Could I remain silent any longer?

How hard Professor Whitney is driven in order to fix any real blame on me, may be seen from what follows. The article in which the obnoxious passage which, I was told, deprived me of any claim to the amenities of literary intercourse occurs, had been reprinted in the "Indische Studien," before I reprinted it in the first volume of "Chips." In reprinting it myself, I had rewritten parts of it, and had also made a few additions. In the "Indische Studien," on the contrary, it had been reprinted in its original form, and had besides been disfigured by several inaccuracies or misprints. Referring to these, I had said that it had been, as usual, very incorrectly reprinted. Let us hear what an American pleader can make out of this:—

"In this he was too little mindful of the requirements of fair dealing; for he leaves any one who may take the trouble to turn to the 'Indische Studien,' and compare the version there given with that found among the 'Chips,' to infer that all the discordances he shall discover are attributable to Weber's incorrectness, whereas they are in fact mainly alterations which Müller has made in his own reprint; and the real inaccuracies are perfectly trivial in character and few in number—such printer's blunders as are rarely avoided by Germans who print English, or by English who print German. We should doubtless be doing Müller injustice if we maintained that he deliberately meant Weber to bear the odium of all the discrepancies which a comparer might find; but he is equally responsible for the result, if it is owing only to carelessness on his part."

What will the intelligent gentlemen of the jury say to this? Because I complained of such blunders as altars being "construed," instead of "constructed," "enlightoned" instead of "enlightened," "gratulate" instead of "congratulate," and similar inaccuracies, occurring in an unauthorized reprint of my article, therefore I really wanted to throw the odium of what I had myself written in the original article, and what was, as far as the language was concerned, perfectly correct, on Professor Weber. Can forensic ingenuity go further? If America possesses many such powerful pleaders, we wonder how life can be secure.

Having thus ascertained whence *illæ lacrumæ*, I must now produce a small bottle at least of the tears themselves which Professor Whitney has shed over me, and over men far better than myself, all of which, he says, were never meant to be personal, and most of which have evidently been quite dried up in his memory.

I begin with Bopp. "Although his mode of working is wonderfully genial, his vision of great acuteness, and his instinct a generally trustworthy guide, he is liable to wander far from the safe track, and has done not a little labor over which a broad and heavy mantle of charity needs to be drawn" (I. 208).

M. Renan and myself have "committed the very serious error of inverting the mutual relation of dialectic variety and uniformity of speech, thus turning topsy-turvy the whole history of linguistic development. . . . . It may seem hardly worth while to spend any effort in refuting an opinion of which the falsity will have been made apparent by the exposition already given" (p. 177).

In another place (p. 284) M. Renan is told that his objection to the doctrine of a primitive Indo-European monosyllabism is noticed, not for any cogency which it possesses, but only on account of the respectability of M. Renan.

Lassen and Burnouf, who thought that the geographical reminiscences in the first chapter of the Vendidad had a historical foundation, are told that their "claim is baseless, and even preposterous" (p. 201). Yet what Professor Whitney's knowledge of Zend must be, we may judge from what he says of Burnouf's literary productions. "It is well known," he says, "that the great French scholar produced *two or three bulky volumes* upon the Avesta." I know of *one* bulky volume only, "Commentaire sur la Yaçna," tome i., Paris, 1833, but that may be due to my lamentable ignorance.

"Professor Oppert simply exposes himself in the somewhat ridiculous attitude of one who knocks down, with gestures of awe and fright, a tremendous man of straw of his own erecting (I. 218). His erroneous assumptions will be received with most derisive incredulity (I. 221); the incoherence and aimlessness of his reasonings (I. 223); an ill-considered tirade, a tissue of misrepresentations of linguistic science (I. 237). He cannot impose upon us by his authority, nor attract us by his eloquence: his present essay is as heavy in style, as loose and vague in expression, unsound in argument, arrogant in tone" (I. 238). The motive imputed to Professor Oppert in writing his Essay is that "he is a Jew, and wanted to stand up for the Shemites."

If Professor Oppert is put down as a Shemite, Dr. Bleek is sneered at as a German. "His work is written with much apparent profundity, one of a class, not quite unknown in Germany, in which a minimum of valuable truth is wrapped up in a maximum of sonating phraseology" (I. 292). Poor Germany catches it again on page 315. "Even, or especially in Germany," we are told, "many an able and acute scholar seems minded to indemnify himself for dry and tedious grubbings among the roots and forms of Comparative Philology by the most airy ventures in the way of constructing Spanish castles of linguistic science."

In his last work Professor Whitney takes credit for having at last rescued the Science of Language from the incongruities and absurdities of European scholars.

Now on page 119 Professor Whitney very properly reproves another scholar, Professor Goldstücker, for having laughed at the *German* school of Vedic interpretation. "He emphasizes it," he says, "dwells upon it, reiterates it three or four times in a paragraph, as if there lay in the words themselves some potent argument. Any uninformed person would say, we are confident, that he was making an unworthy appeal to English prejudice against foreign men and foreign ways." Professor Whitney finishes up with charging Professor

Goldstücker, who was himself a German—I beg my reader's pardon, but I am only quoting from a North American Review—with "fouling his own nest." Professor Whitney, I believe, studied in a German university. Did he never hear of a 'cute little bird, who does to the nest in which he was reared, what he says Professor Goldstücker did to his own?

Χαῖρέ μοι, ὦ Γώλδστυκρε, καὶ εἰν Ἄϊδαο δόμοισιν·

Πάντα γὰρ ἤδη τοι τελέω, τὰ πάροιθεν ὑπέστην.

Haeckel is called a headlong Darwinian (I. 293), Schleicher is infected with Darwinism (I. 294), "he represents a false and hurtful tendency (I. 298), he is blind to the plainest truths, and employs a mode of reasoning in which there is neither logic nor common sense (I. 323). His essays are unsound, illogical, untrue; but there are still incautious sciolists by whom every error that has a great name attached to it is liable to be received as pure truth, and who are ever specially attracted by good hearty paradoxes" (I. 330).

I add a few more references to the *epitheta ornantia* which I was charged with having invented. "Utter futility" (p. 36); "meaningless and futile" (p. 152); "headlong materialist" (p. 153); "better humble and true (Whitney) than high-flown, pretentious, and false" (not-Whitney, p. 434); "simply and solely nonsense" (I. 255); "darkening of counsel by words without knowledge" (I. 255); "rhetorical talk" (I. 723); "flourish of trumpets, lamentable (not to say) ridiculous failure" (I. 277).

What a contrast between the rattling discharges of these *mitrailleuses* at the beginning of the war, and the whining and whimpering assurance now made by the American professor, that he never in his life said anything personal or offensive!

WHY I OUGHT NOT TO HAVE ANSWERED.

Having taken the trouble of collecting these spent balls from the various battlefields of the American general, I hope that even Professor Whitney will no longer charge me with having spoken without book. As long as he cited me before the tribunal of scholars only, I should have considered it an insult to them to suppose that they could not, if they liked, form their own judgment. For fifteen years have I kept my fire, till, like a Chinese juggler, Professor Whitney must have imagined he had nearly finished my outline on the wall with the knives so skillfully aimed to miss me. But when he dragged me before a tribunal where my name was hardly known, when he thought that by catching the *aura popularis* of Darwinism, he could discredit me in the eyes of the leaders of that powerful army, when he actually got possession of the pen of the son, fondly trusting it would carry with it the weight of the father, then I thought I owed it to myself, and to the cause of truth and its progress, to meet his reckless charges by clear rebutting evidence. I did this in my "Answer to Mr. Darwin," and as I did it, I did it thoroughly, leaving no single charge unanswered, however trifling. At the same time, while showing the unreasonableness of his denunciations, I could not help pointing out some serious errors into which Professor Whitney had fallen. Some thrusts can only be parried by *a-tempo* thrusts.

Professor Whitney, like an experienced advocate, passes over in silence the most serious faults which I had pointed out in his "Lectures," and after he has attempted—with what success, let others judge—to clear himself from a few, he turns round, and thinks it best once for all to deny my competency to judge him. And why?

"I do not consider Professor Müller capable of judging me justly," he says. And why? "Because I have felt moved, on account of his extraordinary popularity and the exceptional importance attached to his utterances, to criticise him more frequently than anybody else."

Is not this the height of forensic ingenuity? Because A has criticised B, therefore B cannot criticise A justly. In that case A has indeed nothing to do but to criticise B C D to Z, and then no one in the world can criticise him justly. I have watched many controversies, I have observed many stratagems and bold movements to cover a retreat, but nothing to equal this. Professor Pott was very hard on Professor Curtius, but he did not screen himself by denying to his adversary the competency to criticise him in turn. What would Newman have said, if Kingsley had tried to shut him up with such a remark, a remark really worthy of one literary combatant only, the famous Pastor Goeze, the critic of Lessing?

What would even Professor Whitney think, if I were to say that, because I have criticised his "Lectures," he could not justly criticise my "Sanskrit Grammar?" He might not think it good taste to publish an advertisement to dissuade students in America from using my grammar; he might think it unworthy of himself and dishonorable to institute comparisons, the object of which would be too transparent in the eyes even of his best friends in Germany. Mr. Whitney has lived too long in Germany not to know the saying, *Man merkt die Absicht und man wird verstimmt*. But should I ever say that he was incompetent to criticise my "Sanskrit Grammar" justly? Certainly not. All that I might possibly venture to say is, that before Professor Whitney undertakes to criticise my own or any other Sanskrit grammar, he should look at § 84 of my grammar, and practice that very simple rule, that if Visarga is preceded by *a*, and followed by *a*, the Visarga is dropt, *a* changed to *o*, and the initial vowel elided. If with this rule clearly impressed on his memory, he will look at his edition of the Atharva-Veda Prâtiśâkhya, I. 33, then perhaps, instead of charging Hindu grammarians in his usual style with "opinions obviously and grossly incorrect and hardly worth quoting," he might discover that e k e s p r̥ sh t a m could only have been meant in the MSS. for e k e 's p r̥ sh t a m, and that the proper translation was not that vowels are formed *by contact*, but that they are formed *without contact*. Instead of saying that none of the other Prâtisâkhyas favors this opinion, he would find the same statement in the Rig-Veda Prâtisâkhya, Sûtra 719, page cclxi of my edition, and he might perhaps say to himself, that before criticising Sanskrit grammars, it would be useful to learn at least the phonetic rules. I had pointed out this slip before, in the second edition of my "Sanskrit Grammar;" but, as to judge from an article of his on the accent, Professor Whitney has not seen that second edition (1870), which contains the Appendix on the accent in Sanskrit, I beg leave to call his attention to it again.

WHY I OUGHT TO BE GRATEFUL.

I am glad to say that we now come to a more amusing part of this controversy. After I had been told that because I was attacked first, therefore I was not able to criticise Professor Whitney's writings justly, I am next told that I ought to be very grateful for having been attacked, nay, I am told that, in my heart of hearts, I am really very grateful indeed. I must quote this passage in full:—

"During the last eight years I have repeatedly taken the opportunity accurately to examine and frankly to criticise the views of others and the arguments by which they were supported. I have done this more particularly against eminent and famous men whom the public has accustomed itself to regard as guides in matters referring to the Science of Language. What unknown and uncared for people say, is of no consequence whatever; but if Schleicher and Steinthal, Renan and Müller, teach what to me seems an error, and try to support it by proofs, then surely I am not only justified, but called upon to refute them, if I can. Among these students the last-named seems to be of different opinion. In his article, 'My Reply to Mr. Darwin,' published in the March number of the 'Deutsche Rundschau,' he thinks it necessary to read me a severe lecture on my presumption, although he also flatters me by the hint that my custom of criticising the most eminent men only is appreciated, and those whom I criticise feel honored by it."

I confess when I read this, I wished I had really paid such a pretty compliment to my kind critic, but looking through my article from beginning to end, I find no hint anywhere that could bear so favorable an interpretation, unless it is where I speak of "the noble army of his martyrs," and of the untranslated remark of Phocion, which he may have taken for a compliment. In saying that it was acknowledged to be an honor to be attacked by him, Professor Whitney was, no doubt, thinking of the words of Ovid, *Summa petunt dextra fulmina missa Jovis*, and I am not going in future to deny him the title of the Jovial and Olympian critic, nor should I suggest to him to read the line in Ovid immediately preceding the one quoted. Against one thing only I must protest. Though the last named, I am surely not, as he boldly asserts, the only one of the four *sommités* struck by his Olympian thunderbolts, who have humbly declined too frequent a repetition of his celestial favors. Schleicher, no doubt, was safe, for alas, he is dead! But Steinthal surely has uttered rather Promethean protests against the Olympian,—

Οἶδ' ὅτι τραχὺς καὶ παρ' ἑαυτῷ

τὸ δίκαιον ἔχων Ζεύς· ἀλλ' ἔμπας

μαλακογνώμων

ἔσται ποθ', ὅταν ταύτῃ ῥαισθῇ·

and as to M. Renan, does his silence mean more than—

Ἐμοὶ δ' ἔλασσον Ζηνὸς ἢ μηδὲν μέλει

I confess, then, frankly that, in my heart of hearts, I am not grateful for these cruel kindnesses, and if he says that the other Serene Highnesses have been less ungrateful than I am, I fear this is again one of his over-confident assertions. My publishers in America may be grateful to him, for I am told that, owing to Professor Whitney's articles, much more interest in my works has been excited in America than I could ever have expected. But I cannot help thinking that by the line of action he has followed, he has done infinite harm to the science which we both have at heart. In order to account somehow or other for his promiscuous onslaughts, he now tells Mr. Darwin and his friends that in the Science of Language all is chaos. That is not so, unless Mr. Whitney is here using chaos in a purely subjective sense. There are differences of opinion, as there are in every living and progressive science, but even those who differ most widely, perfectly understand and respect each other, because they know that, from the days of Plato and Aristotle, men who start from different points, arrive at different conclusions, particularly when the highest problems in every science are under consideration. I do not agree with Professor Steinthal, but I understand him; I do not agree with Dr. Bleek, but I respect him; I differ most of all from Schleicher, but I think that an hour or two of private conversation, if it were possible still, would have brought us much nearer together. At all events, in reading any of their books, I feel interested, I breathe a new atmosphere, I get new ideas, I feel animated and invigorated. I have now read nearly all that Professor Whitney has written on the Science of Language, and I have not found one single new fact, one single result of independent research, nay, not even one single new etymology, that I could have added to my Collectanea. If I am wrong, let it be proved. That language is an institution, that language is an instrument, that we learn our language from our mothers, as they learned it from their mothers and so on till we come to Adam and Eve, that language is meant for communication, all this surely had been argued out before, and with arguments, when necessary, as strong as any adduced by Professor Whitney.

Professor Whitney may not be aware of this, or have forgotten it; but a fertile writer like him ought at all events to have a good memory. In his reply, p. 262, he tells us, for instance, as one of his latest discoveries, that in studying language, we ought to begin with modern languages, and that when we come to more ancient periods, we should always infer similar causes from similar effects, and never admit new forces or new processes, except when those which we know prove totally inefficient. In my own Lectures I had laid it down as one of the fundamental principles of the Science of Language that "what is real in modern formations must be admitted as possible in ancient formations, and that what has been found true on a small scale may be true on a larger scale." I had devoted considerable space to the elucidation of this principle, and what did Professor Whitney write at that time (1865)?

"The conclusion sounds almost like a bathos; we should have called these, not fundamental principles, but obvious considerations, which hardly required any illustration" (p. 243).

Here is another instance of failure of memory. He assures us:—

"That he would never venture to charge anybody with being influenced in his literary labors by personal vanity and a desire of notoriety, except perhaps after giving a long string of proofs—nay, not even then" (p. 274).

Yet it was he who said of (I. 131) the late Professor Goldstücker that—

"Mere denunciation of one's fellows and worship of Hindu predecessors do not make one a Vedic scholar,"

and that, after he had himself admitted that "no one would be found to question his (Professor Goldstücker's) immense learning, his minute accuracy, and the sincerity and intensity of his convictions."

By misunderstanding and sometimes, unless I am greatly mistaken, willfully closing his eyes to the real views of other scholars, Professor Whitney has created for himself a rich material for the display of his forensic talents. Like the poor Hindu grammarian, we are first made to say the opposite of what we said, and are then brow-beaten as holding opinions "obviously and grossly incorrect and hardly worth quoting." All this is clever, but is it right? Is it even wise?

Much of what I have here written sounds very harsh, I know; but what is one to do? I have that respect for language and for my friends, and, may I add, for myself, to avoid harsh and abusive words, as much as possible. I do not believe in the German saying, *Auf einen groben Klotz gehört ein grober Keil*. I have tried hard, throughout the whole of my literary career, and even in this "Defense," not to use the weapons that have been used against me during so many years of almost uninterrupted attacks. Much is allowed, however, in self-defense that would be blamable in an unprovoked attack, and if I have used here and there the cool steel, I trust that clean wounds, inflicted by a sharp sword, will heal sooner than gashes made with rude stones and unpolished flints.

Professor Whitney might still, I feel convinced, do some very useful work, as the apostle of the Science of Language in America, if only, instead of dealing in general theories, he would apply himself to a critical study of scientific facts, and if he would not consider it his peculiar calling to attack the personal character of other scholars. If he must needs criticise, would it be quite impossible for him, even in his character of Censor, to believe that other scholars are as honest as himself, as independent, as outspoken, as devoted at all hazards to the cause of truth? Does he really believe in his haste that all men who differ from him, or who tell him that he has misapprehended their teaching, are humbugs, pharisees, or liars? Professor Steinthal was a great friend of his, does he imagine that his violent resentment was entirely unprovoked? I have had hundreds of reviews of my books, some written by men who knew more, some by men who knew less than myself. Both classes of reviews proved very useful, but, beyond correcting matters of fact, I never felt called upon to answer, or to enter into personal recriminations with any one of my reviewers. We should not forget that, after all, reviews are written by men, and that there are often very tangible reasons why the same book is fiercely praised and fiercely abused. No doubt, every writer who believes in the truth of his opinions, wishes to see them accepted as widely as possible; but reviews have never been the most powerful engines for the propaganda of truth, and no one who has once known what it is to feel one's self face to face with Truth, would for one moment compare the applause of the many with the silent approval of the still small voice of conscience within. Why do we write? Chiefly, I believe, because we think we have discovered facts unknown to others, or arrived at opinions opposed to those hitherto held. Knowing the effort one has made one's self in shaking off old opinions or accepting new facts, no student would expect that everybody else would at once follow his lead. Indeed, we wish to differ from certain authorities, we wish to be criticised by them; their opposition is far more important, far more useful, far more welcome to us, than their approval could ever be. It would be an impossible task were we to attempt to convert personally every writer who still differs from us. Besides, there is no wheat without bran, and nothing is more instructive than to watch how the millstones of public opinion slowly and noiselessly separate the one from the other. I have brought my harvest, such as it was, to the mill: I do not cry out when I see it ground. From my peers I have received the highest rewards which a scholar can receive, rewards far, far above my deserts; the public at large has treated me no worse than others; and, if I have made some enemies, all I can say is, I do not envy the man who in his passage through life has made none.

Even now, though I am sorry for what Professor Whitney has done, I am not angry with him. He has great opportunities in America, but also great temptations. There is no part of the civilized world where a scholar might do more useful work than in America, by the bold and patient exploration of languages but little known, and rapidly disappearing. Professor Whitney may still do for the philology of his country what Dr. Bleek has done for the languages of Africa at the sacrifice of a lifelong expatriation, alas! I have just time to add, at the sacrifice of his life.

But I admit that America has also its temptations. There are but few scholars there who could or would check Professor Whitney, even in his wildest moods of asseveration, and by his command of a number of American papers, he can easily secure to himself a temporary triumph. Yet, I believe, he would find a work, such as Bancroft's "On the Native Races of the Pacific States of North America," a far more useful contribution to our science, and a far more permanent monument of his life, than reviews and criticisms, however brilliant and popular.

It was because I thought Professor Whitney capable of rendering useful service to the Science of Language in America that I forbore so long, that I never for years noticed his intentional rudeness and arrogance, that I received him, when he called on me at Oxford, with perfect civility, that I assisted him when he wanted my help in procuring copies of MSS. at Oxford. I could well afford to forget what had happened, and I tried for many years to give him credit for honorable, though mistaken, motives in making himself the mouthpiece of what he calls the company of collaborators.

In fact, if he had arraigned me again and again before a tribunal of competent judges, I should gladly have left my peers to decide between me and my American traducer. But when he cleverly changed the venue and brought his case before a tribunal where forensic skill was far more likely to carry the day than complicated evidence that could be appreciated by a special jury only, then, at last, I had to break through my reserve. It was not exactly cowardice that had kept me so long from encountering the most skillful of American swordsmen, but when the duel was forced upon me, I determined it should be fought out once for all.

I might have said much more; in fact, I had written much more than what I here publish in self-defense, but I wished to confine my reply as much as possible to bare facts. Professor Whitney has still to learn, it seems, that in a duel, whether military or literary, it is the bullets which hit, not the smoke, or the report, however loud. I do not flatter myself that with regard to theories on the nature of language or the relation between language and thought there ever will be perfect unanimity among scholars, but as to my bullets or my facts, I believe the case is different. I claim no infallibility, however, and would not accept the papal tiara among comparative philologists, even though it was offered me in such tempting terms by the hands of Professor Whitney. In order, therefore, to satisfy Mr. Darwin, Professor Haeckel, and others whose good opinion I highly value, because I know that they care for truth far more than for victory, I now appeal to Professor Whitney to choose from among his best friends three who are *Professores ordinarii* in any university of England, France, Germany, or Italy, and by their verdict I promise to abide. Let them decide the following points as to simple matters of fact, the principal bones of contention between Professor Whitney and myself:—

1. Whether the Latin of the inscription on the Duilian Column represents the Latin as spoken in 263 B.C. (p. 430);

2. Whether Ahura-Mazda can be rendered by "the mighty spirit" (p. 430);

3. Whether s a r v a n â m a n in Sanskrit means "name for everything" (p. 430);

4. Whether Professor Whitney knew that the Phenician alphabet had by Rougé and others been traced back to an Egyptian source (pp. 430, 450, 468);

5. Whether Professor Whitney thought that the words *light*, *alight*, and *delight* could be traced to the same source (p. 467);

6. Whether in the passages pointed out on p. 434, Professor Whitney contradicts himself or not;

7. Whether he has been able to produce any passage from my writings to substantiate the charge that in my Lectures I was impelled by an overmastering fear lest man should lose his proud position in the creation (p. 435);

8. Whether there are *verbatim* coincidences between my Lectures and those of Professor Whitney (pp. 425, 470–474);

9. Whether I ever denied that language was made through the instrumentality of man (p. 470);

10. Whether I had or had not fully explained under what restrictions the Science of Language might be treated as one of the physical sciences, and whether Professor Whitney has added any new restrictions (pp. 422 seq., 475 seq.);

11. Whether Professor Whitney apprehended in what sense some of the greatest philosophers declared conceptual thought impossible without language (p. 484);

12. Whether the grammatical blunder, with regard to the Sanskrit p a r i t a s t h u s h a s as a nominative plur., was mine or his (p. 490);

13. Whether I had not clearly defined the difference between hard and soft consonants long before Professor Whitney, and whether he has not misrepresented what I had written on the subject (p. 490);

14. Whether in saying that the soft consonants can be intonated, I could have meant that they may or may not be intonated (p. 497);

15. Whether I invented the terms v i v â r a s v â ś â g h o s h â ḥ and s a ṃ v â r a n â d a g h o s h â ḥ , and whether they are to be found in no Sanskrit grammarian (p. 498);

16. Whether I was right in saying that Professor Whitney had complained about myself and others not noticing his attacks, and whether his remarks on my chapter on Fir, Oak, and Beech required being noticed (p. 500);

17. Whether I had invented the *Epitheta ornantia* applied by Professor Whitney to myself and other scholars, or whether they occur in his own writings (p. 504);

18. Whether E. Burnouf has written two or three bulky volumes on the Avesta, or only one (p. 515);

19. Whether Professor Whitney made a grammatical blunder in translating a passage of the Atharva-Veda Prâtiśâkhya, and on the strength of it charged the Hindu grammarian with holding opinions "obviously and grossly incorrect, and hardly worth quoting" (p. 519);

20. Whether Professor Whitney has occasionally been forgetful (p. 523).

Surely there are among Professor Whitney's personal friends scholars who could say Yes or No to any of these twenty questions, and whose verdict would be accepted, and not by scholars only, as beyond suspicion. Anyhow, I can do no more for the sake of peace, and to put an end to the supposed state of chaos in the Science of Language, and I am willing to appear in person or by deputy before any such tribunal of competent judges.

I hope I have thus at last given Professor Whitney that satisfaction which he has claimed from me for so many years; and let me assure him that I part with him without any personal feeling of bitterness or hostility. I have grudged him no praise in former days, and whatever useful work we may receive from him in future, whether on the languages of India or of America, his books shall always receive at my hands the same justice as if they had been written by my best friend. I have never belonged to any company of collaborators, and never shall; but whosoever serves in the noble army for the conquest of truth, be he private or general, will always find in me a faithful friend, and, if need be, a fearless defender. I gladly conclude with the words of old Fairfax (Bulk and Selvedge, 1674): "I believe no man wishes with more earnestness than I do, that all men of learning and knowledge were men of kindness and sweetness, and that such as can outdo others would outlove them too; especially while self bewhispers us, that it stands us all in need to be forgiven as well as to forgive."

THE MUMBLES, NEAR SWANSEA, WALES,

September, 1875.

Footnotes to Chapter IX (X): In Self-defense

1. See a very remarkable article by Von Hartmann on Haeckel, in the *Deutsche Rundschau*. July, 1875.

2. *Etymologische Forschungen*, 1871, p. 78, tönende, *d.h.* weiche.

3. See p. 348.

4. *Lectures*, vol. ii. p. 157.

5. Having still that kind of faith left, that a man could not willfully say a thing which he knows to be untrue, I looked again at every passage where I have dwelt on the difference between soft and hard consonants, and I think I may have found the passage which Professor Whitney grasped at, when he thought that I knew nothing of the difference between voiced and voiceless letters, until he had enlightened me on the subject. Speaking of letters, not as things by themselves, but as acts, I sometimes speak of the process that produces the hard consonant first, and then go on to say that it can be voiced, and be made soft. Thus when speaking of s and z, I say, the former is completely surd, the latter capable of intonation, and the same expression occurs again.

Could Professor Whitney have thought that I meant to say that z was only capable of intonation, but was not necessarily intonated? I believe he did, for it is with regard to s and z that, as I see, he says, "it is a marvel to find men like Max Müller, in his last lectures about language, who still cling to the old view that a z, for instance, differs from s primarily by inferior force of utterance." Now, I admit that my expression, "capable of intonation" might be misunderstood, and might have misled a mere tiro in these matters, who alighted on this passage, without reading anything before or after. But that a professor in an American university could have taken my words in that sense is to me, I confess, a puzzle, call it intellectual or moral, as you like.

6. *Indische Studien*, x. 459.

7. When I saw how M. Biot, the great astronomer, treated Professor Weber *du haut en bas*, because, in criticising Biot's opinion he had shown some ignorance of astronomy, I said, from a kind of fellow-feeling: "Weber's Essays are very creditable to the author, and hardly deserved the withering contempt with which they were treated by Biot. I differ from nearly all the conclusions at which Professor Weber arrives, but I admire his great diligence in collecting the necessary evidence." Upon this the American gentleman reads me the following lesson: First of all, I am told that my statement involves a gross error of fact; I ought to have said, Weber's Essay, not Essays, because one of them, and the most important, was not published till after Biot's death. I accept the reproof, but I believe all whom it concerned knew what Essay I meant. But secondly, I am told that the epithet *withering* is only used by Americans when they intend to imply that, in their opinion, the subject of the contempt is withered, or ought to be withered by it. This may be so in American, but I totally deny that it is so in English. "Withering contempt," in English, means, as far as I know, a kind of silly and arrogant contempt, such, for instance, as Professor Whitney displays towards me and others, intended to annihilate us in the eyes of the public, but utterly harmless in its consequences. But let me ask the American critic what he meant when, speaking of Biot's treatment of Weber, he said, "Biot thought that Weber's opinions had been *whiffed* away by him as if unworthy of serious consideration." Does *whiff away* in America mean more or less than *withering*? What Professor Whitney should have objected to was the adverb *hardly*. I wish I had said *vix, et ne vix quidem*.